Praise for Edwina Currie
Diaries 1987–1992

'The Diaries are spry and informative ... So much activity, so much plotting, all doomed. Here is the impact of any good diary: a reminder that our ambitions live little longer than mayflies, our worries are as ephemeral as a summer sea fret ... Her plain talking is terrific, particularly as she is standing up for herself against odious, sexist colleagues. [These are] not really political diaries ... they are better than that ... [they are] rich, readable portrayals of life.' Quentin Letts, *Daily Mail.*

'Frank and funny, you can't put her down.' *Time Out*

'Fans of the inner workings of Westminster will find much to enjoy, because Currie is an energetic and sharp-eyed diarist, and her portrayal of Parliament as a rivalrous boys' club is undoubtedly spot-on.' *Sunday Times*

'Her diaries are full of interesting vignettes from her years as a minister and backbencher and they're written in a characteristically forthright style. She doesn't suffer fools gladly and she doesn't pull any punches when it comes to describing colleagues who get up her nose.' *Mail on Sunday*

'An hilarious irreverent portrait of *Yes Minister* proportions.' *Glasgow Herald*

'The frankness pays off, and her humour helps to make this as entertaining as many a novel.' *Manchester Evening News*

'Currie comes across as energetically ambitious and refreshingly undiplomatic in her willingness to insult her peers. Her saving grace is that she recognises her own failings. It makes intriguing reading that puts the turgid style of many political diaries to shame.' *The Observer*

Also by Edwina Currie

Non-fiction
Diaries 1987–1992

Fiction
A Parliamentary Affair
This Honourable House
Chasing Men
A Woman's Place
The Ambassador
She's Leaving Home

Available in e-book by Biteback Publishing
www.bitebackpublishing.com

Edwina Currie

DIARIES VOLUME II
1992 – 1997

Biteback Publishing

First published in Great Britain in 2012 by
Biteback Publishing Ltd
Westminster Tower
3 Albert Embankment
London SE1 7SP

ISBN 978-1-84954-328-6

10 9 8 7 6 5 4 3 2 1

A CIP catalogue record for this book is available from the British Library.

Set in Baskerville

Printed and bound in Great Britain by
CPI Group (UK) Ltd, Croydon CR0 4YY

The secret springs of events are seldom known. But when they are, they become particularly instructive and entertaining ... the great-est actions have often proceeded from the intrigues of a handsome woman or a fashionable man, and of course whilst the memoires of those events are instructive by opening the secret workings of the human mind, they likewise attract by the interest and events of a novel ... If some people would write down the events they had been witness to ... the meaning of an age would be transmitted to the next with clearness and dependence...

   I have been in the midst of action ... I have seen partys rise and fall – friends be united and disunited – the ties of love give way to caprice, to interest and to vanity...

Georgiana, Duchess of Devonshire, September 1782

Author's Note

The full text of this diary runs to 336,000 words. My warmest thanks are due to Biteback Publishing and their editorial director, Sam Carter, and to Adam Sisman, who initially undertook the immense task of editing.

When I started the diary in the summer of 1987, just after the general election, I made myself two promises: that I would always write down exactly how I felt at the time, and that I would never go back to alter anything, however unpalatable or wrong my judgements might subsequently prove to be. During editing we have maintained these principles; nothing has been changed, except where necessary to make sense of the abridged script.

It may startle readers to realise that many Conservatives including myself were strongly pro-European, but this was the party of Harold Macmillan, who had originally tried to join the (then) Common Market in 1961, and of Edward Heath, who succeeded in the following decade. Margaret Thatcher was the driving force behind the Single European Act of 1986, which helped create the modern European Union, the greatest association of free people the world has ever seen. However, as we now know, there has been a substantial degree of difference between its ideals and its outcomes so far.

The originals will I hope eventually be placed with supporting papers in the archives of the Women's Library as part of their collection of twentieth-century women in politics.

ECJ September 2012

Contents

List of Abbreviations

BSE	Bovine spongiform encephalopathy
CBC	Canadian Broadcasting Corporation
CCO	Conservative Central Office
CGE	Conservative Group for Europe
CND	Campaign for Nuclear Disarmament
CO	Commanding Officer
DM	Deutschmark
DoH	Department of Health
DTI	Department of Trade and Industry
DUP	Democratic Unionist Party
EC	Edwina Currie; European Community
EMS	European Monetary System
EMU	European Monetary Union
ERM	Exchange Rate Mechanism
FCO	Foreign and Commonwealth Office
FET	Future of Europe Trust
FT	*Financial Times*
LBJ	Lyndon B. Johnson
LEA	Local Education Authority
LSE	London School of Economics
MAFF	Ministry of Agriculture, Fisheries and Food
MEP	Member of the European Parliament
MoD	Ministry of Defence
NALGO	National and Local Government Officers' Association
NEC	National Exhibition Centre
NFU	National Farmers' Union
NHS	National Health Service

NOP	National Opinion Polls
NUEC	Executive Committee of the National Union of the Conservative Party
OU	Oxford University
PEG	Positive European Group
PES	Public Expenditure Survey
PGCE	Postgraduate Certificate of Education
PLO	Palestine Liberation Organization
PLP	Parliamentary Labour Party
PM	Prime Minister
PPB	Party Political Broadcast
PPS	Parliamentary Private Secretary (Ministerial aide)
PSBR	Public Sector Borrowing Requirement
PUS	Parliamentary Under-Secretary of State
RADA	Royal Academy of Dramatic Art
RCB	Richard Cohen Books
RPR	Rassemblement pour la République (French political party)
RSC	Royal Shakespeare Company
RSM	Regimental Sergeant Major
SDLP	Social Democratic and Labour Party
SDP	Social Democratic Party
SNP	Scottish National Party
TESSA	Tax Exempt Special Savings Account
TORCHE	Tory Campaign for Homosexual Equality
TUC	Trades Union Congress
UDF	Union pour la Démocratie Française (French political party)
WIZO	Women's International Zionist Organisation
WPC	Woman Police Constable

Preface

Edwina Currie's first volume of diaries began in the summer of 1987 and ended in the early spring of 1992, just before a general election. The Conservatives, led by John Major, were hoping for their fourth successive victory; polls indicated that the result was too close to call. John Major had been in power only sixteen months, since winning the Party leadership election after Margaret Thatcher stood down in November 1990. Among the most important of his ministers were Norman Lamont as Chancellor of the Exchequer, Douglas Hurd as Foreign Secretary and Kenneth Baker as Home Secretary. The resurgent Labour Party was led by Neil Kinnock, assisted by Shadow Chancellor John Smith.

At the time of the 1992 election, EC was forty-five. She continued as a backbench Member of Parliament after her resignation from Mrs Thatcher's government in 1988. The following year (October 1989) she published a book about her experiences as a minister, *Life Lines*; and in 1990 she edited a volume of essays, *What Women Want*. Since 1983 she had been Conservative MP for South Derbyshire. She and her husband Ray, a chartered accountant with Arthur Andersen, had been married for twenty years. They had two daughters: Debbie, born in 1974; and Susie, born in 1977. They divided their lives between the Tower House, their family home in EC's constituency in Findern, a village near Derby; a flat in Victoria, within easy reach of the House of Commons; and Les Tuileries, a house in Mouliherne, a village in the Loire Valley. When Parliament was sitting, EC and her husband tended to spend the working week in London, travelling to Derbyshire for the weekends.

1992

Victoria, Tuesday 14 April, 5.30 p.m.

Well: we won the election[1] and I was offered a job, and I turned it down. Next stop, Europe (and clearing my £8,000 overdraft!), I hope…

I certainly didn't want to be Minister of State at the Home Office, under Ken Clarke[2] as Home Secretary. Ken would do all the interesting stuff and there would be precious little left. Prisons and the police, law and order and the Asylum Bill: I just could *not* see myself doing that, answering questions at the Dispatch Box on the latest prison riot, moving the Prison Department to Derby, and no doubt fighting Ken tooth and nail on something he disagreed about (age of consent for homosexuals perhaps? Immigrants? We'd find something…). It's a job that can't be done half-heartedly and it's only worth doing as a stepping stone to the Cabinet – and to choose that route means giving up all hope of Europe before 1999. I want to be part of that, rather than fretting and unhappy in a team of deadbeats led by an aggressive, bolshie egomaniac!

I did discuss with John[3] whether I could do the job and then go to the European Parliament. He felt (1) the ministerial post might interfere with getting a nomination; and then (2) I would have to spend time nursing a seat. Really he was hinting that I wasn't being fair, taking a job path that I didn't mean to continue. I can see his point, but on the other hand he needs strong people he can trust in Europe. He doesn't think Europe will be as important or interesting

---

1   On 9 April.

2   Home Secretary since 1992; Conservative MP for Rushcliffe Division of Nottinghamshire since 1970.

3   Major.

after Maastricht, as the enthusiasm in several countries is cooling, he says. My view on the other hand is that the difficult issues are now replacing the euphoria: that the 1990s in Europe are going to be very tough, but all of us need it strong and successful, and we should therefore put our efforts to that objective. We have such a huge agenda: completing the market; coping with the tensions that imposes, such as human rights and migration, the downsides of nationalism and of the free movement of labour; enlargement; helping the newly democratic countries which are having a very rocky time; accepting the political responsibilities of being an economic superpower – and so on. John just doesn't see it like that, but all the people I've talked to on the other side of the Channel do. Anyway, the weather is better, the money is interesting and the food both, and to me there's *real* politics to play.

I suppose I felt a bit cross, too. I asked if anything else was on offer, and the answer was no, for 'most of the posts were taken already by people they had managed to contact before me.' Now there's a downright lie. I was phoned at Findern at 12.50 p.m.; I'd been in the office at Swad[4] since 11 a.m., and the kids were at home, so it would have been easy to get hold of me any time this morning. I didn't come in to Downing Street till 4.15 p.m., but it would have been quite easy for John to have spoken to me on the phone at lunchtime, had he wanted to.

I suspect some of the Secretaries of State refused to have me. The obvious Department for me is Education, as I was PPS there for Keith Joseph and I'm a former teacher and lecturer. But John Patten, the new Secretary of State, might have worried that I might have upstaged him (I wouldn't have); perhaps MacGregor, the new Transport Secretary, felt the same.

Was it a set-up? John knew I wouldn't work for Ken, I had told him that several times. Did he remember, and put me in a difficult position? Down the end of the line, end of the afternoon – take it or leave it? Or was he trying to be kind? Most of the reshuffle is a balancing act between different factions of the Party, with both

---

4   The South Derbyshire Conservative Office in Swadlincote, Derbyshire.

Jonathan Aitken[5] (anti-Europe) and Anthony Nelson (pro-Europe) in; I don't have a faction or following as such, so nobody would have been upset or surprised if he'd left me out, as in December 1990. I asked him why he didn't offer me something then, and he said he couldn't remember, but I recall how he was when being groomed for Chief Whip: it's become part of his soul to try and satisfy all those who need to be satisfied. If he was going to be kind, or repay a debt, that was the time to do it. Not now.

I do feel annoyed that no one thought what I could usefully do. I'm a fighter, a communicator. Not a civil servant, not an administrator. For thirty years I've been in at the hard end in the fight against socialism and the Labour movement; my target is state corporatism, the notion that the state is all-wise, that the government is here to help you. I share Margaret Thatcher's instinct that there should be as little government as possible (though with record numbers of Bills, she didn't practise it). Here, we have seen off that lefty philosophy with yet another general election victory. There is no battle against socialism in Britain, not for several years anyway; but it's still alive and kicking in the EC, and that's where I'd like to pursue it.

There are two other, lesser reasons for turning John down, which made it much easier than I thought. One is the press, who have been pursuing me since yesterday. Hot news, sweetheart – how does it feel? *Horrible*, is the answer. The team of TV people on Derby Station were ghastly – asking whether I'll keep my mouth shut better than I did in salmonella days. I was tempted to push one young woman off the platform. There stretched before me the prospect of month after month of sleazy scrutiny, pecking away like carrion crows on a living body. I have no techniques for shaking them off and I loathe them with an absolute ferocity. If that is the price to pay, then it is too much. And as a minister I would have no way to pay off my overdraft/buy a new car/pay the accountant or the school fees – so I would be permanently worried about money and frequently frantic.[6]

---

5   Minister of State for Defence Procurement; Conservative MP for Thanet South since 1983; MP for Thanet East, 1974–83.

6   Ministerial salaries in 1992 were £28,175 for a Minister of State.

Finally there is South Derbyshire. I've done everything I can there, to give the area a strong and prosperous future. I could sit back and get fat and lazy. Or I could seek a new challenge, in the fifteen to twenty years left in my political life. And that is what I hope to do.

Victoria, Wednesday 29 April, 8 p.m.

I shall drive up to Derbyshire shortly, but first I must do my diary! It's curious: I started this nearly five years ago in order to wean me off my lover, and to compensate for my need to talk to someone regularly. It's been very cathartic at bad times – really helpful. But the fact that I feel less *need* to write suggests I'm altogether less screwed up than I used to be.

Very much, now, I can put John Major behind me. Thinking more clearly about the way that job offer was handled, I suspect he long since developed a habit of appearing to listen, seeming to take it all in, without absorbing a single word or taking a scrap of notice. Hasn't this happened twice? Firstly, he knew I wouldn't work with Ken Clarke, for I poured out my heart to John on more than one occasion in early 1989. Secondly, he knew I wanted to go to Europe and was on the list, following our discussion in early March. (Even when Margaret Thatcher harangued you, she took note and changed tack, at least until her last year or so, when she stopped listening to anything but the sound of her own voice.) So I was puzzled when he offered me *that* job. If he was trying to persuade me to stay in the UK it wasn't a very convincing performance. No, I think he had not forgotten, but just thought I was as bloodless as he and that my ambitions ran in the same channel. Not any more, they don't. *He* didn't think either of the two points mattered much, so he couldn't conceive that *I* didn't agree. Angela Rumbold[7] says the reshuffle was really the work of Richard Ryder:[8] that figures, for it was a careful, shrewd and cold-blooded balancing act. He probably thought he was doing me a huge favour and that I would jump

---

7   Minister of State, Home Office, since 1990; Conservative MP for Mitcham & Morden since 1982.
8   Chief Whip; Conservative MP for Mid-Norfolk since 1983.

at it, and it didn't enter his mind to check. Well he knows (some) now. I spoke in Graham Bright's[9] constituency last Friday night. An odd event – a Conservative Political Centre supper which turned into an annual dinner, so half were black tie and half (including Graham Bright) in mufti or dull jersey dresses. It was in one of those rooms with huge pillars and whining air conditioning, and the food was a bit pathetic: dried-out breast of chicken preceded by lumpy, lukewarm potato and leek soup. Nice people, however, and looking for a Euro MP. Graham only just held on to his seat, with a majority of 700 or so. 'Was the PM cross with me?' I asked. 'Well, he wasn't well pleased,' said Graham, looking embarrassed. Too bad. Should have tried to find out what I wanted first: at least a little tactful courtesy would have been welcome. The fact that my interview with JM was reported almost word for word in the press next day was *very* distressing, and unforgivable.

Angela Rumbold was treated much worse and is hopping mad about it. She was phoned by Ryder on the Monday night (13 April). 'I hear you are thinking of leaving the government,' said Richard. 'What? No, indeed I am *not!*' said Angela. But the next day, another phone call and she was out. John Major said to me, 'Angela Rumbold is leaving the government to go and sort out Central Office.' Angela and I had lunch at Overton's yesterday, and a very jolly time we both had. She accepted the Deputy Chairman's job because it needs doing, and will do it for a bit, and then will – wait for it – go for a Euro seat, probably Shelagh Roberts's in London South West, which we should not have lost. (Shelagh was poorly during the campaign and went home to rest at 5 p.m. each day. What a remarkably brave woman – but it would have been better for the Party, and kinder to herself, if she had allowed someone else to fight it.) I'm thrilled that Dame Angela (as she is now) is thinking on the same lines; that the battle against socialism is in abeyance here; that it's still on in Europe and that we need strong politicians on our side in the European Parliament.

---

9   The Prime Minister's PPS; Conservative MP for Luton South since 1983; MP for Luton East, 1979–83.

She was entertaining on the subject of Ken Baker,[10] who 'refused to fall on his sword' by accepting Secretary of State for Wales and told her that he wasn't 'another Peter Walker, and intend now to say my piece on the back benches'. She said he's a very self-centred man (presumably why he tried to be magisterial and failed in the leadership contest) and perhaps John Major always had him marked for a fall at the earliest opportunity.

The night Margaret resigned Angela went to her room in the House of Commons and found only half a dozen people in the ante-room, including John Wakeham[11] and Peter Morrison.[12] 'You lot are prize *shits!*' she said, and walked through them to find Margaret alone. They sat and held hands; Margaret cried and Angela comforted her. Angela was angry with Wakeham, who she felt let the PM down. I remember seeing him and his little entourage going into the members' cloakroom about 5.30 p.m. that evening, looking very shifty indeed, a real 'plotting' air about them. Never did he do anything by accident.

Meanwhile we have a woman Speaker:[13] hooray! The Chamber was packed – lots of love and cuddles for our successes, especially those like Graham Riddick[14] who held on against the odds. Sir Michael Neubert[15] proposed Peter Brooke. Tom Arnold[16] briefly seconded, and managed to offend me at least by saying Peter 'looked like a Speaker'. Really, I muttered, and what does a Speaker look like? The answer is, a chap: for even though Janet Fookes has made it very clear for years that she wanted to be Speaker, she 'could not get enough support' to stand. Translated into English, it means the chaps wouldn't have a woman. (Incidentally we *still*

---

10 Former Home Secretary and Party Chairman; Conservative MP for Mole Valley since 1983; MP for Acton, 1968–70; MP for St Marylebone, 1970–83.
11 Former Chief Whip and leader of the Lords since 1992.
12 MP for Chester 1974–92 and PPS to Margaret Thatcher 1990.
13 Betty Boothroyd, Labour MP for West Bromwich West since 1974; MP for West Bromwich, 1973–4.
14 Conservative MP for Colne Valley since 1987. In the 1992 election he increased his majority, contrary to the national trend towards Labour.
15 Conservative MP for Romford since 1974.
16 Conservative MP for Hazel Grove since 1974.

don't have a woman whip; Emma Nicholson[17] and Elizabeth Peacock, both of whom would make excellent whips, are left out of government again. If that isn't sheer, stupid prejudice, then I don't know what is.) So my mind, already keen on Betty, who was easily the best candidate, hardened as I listened to all the claptrap. She was proposed by a Tory: John Biffen, who was excellent, and seconded by, of all people, Michelin woman herself, Gwyneth Dunwoody,[18] who made a splendid speech without a single note. Betty at one time had worked for her father, Morgan Phillips, General Secretary of the TUC. Miss Boothroyd came up the hard way, fighting five times before succeeding. This contest she won easily: 372/238, a majority of 134, with 74 Tories voting for her. What a relief as I turned around in the 'Yes' lobby to find I wasn't the only one! I am genuinely delighted. One in the eye for the stuffy old men.

It's too late for me, though I have at last been allocated a respectable room, Peter Lloyd's old one, so my last years in Westminster will at least be comfortable. Poor Peter Viggers[19] is distinctly put out, as so far he's staying put in the hell-hole. The corridors are full of rampaging bands of new MPs (140 in all) looking for desks and empty rooms to squat in. The signing-in ceremony yesterday was equally a shambles, with much pushing and shoving. It's the behaviour of schoolboys, and I have lost my savour for it. We could all have stood in our places, raised our right hands and been sworn in together; but no, that would be too simple. We might, of course, have our own seats instead of crouching on each other's laps on busy days. But that would take the fun out of it...

Had lunch with Sir Christopher Prout at St Stephen's Club last Friday (24th) – he's current leader of British Tory MEPs. A slight, mouse-like man, dapper, quietly spoken: not much in the way of charisma, no bombast, but nice, and underneath the calm exterior, lots of passion and toughness. So different to most MPs – the nearest would be Nigel Forman perhaps. There are lots of seats coming up,

---

17 Conservative MP for Devon West and Torridge since 1987.
18 Labour MP for Crewe and Nantwich since 1983; MP for Crewe, 1974–83.
19 Conservative MP for Gosport since 1974; he and EC had been sharing a small room with no windows.

7

and some key ones are choosing soon. I would have had to 'come out' before long anyway. I've arranged a meeting in the constituency next Monday night, May Day, to break the news to them. One problem I hadn't realised, it wasn't Prout who mentioned it but William Powell, that strange loopy man who just held on to Corby: a dual mandate doesn't mean twice as much money, it means only 4/3 of a Parliament salary. So after 1994 I would be looking after South Derbyshire for £10,000 p.a., or rather less than a secretarial salary. Of course that is not on! Especially as one would have no time to earn outside. (I was tickled to note that since the election I've earned over £4,000 – indeed it will be £5,000 by this weekend; not too bad, really.) I suppose that's done to discourage the dual mandate, but it does seem peculiarly mean minded. Still by then Deb will be nearer to earning a living and Susie will be away from Repton, so the years of school fees will be OVER! (Last Denstone cheque payment = £5,200. All my parliamentary salary after tax goes on paying fees, every penny.)

I went to a seminar at LSE last night – stuffy, crowded dusty room, no visual aids or slides at all (I'm getting used to industry seminars with all mod cons), with David Butler talking eruditely about the election campaign, and Bob Worcester from MORI agonising about why the polls got it all wrong. Everyone agreed that the campaign in the last week was very different to the earlier weeks. Labour thought they had won and slackened off; the backlash against Sheffield[20] grew, unions like NALGO started big advertising campaigns which reminded the voters of the dogs which hadn't barked until then, and John seized the campaign by the scruff of its neck and talked with conviction about his own policies, his TV/radio interview on the morning before the election being especially effective and showing him in an excellent light.

Now Labour is chewing away at itself as its own leadership contest develops, between John Smith and Brian Gould for leader, and Gould, Margaret Beckett and John Prescott for deputy.[21] What

20 The pre-election Labour Party rally at Sheffield was widely seen as grandiose and damaging.
21 John Smith was elected leader, with over 90 per cent of the vote; Margaret Beckett deputy leader.

a stuffy, dull lot they all seem. Kinnock looks lost; the light has gone out. Major chatted warmly to him on Tuesday and Kinnock looked so *pleased*. In his own party the tide of warmth and approval has probably moved on.

As for me: Hilary Rubinstein is to retire and Lisa Eveleigh will take his place as my literary agent. The (woman) editor at a different publisher likes the stories, but definitely wants a novel first. I have arranged lunch with Hilary and Lisa for 20 May, and I suspect I should turn up with a synopsis for a novel. How about telling it like it is? Yes, that would be very satisfying, a serious novel based in Westminster... a challenge, could be fun, and might just sell a bit too...

Les Tuileries, Sunday 17 May, 4.15 p.m.

Been lying in the sun on a lounger, dozing, reading Nadine Gordimer's wonderful novel *My Father's Son*; but it is quite windy here, and after an hour-and-a-half, first day in the sun, I'm in danger of being burned. I have to get down to work anyway. The introduction to Stephen Parker's collection of political anecdotes[22] was promised for first 1 April, then the 30th, and now I am the only person holding it up. Stephen and Clare, my secretary, urge me not to worry, but the printer is waiting. I wish I had never said yes, as I can't think of anything very original to say, as usual. Also waiting to be born are an article on why Marilyn Monroe is an icon among women (for Tuesday 19th, but that shouldn't be hard), a piece about homosexual law reform for the *Mail on Sunday*, about which more later, and a speech on Maastricht for the two-day debate starting on Wednesday. My head feels full and my programme rather a burden.

I shall be taking a risk next week on the gay law reform issue. I've been a cautious member for some time of the Conservative Group on Homosexual Law Reform, chaired by Sir John Wheeler. We have lost two members to the government: Steve Norris,[23] at last, and Robin Squire, to his delight and surprise; others lost their

---

22 *Three Line Quips*, published later in the year.
23 PUS, Department of Transport, since 1992; Conservative MP for Epping Forest since 1988; MP for Oxford East 1983–7.

seats, most notably Rob Hayward at Bristol Kingswood. We need some new recruits fast. The BBC's *Public Eye* programme asked me for my views – Sam Collins, the producer, turns out to be a small, intense, very bright young man, who makes me feel about ninety. He called back: would I like to go with them to film in Amsterdam? You bet, and off we went, to a cold, windy city. Standing around with cold feet in the rain talking to camera about condoms is not the easiest job I've ever done, but at least you don't feel like breaking up laughing with the sleet sluicing down your neck. I'm keen to see the law on consent changed, preferably to the same as for heterosexuals (sixteen). The practical problem is that the age of consent in Northern Ireland is seventeen, so we might have trouble getting it down further; eighteen must be a genuine possibility. Why do I care about this? Because I hate unfairness and discrimination, simple as that. If John means what he says about getting the best out of everybody, this law should be changed.

In the course of these discussions I was told that Outrage, who have been trying to force allegedly gay people in public life to declare themselves, targeted Peter Lilley.[24] But his friend is said to be the key: Michael Portillo, he of the new hairstyle.[25] Now Michael Portillo is a very tough character indeed, and would sue in an instant.

I took some trouble to get decent coverage last week and it worked a treat. Lots of requests to talk about why I said no to the PM were politely turned down, but I kept the *Sunday Times* guessing. I had first out of courtesy to tell the South Derbyshire Conservatives what I was up to. They were funny and sweet, as much concerned about whether I would cause the hassle of a by-election as curious about my decision. Some understood immediately and were jolly nice about it. The conversation moved on, to my amusement, to the qualities necessary in my successor! Pragmatic bunch.

Within days of the *Sunday Times* article appearing, a letter arrived

---

24 Secretary of State for Social Security since 1992; Conservative MP for St Albans since 1983.
25 Chief Secretary to the Treasury since 1992; Conservative MP for Enfield Southgate since 1984. His new hairstyle – swept back, Heseltine-style – was much commented upon.

from the Cotswold Euroconstituency asking if I would like to speak at a conference in Cheltenham. This is the safest seat likely to come up; apparently Lord Plumb will be announcing next week that he is standing down. The new Vice-Chairman in charge of candidates is Andrew Mitchell, the best of last time's intake in my view – bright, tough and capable; he will work well with the new Chairman, Sir Norman Fowler.[26] There is a slight tricky patch ahead when George Stevenson, our local Labour MEP recently elected to Westminster for Stoke on Trent, will announce he is leaving Brussels; a by-election will result and Sylvia Heal, their defeated candidate from Mid-Staffs, will be put up. But that is a rosy trap for me, and I won't be caught. I will be the first MP to go from Westminster to Brussels in the prime of life;[27] nice to create a precedent, but I won't be the last.

The front-page photos after John had announced his new ministerial team brought home to me exactly what he had done: put the women he wanted in the Cabinet, those he finds no threat. And with two of them there already, a third is unlikely for some time. Mostly I was cross about Gillian Shephard. I like her, but what has she done, ever? Where are the achievements that make her a suitable candidate for the highest posts in the land? When has she stuck her neck out, made a great speech, made her mark on the nation? Answer, she hasn't, and isn't likely to, and that is why she has advanced so smoothly, because she looks (a little) like me, but with none of the disadvantages and the risks my appointment would cause. She went round during the election, a senior minister, introducing herself as 'the one who looks like Edwina Currie'. Never seems to have occurred to her that that's bloody hurtful to the original model still in circulation and makes her appointment an insult, a real slap in the face. I'm not cross with her, but with John.

I can only get frustrated at a government in which no one will stick their head over the parapet, no one will take a risk, no one has a vision. I can't easily or happily be part of a conspiracy of silence

---

26 Conservative Party Chairman since 1992; Conservative MP for Sutton Coldfield since 1974.
27 Barbara Castle had made the same move at the age of 69.

like that. I'd rather leave, go to Europe, and feel the passion and anxiety of new nations being born, new institutions maturing, new principles being established, new laws being made. As the Queen said in Strasbourg,[28] history is being made. I think I shall enjoy it.

Victoria, Thursday 4 June, 11.45 p.m.

My next book will be a novel, tentatively titled *A Parliamentary Affair*, which I agreed with Hilary and Lisa on 20 May. I'm working on a synopsis – really a quite detailed plot and characterisation; a game plan, a recipe. And hopefully a meal ticket. Richard Cohen, now at Hodder, is sniffing around, and so is Sinclair-Stevenson. I'll need some money if I'm to stop footling around speaking at conferences of Architectural Ironmongers, as I did this week.

The week in France with Mum and Zena[29] was a surprising success – in fact they complained they had too much to do! Paris for two days was marvellous: noisy and full of fumes, but such *class*. A concert of Vivaldi in the Sainte-Chapelle will stay long with me, and a morning at Réciproque in Rue de la Pompe, trying on second-hand and sample versions of the great couture names. I look stunning in Balenciaga and Ungaro and Karl Lagerfeld, but not so great in Emmanuelle Khanh, and the Chanels and Yves St Laurent looked ordinary. What a find! What an Ali Baba's cave! Marvellous. I bought three suits and a jacket and two belts = 2,450 francs (i.e. around £250). I shall definitely go again, and probably never shop full price anywhere else… and see if I can persuade the daughters too.

Anyway, in France we got one thing settled. Mum was a lot more disabled than I had realised; she has concealed it very well, but she is slow, deaf and keeps falling asleep and really shouldn't be alone. So she will sell up Liverpool and move to Bournemouth. Probably renting, so that she can afford a decent little flat and be a wealthy woman for a while. Zena will help. That is a big relief.

---

28 Earlier in the month the Queen addressed the European Parliament, in her capacity as UK Head of State.
29 EC's aunt, her mother's youngest sister. EC's mother was then eighty.

Victoria, Thursday 25 June, midnight

Hilary Rubinstein's retirement party at The Orangery in Holland Park, given by the other directors of A. P. Watt, was one of the nicest events I've ever attended. This man (Victor Gollancz's nephew) turned down Jeffrey Archer and said the title *Lucky Jim* wouldn't do; but he represented a host of great names, nurturing Michael Holroyd and Martin Gilbert through years of work to produce 'milestones in literature', and looking after Nadine Gordimer, Nobel Prize winner last year, since she was thirty and first came to England. The room was full of well-known names, mostly attached to unknown faces. Libby Purves is now very fat – pretty face, dry skin, tatty hair, stuffed into a beautiful sequinned jacket. (I may be maligning her if she's pregnant, but I think we're too old – she was only a year behind me at St Anne's.) Brian Aldiss looking scruffy, with a brooch of a pterodactyl or archaeopteryx and a scrawny grey-haired wife. Robert Heller over from the States, next to me: friendly and jovial. Patrick Moore falling asleep, a lump of collapsing foam rubber, in the corner; Godfrey Smith, expansive in a large cream suit, white shirt, and pink and green striped tie (no doubt his club: another bit of the language I don't read). As Oxford undergraduates, Hilary and Godfrey went hitchhiking in Europe after the war with £25 in their pockets: slept in the open in Italy and had one good meal each night. It sounds like an idyllic life from start to finish. Lovely Hilary, been good to me and made my life a lot more interesting, lucrative and fun.

The bad part of the day took place earlier: another of those events where I'm jolly glad I'm not a minister and am only too aware what price my offspring may have to pay for my life. I had been in Birmingham all day doing a very dull conference sponsored by Glaxo at the Birmingham Botanical Gardens (schoolchildren and the Mothers Union on days out, and pathetic, *tiny* glasshouses and gardens. Mine is more lush these days.) When I came back about 4 p.m. the phone went. It was *The Sun*: 'We hear your daughter has been expelled for cheating at her school exams.' But there was no message to phone Ray, or Deb, or Susie, or the Head, nothing. 'News to me,' says I: 'who told you this?' 'The headmaster says he has spoken to you,' the wheedling voice claimed. 'Then he is lying.'

And boy, was I beginning to get angry! I couldn't raise the head-master at school, which in retrospect was a good thing, but finally reached Deb (via the fax!) at Findern. She had made a remark to a friend at the end of the German exam and had been pulled up for talking. As they left the exam room she muttered that the teacher was a 'twat'. He heard and flipped – a pretty stupid thing for a member of staff to do, knowing the kids were tired and tense after exams, with more to come. Deb did her last exam without incident on Monday: then instead of dropping it, the teacher complained to the Head and she was carpeted today. And somebody phoned *The Sun* office in Manchester (her friends, said *The Sun*. A school employee, at a guess). The headmaster was fool enough to speak to the reporter, saying there had been an internal inquiry (ah! No smoke without fire); Debbie was not being expelled (it was considered then?) or suspended (but she has been told not to return to the school? – yes). What a naïve idiot. Apparently Deb exploded at the headmaster this morning and called him a 'fucking arsehole' for making such a silly fuss – and she was dead right. He could have said something positive about a pupil who has been at his school five years; or, if he couldn't manage that, just refused to comment. Ray eventually called at 7 p.m. and took the *school's* side. He sounded imperious and distant and made me even angrier. I told him he sounded just like *my* father, and put the phone down on him.

At times like these I wonder why I stay with him; we seem so out of sympathy. I stay because no one else has ever come along offering me a home (not just no one better – no one else at all. Ever. And he took some persuading.) And because unravelling all the institutional arrangements, property, mortgages etc. would leave us both diminished and unhappy people. And because being alone is lonely and gets worse when you're older, so being with someone is better than nothing. And because being nice to a person, courteous, gracious and considerate, is good practice for me, even (or especially) when I don't feel it or feel like it. Makes me a better person. But oh! how I envy married people who seem to have a meeting of minds and emotions, who know exactly the right thing to say to one another. How nice it would have been to have heard Ray agree with me this evening. But he didn't.

It looks as if I'll be the most senior Tory to go to the European Parliament. Dame Angela has decided against. Well, she will be sixty this year (to my surprise) and can have a bus pass – not the best time to try and start a new career. She says she has been offered 'a good portfolio' of things to do. Henry Plumb on the other hand doesn't look to me as if he is ready to retire: he's sixty-seven, looks fifty-seven, is hale, hearty, competent, busy and *important* in Brussels and Strasbourg and nobody much here. Still, Dame Angela's demise means I can try for Surrey. Andrew Mitchell is keen that the sitting MEP (who is seventy-two) should retire, so we might have some chance. The candidates' list will be ready in September and constituents can choose after that, which I hope will mean after the Party Conference.

House of Commons, Monday 6 July, 11.20 p.m.

Waiting to vote and have just dashed off a cross letter to the *Sunday Times* which has been whinging on about how greedy we MPs are in wanting an increase in our allowances. I put in nearly £3,000 extra from my own pocket to pay for staff last year and that included stopping all spending in September, so I'll vote for almost any decent increase! The article moaned about the so-called 'perks' of the job – car parking, lifts, escalators, offices, phones etc. Wouldn't it be nice if we really were rolling in it; I wouldn't have to earn a living outside at all.

The chances of doing so seem to be increasing. I've had several interesting approaches, including BBC Radio 2 (Brian Hayes), Central TV (*Sunday Supplement*) and from an independent company for Channel 4 or (more likely) BBC, a series of hour-long programmes provisionally entitled *Curried Europe*. Hope these come off.

The PM was on table-thumping form at Thursday's 1922 Committee.[30] It had been a hard and grotty week for him. The previous day, 1 July, was the start of our Presidency of the European Council: there were supposed to be cocktail parties and fireworks and Britain in charge. Instead the gracious appearance of Delors *et al* had the flavour of a schools inspection; meanwhile in the Lords, Baroness Thatcher

---

30 The influential committee of backbench Tory MPs.

of Kesteven took her place and proceeded to lambast Maastricht and everything else. On Sunday's *David Frost Show* she looked quite batty to me, eyes rolling. Maybe it is just that we have grown used to John's style now, and she looks weird and old fashioned. Both the PM and Hurd have fought back, Hurd saying that if we went back on our word we would be 'political spivs'. Still they fail to make the argument *for* the Maastricht agreement: precisely the warning I offered last year. And so they reap the whirlwind of bewildered discontent in the Tory Party and give the impression that ministers don't much like the Treaty either.

Victoria, Tuesday 21 July, 5.15 p.m.

Waiting for Ray to come at 6 p.m. to take me to see Neil Diamond at Wembley. I moaned that most of the theatre we've been to recently was disappointing, like the Shaw (*Heartbreak Hotel – very* tedious) and how it is always me who gets the tickets; and hey presto, he got organised for tonight. Let's hope this continues.

Much amusement at Westminster about David Mellor,[31] a wide boy if ever there was one. Someone tapped his girlfriend's phone and sold the tape to the *People*. Very funny stuff – all about how knackered he was, with two speeches to write. She says it wasn't her, but it all smelt – she's an out-of-work actress – well trained, RADA – some £30,000 has changed hands – he's known her only a few months, seen her two or three times a week, stayed over at her flat (except it was 'borrowed') and entrusted much of his affair to a shady character who, it turns out, works for *Private Eye* and was involved in the 'exposures' of Jeffrey Archer and Colin Moynihan's friendship with Pamella Bordes. This time it's an 'Antonia de Sancha'. Apparently Antonia has a hot temper, had a row with her agent a year ago and hasn't worked since, and is a bit of a fantasist. So she might have been set up too. Anyway, he's been a naughty boy.

He offered to resign, but John Major (predictably) wouldn't have it. The whole business may well be the press fighting back after the *affaire*

---

31 Secretary of State for National Heritage since 1992; Conservative MP for
    Putney since 1979.

Ashdown, and ten days ago the Bottomley business. After altering the 'Health of the Nation' White Paper to include sexually transmitted diseases and abortions and a target for reducing unwanted teenage pregnancies, Virginia forgot to mention that she was an unmarried teenaged mum herself, taking a year off from Essex University to have Joshua when she was nineteen. He is Peter's[32] son and neither parent looks capable of having a child of twenty-five, but there you are: a little sanctity tainted, a little self-righteousness deflated. The public were very sympathetic to Virginia and the press got a lot of criticism; Mellor announced an inquiry into press invasions of privacy, with possible new legislation, so they pushed the button on the tape recorder...

I think he will survive, in part because John Major can't afford to start losing ministers, and in part because the public don't care much. We are becoming more Continental by the minute, and a good thing too!

Frank Delaney took me to Claridge's last week and fed me a load of Irish blarney along with champagne and *medaillons de veau*. It was fun, but he's a sharp character and he was trying to find out what's truth and what's fiction in my new novel. I'm not likely to tell *him*, am I? Still no contract, so I'll just have to get on with it. I've ordered a new computer, faster and quieter and lighter than the old one, so there are no excuses. Please God, support me and help me find a voice.

Les Tuileries, Saturday 8 August

Ray has just taken Susie to the airport to catch her plane back to the UK. We had a lot of fun kitting her out for the sixth form at Repton; there is no uniform as such, but the rules include a blazer-style jacket, a skirt neither too long nor too short, and white blouses with collars. She is now tall and slim and looked like a model: at first she found it a little embarrassing, but after a while rather enjoyed the gasps of surprise from the others and pranced around very happily. She will look good for her university interviews – very grown up indeed.

---

32 Virginia Bottomley's husband Peter was also a Conservative MP.

It's just five years since I started keeping a diary. After we won the 1987 election and I stayed a minister, it was clear I was going to witness interesting events close to. Now I am a long way from power, but I understand how the system works better than most. If I can get it down on paper, in the novel, particularly against a background of the increasing shift of power away from Westminster, I should feel I had achieved something that would last a while. There must be two books there – one based on certain events, the second (if the first is successful) exploring the relationship with a tough, aggressive and chauvinist boss. I might be able to work in a libel case too, to show what such an experience is like.

Looking at pictures of Virginia Bottomley in yesterday's papers, I realised that I could have done that job:[33] but it was not on offer to me and never would be. Virginia is a very tough lady indeed, with the full backing of her family, and should she want it will be a candidate for the leadership next time round. That could be in five years' time, when she will be forty-nine – the same age as Margaret when she became leader in 1975. It's such a pity that I can't stand her – or to be more kindly and accurate, can't warm to her at all. She has developed a style of trying to talk to everyone in the voting lobby, offering a kind word from on high here and there, which I find insufferably patronising: and yet she never meets one's eye.

Les Tuileries, Friday 21 August, evening

Sitting in the evening sun, and sucking a loose tooth. That crown the dentist put on earlier this year is loose, dammit. He was talking politics so much that he didn't do it properly, the root got infected several times and now I think the post has worked its way out of the bone. So I'm having to be horribly careful what I eat until after Bank Holiday, when I've an appointment. Can't have a gap in the front!

Deb got a C and two Ds in her A levels – extremely disappointing. She worked hard from December onwards, but that's not enough to make up for a casual approach over the previous fifteen months. At Denstone only *one* person got a string of As; even Ruth only

---

33 Virginia Bottomley was appointed Secretary of State for Health in May 1991.

managed three Bs and now can't go to Cambridge. This against a background of a record national entry and a record 80 per cent getting A, B or C. So Denstone has a lot to answer for. Deb should not have found herself a few weeks from the exam with any hesitations about German grammar – that should have been sorted out in the first term.

Fortunately it looks as if Huddersfield will take her anyway; when she phoned, the Admissions Tutor told her dolefully that most of the other applicants had done even worse. Her course will be 'Communication Studies with Theatre Studies': God, how tedious, how pointless.

I hope Deb is going to be sensible; at the moment I shall count her career a success if she can earn a living without endlessly coming to me for money! Susie's GCSE results are out next week. Moving her to Repton now seems more than ever a good idea.

My hand and arm are sore from overwork – partly from decorating (finished the big beams yesterday – very satisfying feeling) and partly from around 25,000 words of text created in twelve days, plus the detailed chapter headings which nearly killed me on Monday. However, now I have my framework and some six scenes written. Today I did the rape scene – second go, I couldn't get into it yesterday and writing it was a distressing experience. I'm glad I've got that out of the way.

The evening sun is going down in the gap between the stable and main house, casting long shadows. It's quiet, except for drumbeats in the distance – Mouliherne is having a rock festival this weekend! We've had torrential rain here, day after day – terrible for tourists but it has suited me and my roses and lawn just fine. I was *not* well pleased to find damp patches in several places on the ceiling, and it rains straight down the chimney, spilling wet black waste on the kitchen floor. The chimney breast in the study is also wet and a bit smelly. So we haven't finished here yet.

I can hear an owl calling. It is so nice to be here. I do my bits of grieving here, especially after a modest half bottle of Saumur-Champigny. But I find I am grieving little now, and saving my energy for my 3,000 words a day, feeling satisfied at the end, sleeping soundly without dreams. Time for supper.

Les Tuileries, Wednesday 26 August, 11 p.m.

Last night here. Gone very fast, and I'm pleased with what I've achieved: most of the painting done, bathrooms spick and span, staircase finished and glowing. I can't get back before Christmas, the diary is just too tight, but hopefully the remaining bits such as the kitchen fireplace will by then have been attended to. It has been such fun, such a happy experience doing up this place that a mischievous small part of me wants to do it all over again, and I catch myself looking enviously into estate agents' windows!

Good news on the home front: we have a bid in writing for the novel of £40,000! I was so delighted listening to Lisa that I didn't note who from. Looks like we're in business. Good royalties too and UK only, leaving open the possibility of further income from a TV series and USA sales later. Lisa was also clearly thrilled, as this is our first bid, and an 'opening bid' at that, so perhaps could go higher. Richard Cohen is still interested and so is Frank Delaney, who it turns out is a scout: what a lowly position for such an able and engaging man, not even a proper agent. Hilary Rubinstein meanwhile has been ruffling feathers with an announcement that he intends to start his own agency from semi-retirement. Apparently he's written to all 'his' authors asking them to leave A. P. Watt and join him; as I haven't seen the mail I don't know if I'm one of the chosen few.[34] I'm surprised the directors of A. P. Watt didn't get him to sign a leaving contract preventing him from doing this. Lisa said they hadn't got round to sending him the retirement photo from the party in The Orangery; it will have to be relabelled 'semi-retirement'. She sounded miffed and hurt. I'm not changing – Lisa is looking after me with a great deal of energy, and is likely to be in business as long as I am (whereas Hilary is over seventy), so I'd be mad to change.

Tower House, Sunday 20 September, 3.15 p.m.

An extraordinary week – mind-bending, amazing, exhausting. I started writing a diary half a dozen times, but the events of the

---

34 EC wasn't, but after she teased him, Hilary Rubinstein invited her to join his stable. EC declined to make the move.

hours following made it pointless. I was working on the section in the book linking the summer of 1992 to the autumn and that required rewriting several times too!

So let's start with the devaluation, and sterling being pulled out of the ERM. A blow-by-blow account would start last weekend as the lira devalued and the Swedish krone came under pressure. John Major cancelled a trip to Seville at twenty-four hours' notice. Finance Ministers meeting last week in Bath under our presidency scrapped the rest of their agenda and discussed how to bring the speculators to heel. It was announced that the Bundesbank was considering a cut in interest rates and everyone relaxed: the word 'substantial' was floating around. It transpires that Germany did indeed offer a big cut, but was insistent that the pound was overvalued and must devalue. Our lot said no. It was only a week to today's French referendum.[35] With a little help from our friends, and the increasing hints from France that a yes vote was likely, it seemed a better bet to hold out another week at the same parity.

By the start of this week this strategy was looking distinctly hairy, with a crop of company returns and business reports saying emphatically that the expected boom had vanished and in fact the UK was sliding deeper and more rapidly into a slump, with no prospect of recovery. In the light of these gloomy prognostications the government's policies of maintaining the parity and resisting inflation seemed pretty irrelevant and off beam, no policy at all.

On start of business Monday morning everyone waited with bated breath. The Bundesbank duly did cut its rates – by 0.25 per cent. Enough to give the impression of reluctance, that they were under political pressure to do so. Not enough to help the pound. Around 7 p.m. Tuesday evening (I read in my well-informed Sunday newspapers) German press agencies published an interview with Helmut Schlesinger, the 68-year-old Bundesbank President, in which he said, 'The tension in the EMS is not over yet... this will only happen when there is comprehensive realignment.' That could mean only one thing: that the Bundesbank had expressed

---

35 A referendum on ratification of the Maastricht Treaty, which damaged the market's confidence in the ERM and started the pound's slide.

publicly its view that the pound should be devalued. Everyone now is expressing shock horror that the Germans should so let us down. What a load of nonsense. Sterling has probably been overvalued for some time. Had there been a genuine boom after the election; had the balance on current account moved back into the black, as it is supposed to during a recession; had the UK government's own deficit appeared to be under control instead of climbing unchecked towards £40 billion, then we might have held out.

At Tuesday night the Bank of England still had around £25 billion in reserves, which included £7.25 billion worth of foreign exchange, mainly Deutschmarks, raised the previous week. The government declared itself willing to defend the pound with whatever means were necessary.

This is where it all gets bizarre. Nobody in the Treasury, it appears, seriously discussed devaluation or floating there and then. 'If we had called for a realignment or suspension as early as Tuesday night, the others would have said we had not done all we could to defend sterling,' the *Sunday Times* was told by one official (Burns,[36] the Permanent Secretary? Budd,[37] the Chief Economic Adviser? Bill Robinson, Lamont's Special Adviser – who?) Treasury officials all went home at this stage to sleep. Foreign exchange dealers prepared to come in early. Doug Bate, chief dealer at Barclays, the largest foreign exchange dealer in London, was at his desk from 5.30 a.m. Wednesday till mid-morning Thursday without a break. One gets the distinct impression that people like him were much more on the ball than economic advisers or politicians. The Bank of England did its best, but did not have a chance. In an average week Bate's team will handle about £6 billion a day – enough by itself to swamp the Bank of England in four days' trading. The world figure is about £900 billion per day. The total reserves of the whole EC look puny by comparison, let alone those of a single central bank. When the accounts opened Wednesday morning the money really started to flow from all over the world and everyone wanted to sell sterling.

---

36 Sir Terence Burns.
37 Alan Budd, later (1997) Sir Alan Budd.

At 10 a.m. interest rates went up from 10 to 12 per cent, to howls of anguish, people saying that would put paid to any recovery. I had a phone call from local BBC TV (I was bashing away at the book) and immediately said that it was not enough. By lunchtime they were up another 3 per cent, but the increase was too late and made not a scrap of difference. Bate told *The Guardian*: 'The weight of money was simply monumental and the Bank simply didn't have a hope of matching the market.' In this one day Barclays handled £30 billion: just one bank in one financial centre. The decision was taken to stick it out till the markets closed. It appears a total of £10 billion, maybe £15 billion, was spent by the Bank as sterling fell through its ERM floor.

By evening the extra 3 per cent interest hike had been rescinded and the pound pulled out of the ERM. By mid-morning Thursday it had devalued 10 per cent and interest rates were back where they had started, at 10 per cent.

The nation is reeling and asking what the hell has been going on. Margaret Thatcher in New York is triumphant, failing to mention that it was she as PM who took us into the ERM at 2.95DM in October 1990. She had in the summer enunciated the Milan rules, conditions required before we would contemplate going into the ERM: completion of the single market, inflation down and falling, freeing up of all capital movements and exchange controls elsewhere, an end to other countries subsidising their industries and breaking the rules, etc. Listening to their reiteration at lunchtime today I was struck by the fact that all these conditions have been met, some handsomely, in the two years since. Yet our membership became unworkable, in part at least because those freed-up financial markets are much bigger than one country – or indeed several countries acting in unison. (Both the Bank of France and the Bundesbank bought sterling on Wednesday to help. Another £2 billion worth, which the Bank of England will owe them, but they did try.) We were not wrong to go in, to try. Instead the effort of achieving that Milan position, and competitive pressures, weakened the British economy: or, to put it another way, we failed to rise to the challenge.

Today the French are voting, the vote which started all this uncertainty and instability. I will be commenting on Channel 4 TV tonight on their 'Midnight Special' about the results and their effect on the rest of Europe. Whatever the French are voting for barely exists now. There is no chance of monetary union in 1997, and it would be a miracle if the UK Parliament voted for us to join in then. The timetable always looked ambitious, but German reunification and its effect in destabilising and pauperising the German economy has obliged that country to be much more inward looking. Political union, or at least closer co-operation on defence and foreign affairs, has been put on ice already under the challenge of Yugoslavia: there is still a lot of talking to do on the basic philosophies of recognition, allies and military action. France and the UK co-operate better as fellow members of the UN Security Council than fellow EC members. What a pathetic picture. Major said that Maastricht will not return to the Commons, even if the vote today is yes, until the Danes have sorted themselves out – probably with another referendum there in the spring. He is gambling on having enough time to take the Bill through both Houses of Parliament before prorogation in October 1993. Could be a hairy summer next year.

I do find all this profoundly exasperating and irritating. We are left with no counter-inflation policy at all, though that was supposed to be the centrepiece, the *sine qua non* of policy. We are no longer at the heart of Europe. Major said earlier this year that he wanted sterling to be the leading currency of the ERM – hollow laughs all round, please. I suppose the opening up of competitive markets might well enforce a new counter-inflationary policy, but there is no doubt that it will be much harder for British business to slap on wage increases and price rises when so many other international businesses are hungry for customers too. The oil companies had a 5p rise at once on Wednesday night, the rogues, and said there will be more to come. I think we are heading up towards 10 per cent inflation all over again. That's the way the British prefer it. At several meetings with Tories this week I've faced the question, to me astonishing: 'What is wrong with a little inflation?' The attitude behind it, is the answer. That is also the reason I feel so livid about the criticisms flying around about unhelpful Germany: the attitude behind such remarks is to look for someone to blame, instead of squarely taking responsibility, which is what I thought modern Conservatism was all about. It seems I was wrong.

In the midst of all this faxes were flying around about the book. Quite astonishing! The first bid was £40,000 from Doubleday/ Transworld, otherwise Joanna Goldsworthy who is delightful and whom we met a week Thursday; they publish Jilly Cooper and did a very swish presentation, complete with blue rosettes. Same from HarperCollins, owned by Murdoch in very smart premises indeed down in Hammersmith, our last port of call that hot sunny Thursday (10th), where I met the chairman, Eddie Bell, a small, chubby Scot – they do Michael Dobbs and were full of good ideas for marketing. Their editor for me, Nick Sayers, was a little ducky: frizzy hair, specs and a distant look, much more literary and intense than the others. He asked me a sharp question as to what motivated any of the characters – didn't they come into politics with any kind of principles? As a result I went home and rewrote the conversation between Tessa and Elaine in the café. In the middle of these two was an offer of £20,000 from Random House's Kate Parkin, whose scout is Frank Delaney. The company was neither as well organised nor as keen as the others, and Delaney should know that his efforts are being sabotaged by his bosses. Nice as Kate was, she did not understand much of the point of the story.

The first meeting had been on Monday with Richard Cohen and the top dogs at Hodder and Stoughton. Nothing flash here, just me talking into the very blue eyes of the chairman and showing off a bit. Richard has a permanently pained look on his face but is very able and nice, though I suspect a little indiscreet; it was no surprise to find some details in this week's *Evening Standard* column on Tuesday night. Lisa said he is known as a good 'book doctor': not someone who can nurse a bad book to health and humour a bad but lucrative author, but an editor able to take a book right to the very peak of what it is capable of being.

Lisa insisted that I get the first two chapters written to show everyone, so the week ending 11 September was quite amazing; after twenty-five hours, starting 6 a.m. and tucked in all over the place, I finished and sent it off on Friday morning. The comeback was lovely, with words like 'excellent' flying around – very gratifying. Then the bidding started in earnest. Lisa handled it like a foreign exchange dealer: absolutely brilliantly. We wanted bids by Thursday, but they started coming in on Wednesday night. Random House dropped out: we were not in tune. Soon it was between Hodder and HarperCollins, the former on £66,000, the latter on £60,000. Doubleday then came in with £75,000, payable in quarters. Their marketing presentation was a bit alarming: nudge-nudge, with a lot of emphasis on the scandalous bits. But Hodder are about to lose Lord Archer, who is going in fact to HarperCollins (Lisa thinks because he is close to Mr Murdoch, I suspect because he's being too greedy). Hodder are therefore desperate for another big name, so back they came with an offer of £102,000, payable in fifths, the last part six months after paperback publication. Before they changed their minds we said yes. Joanna Goldsworthy faxed congratulations. Actually I think we have made a very good deal indeed, for with Joanna it would have been more a woman's book, with Nick Sayers it would have been more intellectual but to me he knows little about politics, and with Richard I think I have a thoroughly nice man who could manage both. Lisa thinks he may get twitchy about the sex. We shall see. I want the book to sell, dammit.

That leaves only one simple task, getting it written. It has not been easy this week! I managed only seventeen hours and just under 10,000 words, much of which will have to be rewritten. That is not a satisfactory pace of work at all. Still I have one less thing to worry about, with a sum like that coming in over the next two years. All being well, we could have the text ready for the spring, publish in hardback in October 1993 and in paperback immediately after the Euro elections. Then it will be time to start on the next one, if the first is a success.

It remains only to get myself a Euro seat. I still think this is the right course. Being part of the Major administration, so weak, so woolly, so lacking in thought and bottom and principle and charisma; being unable to influence policy; being nowhere near the centre of gravity and stuck pining, far from the stuff that interests me: no thanks. I do believe deeply, passionately, that we must be part of Europe. When I start speaking on that topic I can feel my heart beat faster, my nerve ends strain to convince and explain: to me that matters, more than mere office.

Victoria, Thursday 24 September, midnight

Just come from the economy debate. Bit of a shambles, but we managed first vote majority of 42 (330 to 288); second vote majority of 27 is also comfortable. I think Unionists voted with us first time on the Labour amendment. Then I went out on to College Green and did some TV (Sky) – pretty disgusted to find I was the only Europhile MP out there, all alone, against a well organised phalanx of Bill Cash[38] and friends.

Debate itself very mixed (I will write about it for book). House packed. Tories pensive, some sullen. John Major hesitant in places. Strong on Europe but not convincing, and I don't think the troops liked it. Lamont closed with a robust, cocky bugger effort which they loved. He is an accomplished debater. In him you can see how good John Major would have been with a Cambridge education. John Smith, in his first excursion as Leader of Opposition, was excellent. Behind me Robert Adley[39] commented that he is the best Labour leader since Gaitskell, but like Gaitskell he could well split his party and see it continue in the wilderness. Ted Heath very good, very funny, went on a bit long – is sure the single market means a single currency and central bank, and it can't come soon enough for him.

Curious incident after debate. The Prime Minister approached me in the lobby and started talking about *Three Line Quips*, the collection of quotations. I said gaily that I have a contract for a fourth book, a novel; a few minutes later he took me quietly back into the empty lobby and wanted to know all about it; when I told him the title he blushed furiously! He must realise he is in it, but I will not let him see any, not even the synopsis, because he would get cold feet and I won't. I told him it was about a 'youngish MP, very green' who gets seduced. Poor man! He may have more than enough to worry about. We talked a bit about the debate – he needs

---

38 Conservative MP for Stafford since 1984; a prominent Eurosceptic.
39 Conservative MP for Christchurch since 1983; MP for Christchurch and Lymington, 1974–83; MP for Bristol North East, 1970–74.

reassurance, conscious that he is not carrying the Party with him. He thinks someone in the Cabinet is leaking stories. I asked, 'Who wants your job?' and he answered, 'No it's not him.' So Major thinks only Heseltine[40] is after his job. I argued that we need a pro-Europe campaign to counteract the Bill Cash onslaught; John said, 'No one takes any notice of Cash, they all know he's loopy.' That's not true either. I'm alarmed that the PM seems out of touch on these two issues. I told him about chasing seats and the need to persuade elderly MEPs to retire. However, now I know that John doesn't take any notice, I don't expect any help from him on that front. I made him laugh and wince and blush about the book, and he called me 'incorrigible'. Unputdownable, he means. Too bloody right.

Outside in the dark I met the *Daily Mail*'s Political Editor, Gordon Grieg, who is the nearest I get to a friend in all this. We discussed the relative performances of the PM and Lamont (who would have been in danger if he had done badly tonight). He feels that the Prime Minister suffers from conspiracy theories, and was sure no one was leaking or criticising from within Cabinet. He said it takes a lot for the PM to feel real passion or lose his cool. On the plane on the way back from Helsinki recently, Gordon, Hurd and the PM got into a big argument; suddenly the PM lost all reserve and shouted 'I've never been wrong on a strategic decision – never fucking wrong, do you hear?' and started swearing 'bloody' this and 'bloody' that. Hurd's eyes rolled and John backed off. Gordon was highly amused, and impressed – but feels that the PM is a bit vulnerable because he is so thin skinned and needs reassurance.

One other nice event was lunch at the Tate with Richard Cohen. We are *exact* contemporaries, both aged forty-five, he at Cambridge so overlapped with Ray, and may even have had same tutor. We had long and fruitful chat about how to handle material – not to revise just yet, but crack on. He wants a new chunk to read by 19 October, which suits me – should manage down to Xmas easily, and that will include seduction which he has not seen. It's still hard work finding hours to do it, and to get any quality in. About seventeen hours this

---

40 Michael Heseltine, Secretary of State for Trade and Industry since 1992; Conservative MP for Henley since 1974; MP for Tavistock, 1966–74.

week so far, and thirty pages. Richard thinks that's a good pace, but I don't.

Tower House, Saturday 3 October, 4 p.m.

A wet day at the windmill, wind blowing dismally around my eyrie as I type.

All around the news is gloomy and I think we're in a great big old-fashioned slump. The government does not seem to know what it is doing. I'm bloody furious at the incompetence and shilly-shallying which has replaced intelligent decision-making among my colleagues. John Major seems to think that long Cabinet meetings are a substitute for strong leadership. His dithering and uncertainty itself is pushing the pound down and making a return to sanity harder by the day.

I have been fighting off redundancies in South Derbyshire, with part of Drakelow and Willington power stations to close and the collapse of Condor the builders. Daw Mill colliery is to close, with the loss of hundreds of jobs in the area. The Prison Department is not to move from London to Derby: good, because at £100 million, the figure given to me by Ken Clarke, it would work out at £50,000 per job moved, an unjustifiable sum. And if the prisons are to be run by private management companies in future, then the current 1,900 civil servants in the Department will not be needed – indeed 190 would be too many, so the project was rapidly heading for non-viability anyway. Ken did the announcements himself, as he did the coming into effect of the Criminal Justice Act, with confusing new rules on sentencing and parole which have caused much controversy. He wouldn't let a junior minister do the presentation. In fact I don't think we've heard anything of Peter Lloyd[41] on national media since the election. Oh yes, that was just the job for me, I don't think.

I did get depressed last week, really crashing stuff, for Lord Plumb has decided not to retire from the European Parliament. I had been hoping to succeed him. In fact he's too good to retire, but he might have given a lead to the other useless ninnies currently sitting on

41 Minister of State at the Home Office – the job that was offered to EC.

good seats. I think we are going to do badly in these Euro elections, which could be against a background of four years of recession. Tory candidates in Labour seats will have a very hard time indeed. It does not make any sense for me to try for one of these, with the possible exception of Midlands Central. I shall just have to stick it out, and wait. If nothing suitable comes along, at least I shall be the best candidate for South Derbyshire, even after boundary changes. At worst I could lose this seat too! And I'd have to write seriously for a living, though by then our expenses would have fallen, with only Susie still at university.

I weighed myself at the gym and have hit 10st 8lbs, a sure sign of things getting out of control, so I can't even console myself with a chocolate biscuit. Indeed I had stopped going to the gym in an effort to increase the hours available for writing, with the predictable result that my productivity and the quality of my work slumped.

The book is going on steadily; I have to send a chunk to Richard Cohen by 19 October, but oh, it is hard work! I found a nice quote from George Orwell in Michael Shelden's biography of him, which I shall copy out and keep: 'Good novels are not written by orthodoxy-sniffers, nor by people who are conscience-stricken about their own unorthodoxy. Good novels are written by those who are *not frightened.*'[42]

Deb is off to Germany next week. She has been much easier to live with since her future plans were settled, but a lassitude and sleepiness has taken over instead, so she has needed nagging to do basic things like opening a cheque account and buying some tickets. She has the use of Ray's lovely new car – I think he is mad – and had a prang last night in Derby Station car park as she was trying to park in the rain. Tears all round, but he was sweet to her. He wasn't as nice to me years ago when I knocked his precious Zephyr!

We have also had a slimy reporter hanging around. Last time Deb was in the papers she had a letter from a man called Darren who wanted a pen pal. It turned out he was a prisoner serving a sentence and had written while on home leave. She asked me what to do: I told her to bin the letter and not reply, but the silly softy ignored

42   From Orwell's essay 'Inside the Whale' (1942)

my advice because she felt sorry for him and no doubt intrigued too, and of course her letters have gone to the press. On Thursday night she was hysterical about it, all alone in the Tower House with this slimy reporter banging on the door. I told her just to ignore him and put the phone down on him when he called. Since I've never seen this correspondence, I've no idea what she might have said. We must have done something right to bring up such an innocent, kind-hearted kid, but I wish she would learn sense.

Tower House, Sunday 11 October, 7.15 p.m.

Dark outside; it has been a blustery day, and I took advantage of rain in the air to plant some more roses in front of the house. Alan Peat, the gardener, has been working very hard, getting rid of the vast awful expanse of gravel and has reseeded the area. I'm left with a tumbledown bank beyond the willow tree, but it will be ideal for rhododendrons next year. Slowly the garden is coming right.

What a strange Party Conference it turned out to be! At least nobody was talking drivel about green shoots of economic recovery this year. There are no signs of recovery at all. Brighton looks like a ghost town. Their unemployment level is around 14 per cent, with 'For Sale' signs everywhere on shops and houses. It looks as if progress has passed by and moved on. All those bijou shops selling dolls and dried flowers; how could they expect to earn a living in a recession? Nor does anyone deny we are in a slump. It can't just be about interest rates; competition has a lot to do with it, as I keep telling businessmen, forcing down costs and reducing overheads. It is very hard on those affected and of course has multiplier effects throughout the economy. Brighton and much of the south has an additional problem, in that they have been very complacent and haven't the foggiest idea how to cope, or to counteract the effects. At least in the Midlands we have been through all this before and are much less affected this time. For years it has been impossible to get planning permission in the south-east for any large scale employment activity, particularly industrial. Hove Council would have had a fit if it had been suggested that Toyota's 600-acre site should be in their area. Planning permission for shops was no problem, so as the shops have failed there is nothing whatever to take their place.

It is the same phenomenon as in the Sherwood constituency, where Andy Stewart[43] was so determined to defend the pits; when they started to close there was no alternative employment. Heavens, we are so much better off with the diversity of industry in this area, and an unemployment rate still around 8 per cent, below the national average.

I put in today for the Midlands Central Euro seat, after discussing it with Ray. I could wait around forever for one of the ancients in the safer seats to retire; on existing form (they were at Brighton) none of them will. I like the name 'Midlands Central' very much; and it is on the right side of the country, with Birmingham International Airport and the NEC bang in the middle, with Peugeot as a big employer, and with lots of successful car component factories selling to Toyota etc. Of the eight Westminster seats in the area we hold five, including part of Coventry, and there might be more than one socialist candidate. Most of all, it is winnable – we should never have lost it – and I am well known there. Back in the days when it was regarded as safe, the selection committee probably wouldn't have touched someone like me with a bargepole. I remember applying to Solihull, and getting a flea in my ear for being so cheeky! The prospect makes me feel excited too. If I get it, I have a platform. If I don't – well, I tried and would have nothing to reproach myself for.

I am in a cheerful mood tonight, for the book went well last week – or rather, I clocked up my twenty-five hours and produced over forty pages all found, getting ready to send a chunk to Richard Cohen. Early morning seems best, and after a run; restoring my gym activities has definitely put my head to rights and reduced the sluggishness. I feel sleepy in the afternoons, so I try to avoid new creations then. We also have *Three Line Quips* coming out on the 19th and that looks very hopeful; it will be nice to get 50p for each copy sold, though at £10.95 I think it is overpriced. If it goes into paperback we may get a better deal. So there will be lots of telly and radio to do the first week we are back.

Did a fair bit this week too, starting with the *Newsnight* debate on the Conference fringe and finishing with *Wogan*, laying into that

43 Conservative MP for Sherwood, 1983–92.

turd Max Clifford, source of many of the stories against David Mellor. The *Newsnight* debate on Europe with Michael Spicer[44] was marvellous: well organised, with Peter Snow in the chair; it rang bells, and reminded me that I did something similar back in 1985 or '86 on health, which also was successful. I agreed with Michael beforehand that we would be nice to one another, which diminished his effectiveness neatly. The official organisers were the Bow Group, who were worried that no one would come – but on the contrary, participants were hanging from the rafters and yelling lustily. Matthew Parris commented in *The Times* later that he was learning to be wary of old gentlemen in military moustaches and blazers shouting insults: a new apparition at Tory Conferences!

Lamont's Conference debate was stirring stuff, but his own performance was lacklustre. By then I was back in the flat and bashing away at the word processor, but even I could see the glum looks on delegates' faces as they heaved themselves to their feet for a compulsory eighty-second ovation, like they had a bad smell under their noses. I suspect John has manoeuvred him to take all the opprobrium, especially if it proves necessary to raise taxes; Lamont will want to stay in power not resign, but I should be amazed if he is still Chancellor by this time next year, or even by Christmas. He is such an arrogant man, so offhand, so unpleasant, with little sly eyes and a small wet mobile mouth like a predatory but lazy fish. His whole manner seems so self-indulgent. How could a fat little jowly man like that understand people who are having to pull in their belts?

I liked Hugo Young's[45] description of most of the PM's speech: 'We were told to get ready for the speech of Major's lifetime if not ours... But this was promising too much. What came out was mostly a recitation of banalities delivered in a sanctimonious drone.' Yes, that was true. What was more disappointing was that most of the rest, on domestic policy, could have been delivered in 1972, not 1992. The section on education, for example; in all the

---

stuff about reading and spelling I waited for acknowledgement of languages, as in Maastricht: nothing. Or getting recognition around Europe for diplomas and training certificates: not a whisker. He seems to have forgotten the urgent need to teach technology and increase the number of scientists and engineers. Increasing the number of motorway service stations is not the answer! But then John himself is not educated. He didn't get much from school, and his domestic policies are still mired at the level of a poor boy from a home in straitened circumstances in Brixton. A quick mind, but not a thoughtful or knowledgeable one. A vision stuck firmly in the 1950s and 1960s. No bloody imagination; no bloody vision.

Victoria, Friday 23 October, 10.40 p.m.

Funny how I used to wait at this hour for a visitor! He might be performing better elsewhere if he still came to see me. According to a monumentally catty article in *The Times* this week, he's lonely and has had trouble eating and getting his shirts washed. When I gave John a copy of *Three Line Quips* yesterday evening in the lobby, I teased him, saying that any of us would make cocoa for him! He responded quite crossly, calling the article 'shitty'. Poor John, he is having a terrible time right now. He looks grey, wan and tired.

Gloom in the Party has given way to panic, indeed to horror. As well as the John Major article in *The Times*, there is a perceptive piece by Simon Jenkins, its former editor, pointing out that 48,000 finance and banking staff and over 120,000 building workers have lost their jobs in the last twelve months. The misery really blew up in the government's face last Tuesday, 13 October, my birthday, with the announcement that thirty-one pits were to be closed, leaving only seventeen open in the whole country. The economic case for closure of at least some pits is very strong. But heavens, was it badly handled, with some Cabinet ministers, including Mrs Shephard,[46] not hearing about it till afterwards. The men were not prepared either, with some pits closed from Friday – a diabolical way to deal with people, especially as many were members of the Union of

---

46 She had been appointed Secretary of State for Employment earlier in
    the year.

Democratic Mineworkers. Scargill has been prancing around like a genie newly escaped from his bottle. The middle class have joined in the fury; from comfortable gas central-heated homes they have written in, wanting to know the economics of spending dole money instead of buying the coal. Because they won't always be on the dole, is the answer, but we can go on buying expensive coal forever. You can have whatever you want, provided you are prepared to pay for it.

Almost certainly our chances in '94 are dished already, but we shall see. Peter Beasley is supposed to be announcing his retirement as an MEP at his AGM tonight. His constituency is Luton and Milton Keynes, both of which are grotty places. Should I try? The majority there is much better than in Midlands Central. However, the latter is closer to home. If boundary changes come up there may be something better in the offing. I wish, however, that I was not bothered by the thought that I could lose in both '94 and '96. In which case I would not return to the House of Commons, but do some TV and another book and hope to try again in '99. It would mean I had wasted the whole of the 1990s and some of my best years. Making a lot of money is not a substitute for being useful. Still I sat in the coal debate yesterday and watched the shambles, the shouting and yelling and posturing on both sides, with disgust and disbelief. It really is a bear garden. The public sit in the gallery, bemused and anxious, even frightened. The Lords in their two rows look decrepit and supercilious. Ambassadors and foreign visitors are puzzled. I am slowly coming to loathe it all, as *inimical* to good debate or serious consideration of complex issues in difficult times. My view was formed before I had sat there six hours waiting to be called. I will not play their games of joining some spurious committee and claiming an empty importance, just to get ten minutes at the tail end of a debate.

Victoria, Friday 6 November, 9 a.m.
Glum faces all round in the Conservative Party about Clinton's victory,[47] but I am absolutely delighted. Bush had lost interest and

---

47 Bill Clinton had won the American Presidential election on 3 November.

looked old and feeble until just the last few weeks. His approach and style seemed so dated. Barbara Bush, deliberately subsuming her brain and subordinating herself to 'George' all her life, was the wrong image; Hillary Clinton, who didn't even want to use her husband's name, who has one child not five, and who is among the US's top 100 lawyers, is a formidable, clever woman who sees no reason to pretend otherwise. For her alone I would have voted Democrat. There is more to it than changing a generation, however. Clinton was seventeen when he met Kennedy at the White House – there was some marvellous archive film of that, with the besotted look on Clinton's face which expressed how all we young people felt about Kennedy. The man *inspired*: ask not what your country can do for you; ask what you can do for your country. That drove so many of us to have an ideal of service, not just self-seeking, not just money. This is what keeps me in politics instead of heading for the media: being useful is more important, more valuable than being rich. Herein lies the emptiness of the last decade; there is no inspiration in the city whizz-kid or Essex man. Even their wealth is empty and shallow. People want and need prosperity, but they need something else as well, some feeling which drives us to help other human beings stay alive, or to reduce their suffering, or to bring them to peace. It was particularly poignant that Clinton was Governor of Arkansas, one of the poorest states, where he piloted anti-racial legislation; he launched and ended his campaign in the state capital, Little Rock, where thirty-five years ago an earlier Governor had called in the militia to defy the Federal District Court's ruling on desegregated schools. I remember being very moved by the image of the terrified little black girl in pigtails being led to school past Alsatian dogs straining at the leash, held by huge state troopers with bursting shirts and menacing grins on their faces. (I must have been only ten or eleven myself at the time.) So this ghost has been laid to rest too, after so long and after such pain. The view here is that the inexperienced Clinton could be like Jimmy Carter – weak, nice, ineffectual. But I reckon the Kennedy model is much the more appropriate, and the fact that Clinton did it without being devious and without all that money is wonderful (and he had a much bigger majority than Kennedy).

It turns out that I must have had the briefest of contacts with Clinton at Oxford, though I don't remember him at all! When I was standing to become President of the Union in 1968, we debated Vietnam. William Waldegrave was in support of the US action and I was against (I don't recall the motion). This was not exactly a fair match, as William's Dad had been in Macmillan's government, whereas I had only the foggiest idea where Vietnam was. And he made much the better speech. I thought the Americans were foolish and their activities doomed to failure, but it was hard to say so without aligning with the left and being anti-war: that meant I had no clear line to take. It turns out that Bill Clinton took part in the debate as a Rhodes Scholar and spoke on my side; one TV company dug out archive film of the event, and there we all were. I hadn't even realised it was being filmed. Bill Clinton went on anti-Vietnam marches in London and grew his hair long; I lost the Presidency and tried to become an accountant.

The man who *is* looking like a Jimmy Carter is John Major. Elected on a niceness ticket, he is twisting and turning, failing to give leadership, duffing it up with incompetence, vacillation, petulance, poor (disastrous!) handling of the media, empty threats; twiddling around in a cloud of dust and getting nowhere fast. The result is lack of action, and exasperation turning to despair. After the coal debate, the Maastricht paving debate[48] on Wednesday. The idea no doubt was to pull off another 244 majority, but Labour promptly announced they would vote against. On the main motion, to proceed, the vote was 319 to 316. The rebels held together very well, with twenty-six Tories voting against on the second vote and six abstaining. David Lightbown[49] missed the vote as he was out in the lobby chasing an abstainer! Our two poorlies, Julian Critchley (back operation) and Don Thompson,[50] were both brought in. Don looked awful – two stone lighter and shrinking, with sagging skin hanging like folds on

---

48 The debate to 'pave the way' for the Maastricht Treaty legislation.

49 A former assistant government whip; Conservative MP for South-East Staffordshire since 1983.

50 Conservative MP for Calder Valley since 1983; MP for Sowerby, 1974–83; a former butcher, he had been a junior minister at MAFF who robustly defended a diet of red meat.

his once pudgy face. He had had chest pains in the summer and went for a check-up; the angiogram went berserk and the doctor refused to let him go home, operating on him two days later for a quaternary heart bypass, a thoroughly nasty job. I like Don, though he was always a bit of a dope. I don't feel vindicated – just sad.

So we fought hard, and we won. Yet within hours it was all thrown away, with the announcement that third reading would be delayed until after the Danish referendum in May. At least that's how it appears. Michael Carttiss[51] was persuaded by the PM to vote with us by being told just that; he took it for a U-turn and so does everyone else. In fact (I suspect) the only change in policy was not to crash through the committee stage with late-night sittings, weekends etc., but to have a half-day's full debate each week, interspersed with other things, including greater attention to the economy. The result will be, of course, that it will take longer. Linking it with the Danes is crass in the extreme. So what was the battle royal on Wednesday night for? And what about the argument that we should not hide behind the Danes? And since the PM argued that all this delay costs jobs, how many more jobs does this (apparent) delay cost? Etc., etc.

I should add that the polls reflect my pessimism and annoyance at the PM. John Major has become the most unpopular PM since polling began, according to last week's *Sunday Times*. The percentage satisfied is down to 21 per cent. It will be even lower next month. Dissatisfied is 72 per cent. You could say that his honeymoon period is over. It feels just like mid-term, not six months after an election. I suppose psychologically, we are dating the handover of power to December 1990. Yet there are signs that the economy is moving – car sales and exports both up in September and October; my secretary Jane Lea[52] was gazumped for a house; repossessions of houses falling; interest rates now down to 8 per cent; inflation rock steady at 3.6 per cent; no plans to cut road-building or capital projects. The US economy grew 2.5 per cent in the most recent quarter; Clinton could preside over a spectacular recovery if he handles it right. The dollar is strengthening, which will help our exports (no sanctions against

---

51 Conservative MP for Great Yarmouth since 1983.
52 EC's South Derbyshire Constituency Secretary.

us, 'because the British believe in free trade'). Against the DM we are still low, around 2.43. If that isn't a raft of opportunity to help us through the economic rapids, then I don't know what is. In a local estate agent in Victoria, one-bedroom flats are being advertised to rent at £180–200 per week. Somebody has some cash.

Victoria, Thursday 3 December, 11 p.m.

Not written any diary recently, partly because I worked hard to send off a chunk of *A Parliamentary Affair*: on Monday off it went, around 55,000 words of it. I have done over 130,000 words in total and it feels as if it really will happen. There are now fifty-one imaginary characters – I have quite a card index, from the colour of their hair and eyes to their bodily functions! I am feeling quite chipper about it. It helps to be reading *Anna Karenina*, which has enriched my life. The technique is so simple, effective and telling, and even the serious bits – Levin and the peasants – extremely well done. The voting episode, in which Levin doesn't know what is going on, is really funny and could be a fair description of procedure in the House of Commons, right down to the whips taking green newcomers by the hand and ensuring they appear in the right lobby.

The Church of England Synod voted to admit women as priests (though it has to go through the House of Commons first – I shall enjoy voting for that). Ann Widdecombe immediately declared that she was to leave the church, and attended mass in Westminster Cathedral. John Gummer[53] has just resigned from the Synod for the same reason, but carefully stays on umpteen committees to retain his influence. Grotty people, misogynists all. May they wake up and find themselves in bed with a black monk: though that might do both some good.

The Maastricht Bill is at last under way, and so is a support group of Tory backbenchers, the 'Positive Europeans', seventy-six in all, no ministers and only one PPS (Graham Bright, who must have checked with John Major first). Only about thirty come to meetings and a dozen or so sat in the chamber for the two days this week and

---

53 Secretary of State for Agriculture since 1992; Conservative MP for Suffolk Coastal since 1983; MP for Lewisham West, 1970–74.

made themselves felt and heard. Lots of old gents uttered words of weak support in meetings, but have shown very little in debate. Their tactics are to keep away and shut up – but all that does is give the Eurosceptics a free run. So instead some of us are having fun, harrying the other side. Cash spoke for three hours and made himself thoroughly unpopular, and then made a complete prat of himself at 9.30 p.m. last night by calling 'strangers',[54] to the fury of harder men like James Cran, Chris Gill[55] and John Butcher,[56] who was seething. I sat behind both Cash and Taylor, wearing brightly coloured outfits, and muttered into their microphones (which is very off-putting!) or laughed at them, or interjected 'poppycock' and the like; and pulled faces, including at one dramatic point as Taylor was calling the wrath of heaven on all and sundry, doing my witch's hex act right behind him, to the delight of all TV watchers. The results were splendid: 416 to 9 against 'strangers', and 296 to 164 on closure. One problem now is simply time. There is no debate on it next week. Maybe one day the week after. There are around thirty groups of amendments: if we have one or two days on each group, that is probably twelve to fifteen weeks' work. There are twelve weeks in the next term before Easter recess on 2 April, so John's promise not to reach third reading before May will be kept. A sleazy promise, and unnecessary too. Last night about 10.30 p.m., as I crossed the Members' Lobby on my way home, Hugh Dykes[57] expressed his disgust that at best only one more day was scheduled for Maastricht before Xmas. He told me the whips were discussing it there and then, so I knocked on the whips' door and found Richard, non-committal, leaning back in a high chair; his dreadful Deputy, David Heathcoat-Amory,[58] who has as much personality as my little finger and wouldn't be where he is if his Dad had been Mr Jones from Cardiff; Tristan Garel-Jones, leaning forward and arguing hard – as the minister in charge of the Bill, he

54 'I spy strangers' is the call used to empty the galleries: a means of delaying proceedings in the Commons.
55 Christopher Gill, Conservative MP for Ludlow since 1987.
56 Conservative MP for Coventry South West since 1979.
57 Conservative MP for Harrow East since 1970.
58 Conservative MP for Wells since 1983.

wants to get on too; and nice, dear Tim Boswell, like a solid English oak, looking troubled, his eyes lighting up as I ventured in. I said my piece about us being fresh and keen, and offered to raise it in Business Questions to Tony Newton[59] today, and did. It's rumoured that Heathcoat-Amory is hostile, so my intervention may have been timely. What a dozy apology for a government.

Bad news: Midlands Central have not called me for interview but are down to their last three candidates. Bit like Northfield[60] all over again, and this time I know better things are on their way. As it happens I am in the Meriden constituency tomorrow at Bickenhill, so I shall have some fun being frostily pessimistic about their chances of winning the seat back.

Tower House, Sunday 13 December, 3.15 p.m.

On Tuesday evening I was one of a delegation which went to see John Major in his room at the back of the Chair in the House of Commons. Our purpose was to urge a satisfactory outcome at the Edinburgh summit, and a rapid ratification of the Maastricht Bill (which has still only done two days in the Chamber in the whole of our Presidency. I think that is a steaming disgrace). It is not only my impression that the PM blows to whichever wind is whistling in his ear, and that therefore the 'pros' have to keep making strong noises or he will bend to the 'antis'. Hence the formation of the Positive Europeans. John was funny, informative, confidential: he's at his best in small groups. But he clearly has no 'vision' of Europe as his own at all. How very, very depressing. He explained he had been straddling an ever-growing chasm in the Party since the summer (I remember telling him to take Cash *et al* seriously in the spring) – 'people have been fed a diet of venom'. Yet it does not seem to have occurred to him that his own prevarication and vagueness provided the opportunity for both bile and wedge-driving; had he shown more determination and leadership, had we got on with the ratification process with energy and dispatch, much more of the row would have subsided.

---

59 Leader of the House since 1992; Conservative MP for Braintree since 1974.
60 In 1982 EC applied but was not selected as the Conservative candidate in the Birmingham Northfield by-election.

None of us dared say so. I got as close as possible by looking him in the eye and sounding a bit hostile as I commented that it was good to see we were no longer talking to 'the biggest Eurosceptic in the Cabinet', the silly remark he made last summer which was intended to appease the Eurosceptics and instead only encouraged them. We came out of there feeling anxious. Nobody quite trusts him any more.

I sent in my application to South Bedfordshire this week, closing date 31 December. Fingers crossed. It isn't a brilliant seat, but should be better with some effort. I need to buy another little black suit.

I went to hear Rabin, the new Israeli Prime Minister, in the aptly named 'Moses Room' of the House of Lords this week. *Very* impressive. At last an Israeli government which wants peace and is prepared to give way to get it. He has stopped all new settlements in the 'Territories' as he calls them and ended grants to settlers to go there. He wants a change from Israeli investment in the Territories to 'investing in the social and economic welfare of people in the rest of the country'. The Occupied Territories should attract investment from outside, he said. The Arab countries have paid only lip service to the notion of helping the Palestinians. Now he envisages big projects, e.g. joining Red Sea and Dead Sea, so gaining hydro-electric power and reducing the salinity of large areas. There are studies which show how a revitalised, peaceful Israel could become the Hong Kong of the Middle East. He has accepted Resolution 242 and is seeking peace treaties with all neighbours on a bilateral basis: 'For there to be peace, the people in the region must make it themselves.' As for 200,000 anti-government demonstrators in Tel Aviv, Rabin said, 'We have taken risks in war; now we must take risks in peace.' He is ready to withdraw Israeli armed forces from the Golan Heights 'to secure and recognised boundaries'. Wow. He has said there should be a date for elections in the Occupied Territories for interim self-government for Palestinians. Trouble is, they see that only as a step towards independence; Rabin sees a federation as more appropriate. Jerusalem to remain whole and Israeli, and so on. It's clear that a great deal of thinking and heart-searching has been going on, and I deeply approve, so now I have joined CFI (Conservative Friends of Israel), which I have resisted doing for nearly ten years, since Begin blighted the land and destroyed hope. Now there's a new prophet singing a new song.

Les Tuileries, Wednesday 30 December, 11 p.m.

Sitting by a bright red fire, toasting… The house has only 12kW of power, which is not enough to have all radiators on, water heater, underfloor heater, cooker, fridge, washing machine, kettle, coffee maker, microwave and toaster all at the same time, as is my wont. So it has to be increased to 20kW, which means a bigger standing charge (and electricity is not cheap here), but it can't be attended to till Thursday morning next week when I'm leaving. Thus I have shrunk my activities to three rooms: kitchen, *lit en séjour* (put-u-up) and bathroom, all of which are kept warm by judicious fiddling with the heaters and turning the water on only at night. To be truthful, the house has now warmed up nicely and the weather has improved, but my first couple of days here felt like freezing for my art. Tots of whisky in hot water a big help! The fireplace has been redone and looks lovely, *so* inviting, but still smokes if the logs are placed too near the front. No wonder the mantelpiece was black – it has given problems since 1810 (you would have thought someone would have rebuilt it before now). The log pile includes pieces of dried old beam, which of course is oak: so I have rediscovered what the English have long since forgotten, that oak is the best fire of all, burning slow and hot and with less ash. Wonderful. All I need is a fat cat and a small dog, and my life would be complete.

I'm here to write, but I can't tell till this time next week how I am getting on. So far so good is all I can guess at. I've done over twenty hours from Sunday to Tuesday inclusive, so I took today off and had a glorious time, catching the 9.35 TGV at Le Mans, which then takes only fifty-five minutes into Montparnasse. Marvellous! I spent an hour at Réciproque and bought a lovely Guy Laroche sequinned top and a black velvet skirt, which will be OK for New Year's Eve tomorrow – dinner at the Carters, about twenty people. And two coats – one posh, long, black, woolly which I promptly wore, and an apricot wool/cashmere mixture, three-quarter length, pretty for spring. Must come again at Easter, preferably a stone lighter. Trying on suits was very depressing. I *refuse* to be a size sixteen, but really I look very dumpy at the moment. All that chocolate I eat at home! Ray keeps giving me bits, as if he wants the reassurance of me the same size as him. Huh!

End of the year, quite a good Xmas: Debbie still somewhat erratic, especially when she has stayed up late or read a book into the early hours. I do understand her moods, but get fed up with them. Being co-operative is no harder than screaming at everyone.

I felt rather wistful on the boat coming over. Some company would have been nice. Couples on both sides of me were talking to each other as we never do, chattering away gaily, sharing all sorts of inconsequential stuff. RFC and I *avoid* such talk. We both have the instinct to contradict and to rule. So we talk hardly at all. That's why I write a diary – I have to have *someone* to talk to that I can expect: (1) not to criticise even when I am being stupid, lazy or disorganised, as usual; (2) not to tell everybody; and (3) not to lie to me or let me down. Awful that there is no human being I feel I can say that of, isn't it? I still feel badly let down by John Major, and had a little weep about it last night. It's soothing that it doesn't hurt so much, as time goes by.

The closing date for the South Bedfordshire Euro seat is tomorrow, so I shall be on tenterhooks till I hear if there are any interviews. Prag[61] is also retiring and I am getting good vibes from Watford, of all places. However if I were adopted for Bedfordshire or Hertfordshire there would be a problem, as I would presumably want to keep the implied promise and stay with them instead of moving back to the Midlands: that means moving house. I can't drive 100+ miles on a Saturday night after late dinner, every weekend. *Not* on. Maybe the expenses would be enough to rent a cottage, but what is the point of marriage if hubby is *never* there?

Nearly midnight. Fire burning low, turn the logs over to coax a little more life into them. It goes cold very quickly when they stop flickering. Munching cherries in red wine and brandy, a real treat; they would be marvellous hot, with ice cream. That's why I've put on a stone since Easter!

---

61   Derek Prag, Conservative MEP for Hertfordshire since 1979.

1993

Victoria, Thursday 14 January, 11 p.m.

Interesting little bit in the *Daily Telegraph* about Jeffrey Archer leaving Hodder to go to HarperCollins, as Lisa Eveleigh thought he would. I wonder how hard they fought to keep him; maybe they could not afford him, especially now they have me. And he has abandoned Richard Cohen too. Apparently all the editorial discussions took place in Archer's splendid penthouse flat, and his last book went through fourteen revisions. I wonder how my efforts will compare. I sent off another 50,000 words or so this week, and some hefty revisions too, so we are over the 180,000 mark and will climb towards 250,000 before the end. That will require a lot of cutting. Lisa guessed at 150,000 words and I said nothing, but that always felt an underestimate. There's so much happening in the book, a complex plot and lots of characters: it doesn't feel like a slim volume. My accompanying reading is Trollope's *The Prime Minister*, which has clearly been a bible for many people. It is a delicious book, vivid and bright and witty. It has helped no end in my drawing of the male characters, especially Roger, who is now much warmer and more interesting.

John Major came into the tea room this afternoon and talked about the Middle East. He is so much better around a table than before the television cameras or even in the House. As he left the table he tried to wink and proffer a little charm but I wasn't having any – I feel I've been had, personally, and I hope he noticed my coolness.

I had Sir (as he is after the New Year Honours) Michael Latham[62]

---

62 Conservative MP for Rutland and Melton since 1983; MP for Melton, 1974–83.

in for supper on Monday night. He shared my concern that the Midlands Central seat had refused to interview any ex- or sitting MPs or MEPs on principle. As a result they have selected, as you would expect, somebody no one has heard of, which makes the seat even more dodgy than now. Michael and I had a good chin-wag; he is an incorrigible gossip, and was full of what he said to Margaret Thatcher in the days when he helped run the Research Department at CCO. He told me he was a member of the 1922 Executive at the time of my resignation and spoke up for me, as did several others, including old Anthony Buck[63] and Anthony Grant[64] (I think). Yet Cranley Onslow still went to Margaret and told her the '22 were unanimous that I should go. I replied rather tartly that I was sunk partly because I had been banned from defending myself in the House on the Monday, and partly because on the Tuesday Margaret herself had derided the whole business by saying she had had scrambled egg for breakfast that morning. She might just as well have said she slept with an HIV positive at the height of our AIDS campaign. I never forgave her for backing away like that. Michael said I could and should have been leader. How curious to be reminded of those days, so long ago.

It can be odd, being on the outside and unimportant. I went this evening to Jonathan Aitken's party in his Lord North Street house (a defence minister should not publicise his home address like this) to celebrate his new book on Nixon. I got a signed copy, of course, though most people there were conspicuous in not doing so. Jonathan was rather drunk and happy, telling me he couldn't attend the official launch on Monday as he was with King Fahd, and he wrote silly nonsense comparing my qualities to Nixon's inside the front cover. I am not sure that the comparison is entirely a compliment! The house is stunning, with a lovely long room with a huge mirror and pink drapes and paintings suitable for dinners and dances at the back of the house where the party was, everyone tripping up over glorious old rugs and carpets – it was a crime to

---

63 Sir Anthony Buck, Conservative MP for Colchester North since 1983; MP for Colchester, 1961–83.

64 Sir Anthony Grant, Conservative MP for South West Cambridgeshire since 1983; MP for Harrow Central, 1964–83.

leave them there under our feet. Champers and smoked salmon and cocktail sausages – all very pleasant. But my current status as an unimportant backbencher meant no one came up to me, to talk; I did the circulating, the chatting. I met Mrs Aitken, who is Swiss and very beautiful, married for thirteen years. Before that she was Jeffrey Archer's girlfriend for about a year. Then she took up with Jonathan. She told me that one day she came back to his house to collect some of her things, and looking out the window saw Jonathan's mother and the Thatchers, complete with Carol, whom he was courting at the same time, having lunch in the garden. The two families were waiting for an announcement of the engagement to Carol. The current Mrs Aitken phoned down and got him upstairs, where he found her furiously throwing all her things into a bag to go back to Switzerland, calling him a cheat and a liar. He made up his mind on the spot and proposed, went back downstairs to finish lunch totally unperturbed, while his Swiss miss sat at the window pulling faces at Mrs Thatcher. The main person hurt was Carol, who went off to Australia and has never married. But Mrs Thatcher never forgave him, and never offered him a job.

Victoria, Thursday 4 February, 10.45 p.m.

I have an interview next Saturday (13th) in South Bedfordshire, Peter Beazley's Euro seat. Part of me doesn't mind if I don't get this one, as the next, Hertfordshire, is a better seat. Madron Seligman[65] has announced he is going at last, but I don't think West Sussex and I would mix very well: it's Worthing, Bognor etc., high percentage of elderly people, little industry, high unemployment and few prospects. However that increases the prospects of Scott-Hopkins[66] retiring, or even pressure on Plumb. At any rate I am feeling happier about it. The preceding day I have three speeches in Oxfordshire which will sharpen my responses, while on Tuesday 16th I'm in Paris, so something to look forward to.

And I have my Toyota Carina: very nice, which is one way of

---

65 Conservative MEP for West Sussex since 1979.
66 Sir James Scott-Hopkins, Conservative MEP for Hereford and Worcester since 1973.

saying a bit disappointing. Dull, as all saloons are. Difficult to manoeuvre and park, compared with my beloved GTi. Pompous dark blue instead of cheeky red. Not me at all. Still, it will serve, and has turned out to be the first car from Burnaston taxed and on the road for a British customer (22 January). I went round the factory on 18 January and must have seen it being made, for Ron Brooks's garage phoned me the following day to say it had been delivered. The factory is quite amazing – huge, light, cavernous, peopled by handfuls of earnest men in white overalls, heads bent over plans and brows furrowed. The balance between capital and labour has shifted decisively, with £750 million spent and only 1,200 employees in there at present, up to 1,500 at Easter. Everything being done at crawling pace this year so that quality is not sacrificed: estimated output approximately 35,000 cars. By 1994 that will increase to 100,000, with the same workforce.

Last week I wrote over fifty pages of the book in nineteen hours – that is over 12,000 words – it just flowed and has come out very powerful, mainly Karen's attempted suicide. This week has been harder, with shooting pains in my shoulder and a largely blank brain, rather as one might expect! However, Richard was very complimentary. He made several sensible suggestions, such as spinning out the climaxes, which I will certainly do. The book will need 20 per cent off, and my deadline for first draft is 25 April. Revision during May. Publication not in the autumn as their list is complete – and, I suspect, money is tight: but OK for early February when we should have a less cluttered run. I asked if there were basic problems and he said, 'I only worry that it may be too commercial. Bit Catherine Cooksony.' That would suit me! He seems to have overcome his embarrassment at talking sex with me (which was really amusing – he is rather proper) and I have stopped intimidating him, not arguing but dutifully taking notes like a disciple. His advice was just to crack on and he'll start editing properly when he has seen the lot. Certainly he seemed a lot happier, so that rubs off on me too.

We gossiped more about Jeffrey Archer. I asked why he left Hodder, and the answer was that when Hodder were in serious financial trouble a couple of years ago (the last time I met Richard), Jeffrey offered to buy the company. Michael Attenborough, the

Chairman, laughed at the suggestion, and Archer was mortally offended. Richard believes that at that point Archer felt he had to leave and find someone else. We talked about Archer's weird boasting. His *Who's Who* entry implies he is an Oxford graduate: no he isn't. He *started* (matriculated) in 1963 at Brasenose but never finished, even though he was President of OU Athletics Club as late as 1966. In fact he attended teacher training college instead. Yet to have overcome these difficulties and risen to become a bestselling novelist – that's an achievement to trumpet. He boasts in *Who's Who* of raising £57 million for the Kurds. Of course he did nothing of the kind; most of it was already pledged by governments. It is still a remarkable achievement: as would be raising £1 million, or even £100,000. What you don't do is *boast* about it, and certainly not in *Who's Who*! He is a congenital boaster. He told Richard that his new novel, *As the Crow Flies*, had sold over 300,000 copies in the USA. Richard checked and it's approximately 230,000. Still remarkable – so why not tell the truth? I think Richard is still a bit naïve and under his spell, for all that he has given up being Archer's editor, for he told me that the whole prostitute story was Archer covering up for somebody else. That, frankly, I don't believe, since if it was true we would all know who it was. Jeffrey is the soul of indiscretion: he is a proven liar and he is no hero, not he.

And so to real politics, before I curl up with *Middlemarch* (which is much harder work than Trollope), and in between I read Michèle Roberts's sweet, sinister little novel *Daughters of the House* and *The Trouble with Harry* by Jack Trevor Story, at the suggestion of Richard, to see how chapters develop. The scandals and writs were flying around last week, with allegations in the *New Statesman* about John Major and Clare Latimer, the cook. There have been rumours for some time, perhaps because Miss Latimer, who is very pretty, forty-one and unmarried, has no obvious escort and is in and out of No. 10 and other private houses late at night. The affair ended before he became either Chancellor or PM, depending which version you read. Well now! I can believe it, yet I don't, because the timing is all wrong. If it is true, it helps explain why he found it so easy to forget his previous one, to the point of forgetting conversations about her deepest fears and dislikes. That was what hurt me the most – the

49

feeling that he had not been listening. On the other hand the articles implied that this started in '88 or '89 and I find that unlikely, unless he was a good deal more duplicitous than I believe him to be. Anyway he flung writs around and received a grovelling apology, and that should still the talk.

We had a lovely weekend with Deb and Susie home and my Mum to stay. She is looking old, shrunken, and is going deaf, which she does not realise, missing great chunks of conversation and talking a bit too loud. Deb is looking lovely – tall and very slim, having lost half a stone since December. I took her to Gatwick on Tuesday morning to see her off to Israel – all a bit emotional. If she enjoys it, it will do her a *lot* of good. Susie was clearly very envious.

Victoria, Tuesday 2 March, 8.50 a.m. (yes, morning)

I'm through to the last round of three at South Bedfordshire. The local Tories are in a fix, as the majority is only 2,000, and two of the UK seats, Luton South and Stevenage, are highly dodgy. So are two of the MPs, Barry Legg (who voted against the government on the paving debate) and Robert Jones, who has told people he will try to stop me getting the nomination. However the other five MPs seem OK or even helpful, Butler, Bright and Madel especially, and I get on with John Carlisle. It is good news that Mather[67] is after it – makes the Parliament a more serious proposition all round. Hertfordshire didn't want to know, I suspect because they've had enough pro-European claptrap from Derek Prag (who told Ian Taylor the committee were being 'beastly' in not inviting me for interview). However the Cambridge and North Bedfordshire seat is also now inviting nominees, and I am to speak in Huntingdon immediately after final selection in South Bedfordshire on 15 March, so we are still moving.

House of Commons, Wednesday 10 March, 11 p.m.

On Monday we lost a vote on the Maastricht Bill, and by the hefty margin of twenty-two. This is the first time we've lost a vote since

---

67   Graham Mather, solicitor; later Conservative MEP for Hampshire North and Oxford.

1986 (Shops Bill) and only the second time since 1979, so it is serious and I still can't figure out why we let it happen. Ryder explained this evening that we don't have a majority even when Liberals vote with us; since twenty-six Tories voted against and another eighteen abstained, there is a substantial gap even with Liberal support. The Unionists are solidly against the Bill, except Kilfedder,[68] who votes with us. I gather that a deal was done over the weekend to obtain Liberal and Nationalist (three Plaid Cymru and four Scottish Nationalists) support; the point they wanted, on representation on the Committee of the Regions, would be conceded *without* amendment, which would produce a report stage and thus another month's delay. The Nationalists stayed and voted with us, but the Liberal Democrats switched sides during the day. The vote was called and we lost, very badly.

What happens now?

1.   The Bill won't finish in House of Commons till June/July.

2.   Given six weeks in the Lords it will just scrape through at last in October *two years* after Maastricht.

3.   That's assuming Danes vote yes in May, of course.

4.   Having lost one, we'll lose others. The Wilson–Callaghan regime of October 1974–79 lost forty-two votes. Only one counts – the 'no confidence' – but some of our boys are so disaffected, and so arrogant, that I wouldn't put it past them, especially as our paper majority falls with by-elections. Some won't stand again and have nothing to lose, especially if they believe the Party needs to have a period in opposition to sort itself out.

Depressed? Yes, somewhat. I'm feeling dog tired, after getting up early, on Monday to write, Tuesday to catch the 7.30 a.m. train to Nottingham for a second rehearsal to present Central TV's *Sunday Supplement* programme, and this morning for a Prime Performers'[69] breakfast meeting, car at flat 7.15 a.m. At least that earned me £2,000. As there'll be no other money in before June and the bank account has only enough to pay taxman and accountant, an

---

68 James Kilfedder, Unionist MP for North Down since 1970; leader of the Ulster Popular Unionist Party since 1980.

69 A speaker agency.

extra bob or two is useful. Meanwhile I'm lunching tomorrow with Richard Cohen, having sent off four more chapters (up to 249,000 words in thirty weeks), and on Saturday we're into the final of South Bedfordshire. Fingers crossed.

House of Commons, Thursday 11 March, 9.21 p.m.

On the backbench, listening to Maastricht Bill, in the middle of the debate on the European Court of Justice. Feeling more than a little spaced out, too, after a straight twenty-hour day yesterday; we did not finish till 2 a.m. If the stupid antics of the left yesterday were designed to delay matters they won't work, but they succeeded in disgusting me. I want out, asap.

I can't quite believe what's been going on this week with our Euro rebels. Yesterday I asked David Davis,[70] the Euro whip, why we went ahead with a vote we could not win on Monday. Before, we have always wriggled to avoid it. Because to do so, we would have had to go on very late, after midnight, long past the time when the Chair would have accepted a closure. If *we* called the vote and lost, then we had not conceded anything, and the delay would have been caused by those who voted against, including the Liberal Democrats who had been so sanctimonious at the weekend about getting on with it. Apparently most of the Liberal Democrats wanted to vote *with* the government as previously, but Ashdown[71] (who is not very bright) said no, and no it was. Davis also said that in the long run the vote would expose the sceptics and destroy the myth that their votes could not cause damage to the government, i.e. we could lose, and badly. They may then come into line.

Well, I don't think much of *that* argument, and neither did the rebels who weren't crestfallen but cock-a-hoop about defeating the government. Most have squared themselves with their constituency associations long since. Most are a bit mad or have strong reasons for wanting to take the government down a peg or two, like Ivan Lawrence.[72] (In case I haven't mentioned it, Lawrence was told on

70 Conservative MP for Boothferry since 1987.
71 Paddy Ashdown, leader of the Liberal Democrats since 1988; MP for Yeovil since 1983.
72 Sir Ivan Lawrence QC, Conservative MP for Burton since 1974.

the Monday after the '92 election to wait by the phone for appointment as Solicitor-General. He waited and the call never came. When he switched on the news that evening, he heard another man's name in the post. So why should he do other than punish the government which treated him so cruelly?) At 2 a.m. this morning in the taxi queue Bill Cash was expansive, offensive and very pleased with himself. There was a wild, hard light in his eyes, and he said, '*We* are the real Conservatives! You – European People's Party! People's Party!' etc. Last time I heard anyone claim to be the heart and soul of their Party when in fact they were a dangerous and destructive splinter group, it was David Owen and the Labour MPs who went off to form the SDP. They split the left-of-centre vote for a decade, and ensured Labour's long stay in opposition. Cash, Taylor,[73] Cran *et al* are perfectly capable of doing the same. It has me worried sick.

Tower House, Sunday 28 March, 11.30 p.m.

The nomination at South Bedfordshire was relatively easy in the end, but I took no chances. The night before I did not want any company so I stayed in London, communing with my God, rehearsing all the difficult questions I might be asked; in fact, all the speeches I had ever made to Tory lunches and dinners stood me in good stead as nothing was asked that I hadn't met before, and I had the confidence to be blunt or funny or to stand my ground when challenged. One chap from the wrong bit of Milton Keynes had arrived determined to move that the whole selection process was a disaster and should be started all over again, but by the end was eating out of my hand; had agreed to work with me and be friends. That's experience, I guess. Rather cruelly I worked on my two opponents' weaknesses, their lack of success at elections; and on their dullness and tendency to speak over other people's heads. My two bits of luck were drawing the lot to go first both times, thus setting the standard to beat. I won on first ballot by a large margin, and now I shall win the seat.

---

73 Sir Edward 'Teddy' Taylor, Conservative MP for Southend East since 1980; a prominent Eurosceptic.

We are also making progress on Maastricht, at last! The government has come to terms with the fact that we have no majority and is now negotiating sensibly with the Liberals. The vote was switched to Wednesday last week and hey presto! we had a majority of seventeen, which included seventeen Liberals and four Nationalists. Twenty-six Tories voted against and more abstained. So business went through the night till noon, and with a session on Thursday all the economic stuff was completed, insultingly debating the EMU in the middle of the night. That leaves relatively little, other than the referendum and the Social Chapter, to vote on in the Commons, so we are on target for the third reading after the Danish referendum, if they vote yes. The whips seem sanguine even about the Social Chapter; apparently there are enough strongly pro-European Labour MPs who will helpfully abstain (some, like Roy Hattersley and Tam Dalyell, instead of following Party instructions to vote against), to ensure that the government doesn't get landed with the Social Chapter and ditch the Bill entirely. It is widely recognised that we will get the Chapter sooner or later anyway.

I wasn't able to stay for the full Maastricht debate this time as at 7.50 a.m. on the Thursday morning, I headed for Königswinter.[74] What a mind-blowing experience. I have written about its short-comings – which are serious – but nevertheless it was terrific to find myself with top-notchers from two countries and able to take part in their discussions as an equal. It helped that I had my Euro-nomination securely under my belt; I did show off and enjoy myself hugely. One Königswinter tradition I was not prepared for was pairing off. Three times I fell in step with some chap, just for company. (Two were distinguished professors, one is about to be.) Three times each one took it I was available and at an appropriate time propositioned me – I extricated myself from the male thigh jammed up against mine in the pub, only to have my hand grabbed meaningfully by a second chap as I headed for the door. One of them was over sixty and a cripple: when I looked at him in total astonishment, he said sheepishly, 'Well, it's a Königswinter tradition.' The sad thing was that the one or two I might have toyed with

---

74 The annual Anglo-German conference.

accepting, people I like and can trust, made no such moves. Maybe that's why I like them. I was so disgusted with this harassment – it was so blatant – that I muttered darkly about it over breakfast to an elderly admiral, one of the old Königswinter hands, who nearly fell off his chair in embarrassment. A British industrialist next to him (who was rather nice, but it was too late by then) nearly died silently laughing. The admiral ('My dear girl') seemed more troubled at the thought I should reject the idea than at his colleagues' presumption. When I hissed that I would never dream of one-night stands, that many of my friends were gay and HIV positive and that was how it happened, he went a weird colour. I enjoyed that, too.

It feels like a turning point. My period of mourning is over; I am no longer stuck in the tomb of the House of Commons, condemned forever to watch the back of the PM's head, and to consider how very disappointed we all are with him, however much we like him. How very let down I do feel, by him, and by the system. Winning my nomination makes such a difference. I have lost over a stone since January and am looking and feeling much better and stronger. I feel less embarrassed, less apologetic, less of a failure. Ready for some adventures, maybe. Who knows? At least I know this period in my life, this penance, this guilt-ridden miserable time is coming to an end, and that I will continue to be useful and happy for a very long time to come. Roll on Strasbourg, here I come.

Victoria, Thursday 20 May, 11.45 p.m.

At the flat, alone and somewhat tiddly after drinking champagne in the Smoking Room. I haven't written for two months because there's been so much going on – even finding time to sleep has been difficult!

Tonight we got through the third reading of the Maastricht Bill by a majority of 180. About fifty Tories voted against us, the Liberals and five Labour voted with, and the rest of Labour abstained – the idea being that we would have less than half Parliament voting for the Bill, which (at present) is still without the Social Chapter. Still 180 is ten times our usual majority of 18, down (1) because we lost the Newbury by-election on 6 May in the most spectacular fashion and there's now a Liberal Democrat majority of more than 22,000;

and (2) because Robert Adley has died, and despite his 23,000 majority, the third-largest Tory majority in the country, there's no guarantee we will hang on to that, either.

The government is in deep doo-doo and it is going to get worse. We're 17 points behind in the polls, the press are filleting John Major for all his failings of leadership; we've done U-turns on educational testing so that this summer's tests will be a shambles, and on rural post offices; and now we are threatening to charge pensioners for their prescriptions. Unemployment fell in April by a minute amount for the third month, but nobody believes the figures, least of all the electorate. We got hammered in county council elections, losing sixteen councils held out of seventeen – the only one left is Buckinghamshire! – and hundreds of seats. We lost nothing in South Derbyshire, holding on to our four seats (out of nine), but all with reduced majorities; John Morgan-Owen hung on to Melbourne by only thirty-six votes. Still that maintains our 100 per cent record of never losing a councillor. So far.

Book going OK – I'm now in the middle of the last chapter and know where I am going. It will be a great relief to finish next week and send it off. It must be done then as I'm off to Israel on Sunday 30 May to see Deb. Should get a chance, with Conservative Friends of Israel, to meet the Prime Minister as well. The London–Tel Aviv airfare is over £800: isn't that a disgrace! I'll hire a car while I'm there and enjoy a couple of days of freedom too. Looking forward to it. Publication date now set for 3 February 1994, so everything shaping up nicely.

Central TV's *Sunday Supplement* started last weekend to general acclaim and amazement – there's nothing quite like it, certainly on tedious Sunday. But to be frank, I hate doing it, which is a real disappointment. I hate being pushed around by Central TV; I hate the *huge* amount of work involved. Since January I've done two run-throughs plus a full pilot and had my hair tinted and highlighted their way three times (Nottingham, two hours plus each time) and spent a day in Birmingham, and Liverpool, and posed endlessly for publicity photos and spent £1,000 on clothes, and all without being paid a penny: this week is the first time I've been able to send in an invoice, for £1,667, which I do not regard as appropriate for two days' (Saturday and Sunday) work each week necessitating two days (Monday and Tuesday) recovering! The original idea was that I was to be one of three presenters, one of whom, Paul Merton, is brilliant and a professional. In fact there are only two, me and Garth Crooks, a sweetie but like me a beginner: so I'm doing most of it, live. I don't mind at all giving my opinions – that's the kind of TV I enjoy – that is what I do for a living. But as a presenter I have to swallow my views, plus learning the details of half a dozen guests, plus looking great (gym, slimming, sunbeds – the works). This is not the career I want, and I could have told Central that to begin with, before they started exploiting me. I tried getting more money out of them but to no avail, so I'm feeling distinctly grumpy and unco-operative about it. Nor is the programme something I can feel proud of – very downmarket indeed. I shall be glad when it is over.

South Bedfordshire is going well, so far. Went to Letchworth last week and I'm in the patch tomorrow too. Totally different to Derbyshire – bright, but educated *and* knowledgeable *and* forward-looking. And well organised – proper agents, the lot. The contrast is profound, as South Derbyshire is not putting up a fight against the Boundary Commission recommendation that we lose Mickleover, which accounts for 2,000 out of our 4,658 majority. I account for much of the rest. Our esteemed Chairman, Alan Griffiths, reckons we'll win it anyway, but it's going to be a juicy proposition for Labour. Maybe I'm leaving just in time?

Postscript

Feeling very flat and sad after the third reading. After all that effort, only a handful of us gathered in the Smoking Room for a celebratory drink. No whips, no Prime Minister (though there were drinks in the Whips' Office – so why not invite some supporters?). I bought two bottles of champagne and that was ample. No wonder this administration is so lacklustre, if it can't celebrate the passage of a Bill so significant and so difficult. I'm disgusted. Edward McMillan-Scott MEP[75] was around, so I took him into the Smoking Room too and got ticked off for it later – isn't it *mad?* Most people thought

---

75   Sir Edward McMillan-Scott, Conservative MEP for York since 1984.

he was a peer; and that includes our own members. Oh, roll on Strasbourg. It could not be worse than Westminster.

Victoria, Thursday 27 May, midnight

The PM did a reshuffle this morning – in the end, a big one. Lamont was sacked (offered Environment but said no) and has behaved like a petulant bully since – no nice letter, just a fax to No. 10 of a press release which lacked only 'get stuffed' for full accuracy. Apparently John Major was very reluctant to get rid of him and was warned by Fowler and Hurd that he had no choice, or he was putting his own job at risk.

The replacement is Ken Clarke. Now his knowledge of economics or finance is nil, pretty well, and this is his fourth Cabinet post in four years. He was turning into a great Home Secretary and was relishing the job, having been Minister of State at the Home Office before. He'll tackle the yawning Budget gap of £50 billion with his customary verve, tossing opponents over his shoulder and chewing up the opposition. The pound should strengthen now Lamont is going, though more companies will be affected by collapsing markets in the rest of Europe. The main problem the PM faces, however, is that Clarke will outshine him instantly, especially with presentational skills and willingness to tackle issues head on. Ken will happily take over the top job whenever the chance appears. He won't intrigue for it – he doesn't need to, and the PM could sack him if he tried. But my only thought was that maybe John Major knows he's running out of steam, and wants a leftish pro-European in a good position to succeed him, rather than a right-winger like Portillo or Howard or Lilley, who would grit their teeth and cut benefits. It's hard to figure out what makes the PM tick or what he believes in, but on certain key occasions he has stuck his neck out when he didn't need to – in 1989, calling for us to join the ERM; as Minister of State for Social Security in 1987, writing the pledge to preserve child benefit into the manifesto – I sat at the same table and watched him adroitly do it – and his strong dislike of poverty, the bitter way he spoke to me of his own nine months' unemployment as a young man.

The rest of the reshuffle is a muddle, from what I can see.

Michael Howard to Home Office (yes, he's a QC); John Gummer to Environment (Good Lord, I think he's been a minister there before, but even so! Apparently Gummer was in line for the chop, but with Lamont he co-sponsored John Major for the leadership contest). Gill Shephard to Agriculture – she has not been a great success at Employment, where the policies on training have been complex, bureaucratic, expensive and largely impenetrable. She chose Agriculture, however, possibly because of her constituency and her French. Her job at Employment went to David Hunt[76] and I bet he is pleased as Punch, though he'd have preferred Environment. John Major has always seemed to have it in for Hunt – always seen him as a rival, even years ago. He seems to have a talent for wanting to put people in the wrong place, or handles them with total incompetence to the point of driving them to fury. I don't believe he can get under the skin of people properly, or perhaps doesn't always bother. Peter McKay in the *Standard* points out that nobody these days speaks up for John Major: well, that's why. He shows loyalty, but not in the right ways, and lacks competence himself. I wonder if he will last to the end of this Parliament?

I certainly need him to last till '95 at least, as that's the assumption in the novel, which I finished today – whoopee! A great weight off my mind. In all I worked flat out for forty-two weeks and delivered 359,000 words. There's loads of revision to do, of course, but that's psychologically easier than having the whole thing hanging over me.

Victoria, Thursday 3 June, 1.30 p.m.

Just back from a super four days in Israel. Deb is well and happy; she settled into the kibbutz within days. I suspect nine years at boarding school prepared her very well for communal eating of poor food and endless chores! She works in the kitchen, six hours per day on her feet clearing the dishwasher. It seems to me mind-numbingly boring, but on principle the work is all done by kibbutzniks instead of giving employment to the poor families in the Arab village next

---

76 Secretary of State for Wales; Conservative MP for Wirral West since 1983; MP for Wirral, 1976–83.

door. Her boyfriend 'Shi' is yet another gangly youth who looks as if he could do with a good meal. She seems to go in for waifs and strays; we clearly don't have the same taste in men! Her course finishes this week, with all the other students spending five days with the Israeli army – of course if any decide to stay in Israel they would have to serve their three years as soldiers – but Debbie got some days off to be with me. We had a lovely time, toddling around the Galilee in a tiny black Fiat Uno I hired. I don't think she will pine much for Israel, or Shi, but she will certainly go back. In answer to my question, she tells me she now feels Jewish. I bet that will wear off back home, too.

Yesterday (Wednesday) I joined the official trip of the Conservative Friends of Israel. We went first to Yad Vashem, the Holocaust Museum, which you can't help but cry over. Some aspects gave me hope – *most* of the German Jews got out: of 500,000, some 176,000 perished. The huge numbers came in Poland, where the entire community of 3 million was wiped out, including the 400,000 crammed into the Warsaw ghetto. Photos taken in there (by a young German soldier on his day off) as people slowly died of starvation were, for me, the most shocking – of beggars and children, all still alive, but mad with hunger, and yet behaving with gentle dignity. As the deportations got under way, one man escaped from Treblinka and came back to Warsaw to warn them, leading to the uprising, the first of the revolts against the Germans. It lasted only a month, but it had three huge effects: (1) it drew attention to what was happening; (2) it spawned many others, elsewhere; (3) it made Jews (a naturally pacifist culture) realise they would have to fight, and train to do it properly, if they were to have their own state. Perhaps it was fanciful of me to see a substantial difference in expression on soldiers' faces as they handled prisoners, between the blankness or sadism of Germans, and the clear distaste of a young British soldier arresting an illegal immigrant (to be returned to Cyprus). The British on the ground must have turned a blind eye so often, for hundreds of thousands got into Israel (Palestine) while officially the government, under Bevin, would not permit it. And it's carping to note that, according to Yad Vashem, only Jews were victims. It was extraordinary to read the words of Pastor Martin

Buber, and not have it noted that he and many like him – Christians and Communists and ordinary people and writers and journalists and free politicians – also died in Nazi hands. Perhaps I was more acutely aware that Yad Vashem is *not* just about Nazis and Jews, but about the depths of human cruelty towards other humans, because to get there I'd driven through the West Bank, through road block after road block bristling with armed guards, several times in scared little convoys of Arab women in veils on their way to work. They never learn, the Israelis. Many of them want a Jewish state based on racial differences, however dressed up: and the veiled women had few rights as they stared down the barrels of those rifles, no vote, no voice, no right to move freely in the land in which they were born. One chap we met at lunch at the Knesset, one of the three religious MPs, wants all non-Jews made to leave Israel. He was quite serious about it – and others, perfectly normal people on the outside, talked of the dangers of keeping the Occupied Territories, with their 1.8 million inhabitants and high birth rate, which will eventually overwhelm the 4 million Jews in Israel. It gave me the shivers, I can tell you. By contrast I felt the utmost sympathy for the three Palestinians we met in the home of the British Consul-General in East Jerusalem (a splendid bloke, sharp as a needle), who talked about how in 1948 they had hoped for a multi-racial Israel in which all could live in peace. I doubt if they said that in 1948 in fact! – but the Israelis have never said it, and they don't want it. After all that was done to them in the name of racial purity. Enough to make you weep.

The meeting with Rabin was a disappointment, partly because the group was too large (nine Tory and fourteen Labour MPs who were also on a delegation). Rabin was critical of Britain's lukewarm approach, which produced a protest from our new Ambassador, Andrew Burns. I remember him from Hong Kong (at least he says I do – I can just about recall the face, but not a single conversation). It isn't done for ambassadors to correct Prime Ministers, especially not when half-a-dozen scruffily dressed Labour MPs are trying to ask questions. To return to Rabin: he's still prepared to accept Resolution 242 from 1967, to give up land in return for recognition of Israel's borders. He said he would expect a full bilateral peace treaty with

Syria in return for the Golan Heights (which would put paid to its inclusion in any Palestine state), with open borders, free movement of trade and people, exchange of ambassadors etc., as with Egypt. For the West Bank and Gaza he'll give 'autonomy' (or 'interim self-government'), with the Israelis deciding only foreign affairs and defence. That doesn't sound like freedom to me – however, the Palestinians would accept even that, at least for starters. They'll both fudge over East Jerusalem too. The problem on the ground is that Rabin's fine words aren't matched by fine actions. The borders of the Occupied Territories have been closed, movement restricted, Arabs not allowed to worship at the Dome of the Rock, etc.

I learned, but contributed nothing. I know whose side I'm on. The Likud MPs we met were all mad and need locking up: a rabid bunch of rabble rousers, too much like the DUP in Northern Ireland for comfort. Labour talked far more sense on security. It was a surprise to our MPs (some of whom struck me as naïve in the extreme) to find that the parties are separated not by economic theory, but by attitudes to security. John Sykes[77] was cheering the arrival of 'the most right-wing MP' in the room until Liam Fox[78] told him of the ethnic cleansing policies emanating from his bearded lips…

Back in England, I attended a splendid event last Friday night (28 May) at Luton Hoo, at which John Major was the speaker. All black tie and glitter and thoroughly enjoyable, though my table had its share of talkative salesmen. Norma was there, looking lovely; she has really grown into the job. John asked Graham Bright whether he was to speak (which struck me as a daft question): when Graham said yes, just a short one, John groaned and said he was whacked, after a day in Paris with Mitterrand. Even so, he droned on for over twenty minutes, with a series of petulant remarks about being unpopular. He doesn't have the right touch, somehow. An example came when he referred to me, as expected, and said 'you always know when Edwina is speaking in the Commons' and 'she'll make a great noise in Strasbourg.' He missed a chance to say something

77 Conservative MP for Scarborough since 1992.
78 Dr Liam Fox, Conservative MP for Woodspring since 1992.

positive about Europe and made me sound a loud-mouthed idiot at the same instant. I was quite hurt. It would have been kinder if my leader had indicated that he agreed with what I said, at least sometimes (and I haven't spoken in the House since January, which shows how much notice he takes of the place).

Victoria, Wednesday 9 June, 8.40 a.m.

Hot, sticky weather; outside they're repairing the road and the sound of a hammer drill is powering its way through the thick air. Inside it's cool and dark and sleepy. I wanted to write a bit now while my brain is fresh, as I think a turning point has been reached concerning the PM. Ironically, I'm to have my photo taken with him at No. 10 at lunchtime, with all the others celebrating ten years in Parliament today.

Last Friday the *Daily Telegraph* published its Gallup poll to find John at 21 per cent approval the least popular PM since polls began 56 years ago, with the Tory Party 24 per cent behind Labour and in danger of slipping behind the Liberals. The poll was done *after* the reshuffle and showed that it had had no beneficial effect at all.

This was followed (for me) by an exceedingly depressing supper at L'Amico on Monday night with the Double Eight Club,[79] attended by Ian Taylor (fresh from writing an excellent pamphlet on Positive Europe – 5,000 copies gone out – I really must find enough brain space to read it!), James Cran, who PPS'd for the PM while Graham was in hospital, Keith Mans,[80] Quentin Davies[81] (as ever, very well informed about everything except politics), Ben Patterson MEP (sweet but tied to the book of rules), and Michael Welsh[82] (who faces the prospect of losing his seat in next year's Euro elections). We tried to talk about the implications of the government's collapsing fortunes for Europe and us positive Europeans, but in the end abandoned ourselves to an orgy of criticism of the PM himself. His judgement is so awry, his personality so weak, his vision so limited and cloudy. A captain trying to be

---

79 A private dining club of pro-European MPs and MEPs.
80 PPS to the Secretary of State for Health since 1992; Conservative MP for Wyre since 1987.
81 Conservative MP for Stamford & Spalding since 1987.
82 Conservative MEP for Lancashire Central since 1979.

a general, it seems like, and really not up to it. And yet... if I'd stayed by his side, would he have retained the imagination, the drive and the risk-taking ability of 1985–8? I'd have tutored him and pushed him and kept him going, and helped him assess friends and enemies. It could have been done (e.g. as PPS in December 1990) and I would have loved it, and him. We'll never know.

Now we face losing not only the by-election at Christchurch (which will be fought in July to get it over and done), but the 1994 Euro elections as well.

Tower House, Sunday 18 July, 8.16 a.m.

My anger and frustration know no bounds! There's almost no thrust from the government on *why* we're in Europe and what we have to do to make it work. I listen for the sound of thunder from No. 10, but there isn't even a faint squeak. On Friday the PM was talking to activists at the Quorn Hotel; he agreed that the Commission has too much power and argued that power should be repatriated to national Parliaments. That's batty. Westminster can't do the job it should do properly – and it has no taste for sensible scrutiny or revision of proposals from a higher power, as Brussels is increasingly (broadly correctly) seen. Westminster activists will oppose on principle and, like now, the government of the day will be engaged in endless battles to get important legislation through unamended. John Major does not seem to have made the connection. But then, like Margaret, it's a very long time since he was a backbencher.

At the Quorn Hotel, John seemed to blame the press for most of his troubles – 'You can make a forty-minute speech or give an hour's interview and it will only make one minute on the TV news.' That's prattish. He's got rid of Sir Ronald Millar[83] – the relationship apparently didn't 'gel'. So we're back to the placid profundities of Graham Bright and the frightened little boy from Brixton's fear of the media. If you want six minutes live prime time, then you give a live interview. Virginia Bottomley keeps doing it, and David Hunt, who is rising fast, and Ken Clarke's based his whole career on it. You don't give exclusive interviews: no other paper will report them and TV doesn't like

---

83 Playwright; Margaret Thatcher's speechwriter.

them. You don't waste your time doing forty-minute speeches – not with nearly three years' experience of Prime Minister's Questions behind you, knowing you're now quite good at answering questions on your feet. There's plenty of effective talent on the back benches who could advise him – Gyles Brandreth,[84] Michael Fabricant,[85] me – but he plods on, looking bewildered and hurt. It's pathetic and makes me *so* cross. And despairing – I feel I could have done so much, could really have helped make this nice reasonable man into a formidable performer. I did, a bit, in the mid-'80s. Oh well: I've done it in the novel, and that will have to suffice.

It looks as if part of my holiday in France will be taken up with intensive work on *A Parliamentary Affair*. Since Richard gets so distracted by phone calls when I'm in his office, which is an uncomfortable and unprofessional place to work, and since he's busy being Publishing Director and seems incapable of compartmentalising his life in London and getting on with what he's promised, the best way is to extract him from that environment. That may mean France. And part of me hopes so. He'd come alone – I invited the family but 'we'd get no work done if they were there'. And Ray will be going back about 15 August. So – who knows? I wouldn't mind... I feel ready for an adventure, almost desperately ready. It's hilarious revising the sex scenes with him – he keeps scribbling 'I'm not being coy' in the margins when I've exuberantly gone over the top. When we start to discuss sex scenes, he starts blushing. If he comes to France at least we'll get the sodding book done, because I'll make him concentrate.

Victoria, Friday 23 July, 12.10 a.m.

We lost the vote tonight, by eight votes. My God, what a mess; I and most of my colleagues are in a state of shock. Three hundred hours of debate, seventy-four separate votes in House of Commons, and the Maastricht Act (as it is now) is still not in force and the Treaty still not ratified.

---

84 Author and broadcaster; world record holder for the longest after-dinner speech; Conservative MP for the City of Chester since 1992.
85 Broadcaster; Conservative MP for Mid-Staffordshire since 1992.

We won the earlier vote on Labour's pro-Social Chapter amendment – at any rate it was a dead heat, 317:317, which meant it fell on the Speaker's casting vote. John Major made the speech of his life – really splendid. But then we lost the unamended government 'take note' motion: 316 to 324, far too large a gap. Four of our side[86] voted with the opposition. Immediately John Major jumped to his feet and put down a confidence motion for tomorrow, to include a reference to the Social Chapter – and this would be enough for ratification, as well as saving the government's neck if it is passed. If it fails, then we have no ratification yet (though it could come later – there's no time limit), but we have no government either – and there'd be a general election next week.

I've had to cancel a planned trip to Venice with the children, but that's the least of my worries. The BBC political correspondent John Sergeant is saying that the rebels (twenty-three of them) looked very shocked at the outcome. We need enough of them to change their vote tomorrow, or we are all in big trouble. A general election now could result in 100 lost seats – more – I have no doubt that the government would be hammered. Seats in the south-west and south coast would fall to the Liberals – perhaps another thirty or so, while Labour would take scads of seats in London and the Midlands. Then Labour would carry a motion in favour of the Social Chapter, and ratify the Treaty.

This evening a grinning PM exchanged banter with John Smith at the back of the Chair, complaining that a day's cricket had been ruined. I'd almost say John Major deserves to lose if it wasn't such a mess.

Victoria, Friday 23 July, 8.10 p.m.

Well, we won the no confidence debate, by 301 to 339 on the Labour amendment and by more, 299 to 339, on the main motion. A majority of forty is highly satisfactory; and because of the wording, it counts as the completion of the Maastricht Bill process through both Houses. Thank God!

---

86 Including Iain Duncan Smith, Conservative MP for Chingford since 1982; leader of the Party since 2001.

I felt *thrilled* as the result was announced. I'd spoken in the debate – better than usual because there was no time pressure. The PM spoke again in his more usual plodding style after his sparkling performance yesterday, but John Smith was superb. He really is very good indeed; it is teeth-grinding that with all our experience we don't have people as good as that. Ken Clarke is the closest, but his greatest talent *in government* is for having rows with people, who stay alienated a long time – nurses and doctors 1988–90, now police officers join prison staff. I suspect Smith is too circumspect to do that, or too devious. Even David Hunt, who spoke last night, hasn't refined his style at all – he simply shouts, and his appearance is ragged and ageing. There were photos of a very sick-looking John Patten in the press this morning: he's been poorly with a bad bug, but his eyes were rolling and for once he didn't look eighteen. Heseltine[87] by contrast is looking much better, though he was 'nodded through' by the whips (i.e. he stayed in his car), in contrast to Labour's Bob Parry, minus his bottom teeth, who shuffled through the lobbies one week after a quaternary heart bypass operation. His eyes were unnaturally bright, but he said to me, 'Just glad to be here, gel' with a cheery smile. Talk about one foot in the grave – Labour brought in Rachel Squire,[88] who has a brain tumour. I looked her up and she was one of my senior social workers in Birmingham back in the 1970s, though she has never introduced herself to me as such. I asked Greg Knight (Deputy Chief Whip) in the tea room why we couldn't at least pair the sick; he looked a little puzzled as if he didn't quite understand the idea, but said it was OK by him. (It didn't happen, though. What a stupid macho bunch the Whips' Office are. It would be different if the Chief Whip was female.)

Up in the gallery this morning sat a disconsolate-looking Norma Major in a pretty yellow suit and white blouse, her son James bored and fidgety beside her – no sign of big daughter. This is, incidentally, only the first time since World War II that a government with a majority has put down a motion of confidence in itself to force its

---

87 Michael Heseltine was recovering from a heart attack.
88 Labour MP for Dunfermline West since 1992.

rebels to toe the line. I was due to do the 6 p.m. BBC TV news, only to get an apologetic phone call saying they'd been offered the PM and would I mind? Hopefully therefore the message has got to John, that instead of moaning about the presentation of his speeches on TV, he should go straight on prime time himself. He was on *Channel 4 News* too and was really good, just like he used to be. He'll need to keep up this higher productivity and quality if all the doubts about his leadership are to subside; next time he stumbles it will all come flooding back.

The PM's libel case against the *New Statesman* ended messily. After obtaining rapid apologies and damages from the booksellers and distributors (this government has promised to change the law making them liable in this way), the case against the *New Statesman* was effectively dropped for a payment of £1,000 in damages to the PM and Clare Latimer. I suspect it was at her insistence, that she wanted no more to do with it. The PM's brother Terry said in an interview that he wasn't surprised John had pursued the matter with such vigour, as their mother was very strict and would have drummed morality into him. Ho, ho! I guess he felt angry on Miss Latimer's part. It reinforces my view that they got the right chap but the wrong lady.

Victoria, Monday 2 August, 11.12 p.m.

I went to Christchurch last Tuesday, and a depressing business it was. Although everyone was pleasant enough, it was clear that people are determined to vote for Mrs Maddock, the mumsy, grey-haired (48-year-old) Liberal Democrat candidate. Poor Rob Hayward[89] didn't get a look in. Even our attempts to set the agenda misfired – choosing law and order as a topic when half of all households have experienced a crime in the last twelve months and crime has doubled in four years was unwise. Our record is, bluntly, indefensible, and it is startling (and telling) that CCO can't see that. Nobody was prepared to attack Mrs Maddock or confront her with her Party's previous advocacy of a carbon tax when she was campaigning against VAT on fuel. Similarly, voters claimed to be

89 The Conservative candidate and former MP for Kingswood.

worried about Maastricht and yet happy to vote Liberal Democrat, even though their policies are more strongly pro-European union. In fact, nobody was prepared to take any risks at all in Christchurch. The previous day the papers were full of unguarded remarks from the PM, who referred to the rebellious tendency inside the government as 'bastards' between interviews on Friday night after winning the vote of confidence. I wanted to call his tough new approach 'brilliant', but was warned off. Lily-livered lot – who are you going to offend, if they're going to vote the other way anyhow? The result was a rout: 20,000 voters switched (and they did switch – the turnout was over 80 per cent, so we have no fallback excuses of apathy); the Conservative vote dropped from 36,000 to 16,000 and the Liberal Democrat vote leapt from 13,000 to 33,000, thus giving Mrs Maddock a healthy majority and no mistake. For the first time in ages I didn't bother to stay up for the result.

And that makes me profoundly depressed, for it suggests we will get hammered in the Euro elections next summer. Barring highly favourable boundary changes (and we won't know about these till September), we don't have much chance in South Bedfordshire. I will go on doing my best, of course, but the nightmare scenario is beginning to look a possibility – losing in South Bedfordshire, then losing in South Derbyshire too. It's all very well us treating the Euro elections as a last chance verdict on John Major's abilities as PM: that abandons those of us fighting the seats entirely. Most of the nation, according to the polls, shares my disillusion with him. He's seen as a weak and incompetent leader with no clear policies or vision, and out of touch with ordinary voters. The matters on which he's hung his shirt – Maastricht and the Citizen's Charter – are widely seen as irrelevant, indeed insulting, when unemployment is still such a present fear. Privatisation is regarded as making unemployment worse, not better (true). Pensioners feel threatened at every turn – whether it's their private pensions as with Maxwell or British Rail, or the falling income from their savings as interest rates have come down, or hints of taxing benefits or cutting disablement payments or of making pensioners pay for their prescriptions. Not to speak of VAT on fuel bills, which most pensioners regard as aimed directly at them. Grey power was always going to make itself felt! Add to that the admiration of many older Tories for Lady Thatcher and sharing her dislike of her wimpish successor, and there's the recipe for continued disfavour. We had already lost much of the working class vote of the 1980s, as the county elections demonstrated in May. Lose 10 million pensioners and we don't have a Party. I feel very fearful.

Richard returned from his holiday and has started slinging paper at me again, but he's probably too busy this week to see me, and I'm set to catch the lunchtime boat Saturday (7th). I don't have much choice as otherwise Ray and I won't coincide, and we have to sign papers at the bank, and get a French will made too: and he returns on the 11th. After that, I can do more revision, but heaven knows when the full operation will be complete. Basically it means no holiday – yet I am quite desperate for a decent break, and a snooze under a tree at Villandry or Azay-le-Rideau, reading a book someone else wrote!

It's midnight and I must sleep, then more tap-tapping early tomorrow. (It is a most embarrassing exercise, revising the novel, because so much of it is crass. Only the sex and violence really sing off the page; much of the remainder is awful rubbish.) The most dismal business of all was that Deb returned and promptly announced that she's going back to Israel for another month, until just before she goes to Huddersfield. I'm scared she will decide to stay. After all, what could be nicer than a louche life on a pretty hillside getting laid by a nice boy whenever you feel like it? I'd taken her out on Friday and agreed to buy her a little car, which she seemed thrilled about. Saturday p.m. we three (Debbie, Susie and me) went to see Spielberg's *Jurassic Park*, which was fun, and then to a Chinese meal afterwards, and that's when she tells me that the kibbutzniks love her more than we do, and she is going back. Apparently we are snobs because we are wealthy. Right, says I, two can play at that game. She had the nerve to ask for money, too. The car was cancelled this morning and I shan't buy her another: if she wants one she'll have to buy her own (she can't take one on to the main Huddersfield campus anyway) and I refuse to have any part in ferrying her to university and back. If she can withdraw, so can

I, so there've been no kisses and hugs since. She doesn't realise how cool I can feel – I've had to protect myself for so long from being hurt by people I loved and now it has become a habit. So I give a big sigh, and long for France.

London, Saturday 7 August, 8.50 a.m.

Sitting in the launderette in Churton Street near the flat, doing Susie's laundry! I catch the lunchtime boat from Portsmouth, so I feel I'm already on holiday.

I've been reading Alan Clark's *Diaries*, which are a joy; if mine get a bit perkier from here on, then it's entirely from his example. He describes events with such panache and people with unnerving accuracy – doesn't rate John Gummer or Ken Clarke, is rude about Tom King, deeply admiring of Parkinson and Tebbit, and fawning over the Lady. His world is Eton, the Household Cavalry, backgammon at his club (he gets into fights and punches people), lechery, often quite casually – on one occasion in a railway carriage, if his account is to be believed! – fine wines, beautiful homes (from Saltwood Castle in Kent to the chalet in Zermatt to Eriboll in Scotland) – all wonderful in itself, but full of added interest when peopled by Ian Gow, Jonathan Aitken and other rogues. He hated the Department of Employment, is refreshingly honest about his failings there, including his 'spat' with Clare Short when she accused him of being drunk. He was – he'd spent the evening at a wine tasting, but worse: (1) he was unprepared – he'd only glanced at the stuff on his way to the House; and (2) he didn't agree with the material, and showed it by the way he mouthed sentences he regarded as rubbish. I remember that evening and it was very funny. What a pleasure to have 300 more pages to come.

Les Tuileries, Thursday 12 August, 10.15 p.m.

Waiting for Richard to ring – the fifth Hodder call and the third from him today. The first part of Chapter 16 arrived this morning and I've already done it. I'll read it through again when I'm fresh tomorrow morning and then post it. The rest, as much as possible, I'll send over on Sunday with someone who's going back to England. Other than that, I can only fax it, pages by the score, which is less than satisfactory.

The expected phone call is to read over to me the revisions of Chapter 16 part 2 (Remembrance Day). I can't believe we're having to do it like this, and Richard has *not* yet finished 16 part 3. I'm keeping up, but he isn't. Infuriating. It could be something to do with the fact that Hodder have let seventy-two people go, and perhaps more to come, so that they're short of spare bodies: but it all seems a bit laid back to me. Jane, his sweet secretary, went off to a christening at 3 p.m. What she didn't do was take the text with her and call me from home; so Richard's trying to do it while fending off other phone calls (I can hear it ringing) and his wife wanting him for supper.

Ray and I had a very good (for us) three days. It must be this place, so quiet and cosy and loving. It's a happy house and makes me feel so relaxed. Over the last couple of years its atmosphere has acted like a healing balm. I certainly appreciate it.

Les Tuileries, Sunday 22 August, 7.45 p.m.

A wet, humid evening, with flies everywhere. My fault for leaving the fruit and cheeseboard out. There was a big rainstorm earlier, not surprising as it has been hot this week: 35°C (95°F) on Friday afternoon. I've got quite a tan now, from only a few hours sitting in the sun.

I've just come back from an organ and trumpet concert at Cunault – most enjoyable, though this year it wasn't the Metz brothers, who play with such spirit, but a tubby bloke who kept going out of time on the first piece. By the end, however – Handel's concerto – they were blasting away joyously. The church is an eleventh-century priory – tall and long and quite spectacular and an ideal site. I took with me a local British family, who had not been to one of the concerts; it was hard to know what they made of it as both are taciturn, and we parted and went our different ways after. I had hoped they would say, 'Do let us pay for our tickets.' (EC: 'No, of course not.') 'Then will you join us for supper?' (EC: 'Thank you, I'd be delighted.') – but neither happened. I can't figure out some people.

Meanwhile I'm clearing the last chapters now, and the typesetting script is arriving in chunks. I hand over everything I've done on my return on 1 September (and I'm free that evening…) All being well I receive the remainder that day; and we hope to have the proof copy on 5 October, the day before Party Conference.

At that point things start to happen, as Lisa sends it out for serialisation, TV etc. I should think we've every chance, and Richard believes it will be a bestseller, 'as you write better than Jilly Cooper, and have written a far better book than necessary'. If we can improve it a bit more he says it would even be 'a good novel'. Wow! Praise indeed…

He's very good indeed at his job, and when working is cool, certain and decisive. He's great company and intellectually very powerful – though with a tendency to jump, scatter-brained, to the next lateral idea. Getting him to concentrate, or to keep to the point, can be difficult.

Incidentally he's not Jewish but Catholic, the product of Downside no less, educated by monks. The Jewish bit is genuine, however – his father was Jewish. My Mum would like that.

Germany, Wednesday 8 September, 11 a.m.

On the Lufthansa plane from Leipzig to Frankfurt, during a lecture tour of Germany. We've already been to Berlin; next step Heidelberg; then Bonn; then Dusseldorf. Back to Birmingham on Saturday p.m.

Richard is disappointed at the outcome of the Hodder merger,[90] where he's still an employee with a boss; he had always been satisfied with that, but two years organising the highly successful Cheltenham Literary Festival has given him a taste for top management and he knows he's good at it. When he lost his job at Hutchinson in 1991 he put together a business plan to set up his own company, but in the middle of the recession could not get backing; now he's beginning to think again seriously. He told me he could put approximately half a million of his own money into a company and has clearly been thinking it through. All very exciting stuff – and I'd give him all the support I could; if *A Parliamentary Affair* is a success and I'm to go on writing then I could move with him when he goes ahead.

---

90 Hodder had merged with a relatively new company, Headline, to become Hodder Headline.

Headline started in a small way and grew fast by clever marketing and he could do the same.

Victoria, Monday 13 September, midnight

I can't find my diary book so I must have left it in Derbyshire by mistake – hope so anyway! It would not be helpful if anyone else were to read it, no sir.

Today is a special day, hence this note. The agreement between Israel and the PLO was signed in the sunshine on the lawn of the White House in Washington this afternoon. With Arafat to his left (first time in twenty years that he has been admitted to the USA) and Rabin stony faced to his right, a bemused President Clinton like a big soft kid walked to the table where the Israel–Egypt peace agreement was signed. President Sadat's widow was there, and Bush and Carter, and James Baker; Kissinger on TV made happy noises. 'We have had enough of killing and blood,' said Rabin – this the man who won the Occupied Territories in the '67 war. 'We want only peace,' said Arafat, looking as if he meant it. And then they shook hands and everyone cheered, and the dancing in the streets of Jericho said it all.

It looks like a PLO victory, and the handshake was certainly warmer on Arafat's side than Rabin's. Yet it was the Israelis who had to give way, or their nation would have collapsed. Arafat is under a different kind of pressure – with no progress, Hamas (extremists) were taking over and he had little time left. I suppose the Israelis should count themselves lucky that the Palestinians are basically decent people – most of the aggression in the last twenty-five years has come from Israel, not from the Palestinians. I feel so thrilled about it all, and hope the leaders will survive the assassination attempts which are bound to happen; for the first time ever today, Arafat wore no gun.

I'm on my own in the flat and feeling a bit blue; my evening meeting was cancelled and Ray appears to be still in Derbyshire. I got a heap of work done; an article for the *FT* on 'If I were Minister for Europe', which only took an hour as it had been humming around in my head for ten days, and another chunk of novel yet again. I can't believe how disorganised this final stage is, and I find it depressing; I would much rather have a long session, and Richard's undiluted professional attention, than all this messing about.

Tomorrow morning I'm with Lord Snowdon for three hours having my picture taken. That means getting to bed now, and dropping off. At least I'll have some new thoughts in my head as I consoled myself this evening with Dr Andrew Stanway's video:[91] and there I did learn a thing or two, and hope I get the chance to practise...

Tower House, Sunday 3 October, 10.30 p.m.

Just ploughed through the usual mountain of paper – invites, moans, queries, requests – but now the Euro seat represents more than half of it, which is how it should be. Clare deals beautifully with all the routine South Derbyshire stuff, very little of which is political, while Emma Joynson-Hicks[92] is at last getting on top of the diary.

Lots happening. Last Tuesday morning, when Ray said he was planning to come back to London that evening instead of staying in Derbyshire, I just cracked. That was the second time in a fortnight.

Deb is settled at Huddersfield; she has got up a women's rugby team – her idea; plans to do Tae Kwondo ('more interesting than karate'); and is a backing singer in a pop group. Classes haven't started yet, 'but there's a distinct lack of talent'. However, that doesn't matter, as she's still in love with Shi. Huddersfield is a bit dull – like Derby, only bigger. She's made friends with a London girl who hates it already and wants to go clubbing every night, which isn't possible in Huddersfield! Her room is on the twelfth floor of a central tower block and is fine, with a lovely view all over the West Yorkshire moors. It's a great relief to hear her bubbling and excited on the phone. Susie also popped home this afternoon, but she looks pressurised, pale and tired. She's an ambitious little madam, and quite determined to get her Cambridge place. I hope she doesn't tire herself out so much that she doesn't perform well at interview.

Steve Norris, it turns out, has added two more ladies to his stable

91 *The Lover's Guide.*
92 EC's new assistant.

and may well have been having it off with four ladies at once: his wife Vicki; his first girlfriend, Sheila Gunn of *The Times*, who's a sad little mouse, despite a good brain, and adores him; a lady from the *Harper's and Queen* magazine; and a House of Commons secretary in her twenties, which has been going on about twelve months. Now that's *really* careless. We can't be the Party of 'Laura Norder and the Family' and have ministers behave like this. Little do they know (though the PM may) that they've both kissed the same girl. Ain't life funny!

This lady is really ready for a move. 24 September I spent at the 'Tenth Anniversary Dinner for the South Derbyshire Conservative Association', which was a deeply embarrassing and awful event at the Stanhope Arms, attended by all of twenty-one people (who included EC and RFC, Tyrone[93] and three of his family, and Jane Evans). Of course it should have been cancelled, but once more Tyrone had arranged that we'd lose a packet if we did. The next night was the Bedfordshire Ball, which was splendid if noisy, and financially a great success. Roll on June.

Tower House, Sunday 10 October, 1.40 p.m.

I felt a bit sorry for Margaret this week, as she'd tried hard to prevent publication of her memoirs until after the Party Conference in Blackpool. She has a right to tell her story in her own way, of course, and can hardly avoid making remarks about erstwhile colleagues. And it's brought her a reputed £3.5 million. But her appearance on the platform on Thursday, after leaked revelations from her memoirs, was a very muted affair, not like the half-mile-long queue which sent me haring off to France two years ago. Only about a quarter of the delegates rose and applauded; most sat on their hands. When the PM came on later, the welcome was much warmer and more sincere; he shook hands with her, but no kiss. Ken Clarke a little later marched right past her. Soon after she left, having stayed only one night and said not a word; but the look in her eyes was desperate and sad.

Conference was awful. Well, for anyone of my sympathies,

93 Tyrone Edwards, EC's South Derbyshire agent.

anyway. Endless bashing of social security 'scroungers', foreigners (including 'Europeans' – this from Peter Lilley, may he dissolve in slime), single parent families – always female – and any thinking not extant in the 1950s when John Major was a lad. One of the prospective MEPs drew a large cheer when he shouted 'European union is dead! The ERM is dead!' He doesn't appear to have noticed that the European Monetary Institute gets going on 1 January 1994, i.e. in twelve weeks' time, that it will almost certainly be in Frankfurt as the price for the DM to be included eventually, and that thus the first steps are being taken which will reduce London to the status of a provincial Stock Exchange. As for European union: the German Supreme Court meets on 12 October to consider the constitutional challenges, and all being well will give me a nice birthday present of throwing them out, with ratification completed on 1 November. At which point the Common Market/EEC/EC changes its name once again to 'European Union', and we're all to talk about 'the Union' not 'the Community'. That'll smack the British right between the eyes! Naturally we'll ignore the change, at least in South Bedfordshire, where the slogan will be 'EC for the EC'.

But it was John's final speech which, in my view, sealed his fate. It appears to have been decided that, in order to keep the Party united, there should be a swing to the right. That means 'old-fashioned' values on the family, education, law and order, sound money, etc. No one seems to have spotted several problems with this (except perhaps Douglas Hurd, who spoke courageously at a fringe): (1) we don't have law and order, we have a crime wave; (2) we don't have sound money, we have a £50 billion deficit, so the failure we're drawing attention to is our own – we're doing the opposition's job for it; and (3) that makes us anti-Europe, which will lose us the Euro elections. Indeed the highly negative tone of John's speech, which drew cheers from his audience, will only dismay large numbers of voters outside the Party. There's no forward thinking at all: no feeling for how the country has changed, no thoughtful assessment of the real options open to us. And of course (4) nobody's perfect, as this PM knows best of all.

Blackpool was a beauty contest, with next year's hopefuls parading: Michael Howard tub-thumping, Clarke impatient but loyal, Lilley defiant, Portillo magisterial. If the contest were held now,

Clarke would get it, so the right don't want it now and are behaving. Nor do they wish to plump for Portillo too readily – they could make the same mistakes as when Major was chosen, too soon, without a thorough knowledge of his abilities and credentials. So we'll have a quiet year, and then a contest this time next year, I predict.

Poor Steve Norris: his wife has left him, and now it seems that he had five women on the go at the same time! 'Mr Norris changes dames', says the *Sunday Times* quite wittily. On Wednesday *Today* had a front-page story 'Minister tried to seduce me', in which I'm supposed to have been prospective victim number six. That comes from the lunch with Paul Wilenius and Jon Craig after I left *Today*. Of course Steve has made it clear that he'd do me a favour any time – and that's how he would have seen it! – but if I want an overweight, middle-aged bloke I've got a much *nicer* one at home.

Derby, Sunday 24 October, 9 p.m.

Polls suggest that we'll get hammered at the Euro elections next June – if the current 14 per cent Labour lead is translated across the country, we'll be left with only twenty-two seats, which sounds plausible to me: but I'd be one of them. The worst scenario suggests only nine seats, the safest, could be held. In that case I'd be out, and the future would be looking seedy.

I suppose there could be advantages in being in a small group – a little band of brothers. If we then did badly at the next general election, which is distinctly possible, the Euro elections of 1999 would swing our way. There could then be a bonus in being a senior member of an enlarged group. I wanted to be an MP when there were only nineteen women MPs; now I want to be an MEP when there are possibly going to be only a score of 'em. Done it before and I can do it again.

Margaret's memoirs were published on Monday. She's been working flat out signing copies and has sold £2 million worth in a week. Good for her. 'Bout time she started raising money for the Party, what? Gyles Brandreth spoke to my South Derbyshire ladies Friday lunchtime, a lovely friendly do in Hazel Salt's house, and confessed on the train that it gave him a splendid excuse for not doing the honours for Margaret Thatcher at the lunch she was attending in his Chester constituency – signing books again. There's something deeply sickening about the whole business, and I have no intention of buying a copy or ever reading it (except perhaps checking my name in the index).[94]

Took Ray to see *Jurassic Park* – second time for me and I enjoyed it just as much, but his reaction was 'I'm disappointed'. That was typical and infuriating; I feel like punching him when he doesn't even try to be enthusiastic. Later *Basic Instinct* was on Sky Movies, Michael Douglas and Sharon Stone in an eye-popping thriller with a tremendous sexual edge; there were some powerful scenes in it, but not a twitch from him.

Les Tuileries, Saturday 6 November, 7.30 p.m.

It's nice to have the diary back – like seeing an old friend! I left it behind in France, along with my cheque books, keys, House of Commons ID and a pile of other necessities.

I came over here last night: a smooth sailing, but as ever too short for a proper sleep. This evening I've been reading in front of a huge log fire; later I'll put a hot water bottle in the bed, then keel over till the morning. As it's Sunday, I'll go for a run, followed by a soak in the bath. Then I'll write all day – I have a short story ('The Birthday Party') to finish and I need two days on the new synopsis, which I'm dreading. It doesn't feel as if it's gelled at all; that will be a real struggle. I leave mid-afternoon Tuesday and stay overnight in Calais, as I'm speaking in Bexley Wednesday lunchtime.

Lisa, Sally Randall (Hodder publicity) and Petra (Hodder serialisation) discussed Richard over lunch at A. P. Watt on Wednesday. They all giggled and blushed at his name, and told me how he helps his authors by getting bits in *Private Eye* about them. Lisa said Giles Gordon (Vikram Seth's agent) does the same. Lisa sent an early short story of mine to Giles, who was then editing the annual Penguin book of *Best Short Stories*; apparently he told Richard that I would write a novel some day. After Sally and Petra had left I asked Lisa why they'd gone girlish, and she told me that she thought he was something of a ladies' man. He has very young children

94 EC later relented and bought a copy. Her name is not listed in the index.

for a man his age. I reckon he played the field a long time before settling down… She also assured me that Richard had, at his own request, discussed his future with Martin Nield[95] in the summer and had been given assurances and was content, with no plans to leave Hodder. That he's thinking seriously about setting up his own business is shown by his constantly working out how much capital he could lay hands on before going to the bank. Golly, I hope it is a goer and that I can help somehow. Lisa says we can have an 'editor' clause in our next contract, i.e. we'll insist on having Richard as editor. Good.

The book is grinding on – should have bound proofs before December. What a business. Two sets of libel lawyers, a recorrected proof, and three weeks for binding. The print order has been raised to 10,000 copies, which (if sold) should guarantee us a spot in the bestseller list. Lisa's started talking to TV people, who seem to like it very much; her partner who will handle it says we're not interested in less than £25,000, but frankly I hope it's a lot more than that. Even if it produces increased sales I won't see any extra money, as Hodder have paid me so much. There are hopes for America and translation sales. I shouldn't be so silly as to worry about these; already I've made a packet out of *A Parliamentary Affair* and it's not even published yet. Paperback possibly next November, so a long time till payment four, and that is a bit of a pest. Anyway everyone who's read the book seems to like it, which is a good sign.

The end of this Parliamentary session (the longest in twenty-seven years) was, by contrast, a wretched scramble to get the Rail Privatisation Bill through. The scenes on Wednesday night were the stuff of pure farce – we'd been voting till 1.50 a.m. the previous night and so there was much bad temper and shoving and cheating and delay in all the divisions, with the gents' loo door wedged shut showing 'engaged' and the door to the 'no' lobby blocked by a bound copy of Hansard, so that the Serjeant at Arms could not enter to investigate. Much doffing of opera hats and handkerchiefs too.[96] Asked,

---

95 The new Managing Director of Hodder & Stoughton, formerly Marketing Director of Pan Macmillan.
96 A means of raising a point of order. These antics were all intended to delay the vote.

as usual, as we voted pointlessly for the umpteenth time, whether I wouldn't miss all this in Brussels, I gave my questioner a short sharp reply!

It could, I suppose, just faintly be in my interests for Ken Clarke to take over quickly next summer as PM, if I lose the Euro seat. One colleague – Tim Devlin,[97] I think – reported that at a recent ministers' meeting Clarke was enormously complimentary about me, deeply regretted I'd turned down the job, and was quite sure we could have worked things out. Oh yeah? He didn't listen the first time, so how come he'd have listened the second? He's sounding much chastened, which is good, but only because there's been a row, which wouldn't have happened at all if I'd accepted. However, I suppose there's the faintest chance that he might offer me a job if he's in, and in those circumstances it would be very churlish to refuse.

Victoria, Sunday 21 November, 4.15 p.m.

I've worked jolly hard this week – being collected daily at 8.30 a.m. to present *The Jimmy Young Programme* was the main demand on my energies, and this time I thoroughly enjoyed it. Live broadcasting for two-and-a-half hours every day is no picnic, but I like the music – honestly – and the audience is friendly and good humoured, while the news items were a worthy challenge. We covered crashes on motorways (a nasty one this week, in which it appears that a teacher fell asleep at the wheel of a minibus – she died with eleven pupils); and the South African interim constitution (good news), and whether there's too much bad news and whether game show hosts are rotten to the contestants – an interview with Bob Monkhouse on his car phone – nice man; and the Queen's Speech, which I missed but didn't miss at all – how silly they all look.

Susie has an offer from Nottingham to read Economics for A B B, which she should get easily, so is understandably chuffed. Deb has arranged a cheap flight to Israel at Xmas, and has changed courses to read English, and thus is much happier all round. She keeps telling

---

97 PPS to the Attorney-General; Conservative MP for Stockton South since 1987.

me I don't know what it's like, being in love, and I bite my tongue to avoid telling her I do.

In the middle of a conversation at Hatchards' party on Tuesday night, Liz Sich, the publicity director at Random House, merrily told me that Richard has been married three times, not twice as I believed. He's lived with at least one other as well. Their names were Francis (named after St Francis of Assisi, but female), Sarah, and now Caroline. The middle one lasted two years 'and was a mistake' he said, quite gaily, when I challenged him – but that makes it three times before he was forty, which takes some doing. He's still great in conversation, though he likes talking about himself, and a wonderful collaborator – quite brilliant. I am very puzzled about what kind of person he really is. Anyway the book is going well – sold to the *Daily Mail* with ten TV companies after it. Whoopee!

Nr Melton Mowbray, Tuesday 30 November, 8.30 p.m.

In a small noisy hotel near Melton Mowbray, otherwise known as the middle of nowhere. I'm here to appear as witness in the magistrates' court tomorrow against a woman who went into the back of my Toyota in April. (The boot still leaks in heavy rain.) She's being prosecuted for careless driving, and instead of pleading guilty did the opposite, bringing everyone to court early tomorrow. Growl! Silly girl. She still hasn't paid me the £100 for which she's liable, the excess on my insurance, so I've no sympathy.

The Budget was very well received on our side, with much cheery waving of order papers and relieved looks, for everyone was ready for big tax increases (they also looked pleased they understood it – real plain English merchant, our Ken). His cheeky-chappy delivery and little jokes, such as increasing the tax on sparkling wines but not till *after* Christmas, went down well, and concealed some sharp policies such as cutting mortgage interest tax relief. He's done himself a lot of good – and could be PM by next year.

It's hard to judge just yet what this success does to John Major, but I reckon it shows him up. I wonder if the electorate will hold him personally responsible for lying to them over tax increases in the general election campaign? We certainly allowed them to think that a Labour government would increase taxes and a Tory one wouldn't, however we fudge it now. His performance at the Dispatch Box is nowhere near as assured and self-confident as Ken's, and his delivery is still strangled and inarticulate, even three years after becoming leader. Oratory we've come not to expect, but competence we have a right to. So I shouldn't be surprised if, as the first VAT-added fuel bills drop on to doormats late in the spring, the voters decide to give us a bloody nose. We'll get hammered – London MPs are expecting to lose Westminster and Wandsworth Councils – and in the Euros too. I still think I'll win mine, and am playing my celebrity status for all it's worth.

I was invited for lunch at No. 10 on Monday last (22 November). There was no starter, but a 'lamb ragout' (actually lamb stew – reasonable but looking a little forlorn in the great silver dishes served by striped-pants waiters: if he wants that sort of nosh he should use cheerful waitresses), followed by chocolate mousse and cheese. Cholesterol level staggering, at a guess. No fruit on the table and, to my amazement and disgust, a dusty arrangement of plastic flowers. I presented him with a proof copy of *A Parliamentary Affair* and the 'flyer' and his eyes popped; that will cause him some innocent enjoyment… He was in chatty mood and didn't look too tired. As we spooned the lamb he said, 'I shouldn't have offered you that job in the Home Office; I'd completely forgotten about you and Ken Clarke…' – yet I'd sat in his office and wept; he'd forgotten. I said, 'It wasn't just him – it was a grotty job.' He contradicted me: 'No, there you're wrong.' (How to explain to him that it would have been an exercise in carrying the can and I wouldn't have lasted five minutes.) 'Anyway,' says I, 'I'm more interested in Europe these days,' a suitable opening – but he's not, and didn't pursue it. I asked him about the age of consent issue and tried to get him to give a lead, but he said about eighty of our side are dead against it. Ah, John, the last thing I thought you were was a coward, and a moral coward at that. You could give a lead, even a hint. You could just make it easier behind the scenes and keep your mouth shut. You could *help*. You could, if you wished, turn that marvellous line about 'a classless society – a society at ease with itself' into a *policy*, instead of an empty slogan. I'm so sick of your slogans; it's the same with 'at the heart of Europe' and now 'Back to Basics'. A man devoid of anything but wiliness, and not much of that, doesn't deserve to be PM. And I don't think you will be for long. In which case you could do something honest and brave, just for once.

I'm now back writing steadily and churning out quite a lot, what with diary, bits of journalism and short stories, of which I've done three recently, the latest for *Family Circle* yesterday, called 'Bump in the Night' – ostensibly about an old lady but really about a young WPC. Hope they like it; it'll go in their January edition, in time for the launch of the novel. On that, good news: the *Daily Mail* clinched it for £25,000 (no, I don't receive that, the publisher does), the Book Club is definitely doing 3,500 copies, W. H. Smith will have a quality paperback at airports at £8.99, and last Friday we had our first offer on TV rights. Hopefully there will be more, no doubt influenced by the success of Michael Dobbs's[98] *To Play the King*, which is infinitely better on screen, and compulsive viewing, than in its rather trite book form. Ian Richardson is simply superb in the lead role – I hope he's being paid a mint for it. The first TV offer is minimum £4,000, maximum £40,000, and they emphasised it was a *first* offer. I expect they'll want to change the ending – but so what, if they make a good job of it? All very exciting and stimulating.

Last week I saw Richard several times: on the Monday night (22nd), when I did a nerve-wracking presentation for the main booksellers, at the English Garden restaurant – very swish, bit like an overblown brothel, gilt swags and painted walls; on the Tuesday evening at Gay Hussar, when I was late, the place was empty and the food disgusting; on the Wednesday, when at Jane Lawson's[99] call I popped in about 2.30 p.m. to check the 'CRC' (camera-ready copy) and sat at his desk – he appeared, looking very bemused, for about seven minutes and then dashed off again. At least now Ray's reading the novel, though he says it's too sexy. Huh.

Susie has her Cambridge interview on 14/15 December, hurrah, and offers now from Nottingham, Durham and Sheffield. Nothing

---

98 Novelist and broadcaster; author of *House of Cards* (1989).
99 Richard Cohen's secretary.

yet from King's/LSE. She wasn't too impressed to hear from St Mary's College in Durham, which is single sex – 'Not sure how I'd cope with that, Mum!' She's on good form and says now she expects she'll go into politics, as it feels 'inevitable'. Ha!

Les Tuileries, Friday 31 December, 4.19 p.m.

I'm working on ideas for a new book while I wait for a phone call, which doesn't come. There have been other phone calls – usually inconveniently when I'm ensconced on the loo! – and I've called home, and spoken to Mum, who is living it up in Bournemouth. Susie has heard from Cambridge: they've put her in the 'pool'. It transpires that only about 30 per cent of applicants interviewed are offered places right away – other applicants regarded as worthy are put in the pool, for less popular colleges to take a look at. Pembroke themselves may have her back for another interview. I think they are mad – at only sixteen and with excellent references from the school, she must be one of the best candidates they have seen. Nottingham, the most oversubscribed university in the country, had no hesitation in offering her a place, and as she has not yet heard from London it looks as if Nottingham might be her best bet. My advice, in that case, would be to try again next year when she has her A levels out of the way, and if she still prefers London to Nottingham, to go for it.

It is pissing down with rain outside; in fact since I arrived on Monday afternoon it has rained virtually non-stop all over northern Europe, causing floods and general havoc. This morning the Loire at Saumur was full, fast-flowing and angry, and looked very dangerous. A lady parking her car next to mine on the river bank said that last week even the car parking areas were flooded. Normally, because the power stations and farmers take so much water, it's a trickle between sandbanks. I watched it, fascinated.

In all sorts of ways this little holiday is not turning out to be a success, partly because of the weather – which is just as bad at home, I know! – and partly because I feel so lonely and depressed. There's a lot on my plate – the novel coming out in February, the age of consent debate in January, the Euro elections in June. And, maybe more: possibly splitting with Ray, and plunging into another novel. It would help if I knew I had to get on with more writing, but I don't believe in working for the sake of it.

So what am I to do about Ray? By this time next year it will have been twenty-five years since I met him. I feel as if somebody up there is asking whether I would choose to spend the next twenty-five years with him. We don't seem to have much in common these days, and you could say that the marriage is drawing to its natural end. We live separate lives. The reasons for staying include my beliefs about marriage – which have kept me there all this time – and there'd be a lot of upheaval and bad feeling. I'm afraid that the girls might get cross with me, especially my little puritan Susie, though Deb may well understand, now she's in love herself. A nasty public divorce is to be avoided. In other words, the reasons for staying are trivial in comparison with the price of staying, which I pay all the time.

The only thing which stays my hand (apart from waiting till the girls have left home, which is soon) is the thought of the loneliness which could ensue. I do not like being on my own. I like to have a home to go to, and a warm body in my bed; I like to have somebody to care for, to look after, to bring little gifts home for, to cuddle and think about and worry over. I like having a shoulder to lean on, and an escort, preferably a handsome one, who admires me, taking my arm, sitting next to me at the theatre, cinema, across a dinner table, getting me a drink from the bar, looking after me. I want somebody around when I'm old and there are no more lovers, only memories. *I like being married.* Yet, rationalising, what I've got now is pretty lonely, like this week. And if I were widowed for years, as happens to millions of women and could well happen to me anyway, I'd just have to cope. So maybe leaving and striking out on my own, while I'm young enough, is not so stupid.

I would not remarry: once is enough. But I would love to set up home with somebody else, or at the least have a regular visitor.

Heavens, what am I to do? What is to happen?

1994

Tower House, Sunday 30 January, 9.25 p.m.

Ray's gone to the pub, Deb is back in Huddersfield and Susie at Repton, after a pleasant weekend lunch – roast beef, Yorkshire pud, roast potatoes, peas, sweetcorn and my special gravy, all munched in silence in front of the TV: we still don't have conversations in this house. Mum has just phoned and is well if a bit shaky. She reminded me that I haven't seen her since May, but we'll meet at the launch party in the House of Commons on Wednesday night. I'm surprised it is so long, but since we talk on the phone every weekend I feel we're closer than we've ever been.

First the good news – Susie got into Cambridge, the little darling, and to LSE, who only want three Bs. She went through quite a punishing ordeal, having to go up for two sets of interviews after Pembroke put her in the pool, partly because she's not doing A level Maths, which they prefer for Economics, and partly because they dislike the deferment. Newnham and New Hall promptly called her and agreed between themselves which was to make the offer. These girls-only colleges are suffering from a lack of good applicants, but Susie said the atmosphere was just like a girls' house in a mixed school, which suits her fine, and 'Cambridge is Cambridge'. She looks very pleased with herself, as well she might be, and I'm thrilled. She is so steady and smart and wise, and such a nice kid. Similarly, Deb is settling down much better in Huddersfield and is enjoying the course. She says her greater calmness and sense of purpose is due to coming off the pill and being in love with Shi, but I reckon she's maturing naturally – at nineteen-and-a-half, it's about time. The current plan involves buying a little house in Huddersfield to share with other students, as their tower block on campus is both grim and expensive; that seems a very good idea. She's taken herself off to estate agents and mortgage advisers and I've promised a £5,000 loan; it all seems both exciting (to her) and highly responsible (to me).

Meanwhile the book comes out on Thursday and it looks as if we are set for the bestseller lists after the most amazing few weeks. I couldn't have picked a better time, really. Back in December David Faber[100] separated from his wife, a very pretty TV presenter, and sued for divorce on the grounds of her adultery with her riding master – shades of Jilly Cooper. Then the dam burst, and since then we've had five mistresses (Tim Yeo[101] 2; Gary Waller,[102] of all people, 2; Malcolm Caithness[103] 1), four illegitimate children (Yeo 2, Waller 2), three resignations (Yeo, Caithness and Alan Duncan,[104] over a row about purchasing a 'council house' in Lord North Street from Westminster Council). Oh, and David Ashby[105] was caught sharing a bed with his (male) psychiatrist when on holiday in France and declared it was just to save money. His nutty Italian wife Silvana has thrown him out. I don't know what was funnier, the idea of David having a cuddle with another bloke, or his furious denials to the press that anything untoward happened. What a shower! I couldn't have made that lot up. At least my characters behave consistently – and none of them fathers an illegitimate child. I didn't think any of my colleagues would be so stupid.

It's blown 'Back to Basics' out of the water, and about time too, but with it the PM's future, I'm afraid. This was to be his great unifying theme for the mid-term legislative programme, uniting law and order, education, and sound finance (not that a £50 billion deficit is exactly that, of course). It was promptly hijacked by both

---

100 Conservative MP for Westbury since 1992.
101 Minister of State, Department of the Environment; Conservative MP for South Suffolk since 1983.
102 Conservative MP for Keighley since 1983; MP for Brighouse and Spenborough, 1979–83.
103 Lord Caithness, Minister of State, Department of Transport, since 1992.
104 PPS in the DoH; Conservative MP for Rutland and Melton since 1992.
105 MP for North West Leicestershire since 1983.

the Conference and the right-wingers – Redwood,[106] Lilley, Portillo – to mean 'back to the old morality': not that the latter is on safe ground, if the rumours are true. So we grind the faces of the poor into the dust and label all single mothers slags and harlots, more or less. I'm sure John Major is correct when he protests that he never intended all this, but he of all people should have foreseen it. The idea is wrong in principle anyway – forward not back, always, for a political party. The whole episode, coming on top of the Public Accounts Committee's criticism of waste and mismanagement of public money and the row over how we tax people more heavily than Labour did, and the Westminster Council fuss,[107] suggests a real failure to get a grip. The Parliamentary Party is furious, and the venom and blame is directed at the PM himself. So after the local and Euro elections, poor John is for the chop. Sad.

Meanwhile... Richard phoned, but the children were making a racket; and again, but could only speak a minute. Losing his job[108] hasn't really concentrated his mind – he slips into a depression and then does nothing, flapping around helplessly and having lunch with lots of people, all to fill the diary tight and convince himself he's doing something. I take it upon myself to chide him gently, but I don't want to add to the misery.

I still think we'll win the Euro seat, if only because all the omens there continue to be good. It's as if we're fighting a totally different campaign to Central Office, much more positive and upbeat, with the right modern, forward-thinking image for the area and the age. It generates *enthusiasm*, and understanding and broad support. I say honestly that I don't know where the EU is going, but we have to be in there to make sure it doesn't go wrong, and that produces nods all round. I only wish we got the same message, loud and clear, from the top.

---

106 Secretary of State for Wales since 1993; Conservative MP for Wokingham since 1987.
107 There were suggestions of gerrymandering by the Conservative-controlled Westminster Council.
108 He had been made redundant by Hodder just before Christmas.

Meanwhile Age of Consent[109] rumbles on. We've had loads of coverage and a lot of fun, with a rally in Trafalgar Square next Saturday, which should be a gas – Deb says she'll come too. We've had an extraordinary mailbag, mostly favourable, with many moving letters, except for the couple with excreta in. If people like that are against us, we must be on the right side.

House of Commons, Tuesday 8 February, 8.10 p.m.

My God, am I feeling depressed. Yesterday afternoon Stephen Milligan, the MP for Eastleigh, whom I've known since we were at Oxford together, was found dead in his flat in Hammersmith. He may have been there all weekend. He was semi-naked, wearing only women's tights and a suspender belt, with a plastic bin bag over his head, tied with a flex which was wrapped around his body and hands. The end of the flex was near his hands, so he could have pulled it tight himself. According to *The Sun*, he had an orange stuffed in his mouth.

It's not yet clear how he died, whether from suffocation, or heart failure, or maybe from drugs; tests are still ongoing and the first post mortem was inconclusive. The police say they aren't looking for anyone else.

I feel so desperately sorry for him. He was a hard-working, unassuming and thoroughly nice man; much brighter than the average here, and destined to be a minister soon. There was never any suggestion of anything odd in his make-up. The only pointers were a high whinny of a laugh as if he were embarrassed rather than amused, and the fact that at forty-five he'd never married (though he'd had plenty of girlfriends). So the possibility is that he was gay, or bisexual – or a loner, so utterly alone that he sought sexual pleasure by nearly killing himself through oxygen starvation, apparently a trick often played in S&M games. A sex game that went horribly wrong, perhaps. What a waste of a good man. I grieve for him, and for all those who can't love in what I can recognise as a normal fashion. Next to this, a pair of gays cuddling seems positively pristine.

---

109 EC was sponsoring an amendment to the Criminal Justice Bill to lower the age of consent for homosexuals to sixteen, the same age as heterosexual couples.

Did he ever love anyone? Did he ever find joy in ordinary sex? If not, he can't for one day of his life have been a happy person.

Everybody at Westminster and in his constituency is stunned and horrified. Ray's comment was an unhelpful 'messy' last night, when I needed to talk about it; one reason for turning to the diary.

It is awful news for the government as well, for it means another by-election, next door to the Christchurch seat we lost so badly last year. Stephen's 17,000 majority looks lost already. There are two other by-elections pending, for Labour-held seats. These are likely to be in May, on the same day as the local elections, and are liable to be a terrible precursor to the Euro elections, where all the polls suggest a disastrous result. Nothing at all seems to be going right for the government at the moment, and the atmosphere is grim. The press are talking endlessly about sleaze, making comparisons with the Profumo affair in 1963. That seems too close for comfort, for the problem then was that Macmillan was losing his grip, and the same feeling pervades now. It seems to have dawned on no one that the bloody 'Back to Basics' campaign is to blame, for it outlawed the one protective factor the Tory Party has always relied on – hypocrisy – and, of course, a sense of humour and perspective.

Meanwhile, everything else appears to be going very well. Last week was just amazing, with the launch on Thursday, the party and dinner the night before which were great, a signing on Waterloo Station which was about the maddest and most exhilarating thing (being dive-bombed by pigeons) I've ever done, and a rally for the Age of Consent campaign in Trafalgar Square with Vanessa Redgrave, Dawn French and loads of people I'd never heard of. I loved the line of one speaker who said, 'Of course it's appropriate for us to be here on Nelson's column. After all, Nelson's last words were, "Kiss me, Hardy."' Mum came down for the party, looking very regal in a new purple wool suit; she is grand for eighty-two, though she keeps shrinking. At this rate she'll be around my knees in a year or two. Roll on the HRT – another good reason for not succumbing to failing ovaries, I guess. Deb made the grandest entrance, just as Tim Hely-Hutchinson[110] – who has a curiously

---

110 Chief Executive of Hodder Headline.

high, squeaky voice – was making a little speech. It was really very funny as this glamorous nineteen-year-old madam in a stunning black trouser suit sashayed down the steps to hold my hand and pinch all the limelight. She came to Trafalgar Square too, which I appreciated enormously. Maybe I didn't entirely imagine the closeness between mother and daughter in *A Parliamentary Affair* as a worthy substitute for a weak marriage.

I suppose the book is doing well, but it will be hard to tell for another few days. The bookshops said nice things, but they always do. Today, however, came my £20,200 cheque from Hodder. I've set aside a bit to help pay Richard for his advice on the new book; he seemed reluctant when we talked on the phone last week to knuckle down to it, but I need his help and am prepared to press him on it. Maybe being paid will embarrass him so much he'll do it. He didn't get the Book Trust job and was depressed about it, but that may turn out to be the best thing for him. He needs a different vehicle – his own small firm; and if it doesn't work, at least he will have tried. Frank Delaney said he should be a writer and that he only lacks the courage and confidence to try; true, maybe, but writing is such an intense and personal (and lonely) activity. Anyway he can't live on what he would earn by his pen, and he wants to waste his time writing about fencing first![111] He showed me a draft of Jeffrey Archer's next book, a collection of short stories. Archer thinks a woman is a 'blond' and has no idea about apostrophes, punctuation etc. His plots are laughably implausible, such as an Englishman getting away for years with the impersonation of a Romanian professor. Apart from these obvious lacunae, his ideas are limited – the stories repeat several themes in earlier collections – but are told with a rollicking good humour that carries suspension of disbelief nicely along.[112] I write much better than that, thank God, and every single reviewer has said so. In fact the reviews have been far better than I expected, except silly old Julian Critchley, who clearly hadn't read the book.

---

111 He did, to international acclaim. *By the Sword*, 2002, Random House.
112 The collection became *Twelve Red Herrings*.

Hertfordshire Moat House, Friday 18 February, 11.45 p.m.
I confess I'm holding my breath at the moment and feel in a complete daze. *A Parliamentary Affair* went straight to *No. 1* in the *Sunday Times* fiction list, which is unheard of for a first novel. This week I understand it's No. 2 to Mary Wesley, which can't be bad, but in compensation we're at No. 1 in W. H. Smith, and that's based on real sales, not the esoteric sampling of the *Sunday Times*. I faxed a copy of the W. H. Smith list to the *Burton Mail*, and to Lisa and Richard; the latter pinged back 'Hooray, Love Richard', which tickled me. Nice man! I knew we were on target for good sales, but it's truly wonderful to be top of the bestseller list. The moment the news was announced, Hodder (in the person of Martin Nield and Sue Fletcher) came winging back with an offer of £250,000 for two more novels. But after conversations with both Richard and Lisa, and following my own instinct, we're negotiating for one only – which Lisa says is worth £150,000 anyway. I didn't like the tone of Sue's fax which Lisa sent me; without seeing any synopsis they want no more than 150,000 words, 'in view of all the trouble with the last one'. What trouble? It went straight to No. 1, dammit. She told Lisa it means no Richard. Ah, but having a success is like winning my scholarship at Oxford: I can insist, and I do. Richard is so stubborn it took some persuading and eventually I wrote to him formally; it still took him twenty minutes on the phone after much circumlocution to get to the point of saying 'yes', on condition that I don't do what Jeffrey Archer did and phone in the middle of the night with 'I'm paying you, so don't argue'. The *A Parliamentary Affair* contract gives Hodder an option within six weeks of receiving a synopsis, otherwise we're free to go elsewhere. After that, I'm free to move. I think they will give in.

The Age of Consent debate is on Monday. And to my utter astonishment, it looks as if we might win it. We've talked about 'over 200' MPs supporting us, which in itself would make for a close vote since there's no whipping at all on our side. By last week we had 270 known pledges, including thirty Tories. But on Wednesday evening Derek Conway, the Home Office whip, told me their calculations were that around sixty Tories will vote with us, which means our support could touch 300, in which case victory is highly likely (since many will abstain). As the vote on 18 follows if 16 fails, and would get through with a huge majority, the age will change by 11 p.m. Monday night – the only open question is, what to. It is quite remarkable. There's been a huge shift in attitude out there. The Stonewall letter-writing and MP-visiting campaign has been sober, persuasive, sensible and very effective. Even if we don't succeed this time, we will before long, and the Currie amendment will go down in parliamentary history. How very peculiar: it wasn't quite what I was expecting to be remembered for!

I was trying to figure out why it made me feel good, and in a way it's revenge, for all the snide remarks, for all the arrogant macho assumptions of Westminster. I've blown the pretensions and prejudices wide open with *A Parliamentary Affair*; if we change the law on gays, that's another smack in the eye for all those men with their Victorian values; and then if I win in June, so much against the odds, it will be two fingers at them with a vengeance. Nothing will so become that place as my leaving of it. Of course I have loads of other, worthier motives, but the worst reasons are often the most powerful and therefore the best.

Victoria, Thursday 3 March, 11.25 p.m.

Well, we didn't win it, but we got damn near. A vote of 280 in favour included forty-six Tories (plus Andrew Rowe[113] as teller), of whom eight were ex-ministers, thirteen ministers including Newton and Waldegrave, and three whips. Another eleven Tories abstained on 16 and voted for 18, so the whips were right that nearly sixty Tories were on our side. We lost by twenty-seven votes, however, because everybody turned up including the Ulstermen, and thirty-five Labour MPs voted against, much to everybody's surprise. That included two frontbench spokesmen, Ann Taylor[114] (education) and David Blunkett[115] (health). I suspect Ann at least will be punished by the PLP in the autumn, and this time Smith will have to drop her.

---

113 Conservative MP for Mid Kent since 1983.
114 Labour MP for Dewsbury since 1987; MP for Bolton West, 1974–83.
115 Labour MP for Sheffield Brightside since 1987.

Most of the Labour antis were north countrymen, so Stonewall has some campaigning to do north of the Humber!

It was a marvellous debate; I feel privileged to have taken part, really. Kinnock and Garel-Jones were excellent, with Tris appealing firmly to Tory principles of fairness and justice. Chris Smith[116] made a moving appeal to be accepted as different but not treated differently. Tony Blair[117] gave a humdinger of a speech, powerful without being mawkish, and held the house through sheer force of personality. He will make a fine and popular PM some day, if his Party have the sense to choose him. Paisley[118] thundered on about the need to 'convert' young men from homosexuality (the word has seventeen syllables the way he says it) by capturing them into a 'happy marriage'. God help us all. The atmosphere was wonderful, and it is a source of great pride that we got a majority of 252 for 18, which in my view is real progress. The success was marred by headbangers in the crowd outside who tried to storm the Commons. But there was a fabulous aftermath, with bunch after bunch of flowers being delivered, as if I was some diva with a first-night hit; by the Wednesday afternoon we were sending them to Great Ormond Street Hospital where Clare's son is now having tests for asthma, poor kid. The flat is *still* full of them, every wastepaper bin pressed into service! And 1,000 letters and cards in three days, most highly complimentary. It took me till 10.30 p.m. tonight, a week later, to shift the backlog.

It felt good to be involved. Electorally I think it will be helpful, as Bedfordshire & Milton Keynes is the youngest seat in the country, with only 14 per cent of population of retirement age, compared with over 20 per cent as a national average and 25 per cent in most Tory areas. So I hope some clean-limbed young helpers will emerge to counteract the whinging old biddies who gain comfort from airing their prejudices in deepest county Bedfordshire (not a hostile squeak from Milton Keynes). We'll find out in June.

---

116 Labour MP for Islington South and Finsbury since 1983.
117 Opposition spokesman on home affairs; Labour MP for Sedgefield since 1983.
118 Ian Paisley, leader of the DUP; DUP MP for Antrim North since 1970, and an MEP.

I sat in on the Employment Select Committee on Monday as they questioned Padraig Flynn, the European Commissioner for employment and social affairs. It was a shambles on both sides. The MPs (mostly Tory) are not skilled inquisitors and let him get away with murder – or at any rate a load of blarney; and only briefly did he rise to the occasion and put a point forcefully, about the need for jobs and competitiveness in Europe. The rhetoric at least was familiar to British ears, but reconciling labour flexibility with high social costs is a tricky exercise at the best of times and a slippery (and perhaps not very bright) Irishman is just the chap to try it. In all, a thoroughly unsatisfactory forty minutes. Anyone could do better. There's no chance of John Major asking me to take on a Commissioner's post, but I suppose a future Labour PM just might. And I'd jump at it. I wish I'd made it to a higher rung in government before I had to leave, simply because I'd get offered better jobs now and in the future.

A debate on industry yesterday had Heseltine on terrific form, rubbishing the opposition, which fuelled press speculation that he's back in the running for the leadership. All very intriguing; he appears to have recovered fully from his heart attack, plus his doldrums after coal closures – he's been proved right a year on. Most of all he's refound his own zest. And curiously it is the *right* who are interested, since Heseltine is sixty-one and he presumably wouldn't be PM for long. That might fill the gap nicely till their man Portillo has grown up enough – say two to three years. And the left warm to Heseltine too, partly because he stood up to Margaret and was unlucky not to win the leadership when she quit, and because his instincts are sound on Europe. Suddenly it looks much more interesting, as poor John Major's position continues to crumble.

Not that I would vote for Portillo. In the tea room yesterday I had a blazing row with him about how we should respond to disquiet over Scott.[119] 'They must wait till the report is out,' he said coldly, eyes glittering. His expression was impatient: 'don't bother me'

---

119 The Scott Inquiry into the Matrix-Churchill affair, which turned on whether ministers had washed their hands of British businessmen whom they had unofficially encouraged to sell arms to Iraq, despite an arms embargo.

almost. 'That's not good enough,' said I, 'it won't be till July and some of us have an election to fight before then. We want to hold our seats' (and I pointed out that Nick Lyell[120] is a Bedfordshire MP). 'You may think winning elections is important,' replied Portillo loftily, 'but there's something more important – honesty, truth…' I was astonished. 'I couldn't agree more,' I said sarcastically. 'That's the whole issue. The public want to know how we could be prepared to let honest men – and patriots – go to jail. What's the answer?' And when I got the line repeated about elections not being important (and implying that I was prepared to lie to win, while he wasn't), I told him he was being offensive. Now this guy wants my vote at some point, presumably, or he thinks I don't matter. I didn't feel angry, just disgusted. On top of everything it is widely believed that he is gay or bisexual, but he never voted for 16 or abstained. Very steely, very cool, and very unpleasant. If that's his style of leadership, I'm glad that I am leaving and won't have to show him any loyalty or regard.

In this week's *Sunday Times*, *A Parliamentary Affair* was still No. 3, after Paddy Clarke[121] and Mary Wesley – well ahead of Dobbs and Crichton. We're now getting in lovely letters from people who have ploughed through all 564 pages. I hope for their sakes I can do a better one next time. Hodder have had the synopsis a week, but not a word from them. All gone cold in that department, after their frantic efforts to sign me up in two days flat. I doubt if Hodder would be stupid enough to let me go, but if they did I could come to Richard for the next book or the one after. He was telling me that Jeffrey Archer let him down over *As the Crow Flies*, after insisting that Richard remain his editor on a percentage of royalties. When Hodder sold the entire Archer backlist to HarperCollins, they sold Richard's contract too. He checked with HarperCollins, who'd never heard of this arrangement. Then he checked with Jeffrey Archer, who said he'd pay direct – so now Richard has to chase that little turd for money, exactly the position he didn't want to be in.

---

120 Sir Nicholas Lyell, Attorney-General since 1992; Conservative MP for Mid Bedfordshire since 1983; MP for Hemel Hempstead, 1979–83.
121 *Paddy Clarke Ha Ha Ha* by Roddy Doyle, winner of the 1993 Booker Prize.

House of Commons, Wednesday 16 March, 7.50 p.m.

The danger of the European elections on 9 June turning into a rout is increasing daily. A *Guardian* opinion poll today shows our support has fallen to only 24 per cent of the voters, only 2 points ahead of the Liberals and a staggering 25 points behind Labour. Given all the doubts about polls – including those who wouldn't dream of voting the other way, but are cross with us at present – nevertheless they make gloomy reading. I suspect we are vastly too complacent about our 'inevitable' political recovery.

I saw Richard on Monday and he was clearly making an effort to be more cheerful and not to wallow in gloom like the previous week (which led to me writing him a real nannying letter, full of pompous good advice). Feeling sorry for himself is a substitute for determined action, yet at the same time the desire to run his own business is hardening into an ambition. I told him that when he has the employment of several people hanging on his actions, he won't be able to swan off or get bored or pine for his freedom: he'll have to knuckle down, be more focused, more single-minded, far more than he has appeared so far. He said he's a hard worker and I don't doubt it, but that is not the same – he dissipates his energies in too many trivial projects. In the business world he could get eaten alive if he is not careful.

After that I went back to the flat, and Ray came home almost immediately. I had lots to tell him, as I'd been up to Liverpool for the weekend (Mothering Sunday), so I suggested we went for a meal to Overton's. I had been assuming all along that he would be upset at what I have to tell him in due course, but maybe I'm wrong – maybe he'll be pleased, or at least relieved. That, I realised with a jolt, would upset me. How terrible it would be if, after all these years, we both discovered that we have been living a lie – that all the words of endearment (which I have stopped using) turned out to be empty. What a let-down – a disappointment – what a failure I should feel. Up till now, I've regarded myself as quite a successful wife. Supposing that wasn't so? Heavens, it would be like a scene in a novel (shouldn't think like that, too bloody cynical). For most of the meal he clearly wished he was somewhere else, and on our return stolidly settled in front of the TV and then came to bed, his back turned the whole time. Once I would have been cursing and tearful. Now I am simply astonished, and rueful.

There were several points of disagreement. I asked what dates he might be available in the Euro election. He named several, but all weekdays. No plans to take even a week's holiday. What about Saturdays, I asked? Then it dawned on me that he'd intended to spend his Saturdays at home in Findern, stretched out in front of the racing on the TV as usual, and that made me quite angry. It's not as if he needs to be home to babysit, as Susie will be up to her eyes in A levels and anyway she usually comes home Sundays. If that's loyalty and full support, then I'm Mussolini.

While I've been typing this Lisa has phoned to tie up some details of the contract for *A Woman's Place*.[122] For the fact is, we've agreed the new contract with Hodder and I have everything I wanted. The overall price is £150,000, a huge sum for a novel and a big increase on the first. It will come in fifths, but the first tranche is £40,000 on signing the contract – whoopee. The line was that I was afraid top-whack income tax was going up and wanted the payments as much upfront as possible; Sue Fletcher was perfectly happy with that. My preferred timing is accepted and my proposed length, which is fine by me. So we're all happy, indeed thrilled. And relieved. I feel a bit like a weary general who has been fighting battles simultaneously on all fronts; then at the end of a long day, he sees his standards, tattered and bloody, being raised all over the battlefield, the enemy is surrendering and there is the sound of distant cheering.

All I've got to do now is write the bloody thing.

Victoria, Thursday 31 March, 2.40 p.m.

Now what I ought to be doing is my accounts for an hour, and *then* the diary, but my mind is buzzing and I can't concentrate; I've spent the last fifty minutes lying on the floor, staring at the ceiling and feeling utterly confused.

I saw Richard yesterday on his return from New York. He was looking tired – 'jet-lagged', he said – he'll never make an international businessman if it takes him two days to recover! – and a bit

---

122 EC's new novel.

thinner. The fencing was fine and he did well, getting to the third round, number 70 out of over 140 fencers of top international class. He's still sore at being kept out of the Barcelona Olympics, but assures me that he's coming to terms with not being a champion any longer. I suspect he says it, but doesn't feel it, yet. We talked nineteen to the dozen and swapped magazines, reviews, ideas, and then arranged today to meet for lunch. Then, this morning, for domestic reasons lunch wasn't possible, though he rang again later and we continued our natter – then he had to ring off in a hurry. It sounds like complete mayhem, and I wonder how anyone can think straight in such an atmosphere.

Still, he is getting on with setting up his business, which he will (wisely) call Richard Cohen Books. Among the ideas he got in New York was a possible biographer for Lucien Freud – surprising it hasn't been done as there was a big exhibition of his work recently. Already he's been promised some financial backing, but he is reluctant to put in his own money. I said he must, or nobody will take him seriously; of course he has to live too, but there should be enough for both. He has given himself to the end of June to get the whole thing up and running.

The book is still in the bestseller lists – seven weeks in the *Sunday Times* list, this week at No. 4. Amazing, really; we have sold over 30,000 in hardback now, and Lisa estimates that Hodder will sell at least 60,000 in paperback. I have worked out pretty carefully what would happen if I win the Bedfordshire & Milton Keynes seat – we could sell the Tower House, cash some of the insurance policies, and split the proceeds. Ray would presumably buy a smaller house up there, and I would lease a Bedfordshire cottage and put the money into shares. What has bedevilled me for the last decade is having so little personal income – the parliamentary salary is so pathetic, one thinks twice even about paying for a meal out. So it would be grand to have some personal capital behind me, which was nothing to do with the company, but the income from which would be mine. Having fewer properties to maintain would also cut my expenses, a lot, and soon no more school fees (whoopee!) – I've paid the bulk of those recently. Then I could live modestly but in comfort.

I have not, however, worked out what happens if I don't win, and there the water is murky. I lose my excuse to leave Derbyshire, as presumably they would want me to fight again. On weaker boundaries we would probably lose it, but at least that would be the honourable position. It's been suggested that I should try for the North Bedfordshire seat, which would be safe, but that implies a commitment I don't feel to Westminster – better, perhaps, to hang around outside Parliament for a couple of years until I could try for the European Parliament again in 1999. The interim I could use well, I am sure – writing, TV maybe, journalism – but I would lose my 'name'. On the other hand it might enable me to regularise my life out of the public eye. Financially, however, it would not be so straightforward.

And losing in June looks a distinct possibility, unless things move fast in the next few days (which they might). I was appalled at the sullen atmosphere on our side at Prime Minister's Questions last Tuesday. We had hardly anyone on his feet trying to get in, and the Speaker ended the questioning after barely forty minutes – unheard of. Before lunch I did *House to House* live TV from Millbank with Ivan Lawrence, who was subdued for him and looking sly, and Michael Clark,[123] a Eurosceptic who abstained on most of Maastricht but who can be regarded as a mainstreamer. I was astonished at Clark's open contempt for the PM and the virulence of his remarks, live on air. At Prime Minister's Questions Tony Marlow[124] demanded that the PM resign (but then he did the same to Margaret). This time there were glum looks of agreement all round. They've all had enough of the PM's incompetence and vacillation. The man has no credibility with the public and now none at all with his own side.

It did occur to me on Wednesday (yesterday), as the PM read the worst press even he must ever have seen, that in some ways it would be better if he went quickly now. I said so in the lobby to Tony Newton, whom I later saw heading towards the Chief Whip – Tony was a whip so he has respected links with the Chief. If we drag on till

---

123 Dr Michael Clark, Conservative MP for Rochford since 1983.
124 Conservative MP for Northampton North since 1979; a prominent Eurosceptic.

the autumn, we will do horribly badly in the local and Euro elections. Better to have a snap leadership election when we return in mid-April, and then we have a reasonable chance of a honeymoon period to carry us over both elections. We can't do any worse, and we might conceivably perform a whole lot better.

Meanwhile I am preparing to fly to France tomorrow morning to rejoin Ray, who went out yesterday with the car. I'll be there till Tuesday, flying back in the afternoon. I really do not want to go to France this time with my husband – much of the time I'm devising excuses for sleeping in a different bed, or pushing him away, or lying still in the hope he'll go to sleep. And counting the months till I can end this charade. Unexpectedly the chances of a clean break while maintaining the girls' friendship became more likely this week, as Susie too is now in love. It means that when I eventually explain to my daughters, there is the faint chance they will understand.

House of Commons, Wednesday 13 April, 11.15 p.m.

I've just been to see the PM. He was nice: gentle, touched my hair and commented that it was a different colour. His face was drawn and grey – the bouncy bonhomie has all gone. Replaced, to my horror and disgust, by a kind of paranoia. If he really believes the things he said to me, then he is more stupid, more foolish than ever I knew him years ago. It was the same, uncannily, with Margaret in her last months. It's as if there is something in the water at No. 10 – a bromide, an insidious inorganic chemical, inimical to life, poisoning, destroying all the natural human qualities that made him so special.

We voted at 9.45 p.m. on the report stage of the interminable Criminal Justice Bill, and I hung around to see if there would be a vote at ten. In the lobby were Nigel Evans,[125] the bright, spunky Welshman who lives in the same block as us in Carlisle Place, and Matthew Banks,[126] another of the new intake, a smooth loyalist but humorous and sensible. We started a conversation about what has to happen, and the sooner the better; the tone and easy vocabulary

---

125 Conservative MP for Ribble Valley since 1992.
126 Conservative MP for Southport since 1992.

suggested that this was one of many such in the Palace's corridors these days. I was startled, as I had been at Michael Clark's bitterness on TV, at how far and how completely the PM has lost their support. Earlier this evening, at a committee meeting of the CGE, we discussed the complete collapse of the group's activities this spring – the PM said he would come to a conference, then let them down, and the upshot was that the whole event was cancelled, leaving them floundering and bewildered.

Banks said he was in the tea room yesterday when Graham Bright motioned him over to an empty chair, and he found himself next to the PM. It was embarrassing and deeply uncomfortable, he said, for nobody knew what to say. This is the first day back after recess, mind, when everyone should be feeling refreshed and ready for the numerous elections which will spoil the early summer. The conversation should flow easily and lightly. The opposite happened. The exchanges boiled down to inanities like 'where are you going next?' Nothing much else. Our youngster told a few funny stories and was thanked later for lightening the atmosphere. Christ.

These remarks dismayed me. The PM has no friends left. What remains is what he can rescue from this mess, for himself as a person, and for the Party. So I asked if I could go in and see him and have just done so.

(Just voted again at midnight – bringing the age of consent in Northern Ireland down to 18 in line with the rest of the country. Big majority. Last night we decriminalised homosexuality in the armed forces and merchant navy without a vote. My goodness, hasn't the steam gone out of this issue quickly?)

We're in his room at the back of the Speaker's Chair, large, featureless, dull: this is a man who fails to impose his personality on the rooms he inhabits, or maybe he has no personality. I used to believe he had deeply buried secret passions, but now I don't think he has any.

EC: 'Have you decided what to do?'

PM: 'I will fight – if there is a leadership contest I will fight. Heseltine would split the Party.'

EC: 'The Party is already split. If you fight you will lose – you will be humiliated. Nobody is telling you the truth; I am not here as representative of any group, just me. It is not for you to decide your successor – that is for the Party to decide, and strictly speaking it's none of your business. You'd have only the same vote as the rest of us. What matters to me – why I wanted to see you – is to ensure you come out of it with your reputation intact... You will be blamed for the poor results of the forthcoming elections. That is inevitable – can't be helped or avoided. They're looking for a scapegoat and it will be you.'

PM: 'Yes' (his expression implied it was unfair). 'So many lies have been told about me in the last two years – lies, innuendo, fabrications... Murdoch... the press have been poisonous – no one should have to put up with all that...'

(He does not speak in whole sentences – just snatches – was trying to be assertive and failing completely – sounded petulant, peevish, foolish instead – like an old man losing his grip. Losing his authority, and not understanding why.)

EC: 'You must not fight. You will lose, and it will be more damaging if you are involved in the leadership contest. You cannot wait until the autumn – we would have weeks of conspiracy and a horrendous Party Conference. Instead, if you do the brave thing and resign immediately after the elections – take responsibility, Japanese-style – everyone will heap praises on your head and it will be the achievements of your four years which will be remembered. That will be your record and reputation in future. The Conference would then welcome the new Prime Minister and you would be loaded with accolades, not least for the courageous way you took it on the chin.'

PM: 'That would be walking away without a fight. I can't do that.' (He said this several times, like a mantra.)

EC: 'They will cut your legs off and make stumps and you will crawl away bleeding. Don't do it. You have a life, interests, outside politics. You should be ready to serve your country in other ways.'

PM (who has obviously been thinking about it – but what showed through was the peevishness again, with no sense of duty – only to himself: here, more than anywhere else, is the reason he has to go): 'I would not stay in politics. I would leave completely – leave Parliament the general election after I left Downing Street, not go to the Lords, not go to Europe, not do anything else in politics ever again.'

I'm left with a bad taste in my mouth and the impression of a man whose current plans are to force an early leadership contest in the summer on a 'back me or sack me' ticket. He is convincing himself that he will win, and that it would then tide him over to fight the general election in due course.

Euston Station, Wednesday 20 April, 9.45 a.m.

After sharing some thoughts with Peter Thurnham[127] last week (Thursday – the day after I saw the PM), I find that he went racing to Graham Bright to say that my views are not representative of most Tory MPs; so I get a phone call from Graham yesterday morning about it, which hauled me cross and dripping out of my bath. I didn't (I hope) imply to the PM that lots of MPs had spoken to me and I'm quite sure I made it clear I was speaking only for myself. But the fact is that John is quite useless as PM and everybody says so. Thurnham is a pain – at the very least he might have kept his opinions – or my name – to himself – it smacks of sneaking, which is surprising as he's generally a genial bloke!

St James's Park, Monday 2 May, 6.35 p.m.

Sitting on a grassy knoll in the park, as the sun begins to sink over Buckingham Palace. It's breezy and a bit chilly, so the courting couples who were lolling around half an hour ago have now gone; the families with pushchairs and tired children are heading for home. I'll give myself forty minutes before I do too.

Election fever is mounting, with the locals on Thursday. I'll vote in Westminster; Ray, disorganised and uninterested as ever, won't be voting at all, as he will be in north Wales with his students. In fact, if we don't get a move on, we won't even be voting in South Derbyshire, as I'm having to nag Tyrone for our proxy votes. Hope the Bedfordshire & Milton Keynes agents are more with it! It looks certain that we will do horrendously badly in both local and Euro elections; the press keep nagging MPs for their comments on Major, but only one or two will come out and say that he must go. But it's surely only a matter of time.

127 Conservative MP for Bolton North East since 1983.

Tomorrow I plan to get on with more writing and finish off Chapter 2; then I can send it to Richard along with his birthday card (9 May).

Victoria, Sunday 8 May, 11.15 p.m.

So far, no response from Richard, though Lisa says he's had his contract this week and is happy with it. That's good news, as he could easily have backed out if he really couldn't abide me any more – much as he refused to do further business with Jeffrey Archer.

All in all, it was a depressing week. The local election results were ghastly. We lost council after council – over 400 seats in all. Westminster and Wandsworth were both OK, but we lost badly in Derby as Chellaston was gained by Labour with a 266 majority – the first council seat we've lost in my eleven years in South Derbyshire. John Keith, the ex-Mayor, came third in Blagreaves (won by Labour with 991 majority); in Boulton ward we had no chance with a Labour majority of 1,269; and we just hung on to Mickleover by seventy-four votes. The first Liberal Democrat on Derby Council, Maurice Bungers, was elected after standing twenty-five times! Overall the city now has a solid Labour majority. There were a few good signs: Clare worked like a Trojan in Lambeth and held her seat with an increased majority. In Milton Keynes the vote was up over last time. That augurs well.

But the pressure is on the PM, not surprisingly. John Carlisle rashly declared he'd stand as a stalking horse if necessary and was promptly denounced in Luton, with his chairman simply calling him a 'fool'. Major wittered on at No. 10 on Friday morning about how the Party had procedures and anyone who wanted to stand would find he'd taken on the PM himself. He didn't actually say, 'I fight on – I fight to win' – but came close. *Stupid.* It is to be hoped that the men in white coats get to him on 14 June before the rest of us do.

Friday night made things far worse for me in the depression stakes, for we went to Northern Ireland to do *Any Questions* – absolutely the wrong place, since the Channel Tunnel was opened that day by the Queen and President Mitterrand. *Any Questions* should therefore have been in Folkestone. Instead we found ourselves a century away, where people murder each other for belonging to a different tribe. The hour's bumpy journey from Belfast to Newry was the least of our worries. There are no hotels in Newry – all bombed out – and only one hopeless steak bar, where my steak was a slab of brown overdone meat *covered* in ground-up parsley, and the salad was mostly bean sprouts. There were police and soldiers around corners everywhere, though they melted away when we appeared. However, as we left the Town Hall after the event I found myself looking down the barrel of a machine-gun carried by a uniformed man (one of ours?) who was pointing it at a jeering crowd of youths. By innocently crossing the road I'd put myself in the firing line. The man and his gun-toting companion quickly got back into their car, a sleek black unmarked vehicle with tinted screens, like something out of a gangster movie. The organisers of the event wanted to celebrate 850 years since Newry's founding, and a sweet naïve bunch of local teachers they turned out to be. They'd sold 500 tickets back in February, but only fifty people turned up – maybe the fact that the first arrivals were the local Sinn Fein councillor and his cronies had something to do with it. The broadcast was a scary experience. At one point as I was talking – live! – all the lights went out and there was a big bang outside. The whole audience jumped a foot out of their seats, their eyes wide and terrified – but no one left, which struck me as extraordinary. It was only a thunderclap, but we didn't know that till later. Then there was a police siren, and the sound of shouting outside – the youths maybe. To cap it all, I got stopped at security at Belfast Airport because of the crystal-handled paperknife we'd all been given. I couldn't get out of there fast enough...

There are grounds for optimism elsewhere. *A Parliamentary Affair* is launched this week in Australia and soon in Canada, Poland and Italy, and has been sold to Meridian TV. It is back in the *Sunday Times* lists this week. And I've been nominated for Bedfordshire & Milton Keynes and the deposit paid. Adoption tomorrow. All I have to do is win it...

Tower House, Sunday 15 May, 8.50 p.m.
John Smith's death[128] has left us all stunned; the Commons paid

128 On 12 May.

tribute, then suspended its sitting, and all campaigning for the Euro elections was abandoned in an unprecedented display of genuine grief. After his last heart attack six years ago, at the early age of forty-nine, he lost weight, cut the food and drink, exercised. But I reckoned he'd slipped in the last year or two, for he'd become tubby again (I used to see him in the House of Commons gym – he was a less regular attendee than me, and that's not saying much). His old conviviality was revived, and I reckon he simply thought he'd beaten it. Yet a photo from last October's Party Conference clearly showed the 'xanthus' – the white ring around the irises, evidence of a cholesterol build-up. When the attack came he hadn't a chance.

John Smith was one of the good guys – clever but not arrogant, tough but courteous, a leader and a team maker. He had every chance of being the next PM, and the mourning for his passing goes far beyond the Labour Party. His way of doing things – his clarity, his commitment, his incisiveness, his persistence – all made our lot look tawdry; all the more so, as *The Observer* this morning published all the vituperative passages from our campaign guide, alongside the PM's generous tribute in the House of Commons.

I reckon the whole sad business now makes Labour more electable, not less, if they handle the leadership contest right – and as an aside, the scope and complexity of their 'One Member, One Vote' system which Smith himself pioneered will make our own, exclusive to MPs, look secretive and undemocratic, not least to our Party workers. Watch for calls for us to change it. If they have any sense, they'll choose Tony Blair. He's forty-one and English, which gives him an edge over both Gordon Brown and Robin Cook[129] if the Party seriously wants to win over most of the electorate, after a Scot and a Welshman as leader. Blair will appeal to Liberal voters – plenty of them, e.g. in a seat like South Derbyshire, would find him far more reassuring than Kinnock – and he'll attract our disaffected skilled workers, who are turning back to Labour in droves as Margaret's memory fades. He could win the next election by a landslide.

---

129 Member of Shadow Cabinet and Labour MP for Livingston since 1983; MP for Edinburgh Central, 1974–83.

It makes our leadership problem even more of a muddle. We can't, now, seek to depose John in June, however awful the Euro results (and they will be), so he's safe till at least the autumn and I reckon till 1995. That means we are stuck with 'state of the art incompetence', as the *Sunday Times* put it recently. I don't think the PM will suddenly grow an extra brain or acquire a greater sense of authority overnight; and once Labour adjust to their new leader, whoever it is, they'll go for our weak links, which include the PM himself.

Michael Etherington, our bright new South Derbyshire chairman, came round and asked that I put on paper my intentions should I not win in Bedfordshire (and the current wave of sympathy for Labour and the reawakening of their voters makes failure far more likely). I have to indicate *now* (not after the result) that I'd fight South Derbyshire again, or the nomination will be blocked. This is where duty calls, I guess, so the letter will be written and sent.

But writing the letter in the terms Michael wants involves several kinds of deception. Firstly, it implies an interest and commitment to Westminster I don't feel. My interests now lie in Europe, and I'd hope to try again in Bedfordshire & Milton Keynes in 1999 if they would have me, but it would be impolitic to tell South Derbyshire voters so. Fortunately it seems a long way off for most people, so the question can be brushed aside. And I couldn't tell Michael about my doubts and fears about staying with Ray and my need to move away. That's easily dealt with if I win Bedfordshire & Milton Keynes, poses problems if I have to fight South Derbyshire again – and if I should win South Derbyshire, I'm stuck with a thoroughly unhappy situation behind the scenes. Still, says my cynical voice, you can always change your mind, but it only works one way. You can persuade them now to accept you as candidate for '96, and you can always pull out if things get impossible. What you can't do is pull out now, and then persuade them later.

Out of the blue comes a message on my bleeper to call Richard. Heavens, I thought, he's pulled out of the contract. Or it's something trivial: maybe the date of Cheltenham has changed. Or maybe the business is up and running – or whatever. But no. It turns out he just wanted a chat, and had tried several times to talk to me at the

House of Commons until it dawned on him I wasn't there. The birthday card was funny, and Chapter 2 is fine, but he thinks we should meet before 14 June just to clarify one or two points and so he can answer my questions about the synopsis, though his advice is to plod on, as before – and so on. I'm bowling along the M1 and for safety's sake pull off on to the A50 to chat, as we slide happily into our usual 'nineteen to the dozen' natter. He was quite insistent on seeing me again soon, though for me the fixed points are 14 June and Cheltenham – we need to rehearse the latter,[130] maybe in July or September.

Nr Milton Keynes, Tuesday 7 June, 10.30 p.m.

We've just had the 'Eve of Poll' meeting which (as usual) I like to hold on the Tuesday night, so everyone spends Wednesday getting committee rooms ready, tellers etc. Had a tiring (if typical) day – got caught in the morning in a small but friendly firm with only a handful of employees; followed around by TV – this time from Greece! – then the pace hotted up in the afternoon at the British Standards Institute, where we met most of the 300–400 staff and my right hand felt like a sponge after. I'm sure we've achieved the target of 25,000 people met face to face during the campaign – that is 1,000 per day, and reasonably easily achieved much of the time. Let's hope it all pays off.

The polls have been quite dreadful, with the *Telegraph* last week predicting we'll get only 21 per cent of the vote, third behind Labour (at over 50 per cent) and the Liberals. If so, then we'll win even fewer seats than the Liberals, who seem certain to take the whole of the south-west, including seats with majorities over 50,000, the north-west too maybe. Labour could find itself with sixty-seven out of the eighty-seven seats, which not even they were predicting before the campaign started.

The problem (in part) has been a truly diabolical campaign, which makes me ashamed to call myself a Tory – and that's saying something. In order to secure the Eurosceptic vote the PM has

---

130 This event, entitled 'Desert Island Books', was to be chaired by Richard Cohen.

been back-pedalling fiercely to the point where, to be quite blunt, I don't agree with a word of our detailed policy on Europe, let alone the general approach. For example, if the veto is so important why don't we use it – or threaten to use it and be believed, which amounts to the same thing?

I should add a word about Alan Sked, who's standing against me for James Goldsmith's Independence Party. Their literature is well produced and Sked did well on a party election broadcast last week. His posters began to appear in Tory houses as we canvassed and I reckon he'll pick up 2,000 votes from our Eurosceptic wing, which would be enough to rob us of victory. I've warned both Central Office and Bob Worcester of MORI to keep an eye open; the former had barely heard of him, yet they plan to put a candidate in every Tory seat at the next general election and could drain away enough votes to make a big difference. The presentation is slick, the arguments (till you think about them) alluring, based on the principle that you can eliminate all the nasty stuff about Europe, e.g. Brussels, by leaving the EU, while retaining all the good stuff which we take for granted, such as successful international trade. Fortunately only 13 per cent of the voters, according to a poll in the *Daily Telegraph* today, seriously want us out, and more than 50 per cent are in favour of closer integration, of whom 10 per cent want full integration. So the nation is still in favour of Europe. The trouble is that while the PM is talking such piffle, the Conservative Party is not.

How very peculiar it all is: I feel reconciled to either outcome! But then when I started it all back in 1991 I wasn't expecting a bestselling novel either, which will pull me back to the UK. And my heart is heavy whatever happens – for if I win, I have to work very hard and will be pushed to justify the £150,000 for the next novel, and if I lose I have to find some way of regularising what goes on at home. The problem is that Ray is being as good and kind as he knows how – red roses last week – and it is almost enough for me to stay.

On the train to Liverpool, Friday 17 June, 5 p.m.

It's humid and unpleasant out there and the land is wilting, but the carriage is air-conditioned, so though I'm still feeling groggy the brain is quietly ticking over. I'm on my way to the Blackburne House[131] 150th birthday party at the Maritime Museum tonight. The original idea was to stay in Liverpool for the weekend to see Mum, but she is off with Zena and uncle Sam to Canada on a coach tour of the Canadian Rockies, something she wanted to do, she told me, before she 'popped her clogs'. So I'll clear off home tomorrow morning, with the not unreasonable excuse that I am dog tired and haven't seen my family much for six weeks.

Of course what I should be tapping away at is the novel, especially as Richard has now set me a deadline for the next two chapters. It's not that I'm feeling idle – rather that it will take me a couple of hours to get back into it, to 'place myself', so anything I did now would almost certainly have to be scrapped.

Anyway I should have plenty of time to get on with it soon enough. On Tuesday morning I sat down with the Tippex and painted out of my diary all the dates for Brussels and Strasbourg, then (having, as my first positive move, booked my boat ticket to France for 27 July) waded through the pile of fresh invitations and entered some attractive items, including guest lecturer on the *QE2* in September/October. With free first-class accommodation, meals and drink, I'll have a week's quiet cruising in which to work, and all mod cons – pool, gym, cinema – at my fingertips. Sounds great. Ray will come one way with me, to do some work in St Charles,[132] and then I'll fly home in time for the Party Conference. In return I have to give two 45-minute talks each way, subjects to be agreed. I shall have a real go at this, as I fancy a repeat invitation!

Our result in Bedfordshire & Milton Keynes was not entirely a surprise, but the size of the defeat, over 30,000, was – and a bitter blow, even though the turnaround of votes was in fact smaller than in neighbouring Hertfordshire, which we also lost. We held eighteen seats, but lost many good people. Both Kent seats fell, two out of three in Essex, Northants, Norfolk – a swathe was cut through the Home Counties. Several were held by the skin of their teeth

131 Liverpool Institute High School for Girls, usually known as 'Blackburne House', EC's old school.
132 Arthur Andersen's American HQ.

or a fluke – Thames Valley by only 700 votes, Graham Mather's seat in Hampshire by the intervention of John Browne, the former MP standing as an anti-Europe, anti-government independent who took 12,000 votes mainly off the Liberal Democrats, to their fury. The turnout was almost exactly the same overall as in 1989, and the national campaigning was pathetic, anti-Europe and confusing. And the overall result was a disaster: with 27.8 per cent of the vote, the government had the smallest level of support of any major party in a national election in recent history, worse even than Labour's 28 per cent in 1983. Norman Fowler fell on his sword last night and announced his resignation.

There were compensations in Bedfordshire & Milton Keynes. We had a higher turnout (38 per cent), higher share of the vote (30 per cent), and lower swing (11 per cent) from Conservative to Labour, compared with 12 per cent nationally and a whopping 15 per cent in London and the south-east. We also had a lot of fun and a fine campaign. Of course I worry that my name attracted more than our fair share of disapproval, and there is no doubt that we were effectively targeted by Labour – otherwise where did they get their 94,000 votes? But the House of Commons Library analysis shows that four other seats had a bigger increase in the Labour vote since 1992 than we did, and two others had a bigger drop in the Tory vote. I may have been responsible for some of it, but I can't be blamed for Essex South, for example, which was worse than us on both counts.

Still, I wish it had been 3,000 not 33,000: we were so badly hammered. It's left me feeling punch drunk. Much of our organisation proved totally inadequate and I wrote a long and cross note to Dawn Bayman, the area office agent, mostly recommending greater investment in training for agents: but I don't suppose she has the budget for it. I also made the point about Central Office not targeting properly (or at all, I thought) and thus leaving a highly vulnerable seat like Bedfordshire & Milton Keynes adrift. Yet a chance conversation behind the Chair with Norman Fowler reveals that I was wrong – they were targeting, it was just that Bedfordshire & Milton Keynes wasn't on the list. That does make me despair. I also felt upset later in the week when it was apparent that the PM doesn't make a habit of writing to candidates, not even me: lots of notes of commiseration came in, with good-luck letters before too – including one handwritten by David Hunt in a helicopter, which was sweet of him. But nothing from John. Nothing at all. And there I was in the tea room on Tuesday, surrounded by kindly words and pats on the back, and the PM at the table opposite, and he didn't even trouble to come over and offer some sympathy or even thanks.

But we are stuck with him, and I suspect he will lead us into the next election, which will not now be till early 1997: as Ken Baker put it shrewdly on the radio this morning, moving the Budget to November makes it very difficult to hold autumn elections. If he does, we will lose by a big margin. The man has no credibility and it will only get worse. Even post-election, he's tripping over the chairs – he's announced there will be a reshuffle, but not for several weeks, presumably to make spoiler headlines as Labour choose their new leader. But that serves seriously to destabilise the government and puts everybody in a tizz till it is done: 'pure John Major – in return for one day's headlines, he undermined his government for the weeks till the reshuffle happens, and ensured further grief when the changes fall short of the expectations he has raised', as *The Economist* gloomily put it.

I am deeply conscious now of being distracted from politics and becoming much less single-minded about it, as work elsewhere, both writing and TV appearances, is more fun to do, relatively easy and lucrative. If success eludes me on the hustings we have had plenty of it in the publishing world, for example.

Richard and I met for tea as planned in the Goring Hotel; he was early, sipping a cool lime juice and soda. He'd been at his son's sports day in jeans and T-shirt but had changed into a grey suit for our meeting, which led me into teasing him. His business exists; we talked as we have before about how he will have to be single-minded if it is to succeed. Last week when I heard from him that he had been paid, which meant I had, I promptly sent him a cheque for £5,000 for shares in his company. It turned out I was the first, so I've gone up in his estimation – lots of others have made promises, but nothing else so far. A prospectus is going out about now and he will make an announcement to the publishing press when he has secured £300,000 of funding. His first list will be next summer. I put it to him that his foray to Canada for the Commonwealth fencing games should be his last competitive outing, as his investors work very hard for their money and will expect him to do the same.

Meanwhile Ray has made a bigger effort in the last few days and I think I am going to pluck up courage to talk to him. If I have to strike a delicate balance in the next few years, since I am stuck in England, then it will be easier if there is a friendly *modus vivendi*.

Went to a horrendous lunch with Stanmore WIZO – invitation via Michael Howard's Mum, who was sweet – on Wednesday. I was much too tired and should have jacked, but after earfuls of aggressive abuse of the government, the Party, the Arabs and everyone who like me is not particularly pro-Israel, I walked into a psychological brick wall and left in a paddy.

The Tower House, Saturday 2 July, 9.15 p.m.

I have made a resolution to spend a couple of hours every weekend doing the garden! I enjoy it – the physical sensation of working hard, and being in the open air, and the comfortable satisfied feeling afterwards of being too tired to do any more; the maintenance of an asset at the same time as the honing of a skill – I could make a garden anywhere now, having done it twice already. It's an essentially lonely, solitary activity which gives me plenty of time to chew things over. I don't have to perform or talk to anyone. And if I didn't do it, the garden would deteriorate and I would kick myself. Nor is there any likelihood of Ray doing it, apart from trundling around on the lawnmower.

I'm also collecting reasons for swapping my dull car for a much flashier version, which is probably going to cost me more than I want to pay. My Toyota Carina, which was made in January 1993, was one of the first production models, and the first to be sold to a British owner. I have tried to sell it to Derby Museum, but Toyota had beaten me to it with a free pre-production car. Two weeks ago I'd asked Ron Brooks's garage in Ilkeston to send brochures for the latest version of the Corolla which I had loved so much: but nothing came, and when I asked again I was told they hadn't any.

Odd: this is the world's bestselling car and they've no leaflets? So I went up there yesterday, but their attitude was distinctly tired. The car I was interested in was still in its protective wax coating. A nose was turned up at mine (which I'd bought from there only eighteen months ago and paid £15,000 for) and the derisory price of £8,750 max offered, with no discount on the new car or air-conditioning.

Somewhat disgruntled, I headed for Mann Egerton in Derby, the main dealers, on the principle that they would have more models. They did, including exactly the red GXi number I might fancy, and out for a spin we went. But also in their car park was another red racer, a second-hand MR2, a two-seater with a two-litre engine and a different kettle of fish entirely. A purely selfish car – no ferrying of kids or humping baggage! A test drive in that was a delicious experience and the price, for an L-reg demonstrator, could be comparable. And they keep their value better, so what I don't lose in depreciation I can spend on upgrading. The sales manager comes round tomorrow to lend me an MR2 so I'll have it in London all week, and I think I am going to enjoy myself. He has a customer, either way.

And Susie (who came with me and kept making remarks about how the MR2 wasn't suitable for a 48-year-old woman – huh) has now finished all her exams and left school, so for the first time in twenty years we have no school fees to pay. She is whacked, poor girl, but all the signs are good for her grades. In late August she will be working in London for ZDF, the German radio station, and asked if she could share a flat with a school-friend, whose gap year will be spent entirely in town. But her share of the rent is likely to be £30 per week which she doesn't have, as she isn't going to be paid. I felt mean explaining the facts of life to her.

Yesterday was our wedding anniversary – twenty-two years. Ray kept cooing 'twenty-two years, Boot!' and he gave me a couple of books and a silver photo frame as gifts. We decided to go out for a meal and I insisted on somewhere new – Indian – the Full Moon in Normanton Road. Good food and not expensive, and the service cheerful if slow and slapdash: but so typically Derby in the complete lack of any staging or atmosphere, just cream walls and brown paint.

There was a water feature next to our table and we asked if it could be turned on. The waiter obliged, then after a couple of minutes, presumably having shown us that it worked, it was switched off again. Even the music was wrong, and I longed for the exotic opulence of Rajdoot in Birmingham or the style of the Red Fort (which is dear these days). So I was bored, and tired too, and found myself increasingly silent as Ray and Susie held staccato inconsequential arguments, mainly about who did what some time ago or sport or people I didn't know. It's good that the two of them are close, of course.

Meanwhile I am writing and have settled back into a routine quite well, with more than fifteen hours under my belt this week and most of Chapter 3 done. In the next two weeks Chapter 4 must be completed and sent off too. Anyway I managed to put some sex in – about the right stage in the novel, I think. My next scheduled meeting with Richard is at end of July, the day before I go to France.

Victoria, Monday 4 July, 10.25 a.m.

Had to leave the piece in a hurry as the family arrived home. Ray asked curiously what I had been working on, but nobody knows about this diary, and I'd rather keep it that way.

The MR2 demonstrator came, a sleek blue beast, and I drove it to London. Oh, gorgeous. A car like that says 'I am' very loudly. (It also says 'no more school fees'.) I could fall in love with it – particularly the way it turns heads as it passes. So, if I can't have all the other things I've worked so hard for, or love – a flat in Brussels, the chance to try every kind of hire car at Le Mans Station, a good marriage – maybe I can have a glamorous consolation prize and lavish my love on that instead.

Another letter arrived from Richard today, full of energy, on Richard Cohen Books notepaper. He needs to remember that there's more to setting up a business than visiting the printer's.

Victoria, Tuesday 19 July, 11 a.m.

There's a reshuffle imminent – it's being billed as the biggest in years – probably tomorrow, so that the headlines on Thursday (21st) eclipse the results of Labour's leadership election. But what a way to acknowledge the supremacy of (1) the press and (2) the

Labour Party in British political life. Blair's background is curiously similar to John Major's and will make very interesting reading in the tabloids on Friday, when the reshuffle – exchanging one bunch of tinny dullards for another – will have faded very quickly. His father, it turns out, was a self-made businessman and Tory, but his grandparents (whom he never knew) were music hall stars, just like Major's parents. Accounts for his good looks and controlled performances, perhaps? And he's *very* articulate, much more so than Major. Parliament finishes tomorrow, effectively, so there'll be no Prime Minister's Questions for Blair till October. By which point the reshuffle will have been completely forgotten.

Richard has been in touch with my assistant Emma, and named the Connaught as the place for our lunch. I've rebelled and said no – I'd have to dress up and perform, and given that Parliament is well and truly finished, I'd much rather get out for a picnic in Richmond Park if the weather permits. What's he doing, suggesting the Connaught? Not trying to impress me, I hope: but certainly setting up a very formal and public meeting instead of the friendly discussion I'd hoped for.

I got furious with Ray last week. The house is so dilapidated – there is so much to do – and he's even delegated the job of grass-cutting to Susie. He doesn't seem to realise how hurt I was that he helped so little in the Euro elections. He can take holidays – whole days or a week – to go to Lord's or racing in York, but not a single day off did he manage in the entire five weeks' campaign. It's enough to make you weep, and I do.

I bought the blue MR2, which is a simply gorgeous car and makes me feel young and vibrant! As the registration number is L251 OTO it will be known as 'Otto, the boy racer'. I'm desperate to show it off to Richard, as he'll laugh like a drain and then share my pleasure in it. I've picked up £10,000 of work since the election – speeches and articles – so I reckon I can afford it; and I'm back making speeches again, on reasonable form after the disaster at Stanmore WIZO.

Les Tuileries, Monday 1 August, 12 noon

I've just finished polishing the floor of the long room and Ray has gone off racing at Lion d'Angers for the day, so it's time to catch up a bit before spending the afternoon by the pool at Longué, if the weather stays reasonable. Huge storms over the last couple of days have left everything fresh and green and my roses perking up happily. Last night as we came home from supper at the Carters', (much of it in a thunderstorm which drove us, screaming with laughter, indoors) we were dive-bombed by little fluttering bats; they set off the security light outside, which attracts bugs, and then they flit around eating their dinner. After rain the night sky is like black velvet studded with sequins. Marvellous.

The reshuffle has been and gone, mostly uninteresting, though a total of twelve new junior ministers have been appointed, including Angela Browning[133] and the splendid Ian Taylor, and James Paice,[134] both Double Eighters. Brooke and Patten are out as expected, but Tony Newton stays put and Waldegrave survives to go to Agriculture. Gill Shephard goes to Education, and there I felt a twang – that job I should have liked, and the timing would have been nice: but it was not to be. David Hunt has effectively been demoted though he was putting a brave face on it; he's to be Chancellor of the Duchy of Lancaster, and chair of most of the Cabinet committees, a sort of 'chef de Cabinet' for the PM, to ensure that policy-making goes more smoothly – but he would surely have preferred Education, or Environment, where the out-of-his-depth Gummer remains. There are five new Cabinet members: Mawhinney[135] in Transport, Dorrell[136] in National Heritage, Cranborne[137] in the Lords, can't remember the other for the moment – just shows you! – and best of all, Jeremy Hanley[138] as Party Chairman, an excellent choice. He has a grotty job ahead, but will be robust, cheery and wise (married

---

133 Conservative MP for Tiverton since 1992.
134 Conservative MP for South East Cambridgeshire since 1987.
135 Dr Brian Mawhinney, formerly Minister of Health; Conservative MP for Peterborough since 1979.
136 Stephen Dorrell, Financial Secretary to the Treasury since 1992; Conservative MP for Loughborough since 1983.
137 Viscount Cranborne, heir of the Marquess of Salisbury, became Lord Privy Seal and leader of the Lords; before being summoned to the Upper House, he had been Conservative MP for South Dorset, 1979–87.
138 Conservative MP for Richmond & Barnes since 1983.

before, and his wife, so no more nonsense about back to basics, I hope). I noted that Dame Angela Rumbold is no longer Deputy Chairman – that moment of glory didn't last long, and she didn't seem to have changed the Party's attitudes to women. The new Deputy Chairmen are John Maples and Michael Dobbs, the latter again an inspired choice.

Sue Fletcher tells me that we've sold 59,000 copies of *A Parliamentary Affair*, of which 25,000 are through the book clubs, 'and they keep coming back for more'. Fifty thousand copies of the paperback have been printed. Yesterday I sent off another article for *Hello!* – my second – and last week one for the *Sunday Express* Magazine, both of which may become regular occurrences. At £600 for *Hello!* and £500 for the *Sunday Express*, that's grand – easier, and much faster, than reviews, which usually take me two weeks and bring in £400 if I'm lucky.

It turned out that Richard's suggestion of the Connaught was intended as a treat, as I had mentioned that I'd never been there. He sounded quite hurt that I rejected it! He also promptly cancelled both his morning and afternoon engagements, without any urging from me, so we ended up with five hours together, 11 a.m. till 4 p.m., and great fun it was too, for I inveigled him into the car and we went into Richmond Park for a picnic. We talked shop; the new chapters from *A Woman's Place* are fine, but I was disappointed that Richard says I am still overwriting, whereas I thought these recent chapters were much better. Not ready for the Booker Prize yet, obviously!

He is getting on famously with his company and has raised close to £200,000 in funding. Much of that will come from his own funds – the shares he holds in his father's company – but around £70,000 comes from people like me. With some energy he said I shouldn't underestimate the excitement being generated by Richard Cohen Books in the publishing world. He talked non-stop for ages about the deals he's doing, and the one that got away. For the first time, he sounds like a businessman, and that augurs very well. I am genuinely thrilled for him, and apprehensive.

We talked other books. Fay Weldon has lost her husband, the

subject of her last novel *Affliction* (he's died), and married her toy-boy; I showed Richard an interview with her in the *Express* in which she sounded very chipper, but he said her friends are concerned – she has sacked her agent, changed publisher etc. Yet I recall him also saying Fay's career had taken a turn for the better recently and she was selling well. To me she looks happy, and I said so.

Richard said he had been thinking about me during the previous week, when the reshuffle took place on the Wednesday (20 July), the same day that the new European Parliament met. Richard hadn't picked up the latter point, but understood immediately how much worse that made everything. My resolve not to get upset and to put all those hopes of preferment behind me cracked a little, for now both dreams have been shattered: and with the likelihood of losing South Derbyshire, my political career is virtually at an end. Richard thought about it without any prompting and with gentle question-ing got me talking, which helped. The contrast with Ray could not have been greater. On the Friday night at home, as he slouched in front of the TV (yet another athletics competition), he said, as in a ritual, 'Had a good week?'

'No,' said I, bluntly, having just finished talking to Richard. 'Oh?' says Ray with a puzzled air, and does me the courtesy of turning the sound down, though physically he doesn't budge. 'The reshuf-fle, and the new Parliament,' I answer. 'But I thought you'd given up hope of that...?' he asked, seeming puzzled. 'I had, but it still hurts.' Silence for a moment. What he should have done, of course, was get up and come and give me a cuddle. No chance. 'Oh,' he says once again, and returns to the TV. I fled. What do you do with a man who can only say 'Oh'? I know now why women run into the kitchen and grab the frying pan and hit them over the head.

Les Tuileries, Saturday 20 August, 11 p.m.

I've just come home from supper chez Carter: a lovely meal of lettuce soup, beef Wellington and apricot pavlova (and I took a *tarte aux prunes* I bought in Saumur market today, also delicious). Also there was yet another couple who have moved out to France with no clear idea of how to earn a living here. On my first day here in July I was met – hardly out of the car and still unpacking – by a gaunt stick of a man, who'd bought a house in Mouliherne last year and no sooner settled, planning to survive on the income from capital and on building work, than he went down with (treatable) cancer. At this point – having sold up everything at home! – he discovers that he's not entitled to UK social security or sick pay, having long been self-employed; indeed to qualify for any help he'd have to lie about his intention to emigrate. Most of his savings have gone, too. I felt so sorry for him and put him in touch with his MP at home. There should be a government health warning on every paper to be signed by Brits who come here to settle, asking them whether they have fallback plans if anything goes wrong. They wouldn't expect to move to Margate in such a casual fashion, so why aren't they more thoughtful about moving to another country?

I came home a bit early: partly because I'm tired – I tore my calf muscle badly a couple of days ago, and walking on it, as I did around Saumur this morning, leaves me whacked; partly because I want to do four hours' writing tomorrow morning before anything else, otherwise (like today) nothing gets done and I feel guilty all day.

Not only did Susie get all her four grade As and her S level with merit, but came in the top three of the Oxford and Cambridge Examination Board for her Economics, and in the top five of the Associated Examination Board for German, and has certificates of excellence – effectively starred As – from both. Whoopee! Cambridge confirmed her place immediately. In fact she found out via the press: the headmaster had given some of the best results to the *Burton Mail*, who telephoned her and asked for her response and which university she was going to, to which she said, 'I'll tell you that if you tell me my results!' Yesterday there was a nice photo of her in the *Burton Mail*, and the marvellous news was picked up by the *Derby Telegraph* and the *Daily Mail*. Apparently record numbers of students sat A levels this year – about 300,000 exams were taken – and over 80 per cent passed. According to that hairy-faced prat Sir Rhodes Boyson,[139] it's because the exams and examiners are getting easier. That's pernicious rubbish, to my mind. The courses are much more interesting and better thought out than when I was

---

139 A former grammar school headmaster.

doing them, with a wider choice; the students are better motivated. I am very proud of her, and so pleased, both for her, and for myself: it feels like a job well done.

The new novel is going quite well. On the positive side, I find I can get the characters to talk to me and tell me what they're doing and thinking. The scenes come relatively easily and there's not much rewriting; about twenty hours per chapter sees me through, with another couple tidying up – so two hours per thousand words is still a fair guide. I enjoy it while I do it and the time flies. On the other hand, it doesn't sing like the first one did: it doesn't burn to get out of me, and I don't feel I'm crossing any thresholds, rather trying to do a workmanlike job. The challenge is muted and I'm fearful that this faint ennui is bound to show in the writing. Partly it comes from fear of overwriting – of writing too much, or of using the presence of the screen to put stuff down which is irrelevant to the novel but interesting to me. As a result this one is going to turn out much smaller and we'd be hard pressed to dub it a blockbuster. It sure as heck isn't worth £150,000. But it is better crafted and certainly better written – proof-reading *A Parliamentary Affair* for the paperback edition is making me cringe, though it gets better halfway through, when I had a clearer idea what I was at.

I wanted to record the most spectacular Gallup poll for the *Telegraph*, published 5 August and carried out between 27 July and 1 August, just after Parliament rose. It showed a Labour lead of 33.5 per cent, the largest either of the main parties has ever had over the other. Labour have over 56 per cent support, so their honeymoon is continuing, and no doubt will fall back. What struck me most forcibly was that our support had hardly budged – well, it's fallen from 26.5 to 23 per cent, but the main shift is a fall in the Liberal Democrat support to 14.5 per cent, with Labour being the gainers. Now we know that if the Liberal vote falls in a seat like mine, it will go to Labour, not to me – and that's goodbye South Derbyshire.

John Major has let it be known that his preferred successor would be Stephen Dorrell, but for the life of me I can't see it. He's nice, and intelligent, and wet, and fine on Europe, but always looks tired and a bit out of his depth, in the wrong business, as if the Assistant Professor of Aeronautics at Loughborough University somehow found himself in charge of policy at the Treasury. There's no charisma, or toughness, no sense of authority, and no leadership qualities, though I doubt if he'd be quite as hopeless as poor old John Major. John would have done better to say nothing. And it confirms my suspicion that he's ruled out David Hunt, which is cruel and wrong. If David has any sense, he'll stick at it. He would be a more attractive and emollient candidate for the left/centre than Clarke. And I suspect that Hezza still thinks he'll have his chance, though his health and age will prevent it. We should have had him in 1990, shouldn't we? What a mistake we all made, me most of all.

Ferry from Le Havre, Friday 2 September, 5.15 p.m.

Well, that's the holiday over. It's been productive, and wet (the two are related), but I'm brown and feel relaxed and rested. My torn calf muscle seems to be healing; I will test it out gingerly at the gym on Wednesday (7th), so fingers crossed.

I've been invited to Moscow for the week beginning 17 October, by the Future of Europe Trust, the all-party group chaired in the UK by Calum Macdonald. If I can get a pair – and it could be Dale Campbell-Savours,[140] who would be an intelligent companion – it could be a terrific trip. The Trust's aims are to promote democracy in the newly democratised nations. It brings rising MPs to the UK (and I presume to various other western countries) as part of their political education. No doubt we'd have to do some talking when we get there. Hope so!

It could make the autumn a very busy time indeed, what with the paperback launch (15 September), the *QE2* (29 September–9 October), Party Conference (11–14 October), Cheltenham (14/15 October), Russia (17 October on) and Italy for the Italian launch (mid-November). Question – will I get any advice bureaux done at all? Will I get any writing done? (Yes, to the latter.) Richard tells me I'm performing at 8 p.m. on Friday 14 October in Cheltenham: would I like to stay in a castle that evening? Yes, rather! His piece is at 11.30 a.m. next day, but although I'll stay for that, I'll

---

140 Labour MP for Wallington since 1979.

clear off afterwards, as Caroline and the children are coming, so I won't want to be in the way. He and I talked long on the phone several times. His company is making progress. But: no premises yet, and the deal with Reed fell through, and though talks with Anthony Cheetham at Orion are promising, there's nothing concrete yet, and his attempts to cash his A. Cohen & Sons shares[141] came to nought – they're worth £400,000, but his cousins have blocked them. So Richard Cohen Books still has a long way to go yet.

The novel itself is piling up – now over 60,000 words, of which about 30,000 were done in France. I have real trouble, however, making it come to life. The only bits I feel happy writing are the sex scenes. Isn't that a disgrace?

Tower House, Thursday 8 September, 10.15 p.m.

I've just finished Andrew Davies's *B Monkey*, which is sexy, frightening and sad, so that I can hand it over to Deb tomorrow (we're going shopping in Meadowhall, Sheffield). But the ending, when the man Alan says, 'Where does it go, when it's gone?' suddenly overwhelmed me, and I had to put my head down on the kitchen table, in this house I've loved so much, and weep.

I feel so very sad about Ray. All our love – where did it go? It's as if we woke up one morning to find that it had stolen away quietly in the night: from then on, having him touch me, or make love or any intimacy, just felt wrong, as if I was doing it with a stranger, or even with a taboo person, such as my father. But it's more, far more than just the physical side, as I started explaining to Deb on Sunday, under a tree up Dovedale, listening to the rain hissing past and knowing we had to get wet before we could get to the car – just as I know there is a lot of pain, a lot of tears to come, before I can reach calm and contentment.

'I'm not surprised,' she said, 'you two never do anything together.' That's not strictly true: we'd been to the movies the night before. But, for example, he made a point of going to France and returning at different times, of having his own car there, a terrible waste of money.

---

141 The Cohen family company, started by Richard's father.

An incident in France made me think – we had supper at the Carters' with Claire and Georges Ernoul:[142] it was the first time Ray had met them. Four years ago I bought a house and spent ages planning, thinking, plotting, with Georges, but Ray said he wouldn't come until the WC was installed, and so missed all the fun. More significant, I now realise, he failed – indeed refused point blank – to partake of my life, of a big chunk of what I was thinking, dreaming, achieving. When I wrote *A Parliamentary Affair* he wouldn't look at it, not a word, till it was finished, despite having a degree in English – so he missed a year of thinking, living, agonising (and he could have helped). When I stood for election in Bedfordshire he stayed there not one single night, and we were never alone together. So he heard nothing of my inner feelings.

Richard came to the flat at lunchtime yesterday and we talked – mostly about his company, which is coming on really well – he's a bit stuck on a sales and distribution network as he's too small to create his own, but too big to be taken on easily by e.g. Reed or Orion, though at least the latter were friendly. Money isn't a problem any more and he has fifteen marvellous books signed up, including some sure-fire winners. As he talked about this he paced up and down, agitated and excited – when he sat down and ate, he nearly choked for being in such a rush. It's marvellous to see him like that, like a big kid, his head full of projects. Then he settled and we talked about *A Woman's Place* and made progress.

Deb was funny. 'Will you have a boyfriend?' she asked, as we drove home from Ashbourne. 'Why do you ask?' I said. 'Well, won't you miss the sex?' I smiled ruefully. 'Ah, young lady, I shan't tell you the gruesome details, but I miss the sex now.' (That clearly hadn't occurred to her.) Silence. So I asked, 'How would you feel if I did have a boyfriend?' She grinned: 'Yeah, that'd be all right.'

Tower House, Sunday 25 September, 10 p.m.

I've just finished revising the nine chapters done so far of *A Woman's Place*, ready to send or give to Sue Fletcher, with whom I am having lunch on Wednesday. That'll impress her. She's taking me to Le

---

142 Georges Ernoul was the architect who supervised the modernisation of Les Tuileries.

Caprice, where I've never been, presumably to impress me. But she can't write, and I'm up to nearly 75,000 words, so I guess I know who'll win that contest, at least this week!

Richard was not pleased that I hadn't completed another chapter as planned, so I got my head down this week and churned out the 12,000 words of Chapter 9, finishing with a bit that should become famous, tiramisu and chocolate sauce and sex. It felt a bit like writing to a formula, but it was fun to do and should still be a surprise to the reader, though vintage Currie.

I've been reading the extracts from Alan Bennett's diaries in *The Observer*: beautifully done, all nuggets of insight and wit. Yet his personality seems so erratic – failing to show any sympathy with Tebbit in the bombed-out hotel, yet pages of weeping with the dying Russell Harty. He doesn't go into his own love life – maybe the full diary does. As ever, when reading the jottings of somebody who can really write, I resolve to do better myself.

QE2 – Day 1, Thursday 29 September, 10.35 p.m.

Oh God, it's awful – just awful. This was a big mistake. I am terrified I'm going to waste the next ten days, half pissed, and feeling distraught like now.

What's wrong with it? Firstly, if this is a first-class, five-star hotel, it isn't a very good one. The cabin isn't clean. The furnishings are drab and – unbelievably! – stained. The bed coverlet, for example, has a large stain on the flounce. Coffee? Blood? Who knows? One of the armchairs had a stained seat; I made them take it away. The net curtains are dirty. Fingermarks on the coffee table glass top. Glass shelves in bathroom dusty. No laundry bags. No flowers or fruit in the room (there are now, but the steward tried to palm me off with a black banana – unbelievable). *Nothing* in the mini bar but half bottle of champagne – in fact they'd forgotten Ray entirely, so there aren't enough towels either. No bath robes. No kettle or coffee maker. The dining room ('Queen's Grill') is posh, but the food ordinary – my grilled chicken was dry and I didn't finish it. Most of all (nothing to do with the service), I don't know anybody, and can't see a single friendly or interesting face. 1 thought we might find ourselves on the captain's table, or (more interesting) the chief engineer's, but we have a table allocated to ourselves, so I'm obliged to make conversation with Ray. Tonight I made it to the Irish coffee, then fled. It isn't even possible to chat to a neighbouring table – though most of the couples look bored already. Like being in a straitjacket. *Awful.*

Enough whinging. At least this way across I get an extra hour's sleep each night. But the noise of the TV is now coming from the cabins on both sides. Oh, heavens. I think I'll get drunk.

QE2, Tuesday 4 October, 9.25 p.m.

The Big Apple was gorgeous this morning, sunny and bright: absolutely at its best, which made our dawn arrival past the glittering Statue of Liberty a magical experience – the torch really did seem to be aflame, and the golden light moving across the face of the skyscrapers made it seem a magic city. I landed at about 10 a.m. and for a while wandered around rather aimlessly with Ray – his hotel room at the Hilton wasn't ready. Eventually I pushed off towards Central Park, and sat on a terrace for an hour or so watching a Tae Kwondo class. About 200 men (mostly) and girls performed exercises and shadow-boxed and bowed to instructors – all very energetic and rather splendid. Nice to sit and watch harmlessly a collection of attractive athletic blokes, tanned pectorals heaving out of white jackets, neat bums in white trousers. I was tickled that while the venerable master was clearly Japanese and a couple of his sidekicks Korean or Vietnamese, the main instruction was given in Spanish – I guess that a lot of the guys were waiters. Then I met Ellen Levine (she's the A. P. Watt New York agent) for lunch – she is so tiny and has so much black hair and huge specs that it's hard to see her face at all. She was gracious enough to let me do most of the talking, and listened politely to my dafter stories.

The cabin is quiet, or maybe I am used to the constant noise by now! The propellers churn and the wind slaps waves in a regular, hypnotic rhythm against the side of the ship, not far below the portholes. I can't get the room temperature right – either it's too cold, or, like now, after turning it up a couple of degrees, sweltering. Still, it isn't as bad as when we first embarked less than a week ago, though it now seems like a month.

In the days when this was the only safe way to cross the Atlantic, it must have been marvellous. Photographs confirm the regular star-studded passenger lists of the *Queen Mary* and *Queen Elizabeth*. But these days there aren't any glamorous passengers. Anyone busy will go by Concorde. Only the retired or unimportant (like me) travel this way. If, on the other hand, the cruise is simply for relaxation, then standards are nowhere near high enough. In a first-class hotel there would be flowers in the cabin, and fruit, and dressing gowns and enough towels, and a full drinks cabinet (even if you have to sign for what you use – that's OK), and a hairdryer and kettle and mini sewing kit; none of these were available without asking, though cheerfully enough then provided. That's because what is on offer isn't comfort but service. Similarly there is no running buffet anywhere in the ship (except maybe crew quarters?); meals are served in very formal surroundings at set times, and woe betide the passenger who's too early or too late. So there are queues in first class every 1 p.m. for the main lunch buffet – old ladies staggering around under the weight of their diamonds and trays – unbeliev-able! Three nights on the trot I could only get served in the Queen's Grill if I dressed to the nines in sequins and pearls. Last night's pudding was tinned peaches and defrosted raspberries, albeit flam-béed with great aplomb.

Just before I left Sue Fletcher told me that we were up to 92,000 copies, so hopefully we'll hit the 100,000 mark by the return. Ain't that nice? The next two talks are 'A Woman's Place...?' and 'The Crazy World of the House of Commons', into which I'll weave more salacious readings from *A Parliamentary Affair*, to sell the rest of the *QE2*'s stock... I haven't managed to do a great deal of writing so far, but now that I have the cabin to myself for the return leg, my excuses have disappeared. I managed two hours tonight before succumb-ing to a rather dull hamburger and good chips via room service, so maybe one chapter will get done, but not the planned two.

QE2, Thursday 6 October, 11.10 p.m.
Much excitement earlier this evening. The *QE2* intercepted a Mayday call from a fishing vessel on behalf of a sick seaman. We changed course and belted along, to make our rendezvous in heavy seas at around 9.30 p.m., with a running commentary from the

captain – so the dining rooms emptied and a thousand bejewelled passengers leaned over the rail, shouting encouragement, laughing and applauding every move. The trawler had no small boat suitable, so a motorised dinghy picked up the sick man strapped in a stretcher, and brought him alongside. At that point we all realised how ruddy huge this ship is, and how terrifying for the tiny boat alongside; each heave of the seas sent it up in the air about twenty feet and forward about twenty, so getting the stretcher on board needed courage and skill of a high order. Much cheering from us as the manoeuvre was successfully completed; then the dinghy hung about for a bit, waiting for the return of the stretcher and lifejacket. Its three-man crew smoked and joked with passengers high above them who were taking their photos, then stood off for a few minutes while the guy in their bow took pictures of us! One crew member told me it's only the second time he can recall this happening in eleven years' sailing, so it was quite an event for them too – waiters and other staff crowded deckside with passengers in the most natural event we've had all voyage.

On the outgoing journey I managed only five hours' work and felt very grumpy. So far on the return it's nearly nine, with more to come. And that is partly because Ray is not here, and partly because I did as I had promised myself, and talked to him on the last afternoon of his stay, although my nerve nearly failed me.

How very strange, and sad. As I said to Deb on the phone from New York, while it was a relief that he didn't scream and shout, it was also a tragedy. It would have been better if he had got upset. But he didn't – or if he did, he hid it pretty well. He had no idea that I was unhappy, he said; he was shocked (and even that had to be dug out of him in response to a direct question). He seemed quite surprised that a wife should want her husband to be actively involved in the same things, to be genuinely interested in what was going on in her head. I pointed out that we share nothing, and that he hasn't the foggiest idea what interests me, or what takes my time and attention – the novels, the French house, the election, even doing my accounts – how nice it would be if my qualified and experienced husband, seeing me struggle, had said, 'Leave them – I'd be happy to do them for you.' At this Ray looked astonished, as if that way of looking at it had never occurred to him. He had no response to my point that since we don't talk and we don't share anything, we don't have a marriage, and haven't for ages.

I asked if he had noticed anything wrong, and he answered, well, yes. He hoped it would right itself on the voyage. At which point, I swear, he demonstrated everything which has driven me crackers for years, and just gave in. Not a word of reproach. Not a plea. Not a single 'I love you – please stay.' In fact the word love wasn't mentioned once. A brief apology – but no offer to try to do things differently. And that was it, all over in twenty minutes.

There was a postscript, in that on my return to the ship the next day a bunch of flowers was waiting for me in the cabin, with a card in his handwriting – but no message, no letter.

It is bizarre. A quarter-century disappears, just like that. He seemed numb. Of course it is partly my fault. For a long time it suited me to be allowed to go my own way and not be interfered with by my husband. His tolerance and easygoing manner, his casual acceptance of everything I did, was perfect. But he needed to be warmer and more supportive. So when I got to Westminster and found men who scored more highly on both counts, I was off. Then, in the years I was a minister, I was so damn busy that his benign neglect didn't matter. A more loving husband would also have been more demanding, and he (helpfully) wasn't. The trouble only really started after I left the DoH and needed strong support, which wasn't forthcoming. And I realised, too, that so many of my expectations had not been met. It would have been much easier to have made it to the Cabinet had my partner in life been as ambitious as me, for me; had enjoyed the company of politically active people; had been able to make contacts and to provide a strong backdrop of solid networked support when it was needed. But none of that ever happened. On my own it wasn't impossible, as John Major has shown, but I would have needed to be much cleverer myself, as indeed John was.

I always said to myself that I stayed because I'd never found anyone better, and that was true; there are advantages in being married to a nice guy, and my feelings for him continue to encompass real affection, though I don't love him any more. But I began to switch off in a big way. It became only a matter of time, and opportunity.

And then came the success of the novel, which makes it possible to get away.

Tower House, Sunday 16 October, 10 a.m.

Trying something quite new: I am in bed in the spare room, where I spent the night, and (unable to go for a jog because that calf muscle is still jippy) have the computer on my lap. This room is lovely – much warmer than the round room next door, cleaner and less cluttered, and lighter. I slept like a log, and without any guilty feelings either. Yesterday I seriously contemplated moving all Ray's suits out of here and all mine in; that would give him an empire of his own next door and mean I didn't interfere with him. It would almost be doing him a service to let him be; it certainly makes me less angry and frustrated. A peaceful atmosphere is much to be desired.

Party Conference was unpredictably fun this year. Isn't it odd? Last year was all adulation and frenzy, targeting the sick (invalidity benefits) and the unfortunate (single parents). This year, though the sentiments were no less immoderate in some quarters, a more sensible air prevailed; the fightback has begun. The Eurosceptics tried hard and initially made a tremendous impact but – at last – went too far. In a fringe on Monday night Norman Lamont declared that we might eventually have to leave the EU and go it alone. Hooray, some cried, at last a senior figure has given respectability to the opinion no one dare utter. Immediately, however, the Party machine pitched in; the idea of leaving was out of the question, clearly also the view of most of the delegates. That's progress, believe me. Then Portillo pitches in, saying Europe isn't working, to the delight of large sections of the audience, who gave him a hugely enthusiastic standing ovation. But that was engineered, was the comment of the press; his fans would have made a splash whatever he said. Portillo's unpleasant xenophobia, which was not rejected by anyone else from the platform, his humourlessness and his peculiar narrow hardness – he is the Robespierre of this government – are combining to make him an offensive figure, one inviting resistance rather than affection. The result has been, for the first time, an increasing determination to fight the corner against him.

The problem, in part, is that for the moment he is the only contender. He and Lilley take no notice of the government line, but peddle their own philosophy. Douglas Hurd is losing interest fast and indeed, after his speech on Tuesday – bland and unimpressive – he cleared off to the Gulf for a photo opportunity. Heseltine, who wowed the Conference immediately after Portillo, still wants the job, but those of us with a vote on the matter would seriously doubt the ability of a man with heart disease to cope. It is not as if we all love him and admire the man so deeply that we'd be prepared to take the risk, as with Churchill. Then there's Ken Clarke: he has all the abilities of punchy speaking, courage, a clear mind, pro-European sentiments, and makes glorious fun of Bambi[143] and the socialists, but he doesn't know how to stroke people in public or in private, and can't be bothered to find out. Allied to a fine brain is a lazy character, typified by his not reading anything in his box other than what is really necessary, and by his utter insensitivity to the feelings of others. If Ken wants the top job, he will have to work a bit harder for it.

Tom Spencer[144] asked me for breakfast on the last morning of the Conference and Maurice Fraser, the extremely bright and nice special adviser to Hurd, joined us. Tom interrogated me closely on my intentions over the next few years, and soon it emerged why. After his three years as Chairman of the CGE, Bob Walter is due to step down in June; and the current notion, Tom told me, is for Whitney[145] to take his place. That would be a disaster. We could kiss goodbye to the election, and to any future influence in Europe as Tories – and possibly to the free trade, open Union we right-of-centres want. So the stakes are bloody high. I'd do it, I told Tom, it is important enough to me, and at the rate I'm writing it, *A Woman's Place* will have been put to bed by then. So count me in. It'll all need a mass of plotting – not just the chairmanship, but the fightback

---

143 A nickname for Tony Blair, the new Labour leader.
144 Conservative MEP for Surrey since 1994; MEP for Surrey West, 1989–94; MEP for Derbyshire, 1979–84.
145 Ray Whitney, Conservative MP for Wycombe since 1978.

as a whole. Tom will relish it, and it's good to be on board with him. Ha!

Enough of politics. The Cheltenham Festival of Literature in most ways you could describe was a disaster for me – isn't life odd, in that the Conference, which I dreaded, should have made me so much more optimistic, while the Festival, which I was looking forward to, was just awful, and may have caused permanent damage to my relationship with Richard. It was partly that I was very tired, getting to bed after 1 a.m. and up at 7 a.m. for breakfast meetings and TV – and I don't have the stamina, quite! A three-hour drive on narrow twisting roads from Bournemouth to Cheltenham was ghastly, exhausting in its own right. The rehearsal for my event was dismal, as Richard was trying to change the order of books which I had quite carefully chosen and already changed on the suggestion of the actress who was to read the extracts; I knew I was too tired to cope with any further fiddling and put my foot down, a little too close to tears. The actress was a big mistake, too, but we only realised with falling spirits too late during the presentation, for she read very slowly and portentously and turned everything into a dirge – in desperation I grabbed *Cold Comfort Farm* at one point and read out a paragraph to lighten the atmosphere. Then the timing turned out to have been the worst possible, for it coincided exactly with *Any Questions* coming from Cheltenham Ladies College up the road, so (although 200 tickets had been sold) there were, at a guess, only 120 or so people in a vast tent, and all I could see were rows of empty seats. The Festival organisers missed a trick, and *Any Questions* got it wrong too, as they brought three writers up to Cheltenham who had nothing to do with the Festival – Michael Dobbs, Ken Follett and another that I can't remember now. Dobbs was twenty minutes late for the programme as he got stuck in awful traffic too. So I could have done the broadcast, and stayed in a hotel in town which would have cut my chasing round, and done 'Desert Island Books' on the Saturday morning when I was much less tired, and altogether enjoyed myself. Instead it was all ghastly.

The biggest mistake of all was staying in Sudeley Castle. I had imagined Lady Ashcombe (an older woman, an American literature buff, Richard had said) as bouncy and wisecracking and warm;

instead she was small, beautiful and very formal. I knew everything was wrong when strong, neat lapsang souchong appeared and high tea was neatly laid out in a gleaming kitchen, smoked salmon sandwiches already cut, pieces of cake in regimented rows on a platter, thick napkins folded on side plates. Oh, no. I've never tried lapsang souchong tea before, and it's like a tisane and disgusting – may I have ordinary tea, in a mug, I pleaded weakly, and out came the teabags. The house is stunning – much too so – velvet drapes and hangings everywhere, the most staggering art, all in perfect nick and layer upon fabulous layer of it, even in the private rooms and, worst of all, in the bedrooms. I can't believe anybody feels comfortable living like that. I certainly began to feel quite desperate. The huge shiny copper tub in my bathroom was instantly unusable as far as I was concerned and the bedroom was stuffed with feathers[146] – pillows, eiderdown, the lot. During the night, to recover my sanity, indeed, I stripped the bed completely and slept on the floor.

I know it is hard for Richard and that he is under tremendous pressure. The business is taking shape and on Friday morning he signed at last an agreement on marketing. At Frankfurt he got agents in all the main regions of the world, and had many expressions of support. All he has to do now is to arrange his distribution network, and raise half a million by the end of the year – but both are well within his capabilities. His first book will be published next June.

Victoria, Wednesday 26 October, 10.30 p.m.

Last weekend Deb came up to London for a Stonewall concert in the Albert Hall, and we had a long natter. She's about to break up with Shi, who she's got fed up with: she has been to Israel five times and he's just cancelled his trip to Europe. Poor lad – after the kibbutz he'd hate Huddersfield – he's never been further than Egypt. No tears, just exasperation. So a new love, nicknamed Brownie, who's the head of security at the nightclub where she works, and is a car dealer and has lots of money and is lovely and has a beautiful body and is black. I raised an eyebrow, but it clearly doesn't matter a *jot* to Deb; I'm glad about that, though she does seem to cast her

---

146 EC is allergic to feathers.

loving net wide. The concert was simply marvellous – Elton John prancing around singing 'I Feel Pretty' was the funniest thing I've seen in ages, and he *looked* so happy too; Sandi Toksvig told lesbian jokes, Sting did a striptease, Ben Elton and Stephen Fry told funny stories, and the music was great. At a party on the roof garden above Derry and Toms afterwards, the vodka flowed, the drag queens gyrated, Vivienne Westwood nearly fell over several times and was only saved by her hirsute young toy boy, and Deb danced with Sting… He must have been quite relieved to be approached by a pretty young het! She's looking lovely, very slim and pretty, and I feel so proud of her.

Victoria, Tuesday 15 November, 9.20 p.m.

Ray is at an accountancy dinner tonight so I'm to expect him home late. The relationship is amicable enough, polite, almost warm: we went to a movie (*Frankenstein* with Kenneth Branagh) on Friday night, and I cooked roast beef lunch for us both ('splendid') Sunday afternoon. He still hasn't said a word: not even 'are you still planning to go?'

Moscow was wet and cold and chilly and dirty, everywhere neglected and dismal and broken down. Yet much better than it must have been quite recently, with bright shops, plenty of kiosks, bustling markets, Irish supermarkets and pubs, loads of traffic, no shortages. Most of the produce we saw, coats and suits and electrical equipment, is clearly made locally, in the Moscow No. 3 Tank Factory or the First Uniform Factory, on the side. Clothing design and finish quite good, but at £25 for a ladies' coat it isn't coming from Italy. Dale Campbell-Savours was amused, when buying a Russian electric shaver as a souvenir, to watch the woman assistant try several before she found one that worked – and put the others back on the shelf! I looked at prices, many of which are now at world levels, so didn't buy much – $80 or more for a fur hat which won't be worn seemed pointless, so I brought back vodka and trinkets only. (Got a taste for the Stolichnaya – sweet and warming!)

The impact of western culture is already enormous. The only proper queue we saw was at McDonald's (there are now three in Moscow). And my abiding memory is of belting down a suburban road in our Mercedes (they drive like the French used to) with Donna Summer blaring out of the car radio, a Nissan in front and a Toyota behind. Yet the ordinary people have a solidity which won't easily be eroded – e.g. the chubby cheerful butcher women in the market asking that their photos be taken and sent to them, showing off mouthfuls of gold teeth! The babushkas standing on the pavement near a busy intersection, stamping their cold feet and selling whatever their shopping bags could carry: I watched one large lady quickly sell the four cabbages she'd brought, and cross herself as she got shot of the last one. Dale and I watched fascinated from a car. We worked out that they must have gone to the early morning wholesale market, and would make enough each day to put a chicken in the pot, and to make up a meagre pension. Mostly they seemed cheerful enough and had their 'regulars' – but those who are too old end up as beggars and we saw a few, huddled shadows in the archways of the metro, and beggar gypsy children too. Yet none of the able-bodied homeless you see in London, and nowhere like our numbers. Many of the salaried people I met (e.g. MPs) are supporting elderly relatives – up to nine people dependent on one head of household. Most of the MPs have outside interests on which they pay no tax – but then nobody does.

I feel curiously unmoved by the visit; I shan't care if I never go there again. Whereas Romania was beautiful but nasty in places, Moscow was callous and indifferent, its treasures artificial and humourless, its general air drab, its politics and economics sleazy. It was good to come home. The plane was full of Scottish roustabouts returning from oil rigs near Murmansk with lurid tales of cold and hardship: I felt warm even to them, until they got drunk.

There's quite a row going on outside the flat (it's 10.35 p.m.). Someone is yelling and kicking over bins. There were loud sirens earlier – all queer, and unpleasant, and troubling. I don't like this area now; day and night there are drunks and layabouts and strange puddles and tell-tale smells, and nobody seems empowered to get them into hostels and day centres and clean the place up. My flat-hunting is turning up much nicer places than this, bigger and more comfortable, with trees and greenery, especially around Clapham Common. The bank are willing to lend me £100,000, which means

I can go to £125,000, and do repairs and redecoration later as more money comes in.

Victoria, Sunday 27 November, 7 p.m.

Feeling grotty. Another period started today – the third in five weeks – my system is going haywire. I am reluctant to ask my young GP for help, since (1) he looks like an angelic choirboy; (2) generally I'm bursting with health and almost a stone lighter than on my return from the *QE2*; and (3) the hormone test last summer was normal. So I'll have to put up with it. If it's fibroids, then the answer may be surgery – a hysterectomy – and I don't fancy that either. Maybe the system's just objecting to being starved of its most essential ingredient – TLC!

Saw Richard about ten days ago. He's feeling chipper about RC Books Ltd, for which (as at Thursday) he's now collected around £200,000 out of the £500,000 he needs. In fact he could raise most of that from his own resources. He's had modest cheques from Victoria Glendinning and Sebastian Faulks – who also sent seven postcards written to friends urging their support, to be clipped to seven prospectuses: *what* a nice move. Susan Hill and Jeffrey Archer have promised support. A left-wing publisher hinted at £250,000 as long as Richard publishes lots of new left-wing authors, which didn't seem like a viable business proposition – and is the kind of influence purchase more common in my Party! How coy champagne socialists can be. He's taken the premises in Manchester Square; typically Richard got the postcode wrong – they're as posh as you can get in W1, not downmarket WC1. He also managed to misspell my name in the prospectus, which embarrassed him enormously. As his business was officially launched on 17 November I gave him Blake Morrison's *When Did You Last See Your Father?*, since it was his father's money which made it possible. He was very pleased with that. The novel is still moving ahead reasonably well, though I must get on with Chapter 15 this week. I've also been commissioned to write the *Daily Mail* Xmas story, at £1,700 for 2,000 words! Norah of A. P. Watt says she'll be demanding £1 per word for me soon, but in fact I already get that: *A Woman's Place* is £150,000 for 150,000 words, and a *News of the World* article is usually £1,000 for 1,000 words. 'Toy Boy'[147] seems to have had quite an effect on commissioning editors and speaking agencies. What also will help is my being chosen as 'Campaigner of the Year' for my work on gay rights in '*The Spectator*/Highland Park Parliamentarian of the Year' Awards. That did please me inordinately, as I confess I was a little hurt not to have been given something (even shared with lots of others) at the Equality Show – instead they honoured Gay Switchboard, which will certainly be around another year.

Today is the fourth anniversary of John Major becoming PM. Yet his authority is virtually non-existent, and his admirers are reduced to the staff he appoints to his office. They're changed recently too – Jonathan Hill's gone back to his PR company and Sarah Hogg's given up. I never thought much of her, I confess. She couldn't see the depths of the recession coming or the yawning gap on public spending which has caused us such anguish. She's failed to prepare the country for the single currency, failed to extol the benefits of Europe, and allowed the PM to get away with the ill-begotten Citizen's Charter as his flagship policy. David Hunt has shown what he thinks of that by delegating it to Bob Hughes,[148] his very junior minister; David realises that he's been sidelined since the reshuffle and he's very upset about it. And that was stupid of the PM, as Hunt is able, and can turn a phrase and has some views; we are short of such talent, so it's the same mistake as misplacing me (and that's not being conceited, I hope, just realistic).

Tower House, Wednesday 30 November, 4 p.m.

At least if I'm tapping away at the machine in my eyrie, I can kid myself I'm working! And get back in the mood to start on Chapter 15. I wish I felt more enthusiastic, but this is the dogged bit; once I get started, I enjoy it.

Hugh Dykes asked if I'd be interested in something else after March – the chairmanship of the European Movement, which he has held for six years. It's not that likely that I'll get the job. Officially the European Movement is an all-party affair, and its

---

147 A short story printed in the *Daily Telegraph*.
148 Robert G. Hughes, Conservative MP for Harrow West since 1987.

role will be significant in the referendum on the single currency, which is looking more certain by the minute, so there might be both personal objections to me, and the feeling that it's time for a non-Tory. However, Hugh says all the other possibilities are weaker personalities, so maybe I'll be asked. And, truthfully, I'd be thrilled – that's my métier; I could feel very comfortable arguing for a stronger Europe, and it'd stop me getting bored, which happens all too frequently, especially when the only thing on my plate is Chapter 15.

The Eurosceptics had a field day on Monday night on the Bill to increase Euro spending. We won the vote on a Labour amendment by 330 to 303, a majority of twenty-seven, thanks to the support of the Ulster Unionists, who don't want a general election any more than we do, and the main motion passed with 329 in favour and only forty-five against, as most of the Labour Party went home – their Euro MPs are keen to have the extra money. Seven Tories abstained on the first vote and only one (Carttiss) on the second; all have lost the whip, after being warned that this would be the consequence of their action. Another, Richard Body[149] (mad as a hatter; he it was of whom the PM said, 'When I think of Richard Body I see men in fluttering white coats'), voted with us, then resigned the whip in protest, he said, at the strong-arm tactics used to win. So we are in uncharted waters. This is the first time since 1942 that any Tories have lost the whip, with the sole exception of Rupert Allason[150] last year, who hardly counts. Even when Churchill opposed the Munich Agreement in 1938, the whip wasn't withdrawn, though Central Office tried to get his association to deselect him. Macmillan, who'd been a rebel himself in the 1930s, was relaxed about rebellions. Enoch Powell was allowed to vote against the government 115 times – and during the Maastricht votes, many of the sceptics must have got over the 70 mark. So it's a bit late – and a bit strong – to discipline them now: but necessary.

Thus we now have ten parties in the House of Commons (assuming

---

149 Sir Richard Body, Conservative MP for Hillard with Boston since 1966; MP for Billericay, 1955–9.
150 Conservative MP for Torbay since 1987.

the rebels are organised enough to stay together), and none has a majority: there are only 321 official Conservatives, and 325 others, so we're five short of a majority, not counting the Speaker and three Deputy Speakers, who don't vote. What happens now? Nobody knows! It depends a bit on how strong the MPs are in their own patch. John Wilkinson (Ruislip) and Nick Budgen (Wolverhampton SW) aren't, and will be under pressure to behave or retire, especially John Wilkinson, whose people are angry. Teresa Gorman,[151] Tony Marlow, Teddy Taylor and Chris Gill all have local backing and presumably will continue to vote against the government; their local associations may find themselves struck off and, ultimately, with official candidates against them. That could be entertaining, especially in Billericay – and Teresa is stupid enough to be a lone outpost. Carttiss seems OK too – he's such a peculiar character, given to robust and idiotic opinions, a throwback to an age when brains were a disqualification for Parliament. But we have our martyrs, which must make Bill Cash, Michael Spicer and a few others who hate Europe as much but voted with the government grind their teeth in rage. Abandoned their principles and lost face too, poor souls. Almost makes you feel for sorry for them.

House of Commons, Wednesday 7 December, 6.50 p.m.
I'm about as tired and dispirited as I can be. Last night, for the first time anybody can remember, we lost a vote on an important element of a Budget. The proposal to increase VAT on domestic fuel bills was defeated by 319 to 311. Fifteen Tories either abstained or voted against, including most of those who lost or gave up the whip last week – only Budgen voted with the government immediately after Ken Clarke announced that the government were abandoning the increase. First thing this morning interest rates rose 0.5 per cent, so that's a merry Christmas to all mortgage holders. On Thursday Cabinet will decide what extra measures are required to bring in the £1.5 billion p.a. which has been lost. Fortunately the pension books, including the increased compensation for the fuel tax, have already started going out (that is a six-month exercise), so

---

151 Conservative MP for Billericay since 1987.

we can't be asked to vote to take money out of pensioners' purses. Otherwise even I would dig my heels in.

Politically it was so dumb. From the moment the rebels lost the whip it was clear they would take their revenge. And you could see people sniffing the wind – if we were to lose, they wanted to be on the winning side. It did occur to me that if Labour were minded to be cute they might send some of their chaps home to ensure we won, so that then we would be saddled with the burden of 17.5 per cent VAT on fuel from there onwards. As it is, we're saddled with the idea, and it will haunt us. In that case, we would have done better to squeeze some political advantage from the mess – and cheerfully abandon the thing in the Budget speech last Tuesday, saying that the forecasts were so good that we didn't need it any more. Instead, Ken went his usual macho way, punching in all directions and knocking himself over in the process. He was still shooting off his mouth as he arrived back at No. 11 last night, saying it was a defeat for common sense and he'd never been beaten by worse arguments. Showering your opponents with abuse is not guaranteed to turn them back into friends. Fool, idiot, imbecile: he has the political nous of a three-year-old. And the PM has none at all.

So now we have a government that can only get large chunks of its programme through with the support of the Ulster Unionists; and when that's not available, can't get it through at all. Some of the rebels were making a point, that having been deprived of the whip, they were in a position to punish the PM. Some have nothing to lose: they will either be deselected, or will retire (Body) or will be defeated at the election (Sumberg,[152] for example, whose majority is only 788). For these people there are no sanctions the government can offer.

Aren't I lucky that I can now earn my living in other ways. This morning I rose early (hadn't been able to sleep, in fact) and finished off the *Daily Mail* Christmas story. It's not too bad; Clare liked it, anyway. On Monday, knowing I was to see Richard yesterday, I worked flat out and produced 4,000 words to finish Chapter 15. I feel real progress has been made: about 122,000 words done out of 180,000. Richard wants Chapter 16 by the time we meet again,

---

152 David Sumberg, Conservative MP for Bury South since 1983.

and he will have it, if we don't find ourselves embroiled in a general election in the meantime.

I saw his new office for the first time yesterday. Very posh location, splendid front door, and he can use the boardroom on the ground floor belonging to his landlords. He has the basement with its own entrance. There are four tiny rooms, which will be cramped; but most meetings with authors and investors will be elsewhere. Manchester Square is splendid, with the Wallace Collection right opposite; before our next engagement I intend to go inside and explore (I recall spending time there as a student at LSE and loving it, but can't remember a single painting). We went for lunch in Selfridges nearby – downmarket but nicely served and surprisingly good food, two of us for £29. Richard is now looking immensely cheerful about the business and has raised nearly £400,000, with support from a dozen authors – Archer put in £25,000, which I thought was miserable. He'll need more capital later, but once he's up and running angels will come.

Just been nattering with Deb on the phone. Steve the fireman is still in the picture, but keeping out of the way. And there's Brownie too, who still fancies her; but he flits from girl to girl and is not good news. 'Mum,' she tells me, 'the trouble is that the risky guys are always the most attractive' – don't I know it!

Victoria, Sunday 18 December, 7 p.m.

I came down yesterday to collect Susie from Heathrow – in fact she arrived at 7 a.m. this morning to a cold and sodden welcome – and arranged a bit of TV recording last night with Terry Wogan to fill time. It's called *Do the Right Thing*, has no intellectual content whatsoever, and paid £1,500. Not bad for three hours' work.

Susie is as bouncy, edgy and aggressive as ever. When she phoned Deb this morning the latter called me to the phone and hissed, 'Have you told her?' – to which the answer was no, I haven't managed to get a quiet word in yet. But before bed tonight I will. Apart from anything else, she's planning to spend most of the next two weeks buzzing around seeing her friends; after we've talked she may see value in spending a little time with her family and not taking us quite so much for granted.

Another ghastly week for the government. We lost the Dudley
West by-election by a huge 20,000+ majority (the Tory vote was
down from 34,000 to 7,000), with a swing of 29 per cent. On that
figure we'd have a wipe-out of Canadian proportions[153] at the
general election, and although no one seriously expects that,
the prospects of pulling back to success are growing dimmer.
Party Chairman Jerry Hanley said gaily that Labour lost votes in
Dudley. In fact they *held* their vote to within a few hundred, while
ours disappeared.

What's happening? The *Blair factor* is the answer. For the first
time in over a decade the Labour Party is led by a clear-headed,
intelligent, articulate middle-class Englishman, with an English
accent and an English seat. England is where 40 million of our
58 million people live; and one-third of the entire population lives
in southern England. For the English middling-off, Blair is good
news and very reassuring. His concern about law and order meets
their preoccupations; he knows they can't afford private health
or education and don't want those services privatised or messed
around any more. His decision to send his son to the Oratory, a
grant-maintained school, helps reassure them on the future of such
schools and suggests that he will *not* bow to pressure from his own
left wing. His efforts to reform Clause IV, which John Smith had
largely abandoned, indicate that he's trying to turn Labour into
a modern social democratic party which understands the market
economy. If he's successful he could be in power for a decade, and
I could be sixty before we next have another Tory PM (which then
mightn't be Portillo, but someone coming up behind him).

The current atmosphere is just like 1976–7. The Labour Party lost
its parliamentary majority in 1976 and survived till 1978 in a pact
with the Liberals, though Callaghan reneged on his promise to make
David Steel a minister. The winter of discontent 1978–9 showed
the PM had no power or sense of direction at all. Meantime Mrs
Thatcher, who had become opposition leader in 1975, had started

---

153 In the October 1993 Canadian election the ruling Progressive
Conservative Party was reduced to only three seats. The Prime Minister
Kim Campbell lost her seat.

very slowly: in the background Keith Joseph and Alfred Sherman were developing a new Tory philosophy in the Centre for Policy Studies. By 1977 voters were turning to the Tories in droves, and it was with some impatience that they waited for an opportunity to get Labour out, in 1979; and they've remained out ever since.

1995

Pride of Le Havre, 1 January, 8.30 p.m.

New Year's Eve was fun, in a slightly dotty way. Susie came to London on Friday (30th) and we went to see Sue Townsend's *The Queen and I*, which was utter rubbish. Only about 10 per cent came from the book. The rest was culled from 1994's royal revelations so it sounded like bad *Private Eye*; and as it had been developed as a play in one of those sloppy, ill-disciplined drama workshops in Leicester (what do they know about the arts in *Leicester*, for heaven's sake?), it ended as a dismal polemic on the evils of poverty, as if they were all Margaret Thatcher's fault. Having survived a Liverpool childhood, naturally I have other views. Come the revolution – which is, after all, what is supposed to have happened in *The Queen and I* – there'll still be lazy good-for-nothings. I fell asleep in both first and second acts. Yuk.

On Saturday (yesterday) Susie and I packed, then went to a movie (*The Last Seduction* – brilliant), followed by a meal at TGI Fridays (noisy, busy, very hip), and Trafalgar Square, where we stood with thousands of others trying to see the fun. But since *everyone* was doing that, there wasn't much fun! All very sedate and dull. There wasn't even an amplified Big Ben, so nobody knew exactly when midnight was. No singing, no music, no countdown. Very anti-climactic! Still, it was good to be with so many (mostly) young people, all wanting to celebrate and wish each other a happy 1995. Afterwards Susie and I walked back to the flat and slept for a couple of hours, before I drove her to Heathrow to catch the 6.55 a.m. plane to Hanover on the next stage of her gap year. Then I drove to Portsmouth to catch this boat.

Susie now knows about her father and me. She was upset and didn't really understand – we aren't 'splitting up' and we don't fight or hate each other, in fact we get on quite well. Christmas this year wasn't bad, as we were all trying to be nice to each other. On a superficial level therefore it's rather pleasant being together – a bit like staying with in-laws you like but with whom you have little in common. So conversation is warmer than polite. A real effort is made to give presents that will be welcome. (I gave Ray a new biography of Presley and the life of Robert Louis Stevenson and an updated version of Peter O'Sullevan's autobiography – apparently I'd given him the original in 1989, though I'd forgotten.) The atmosphere's quite relaxed. People pitch in without being asked – lay the table, load the dishwasher, empty the bins.

I get back on 10 January when Parliament restarts, and then the first priority is a new flat. I went to look at the only new-build in the neighbourhood of Clapham Common, 'The Nightingales': nice but expensive. That might be what I want, though the asking price of £153,000 is a bit high; but the location is perfect and it would be fun to turn something new and plain into a comfortable home. It has a shower, and two decent bedrooms and a lovely big lounge and a decent view, so maybe.

Les Tuileries, Friday 6 January, 6 p.m.
Sitting by the fire: cosy, warm and quiet. Behind me a glorious red cyclamen I rescued from SuperU in Longué, where it was very dilapidated and sad. On the table my word processor, closed for the day. The novel is coming on quite well; I've been hammering home how horrible it is to be the subject of press attention, and trying to explore the state of mind of 'Anthony'/Stephen Milligan/Jocelyn Cadbury. Since I'm neither screwed up about sex nor have ever been suicidal, it's tricky: neither my imagination nor my writing skills are really up to it. Yet I'm still churning out quality copy (much better written than *A Parliamentary Affair*) quite fast: twenty-two hours this week so far, 11,600 words, so still two hours per thousand words. It has less buzz for me, however, than it did. I suppose because two years ago I was (1) in uncharted waters; (2) running away; (3) getting things off my chest: my writing was a refuge from the awfulness and uncertainly of my political life. Now the writing is centre stage and politics is clinging on as a hobby: so the authorship isn't so much

fun, the secret naughty place I've found to hide, as my cash-earning job. I should be grateful. But I feel somewhat bereft.

I'm into Alan Bennett's *Writing Home*, a curious but tantalising mixture of diaries, eulogies, articles, film and TV scripts (with added comments), rehearsal notes etc. – a ragbag, but beautifully written and full of wisdom. He keeps a diary, he says, in order to have a conversation with himself, and to slow down time. Maybe my efforts, confided in the heat of the moment, may have some permanence and some interest eventually in decades to come, either to myself when I'm old, or to other people. Maybe I'm just more honest than Mr Bennett in admitting it.

The fire is wonderfully hot, but it's the only place in the whole house which is! Paris and most of France are covered in snow (9 cm last night), but we're too far west, so we've had torrential rain, freezing fog in the mornings and bright crisp sunshine the rest of the time. The forest is beautiful, full of colour, the grass is still glowing, and my geraniums, though nipped by frost, are far from dead. Every time I come here (especially in winter) I wonder why on earth I bothered to buy such an outlandish property so far away. Then, after a few days, the peace and calm blanket me. So this is a place for reflection and healing, and without it I'd be some kind of nutcase. Here I did all my weeping over John Major, and what hurt the most – not being invited to join his government at the first opportunity, and then being offered the one job in government I would not and *could* not accept. Here I ground through my fury at Ray's increasing emotional absence from my life, and came to see that (since he barely lived with me) I could live without him, and might prefer it. Neither subject has bothered me much this winter, so I suppose I'm 'through' those bad patches.

I think a lot about getting older and about being self-disciplined enough to keep age at bay. I wish I could stop nibbling and gener-ally overeating: although I'm fit, ten-and-a-half stone means a thick waist and a big bum. There are more significant signs of middle age: for example, if at any time between 3 p.m. and 6 p.m. I lie back and close my eyes, I'm asleep for a couple of hours. If I'm writ-ing between those hours I start to drift, while car-driving is quite dangerous. I don't remember being like that twenty years ago.

It's 8 p.m. but I'm not hungry, partly because I treated myself to lunch today at the Cheval Blanc in Mouliherne – for 48 francs I had my choice of dozens of *hors d'oeuvres* (mostly homemade and fresh), a grilled gammon steak, a platter of chips enough to feed a family, a cheese plate which would have graced the Ritz *and* puddings. The little dining room was busy with short thick-set men, very solemn, who entered in threes and fours, shook hands with their mates and then settled to eat in great dignity. I guessed they were local work-men – foresters or farmers, perhaps; in sweaters and rough cordu-roys, one in wellies. None of them would have got near the dining area of a pub in Britain, yet they knew their food (the other *plat du jour* was a *huge* bowlful of mussels which required great concentra-tion and much slurping to eat: watching one large man on his own doing this and reading *Figaro* at the same time was a delight).

I'm still not hungry. That must have been one hell of a lunch! *The Times* for 31 December also tells me that in May we celebrate the 200th anniversary of Boswell's death, 'the original Scots yuppie, his nose covered with the boot polish of the famous… [who] chased celebri-ties with the frenzy of today's television researchers'. Johnson told him 'that whatever strikes strongly should be described while the first impression remains in the mind'. That by itself is sufficient justification for a diary: the vividness of immediate recollection unsullied by afterthought. This practice, comments *The Times* with delight, 'creates immortality'. So that's what we're all up to! Mae West it was, I think (not attributed in *The Times*), who said 'keep a diary and some day it'll keep you.' It is obvious that the leader writer either keeps one, or at least admires those who do. I'm very glad I do: it's like having an old friend, but one who, understanding exactly how I feel, is sympathetic and kind at all times, and laughs at my jokes.

Liverpool, Sunday 22 January, 9 a.m.
It's Mum's eighty-third birthday, so I've come up for the weekend; yesterday I took her to the Marie Curie home at Sunnyside (cheer-ful thing to do!) for tea, and last night to see a movie, *Forrest Gump* with Tom Hanks, which she loved.

I did *Question Time* from Southampton on Thursday night with

Michael Meacher[154] and Matthew Taylor.[155] David Dimbleby is now turning into a less pugnacious version of Robin Day – he is much pleasanter than his rather obnoxious brother Jonathan, he of the Royal persuasion. In fact it went so well, and I was so pleased with my performance, that afterwards I felt terribly depressed that I'm not getting (and never will) the chance to do this as a senior member of the government: I'm not where I still feel I should be. Everything else has been a success, but is nevertheless a substitute. Thursday night/Friday morning was a bad time.

The fourth member of the panel was someone I hadn't met before – a tall, willowy lady called Gwynneth Flower, very handsome in pink, the Chief Executive of Central London Training and Enterprise Council (TEC). I was puzzled that I'd not met her before, and in the taxi from the station asked her about herself. Engineer; ex-Army Colonel (Intelligence); has been a senior engineer at Marconi till four years ago; headhunted at various times and now in charge of the TEC, of which Lord Stockton is Chair. That all seemed even odder, for a woman engineer at such a level, with a remarkable career behind her, I'd have known, or met (e.g. at 'Woman of the Year'). Turns out she was a bloke, doesn't it! The surgery took place only four years ago, so most of her life he was a tremendously successful high-flying *chap*. It shows (in part) how hard it has been for women of talent to make a go of it, that I'd automatically assumed such a female person would have been unusual and therefore singled out, noticed, fêted. What courage, to go through all this. He was married, with four grown-up children, and is now sixty-two. I suppose that when the last child reached adulthood he must have thought 'now or never'. Anyway, I'm fascinated, so I'll write a supportive note, and ask her to lunch.

My latest pet 'subject', Gulf War Syndrome,[156] is demanding a lot of work and thought. Tomorrow (Monday) I have meetings at

---

154 Member of the Shadow Cabinet and opposition spokesman on transport; Labour MP for Oldham West since 1970.
155 Liberal Democrat spokesman on education; MP for Truro since 1987.
156 In December EC had called a Commons debate on this apparently mysterious condition.

British Legion HQ and with Nick Soames.[157] So far about seventy soldiers have been through the full assessment and most have some recognisable condition. It's irritating that the Gulf War itself is still being denied as the origin, but I shall put to Nick that if the 400+ veterans suing the MoD, with the tacit backing of the Royal British Legion, win their case, it will be bad politically and cost a packet. Better to prepare for an orderly retreat, in my view. This last week the Defence Select Committee announced it would investigate (I've been bombarding the members with paperwork for weeks, quietly, all of them), and on Tuesday, the fourth anniversary of the outbreak of the Gulf War, the Labour Party held a press conference and demanded an inquiry. They did not invite me to attend, but because of the adjournment debate in December the press came on to me in droves.

Meanwhile *A Parliamentary Affair* is still going strong: 129,000 sold as at 18 January, according to Sue Fletcher (who took me to lunch at Le Caprice again), including 22,000 sold in Australia, where it's quite a hit.

Last Friday I paid the reservation fee for Flat 5, The Nightingales. It's a perfect location for tube and park. The flat is brand new, nothing to be done, clean, no dust, and should have investment value. It's big – just under 1,000 sq. ft, and well designed – two bathrooms – and has a huge living room; it should be warm, comfortable and reasonably cheap to run. Anyway it'll *do* for a while. Of course I'd like something bigger – an extra bedroom or study – but that would cost more; and anything else I've seen in my price range is in the wrong place or needs time and effort and cash spending.

Victoria, Saturday 28 January, 10 p.m.

I'm here tonight to do *On the Record* tomorrow – a live lunchtime hour, nationally set in 1997 with the single currency referendum under way. I'm on the 'yes' team with Roy Hattersley. Iain Duncan

---

157 Now a junior minister at the Ministry of Defence; Conservative MP for Crawley since 1983.

Smith and Peter Shore[158] are the 'nos'. We both have a PPB – ours shows the antis as Neanderthal men, literally. Given that Roy has made no attempt to contact me, and didn't turn up at the BBC for our (only) prearranged meeting, I'm not hopeful of a good outcome. The 'official view' is turning against the single currency, or at least against our joining it: sovereignty, the Queen's head on the coinage and all that junk. Makes me feel nauseous. Then they have the gall to ask why their pensions are worse than the Germans' and our trains slower than the French. Because the others don't breakfast, lunch and dine on nostalgia, that's why.

It's been a bad couple of weeks for pro-Europeans. The PM did a *Breakfast with Frost* interview in which he projected that nothing substantial would come out of the next Euro summit – and if it did, he would veto it. Michael Portillo announced he was 'much encouraged'. Palm fronds of peace were offered to the rebels, who promptly voted against the government over the fishing issue. Yet the PM is still making purring noises in their direction, and sounding more and more like 'one of them'.

Andrew Marr in *The Independent* on Tuesday got it right. The PM has simply looked around the playground at the various groups of school bullies – Eurosceptics or Europhiles – and joined the nastier group. Policy is driven not by what he believes on Europe, or what is best for the country, but on what John Major needs to do to survive. We Europhiles are not fighters. Ray Whitney is still the prime mover in the Positive Europe Group and he's all vague smiles and catchphrases, the quintessential diplomat. Similarly the European Movement have decided to have Giles Radice[159] as the next Chairman after Hugh Dykes. Radice is limp and laid back, again with no ability to inspire or lead. I despair!

Marr's remedy for us is to start rebelling and voting against the PM. I can't see that happening at all – we're too wet (in Margaret Thatcher's original use of the word, i.e. not strong) and very loyal.

---

158 A former Labour Cabinet minister and a prominent opponent of the European Union; MP for Bethnal Green and Stepney since 1983; MP for Stepney and Poplar, 1974–83; MP for Stepney, 1964–74.
159 Labour MP for Durham North since 1983; MP for Chester-le-Street, 1973–83.

To rebel would split the Party wide open and send us all to oblivion. So indeed will a drift of policy to the right, of course – every voter in South Derbyshire would go the other way. If Portillo becomes leader, then we are out for a long time. But there's no one else, and no coherent movement to pitch behind an alternative. So we're stuck with Major and his vacillation and his short-sighted unprincipled inconsistencies. This is not the man I once knew. His ambition then was strong but modest, his ideas and beliefs deep rooted and based on compassion. This man is all hot air and cunning, a truly hateful combination, motivated only by the will to stay in office.

Susie has written from Hanover; she seems to be surviving, and comments about Ray and me: 'You know I wish it wasn't happening, but I also know that if I were in your position, I would probably do the same.' That is reassuring, and in its own way comforting. Ray hasn't said a word to either of his daughters, even though he's aware they know. Deb is OK too, in her little house: I took Mum across to Huddersfield on Sunday and Deb cooked us large platefuls of microwaved frozen quiche and baked potatoes, quite competently. My Mum was thrilled, really – Deb's house is much larger and more comfortable than her own. I was ashamed to realise I'd only seen Mum once last year (though on the last occasion I was in the 'Pool she was in Canada), so I've put four more dates this year's diary to go there. Yet Liverpool is still awful – greedy envious eyes on the car, so you're scared to leave it out of your sight. As we drove home from the cinema, Mum and me, we were 'buzzed' by a police car in Queen's Drive. I suppose they thought the Toyota must have been stolen. I slowed, they drew alongside. I waved; they collapsed in giggles. Poor lads, must be a thankless task on Merseyside.

Victoria, Tuesday 31 January, late
I had dinner this evening with Michael Spicer in the Members' Dining Room from 8 till 9 p.m. Also at the table Roger Evans:[160] found we had much in common, though of course we disagreed

---

160 PUS, Department of Social Security; Conservative MP for Monmouth since 1992.

on a good many issues. It was all jolly and thoughtful, until at the end joined by a very oily Home Secretary, Michael Howard. The conversation disintegrated very quickly. 'But that's what we are doing!' he cried. 'We have made it quite clear that if we don't like what the other Europeans propose we will use our veto!' You're on a hiding to nothing, I wanted to say out loud. But he was not in a listening mood. Instead I patted his hand with as patronising a gesture as I could muster, said 'You're too smooth for me, Michael,' and left.

Train to London, Sunday 12 February, 7.25 p.m.

My car is in for service, so I'm trusting to British Rail – or the Midland Main Line, as this bit is now known. I wonder if the government realises the extra costs incurred in splitting BR into dozens of separate companies? Plus the uncertainty of the last couple of years over privatisation. The result is unhappy, and shabby, and crying out for money to be spent on it. Dismal.

Still, it's been a grand week in many ways. I took Clare down to see The Nightingales and we ended up with the site manager at a warehouse in deepest, scruffiest Wandsworth which recycles old wood (and door handles and ironwork and anything else you fancy – a real Aladdin's cave). The hunt for my floorboards was on. 'What's that?' I pointed upwards at samples on a wall. 'That's French oak,' was the answer, and it gazed down at me, blond and beautiful and hard as nails. So after some haggling we settled on £3,400 for the 77 square metres I want, and aren't I a happy piggy! I'd love to spin a tale that it comes from the chateau in which Marshal Pétain died (or de Gaulle, or Voltaire, or whoever) but in fact EC fire regulations have required refurbishment of stock carriages, so it's been liberated from a French cattle truck.

Richard's company had its first party on Friday night, with around eighty people – most of them investors – and authors and other friends. Quite a gathering! Sebastian Faulks was there – 'Author of the Year', to whom I'd presented his 'Nibbie' award at the *Publishing News* dinner at the Hilton the night before; and Christopher Potter of Fourth Estate, 'Editor of the Year' (he did *The Shipping News*). Jeffrey and Mary Archer graced the basement, and Jeffrey peered out of the window and said the view wasn't as good as from his place, the silly show-off. He has been away writing and came back with a 140,000 word novel. It will go through fourteen drafts, he boasted, to the smothered snickers of his listeners, as if he didn't realise that *fewer* drafts are more impressive. (As he toddled off one lady raised an eyebrow at me – 'Why fourteen?' she murmured. 'Because he can't spell,' I told her.) One delight was meeting Linden Stafford,[161] whose voice I instantly recognised and gave her a big hug. She's not at all as I thought – short, dumpy, frumpy, frizzy hair and specs, but friendly and warm and a bit shy. And John Walsh, who came as a guest of Corin Redgrave (the author of RCB's first book, a biography of Michael Redgrave, sure to be a big seller). Again, I'd imagined John as a slim, balding man in his fifties, but he turned out a big blond hunk, chain-smoking with Victoria Glendinning. He's no longer at the *Sunday Times*, but currently runs the *Indie* magazine and soon will be Literary Editor in place of Robert Winder. I think John Walsh was a little taken aback at this fierce dame wafting away his cigarette smoke! All in all, it was a marvellous evening.

Richard asked my opinion on a £50,000 investment he'd been offered via a woman judge from her friend who wanted Richard to publish his books. 'Vanity publishing,' I sniffed, 'If the books are any good you'll publish them anyway. If he thinks he's buying you, that's a big no-no. And if his ideas are that strange, he could pull out on a whim and demand his £50,000 back. So don't touch it.' And he didn't – but he may get some of the money anyway, as the judge was impressed by his refusal.

Ructions elsewhere – my Mum was nearly arrested about ten days ago over the M&S store card I gave her for her birthday. It turned out I sent her mine, not hers, and the shop was not impressed when she turned up waving someone else's card and demanding to spend money on it! I got a frantic phone call at the office, and it took some time to establish the connection. At this point tempers cooled. 'Are you really Edwina Currie's mother?' 'Of course I am.' 'Ooh. Sit here, Mrs Cohen. Can you get us her autograph?' It didn't help

---

161 A freelance copy-editor who had worked on EC's novel.

that (at the age of eighty-three) she couldn't remember my home address or phone number.

The MoD announced on Wednesday (in answer to my probing parliamentary question) that independent medical audit would be sought on Gulf War Syndrome and the results published in the *British Medical Journal*. This is the first time in history that the MoD has obtained civilian help. The Royal British Legion are cock-a-hoop, as it sets a splendid precedent. We've a big event at the House of Commons on 27 February (the eve of the end of the Gulf War). The assessments are in hand – the men are no longer being fobbed off. I took Colonel Terry English and Brigadier Tony Dixon to lunch with Lady Mar[162] the day of the Select Committee hearings and made notes: and as I read them back Tony murmured in appreciation, 'If you'd been in the Army you'd have been a general by now.'

The net result of this was an 87-hour week from 30 January. Last week was better, at around sixty-two, but I'm still very tired. Partly it's because my periods are now coming every seventeen to nineteen days, so I moaned to my GP and he's sending me to see the gynaecologist Joe Jordan on 25 February. We'll try hormones (tablets? patches?), but since I have fibroids, a hysterectomy is highly likely. Oh dear, that scares me rigid. What would I be like afterwards? Would I still be as energetic, as youthful? It's not losing my womb I worry about, it's losing my personality. I feel a sense of frustrated rage, after all the efforts I make to keep fit. And will I be interested in a sex life afterwards? Or any good at it? Will the urge go? Will I still have orgasms? (Hope so!) It would be major surgery and carries a big risk (look what happened to Judith Chaplin[163]) and would take three months to recover. *Not* funny.

The Party is falling to pieces over Europe, with open fighting between Cabinet factions. Portillo openly criticises Clarke, who argues for the benefits of a single currency. Jonathan Aitken comes out against (one of Clarke's team). Redwood smarms around. The

162 Margaret, Countess of Mar, Patron of the Gulf War Veterans' Association.
163 A few weeks after being elected to Parliament in 1992, Judith Chaplin collapsed and died following minor surgery.

PM does nothing. It is *awful*. I can't believe how leaderless we are, or how far the Party is slithering to the right. Charles Wardle resigned yesterday,[164] concerned that our immigration controls will disappear (good thing too) – that threatens to be an election issue. Stephen Dorrell came to a South Derbyshire Conservative Association dinner and promised me that the PM is really left of centre and will be there for years. But I think the sceptics are planning to have him out in November and put in their own boy (Portillo).

Tower House, Friday 24 February, 8 p.m.

God, I feel rough! Another very heavy and painful period today, but at least this one was more or less on time, at twenty-six days. Tomorrow morning I go see Joe Jordan in Birmingham and then we should get some help. Meanwhile the only things that appeal are hot tea, toast and honey, and chocolate – comfort eating, in other words, satisfying both my hormonal cravings and my most childish weaknesses!

It doesn't help that during the week I was waking up at 5.30 a.m. with my brain racing – maybe it's related. But the stress level is horribly high at the moment. One stress factor is the flat – on Wednesday I signed the contracts, which have now been exchanged, so we're on our way. It's in a Conservation Area, apparently, which can only add to its future value. Yet that brings closer the dates for packing up and leaving, as opposed to just thinking about it. Ray has continued to be in London only two nights recently, Tuesday and Wednesday; Thursday he is usually home and he tends to take odd days of holiday owing to him on Mondays. When he is in the flat, all I get is a grunt. And yet… I know as I pack those boxes I will be very tearful. I do so wish it hadn't come to this.

Last Thursday in Neil Kinnock's patch[165] we polled only 900 votes, came fourth and lost our deposit. We will be wiped out in Scotland and Wales. The Party nationally is still stuck at 22–24 per cent, even with MORI, who are generally favourable. Hence the

---

164 From his job as PUS at the Home Office. He had been Conservative MP for Bexhill and Battle since 1983.

165 The by-election caused by Kinnock's appointment as an EU Commissioner.

atmosphere at Westminster is gloomy and resigned. And Blair goes steaming ahead. He wants to be in power a long time, not just once. So I expect they'll keep trying until the thing cracks and the government loses a confidence vote. I seriously doubt that we can survive into '97, and possibly not far into '96. The novel could get in the way a bit of the election – or do I mean the other way round?

A Parliamentary Affair has been sold to Russia (whoopee!) and is already selling well in mass market paperback in the airports – it's W. H. Smith's No. 9 already, though the launch isn't till 20 March. I'm working hard putting stuff in the can – did a *five-hour* photo shoot for *Bella* today. Richard is also working flat out. We had only the briefest phone conversation this week as he had a heavy cold – business is going well.

Victoria, Sunday 19 March, 7.15 p.m.

I'll have to be quick as Ray is on his way. I'm about an hour ahead of him!

Progress – Joe Jordan put me on HRT rightaway, pooh-poohed the idea of surgery and everything's fine. What a huge relief. He handed me a pile of tablets, try these. I took one Premarin (oestrogen) and one noresthisterone (progesterone) as I left his consulting rooms in Birmingham, and by the time I reached Derby the pain was going and I was feeling much perkier. Now I'm back where I was before last summer – bags of energy, clear brain, body under control, six hours sleep a night and no drowsiness in afternoon. Oh, the joy of feeling *well* again.

The alternative career also makes progress. We're now busy promoting the mass market paperback of *A Parliamentary Affair*: tomorrow is London Book Fair at Olympia: I'll arrive on board a red double-decker London bus plastered with the legs.[166] Sue Fletcher says we've already sold 125,000 copies of the mass market paperback. Crumbs. Meanwhile I'm over 160,000 words on *A Woman's Place* and got a bit stuck (one reason for coming down early tonight) until I realised that this is the resignation chapter, which

---

166 The book's cover shows a pair of stockinged legs, tapering down to bright red high-heeled shoes.

I'm not so keen to do. After that, though, it should be a doddle. Richard keeps saying the stuff is 'strong' and I certainly find I enjoy reading the chapters. The big sales of *A Parliamentary Affair* suggest we have got something right – very reassuring.

Especially in the face of the virtual collapse of the government. We've lost three ministers since Xmas – Allan Stewart,[167] for getting into a row with a roads protester, Charles Wardle and Bob Hughes, of all people, with girlfriend trouble. He's on his second marriage (she was his secretary at the Commons) and drifted into an affair with a constituent, whom he then employed, and who on being sacked by Mrs Hughes buzzed off to the *News of the World*. He is a silly prat. He was only Citizens' Charter Minister, but might have hoped for more. Maybe they've too little to do in that department! Makes me wonder how close I get to the truth in my novels: how depressing. But I wish it hadn't been Bob, whom I like.

Meanwhile the Grim Reaper is also catching up. Nicholas Fairbairn[168] died, as expected, of liver failure at the age of sixty-two. I'm surprised he lasted that long! That brings down the majority to twelve, then to eleven once we lose the by-election to the SNP (and we'll come fourth). We are in no hurry to call the contest, of course. (Nicky called our candidate, chosen to replace him, an 'unelectable clone'.) On average ten MPs a year die or leave. Half will be ours. Already we have several known to be ill – Geoffrey Dickens has cancer, Jack Aspinwall[169] had serious heart surgery, Julian Critchley's in a wheelchair, though still perkily *compos mentis* if his book reviews are any guide. (He was very dismissive of Lord McAlpine's new novel, *Letters to a Young Politician*.) Others on the green bench don't look as if they'll last to me. So I think we'll be in general election territory by this time next year. This last week Ken Clarke admitted that the 'feel-good factor' could take another couple of years to develop, thus taking us well beyond the election. You'd have thought he was actively planning to lose from the

---

167 PUS for Scotland since 1992; Conservative MP for Eastwood since 1983; MP for East Renfrewshire, 1979–83.
168 Sir Nicholas Fairbairn, Conservative MP for Perth and Kinross since 1983; MP for Kinross and West Perthshire, 1974–83.
169 Conservative MP for Wansdyke since 1983; MP for Kingswood, 1979–83.

reaction. It didn't help, of course, that in his efforts to boost confidence he spoke of the booming industries of Consett, including steel (closed fifteen years ago) and a nappy factory (folded 1991). He's so laid back, is Ken, that he probably hadn't read his brief – or bothered, indeed, to ask for one, and remembered bits vaguely from DTI days.

It makes you want to tear your hair out. In an article in the *Sunday Times* today Roy Hattersley, who has spent twenty out of his thirty years as an MP in opposition, warned those Tories who yearn for a short cathartic period out of government that it's frustrating and depressing out there. Yet it should have been a grand week, for unemployment is down again on a strong, steady trend, and Toyota announced the hoped-for £200 million expansion at Burnaston, to give a thousand more jobs next year. It won't be the Carina, which is a bit of a flop, but a new Corolla – so very good news indeed for South Derbyshire. Even if they throw me out at the polls, I'll have done something there to bring long-term prosperity.

I've no doubt now, and neither has anyone else, that Labour will win the next election. And we'll be out a long time. The nice people will drift away to run their businesses – they already are doing so – and the nasties will remain, with Portillo at their head, and eat away at the Party till they're transformed it into a parody of its former self, an anti-Europe, small-minded, snide little negation of a party, which could do even worse at the election after this. I can't help but admire Blair's courage, determination, clarity of language and firmness of purpose. He's acting like a PM already, and even Tories think so.

Gwynneth Flower came to dinner at the House of Commons on Wednesday and was most entertaining. She is handsome and tall but now *clearly* transsexual – anyone that sexy wouldn't sit so demurely, for example. Her conversation was full of sexual remarks and references, mostly uttered in a high braying voice which made other diners turn round in curiosity – I spent most of the meal in fits of embarrassed giggles. I told her to write everything down, and when she's ready, in maybe five years' time, she could publish an autobiographical account. Her views on a woman's world in particular would be very intriguing – Jan Morris was and is operating in a much easier profession, journalism and literature, whereas Gwynneth was a very macho bloke and is successful as a female in a very macho world still. She said wistfully she could understand why 'Jeff's wife' was so upset, for 'Jeff' (her previous incarnation) was rather gorgeous. How very amusing: and how deeply tragic, all of it, underneath. She has men friends, full sex etc. – but the moment they realise the truth they vanish. Her best male friend is gay. She's too sexy for her own good, I wanted to tell her. Being female involves more disappointment and rejection than she realises.

Victoria, Thursday 30 March, 10.20 p.m.

Absolutely *whacked*. The tablets may be working, but I can still overdo things! The promotion effort for *A Woman's Place* has been horrendous: successful, I hope, but then it's a lot easier to sell at £5.99 than ten quid dearer. I was at the Ideal Home Exhibition today doing virtually a 'Roll up – roll up' act; we shifted 'em at the rate of one every two minutes. Satisfying.

And I managed at last to get Chapter 22 done, the resignation. The ending is really tearful – the PM in love with her – and the actual resignation, the collapse of will, is exactly how it happened. I didn't go and talk or moan to anybody in December '88. Perhaps if I had, I might have rallied some support. Michael Jack[170] (now Fisheries Minister and the chap who took my place in April '92, a pleasant, unobtrusive, forgettable sort of chap) asked why I didn't retract. The answer's twofold: (1) I didn't want to; (2) I couldn't anyway, as I was prevented from speaking. I've made 'Bampton' stupider and crueller than Ken, but I guess comparisons will be drawn. Hope the lawyers let it stay.

Anyway we're in striking distance of 'THE END' – hooray! At 176,000 words done (or around 90 per cent) I should finish over Easter. Deadline is when Richard returns from Liège, as I have to start editing then. All being well, I'll be in the new flat.

I now actively dislike and deride the House of Commons. I'm not alone – yesterday was an Opposition Day debate on education, yet for much of the time only two Labour MPs were in the Chamber.

---

170 Conservative MP for Fylde since 1987.

If I want to get a point across, I do TV or radio – I certainly don't waste my time in debates trying to get called. The whole place is becoming devalued. It is wearing and stressful to attend a job day by day when I feel such active distaste – for the main activities, the ethos, the style and the people. If you're not happy at work, it shows.

House of Commons, Thursday 27 April, 6.25 p.m.
First draft of *A Woman's Place* complete! 202,000 words, finished last Sunday lunchtime. Richard said Chapter 25 was 'extraordinary – almost too strong', and that as he read it he realised I wasn't restricted to writing about politics but could write about anything.

Most of the stuff in The Nightingales now unpacked. I slept there for the first time last Thursday (20th) and all this week. Kitchen, bathrooms, heating and hot water all fine. Bookcases erected – well, some of them. I can find most things in my study and work there. Ceiling lights remain to be fixed, but I am threatening that if I have to do that I'll fuse the whole block. Neighbours moving in. Posh automatic doors on car park a bonus, but kept me out for two days! Clare brought flowers, Richard Californian bubbly. I've cooked several meals – grill is brilliant after the smoky mess at the Tower House and I didn't have one at all at Carlisle Place. Fridge and freezer full. Dishwasher and washing machine operational. Phone in (need to get one more handset). At present only furniture is bed (they delivered two – hopeless!) and two tables urgently bought from IKEA (good) and Argos (rickety). More serious stuff comes next week. Have to get carpets. Curtains are ordered. And so on...

What a business, moving house and finishing a novel at the same time. Yet the burden *has* lifted, for now I'm not tiptoeing around Ray all the time. As I rather expected, when I don't see him I don't think about him.

Portsmouth, Friday 5 May, 9 p.m.
Baking hot day: the air in central London sticky and yellow with fumes which made my throat itch.

Yesterday's local elections were grotty. Overall (England and

Wales, not London, not Scotland) we lost 2,027 seats out of 4,000 defended and are now in control in only eight councils. Labour got most of them (1,500), and won some from the Liberals as well (who had 800 gains). We lost places like Basildon and South & Mid Bedfordshire. In Derby we had six seats to defend and lost the lot. Nationally Blair got 47 per cent, we had 26 per cent and Liberal Democrats 25 per cent. So our percentage was even lower than in the Euros. What also struck me is that some of our pledges are lying to us. In Chellaston we were running at 47 per cent all day – and they're competent canvassers – so we should have won, given that we count only known pledges. Yet we lost quite heavily. We've always rather assumed that people would lie to the pollsters and tell us the truth. Now, I fear, it's the other way round.

I predict we could be left with fewer than 200 MPs after the election. If the odds and sods get fifty or so, then Blair will go to 400 – and a majority of around 150. Not impossible: that was the 1983 result when we had a majority of 144, simply because the opposition was split down the middle. The same could happen again, with Blair taking 45–50 per cent overall (Scotland is heavily his, and London is more Labour than much of England), while Tories and Lib Dems split the rest evenly and disastrously. Mine would go, of course.

What a dismal way to face the next eighteen months or so. Yet I feel curiously philosophical and resigned about it. There's nothing whatever we can do, and if by some miracle we were elected we'd be just as hopeless at government as we are now. Clueless! How ironic that in our search for a classless society we Tories came so downmarket as to choose as our leader a man with no education; and the end result will be the elevation of Blair, public school and Oxford, class oozing from every middle-brow pore.

Nor would things improve if we changed Major for somebody else. Much too late for that. Polls indicate there'd be no lift in our popularity. Portillo is arrogant, and a hypocrite, and far too right wing for the country; and Ken Clarke is also incompetent – he got into a mess this week for not reading his brief, which led him into contradicting the PM – and he's a bruiser. Gill Shephard and Brian Mawhinney are the names now being tossed about, but neither is front rank, I think. Gill would be a competent stopgap, but she doesn't think women with young children should work – so much for recognising the aspirations of today's families. Mawhinney is ambitious and wants it, but he's a fundamentalist Christian (voted for 21) and a Protestant Ulsterman, a lay preacher of the kind who gives me the willies. OK if you keep him away from any social engineering, but bad news (for example) in education or social security. Anyway JM has said repeatedly that if he was challenged he would fight, though I suspect he's forgotten what he'd be fighting for, except merely to retain office. A contest would split us down the middle and set candidate against candidate. In our Party the modernisers (me *et al*) have lost, I'm afraid, and instead of imposing an electorally attractive stamp on us all as Blair has done with his lot, the PM just goes for the easy option of appeasement of the rebels (who are back in, with the whip rammed down their throats) and a silly grin on his face.

I give up. I think I'll put a bet on Labour. Then at least I will win something!

France, Monday 8 May, 6.30 p.m.

In Gacé, on the way back to the boat. It's been a baking hot day and now is a balmy, slightly breezy evening. I'm in the grove of pollarded trees off the main road, surrounded by birds; a group of children in shorts and T-shirts and their parents wend their tired but happy way home; from an upstairs window in an old house an old lady regards me curiously. In every village the flags are flying and flowers adorn the war memorials. For today is the fiftieth anniversary of the end of the war.

I couldn't bear it in the UK. The tone was so triumphant and backward-looking – harking back to the days when we beat the Germans and lorded it over an empire, when Churchill (single-handed) was the saviour of freedom. Yet – within three months of VE Day Churchill was defeated as the people voted *not* to go back to the old days; within nine years (1954) the Japanese had overtaken the UK in shipping tonnage launched; by 1955 there was already talk of the German economic miracle. That was also the year we pulled out of the Messina talks, which led to the Treaty of Rome. While other countries built a new Europe we sat back, convinced we were invincible and indispensable, whereas our behaviour proved the opposite.

The celebration in Parçay-les-Pins showed up some of these points. The Mayor is also President of the *conseil-général*, which covers fifteen communes including Mouliherne. He heard of my comments that it was sad nobody celebrated the Liberation of August 1944, counted Parçay's pennies and set to. Mass was at 9.30 a.m. (still getting dressed with a hangover), then speeches, presentation of medals, the Last Post, laying of wreaths and bouquets on the war memorial (all flowers: red, white and blue) and the band and a *troupe* of real soldiers from the barracks in Saumur whose captain is a local man – and the children and balloons and racing pigeons released, and a *vin d'honneur* or three, and a big well-stocked buffet down in the Salle des Fêtes supervised by Nicole from the café looking cheery, fat and harassed. Even an accordionist and much cheery jigging about, French-style. Hilarious! The band played the 'Marseillaise' and several jolly marches with gusto and a complete lack of musical sense – the two saxophonists were both badly out of tune, and only the elderly band leader who played the cornet had any command of his instrument. It was clear each player had his own idea of the French national anthem, and that they never practised (or at least, not together). The Mayor had insisted on inviting every English family he could lay hands on in the area including those in *gîtes*, who probably thought this sort of thing happened every holiday. He then wanted a speech from me, and our own national anthem. Problem: the band could manage 'Land of Hope and Glory' but not 'God Save the Queen'. A tape had been brought from England. At the last moment the tape recorder refused to function. So at his insistence all the Brits (including two magnificent kilted Scots sporting their national service medals, and who were both respectfully addressed as 'Colonel' by every Frenchman in sight) lined up by the mike and in some embarrassment sang it without accompaniment. And then the French applauded us. Oh, my. Well, it all made for a moving moment, and as I said to them, 8 May '45 ushered in an extraordinary era, of peace and friendship between nations: we thank those who bequeathed it to us, and pass it on with enthusiasm to our children.

The weekend offered an unexpected bonus: yesterday (Sunday) was the second, final round of the French Presidential elections. To everyone's surprise the Socialist Lionel Jospin topped the poll on the first round (23 per cent), with Chirac, the favourite, second. Balladur had 18 per cent – he had never seemed comfortable campaigning and had no clear message. Then Le Pen 15 per cent, the Communist 11 per cent, I think, and so on. Le Pen had suggested that the problems of 3 million unemployed could be solved at a stroke by repatriating 5 million immigrants: or rather, the twin and related problems of the *'exclus'* (those cut off from the good things in French life – the homeless, druggies, people on social security etc.) and the high level of unemployment especially among the young. Chirac homed in on this too. After the RPR/UDF right-wing alliance won the national elections two years ago Chirac refused to be PM, installed his pal Balladur as a safe pair of hands, and set off to discover modern France. As a result his remarks, especially a speech in February, struck a real spark especially with young people who formed up enthusiastically for him ('JAC = Jeunes avec Chirac' on lots of cars, posters etc.).

So I contacted the RPR office in Saumur and was invited to join in. What a lark! From 4 p.m. till the polls closed at 6 p.m. I sat in the polling station at the Théâtre in Place de la République. Then I watched as the box was emptied and the count commenced. As soon as ours was done (55 per cent for Chirac – but would it be enough? Saumur always voted right of centre), we went to the Mairie in the lovely old building on the *quai*. The place was packed and sweltering with excitement and fear. Jospin was a dangerous man, I was told, a real old-time Socialist of the old school. In his last speech he had promised everybody everything including tax cuts. This would tempt voters elsewhere. A big TV screen broadcast the debate in Paris – the tension mounted – the results were relayed, one polling station at a time, by computer to Paris – then at 8 p.m. a silhouette flashed on the screen – who was it? Who would rule France for the next seven years into the next century? Then everyone started screaming and jumping up and down and the Gaullists were chanting, *'On a gagné! On a gagné!'* and everybody was kissing everyone else – and I'm not sure I remember much after that! We made our way to the Château, where the party started as soon as the Saumur Mayor arrived – he's RPR and a Senator and going places, handsome and young and nice. Loads of alcohol and food and horns blowing – the students, led by the Mayor's son, arrived and danced around wrapped in the tricolour – I was presented with a bottle of special edition Chirac champagne and kissed repeatedly – *oh, là là.* Driving home was an experience: I felt like Damon Hill until I realised I couldn't overtake the car in front as I'd forgotten how. And my head this morning…

It showed me why we'll lose. Nobody feels that way about us at all. Especially not young people. And without them we have no future – only nostalgia and unpopularity. A weekend to remember.

Clapham, Friday 26 May, 10 p.m.

What I ought to be doing is putting up the living room curtains, but I'm tired and full of steak, salad and 'chunky monkey' ice cream – banana flavour with walnuts and chocolate, utterly wicked. And it has been a long day – opening Willington Station with Bob Horton at 11.30 a.m., then a dash by train to London, finished off and faxed a review of *Stranger than Fiction,* Michael Crick's biography of Archer, sorted out my expenses for 1994/5… I feel brain-dead and capable only of reading an Archer novel.

I asked Richard to check my review and when I received his comments I realised he doesn't condemn the man as I do. They worked together for eighteen years and seven books; Richard doesn't like negative or unpleasant remarks about Jeffrey. Which is odd, as J's moans contributed to R being given the push when the recession began to bite. I don't suppose J realised, and wasn't being vindictive, just his usual overweening and insecure self. But (even though J kept him as a freelance editor) his criticism started R going downhill. If it were me, I'd be bitter. I'd certainly have had long conversations with Crick – yet R refused.

Personally I think Archer is ghastly. Not just a fool and a rogue, but a miserable liar. If he seldom acts with malice, he as seldom displays honesty or integrity. In politics that's dangerous – one wonders exactly what he'll get up to next.

It was fun opening the new station, which is part of the new Ivanhoe line from Derby through Burton to Leicester and Loughborough. We are reintroducing to passengers a line cut to freight by Dr Beeching only thirty-five years ago. Bob Horton, the Chairman of Railtrack (who I met years ago at BP), looking fatter, greeted me with a hug, to the amusement of Mavis Davidson, and other Willington Tories gathered to watch. Yesterday was another coup, when Roads Minister John Watts[171] opened the Derby southern bypass, £30 million worth. Two years from now we'll have most of the M6–M1 link open. The economic effect in South Derbyshire should be dramatic.

I've been in the press a lot this last week or so – partly coincidence, such as 'Relative Values' in the *Sunday Times* which was set up two months ago, and partly because I got bored with the endless grind of editing and accepted a couple of commissions: *The Guardian* (£250) last Saturday on the whips' office (Michael Cockerell's TV study was on Sunday night), *Sunday Express* (£1,000) about the wonderful TV series *The Politician's Wife* with Juliet Stevenson and Trevor Eve, who are both spot on – they even look like the Mellors and Norrises. ('Chatterley', the adulterous minister in *A Woman's Place*, has now become 'Mellis'. Both Richard and Clare like that. I think it's a bit cheap, but my readers may think it's rather clever!) Then the *Sunday Times* (£500) came up with the Archer, and 1,000 words on the front page next week all being well, so who could resist that? And Barbara Kelly wanted me to give a big speech on 8 June for £3,000. Flush with cash, I doubled my investment in RCB from £5,000 to £10,000. Then the speech fell through. Oh well, I can manage. And it did boost him at a tricky time.

We met here and talked Monday and Wednesday – editing demands constant contact – and I still find his mental approach marvellous.

After he'd gone on Wednesday I realised my chest and throat were hurting and my pulse was up: I was heading into a full-blown infection-induced asthma attack, the kind I only get under extreme stress. Last time was May/June 1993 when I was getting no rest, and worrying about *A Parliamentary Affair* and Maastricht etc. So I

---

171 Conservative MP for Slough since 1983.

bunged myself full of Distaclor and slowed down a bit – which is why I'm sitting here quietly, not heaving away at the curtains. I've no desire to end up in hospital with pneumonia.

What it made me realise is how much stress the separation is causing me. My own failure has been long drawn out, slow, almost dull, but it's still been an ending and made me very sad. (It also causes endless problems of detail such as addresses for banks, and generally keeping it a secret. And having four houses, three washing machines, three faxes etc. makes life complicated, drains energy and takes time.) Brussels would have solved a lot of problems – plenty of money, a good lifestyle, new friends and a new role in life, a lover or two etc. Yes, that would have been fine – it was a good plan. What wasn't, was to lose.

I would feel better too if RCB was in a sounder state. But *Hitler*[172] was published in a ham-fisted way with no trumpeting or publicity – Richard was just so thrilled to get it out and so pleased with his coup. It's hardly been reviewed and subscriptions have stopped at 3,000: enough to make a small profit, but it should have made millions and now won't. The Patrice Chaplin[173] book is going to lose him £40,000. It isn't a proper biography, only a pen portrait, so has been turned down by agents in the USA. Richard is very crestfallen and says he was 'too soft', but he could easily have offered a contingent contract – Patrice was never going to go elsewhere with her tale of woe. His doings in fact make me realise just how well paid I've been – the serialisation offers for several RCB books are less than £1,000. He has taken on too many, in my view, and needs to concentrate harder to make each a success: and I itch to run that office for him, as his staff are useless. Silly things make them seem so amateurish – like not being able to work the fax properly – his call I.D. at present is 'Vickery & Co', as nobody knows how to change it! I made Richard laugh on Thursday (coffee in Selfridges) by saying that if there were an election next month and we lost, Clare and I could march into 7 Manchester Square and sort them out.

---

172 *The Death of Hitler* by Ada Petrova and Peter Watson, the first book published by Richard Cohen's new company.

173 A biography of Oona Chaplin, Charlie Chaplin's wife, by her former daughter-in-law.

Tower House, Sunday 11 June, 11 a.m.

And there was I thinking it had been a good week. Monday was the official launch of RCB at the Globe Theatre, which went very well: Redgraves everywhere, Lisa, Giles Gordon, Simon Hoggart doing the vote of thanks. The Redgrave book has had excellent reviews, though sales are poor – probably because there's been a plethora of Redgrave books including one by Deirdre, Corin's first wife, which wasn't very flattering!

On Wednesday we relaunched the 'Britain in Europe' campaign for the European Movement: good press, went off well, and there was a distinct sense all week of the pro-Europeans fighting back. The Double Eight dinner on Wednesday was predictable – depressing yet comforting, with Ian Taylor (now a DTI minister) telling us that nobody in government takes the slightest notice of the PM any more. Heseltine won't force a contest, but would stand if there was a vacancy. Hezza was in fact in South Derbyshire on Friday afternoon for a tea party. He was on good form: spoke twenty minutes without a note, thoughtful and interesting, and looks very well. The first question was, 'Michael, how is your health? What do your doctors say?' Trust South Derbyshire to be direct! He did not flinch, but answered that he was fine, and no more damage would be done by a full return to work than by retirement. I noted, however, that he had no evening engagements and was going home after a relatively light day. 'Friends for dinner,' he said as he left.

A Woman's Place comes on apace: the week in France was very fruitful, as I cleared up to and including Chapter 12. I hope to have most of it done before I go to Washington on 28 June, though we'd all have to get a move on to do that. However, as I've agreed to babysit Deb's house and cat 20 July to 4 August, and not go to France till all done, the timetable isn't slipping too much.

I thoroughly enjoyed my other activities last week, which also included more on Gulf War Syndrome – Select Committee on Defence grilling the MoD doctors again to my great pleasure, and a breakfast planning session at the Royal British Legion on Thursday, the side table piled high with sticky cakes to the great amusement (and disappointment) of the ex-soldiers present who had been expecting bacon and eggs – and so had I. (And I lost 5lbs from the 11 stone recorded in the gym on Monday morning, and have behaved ever since. I *will* get that saddle off. I do feel far more in *control*. That's what made it a good week.)

Deb's angry riposte to Lynda Lee-Potter[174] was published with a photo, half the letters page, with the headline 'Why Edwina is the Best Mum in the World', which made me feel very proud! (It wasn't written with publication in mind, but was first class.) Susie's interview on life with a famous parent was in *Mizz* this week. The photo was lovely, and she sounded well balanced and mature. Susie did, however, indicate an interest in politics as a career. That has implications for me and includes supporting her, both emotionally and financially, and not embarrassing her, e.g. will I want to publish my journals when I'm seventy (plan: to provide pension!) when she'll be forty and possibly at the height of her career? She's so able she could do anything, and that creates an obligation on my part.

Meanwhile the government continues in deep doo-doo, with the polls showing Labour ahead by almost *40 per cent*: they've been 20 or more points ahead for nearly eighteen months – pre-Blair – and the PM's approval rating has been below 25 per cent for over two years.

Clapham, Tuesday 20 June, 9.15 p.m.
Yesterday I took over as Chairman of the CGE at its AGM. My speech was a rehash of one I had prepared for a debate in the House but was never called to give. It'll be rehashed tomorrow in another Euro debate in the Commons; if I'm called it'll be the first time this year. Yet the media identify me with the cause – shows how irrelevant Parliament has become in the face of competition from TV etc.

The Party is now seething with serious talk about getting rid of JM. Several things have occurred in quick succession. Ten days ago the barmy Baroness launched a full-scale promotion offensive for the second volume of her memoirs, giving TV interviews at her most ferocious – attacking the government (mostly correctly) but worse,

---

174 Lynda Lee-Potter had written that it must be awful to be one of EC's children.

reminding everyone what charisma is all about. On Tuesday out of the blue Michael Heseltine is on his feet, sanctimoniously and amazingly blowing the whistle on arms to Iraq and Jonathan Aitken. The Scott Report is nearly ready and is being leaked all over. Hezza intends he'll emerge clean. The result is that MPs' sleeves are being plucked by constituents who still prefer him and can't figure out why we chose John (because he wasn't Hezza, of course). Also on Tuesday the Fresh Start group, approximately fifty MPs anti-Europe, went to see the PM. When he wouldn't give in to their demand and rule out a single currency forever they harangued him, then came out spitting tacks and talking of a dream ticket of Hezza–Portillo: i.e. withdrawing their support. As the Hezza bandwagon began to roll, however, they got scared and began to backtrack and say we should support the PM. The Party at present does not present an edifying spectacle.

How might it happen? And would it make any difference? Well, on today's performance at Prime Minister's Questions John might just throw in the towel. He was average (i.e. not good enough), but our side were dire, with quotes about 'losing your head' (Kipling) and 'The dogs bark but the caravan moves on' (*sic*) which produced much Labour hilarity. We did look a shambles, even to ourselves. (Virginia did Health Questions beforehand in a virginal white suit, the effect spoiled by frantic red fingernails. So now she not only sounds insincere, but looks it, too.) A reshuffle is due soon: Douglas Hurd has said he's had enough, Hanley must be moved, ditto Virginia. They all look *so* tired.

The House of Commons today was full. 'They've scented blood,' murmured Michael Fabricant at my side. The battle ain't over yet, but it won't be long now, I hope.

Clapham, Monday 26 June, 11 p.m.

I don't know whether it's always a good thing to be close to the centre of events. It leaves me deeply uncomfortable, as if one false move or word, quite inadvertent, might tip matters the wrong way – like the character in the story who goes back in time and crushes a butterfly, only to find on returning to his own time that he's changed the course of events entirely. Not that I matter at all, which is both a relief and a source of wry reflection. *If* John Major had offered me a job in December 1990 – or a proper job in 1992 – if I'd done well – I'd have been in the Cabinet by now – and who knows?

On Thursday JM dropped a bombshell: he would resign as leader of the Party (but not as PM) and force a leadership election. Backbenchers were told the news at the 1922 Committee, in the form of a letter from the PM to the Chairman, Marcus Fox. It was clear that about half those present knew what was coming, and dutifully banged their desks. I didn't. It was clear what the PM *thought* he was doing: putting our backs against the wall, in what I regarded angrily as a form of blackmail. So 'loyalists' were delighted that he was at last going to nail his critics, Eurosceptics and press alike, by trouncing any opposition and reasserting his authority in triumph. Who, indeed, would stand against him? No one of significance. Thus his victory, and enhanced status, were assured.

The next day it started to unravel. Douglas Hurd announced his resignation. It was intended to be helpful to the PM, I guess, as clearing the decks a bit, but instead it looked as if Hurd thought the game was up. Then serious names began to be tossed around as possible candidates to stand against John, such as Norman Lamont – ex-Chancellor, and a stalking horse of some weight. And today, after days of fevered speculation, a cool John Redwood resigned from the Cabinet and declared himself a candidate, surrounded by cheering Eurosceptics, with Lamont at his side looking very pleased with himself – Redwood has promised him a Cabinet post.

Redwood won't win, but he can deliver a mortal blow. Three hundred and twenty-nine MPs can vote: the PM has to take 50 per cent + 15 per cent, i.e. two hundred and fourteen to be the technical winner outright. I think he'd attempt to carry on, even without the support of one-third of the Parliamentary Party, and it would take more resignations and the most almighty row to unlatch his fingers from the reins of power. But if the first ballot is indecisive, both Hezza and Portillo would be keen to elbow JM out of the way, so I can't see him surviving.

The main loser from Redwood's pre-emptive strike is Portillo, who has been looking very glum all day. The gainer I think is Hezza, as there's no love lost between Redwood and Portillo and it's unlikely one would stand down in favour of the other. So the right is split. Redwood has been very resentful of the attention given to Portillo, whom he regards as a bit flash; and I suppose he's had his fill of Wales, anyway. He was peeved, understandably, when after a long private conversation with Major on Wednesday he wasn't told till 4 p.m. Thursday, and then by Michael Howard: as a Cabinet minister he felt he deserved better. (Nothing was said at Cabinet Thursday morning.) This lack of attention to detail is typical of the PM in recent years.

As for me – I don't want either Redwood or Portillo to win. That would lose us the general election worse than the current incumbent. The only chap who would give Labour a moment's pause for thought is Heseltine, and he's not a candidate – yet.

It is so extraordinary – in the last ten years I've been close to two men and each is in crisis this last week or so. One's been left by his wife (Ray) – though it only just seems to have dawned on him – and one's about to be abandoned by his Party (John).

In addition, poor Richard has just split with his wife. He had in fact left just as I was writing my last diary piece. He's staying in Belsize Park with the Garlands[175] – the new Mrs Garland is a therapist, so understands he needs to be left alone; and next week he moves into a flat near work. He intends later to get somewhere closer to the family in Wandsworth (that's what he should have done right away – he does make life harder for himself).

House of Commons, Wednesday 5 July, 12.35 a.m.

I'm in the Library: if I do a little work, no sooner will I settle but the bells will go, whereas if I drift into the tea room it'll take hours. We're voting on the Pensions Bill, a long, complex and necessary reform both to protect pension funds after the Maxwell raid and to raise the state pension age to sixty-five for women. Their Lordships have hung goodies on it like the proverbial Xmas tree, including the right of divorced women to have a share of their ex's pension (might be useful), while pressure groups want better war widows' pensions etc.

Bell's gone! Now didn't that work like magic? So Major got

---

175 The cartoonist Nicholas Garland and his wife.

218, Redwood 89 and abstentions 21. I was in the end the only MP who didn't vote, apart from Richard Body, who's refused the whip and can't. Unexpectedly high for Redwood, but most of the likely abstainers voted for unity, loyalty and the devil they know. It turned out a pro-European victory, as the PEG gave JM enthusiastic support – I just hope he realises and stays on our side.

My estimate is that the euphoria and relief won't last. If JM showed in normal times half the energy, courage and decisiveness on show this week, there'd have been no contest. If he was as firm with all his opponents… oh well, I won't go on. Off to vote.

House of Commons, Monday 10 July, 10.35 p.m.

After John won, Heseltine became Deputy PM and turfed out the Deputy Secretary[176] to take the most magnificent suite of offices in Whitehall overlooking Horse Guards Parade and the Park. He has access to No. 10 by means of a swipe card, according to a thorough and speedy briefing given to the press – he'd gone scouting around on Monday and Tuesday even before the vote, it appeared. The general view is that he has taken over.

The low level of abstentions was due to Hezza voting very publicly for JM at 2.30, to be followed soon after by twenty to thirty Heseltinies who also ostentatiously showed their ballot papers. That a deal had been struck could not have been clearer, though of course denied by all and sundry. The reshuffle confirms a shift back to the centre: most of the new ministers are loyalists, though James Cran comes in just to maintain balance (but not Bernard Jenkin,[177] who's much more able). Two women are in – Angela Knight[178] and Cheryl Gillan,[179] both of whom I profiled in a recent article, but still no female whips.

Clapham, Thursday 13 July, 11.25 p.m.

I delivered *A Woman's Place* yesterday, haring round London in a taxi laden with folders. Lisa I'd missed – she went on holiday yesterday for a fortnight. Sue Fletcher did not have time to see me – 'still

---

176 A senior civil servant.
177 Conservative MP for Colchester North since 1992.
178 Conservative MP for Erewash since 1992.
179 Conservative MP for Chesham and Amersham since 1992.

at lunch' said an aide, though it was 4 p.m. Only Richard made me feel a bit special, telling me it was wonderful, amazing, he was deeply impressed etc! He wants to take me out to celebrate on Sunday night, after he comes back from the Archers' summer party in Cambridge. Only he knows how I had to pull out all the stops to finish on time. And I know what he went through, too: he went AWOL for four days (Sunday 2nd to Wednesday 5th last week), just vanished – 'out of London' according to Nick Garland, whom I phoned in some anxiety on Tuesday night (4th). Should I be worried about Richard, I asked? No, was the answer. And so it proved, for he had done the editing, which he produced with a flourish.

Wonderful feeling to have got rid of *A Woman's Place*, though also sad. I know what happens to the characters now: I know how they feel and how far they could get. The daily process of exploring them was immensely satisfying. Now I have loads of other things to do for a bit (including some revision, of course) and hope to read other people's books for at least a couple of weeks!

I was right, I'm sure, about the leadership contest being a big mistake. A *Guardian* poll yesterday suggested we'd moved ahead 1 point (to 25 per cent!), but are now seen as far more divided. Most telling, however, was the PM's own performance on 6 July at a hastily convened victory rally at the Queen Elizabeth II Centre. His speech started off well, but soon became his usual dreary, intellectually vacuous stuff, and I found myself struggling to stay awake. It's no good saying he's no orator – *he* wanted the event: and he simply does not improve. It's adolescent stuff. The content, too, made me squirm: (1) £1,000 vouchers for nursery education, which is the cheapest and scrappiest way to keep a promise to have every four-year-old in a nursery class (now extended to playgroups – hence cheap, but not effective), even as average class sizes climb; and (2) the intention to abolish capital gains tax and inheritance tax, though he didn't know when. Even the attendees looked puzzled at this; it had the sound of a policy made up as the speech was written. And Ken Clarke has rubbished the idea since, so clearly it wasn't a Cabinet decision. But worse: (1) we can't afford to do it, with a deficit still over £35 billion and the economy faltering again; and (2) it appeals to the wrong bit of the electorate, those who'd vote for us anyway as they have too much to lose under a Labour government, instead of (e.g. cuts in income tax) appealing to the middle ground, the skilled working man, who has no worries about capital gains tax or inheritance tax. It makes us look as if we *only* look after our friends. I for one resent that.

Huddersfield, Tuesday 25 July, 8.35 p.m.

Deb's house is a nice place – even better after I'd spent £100 on the garden and taken most of yesterday afternoon to plant roses, buddleia, lavender and pinks, which should survive the most malign neglect. It's been so hot today that the roses got scorched. And the kitchen will show improvement by Thursday too, when the new gas cooker arrives: I couldn't bear to touch this one, it's so disgusting and the grill is burned out. So unless I was prepared to live out of the microwave (also caked in food, but at least that yielded to a good scrub), then it was off to the gas showroom and the cheapest model in the place. I feel virtuous and pushy at the same time. Funny how I've resisted domesticity all my life, but at Clapham, France and now here I'm content. Playing at dolls' houses, I guess.

Saw a huge dolls' house on Sunday and the doll who owns it. I took Mum to Nostell Priory, the nearest National Trust place to here, and we found we'd walked into a huge VE/VJ Day celebration with thousands of Royal British Legion members. Splendid, noisy, packed, cheery, good natured: but we'd only come to see the house, so after fighting our way through we started our tour by gaping at an extraordinary Holbein of Sir Thomas More and his family. It's a fascinating work. And so was the next face we saw – 'Hello, I'm Diana St Oswald' – and Lady St O had been told of our presence and had glided in. Fifties (late), short, dumpy, elegant in dark-blue spotted silk, and with small, pretty feet and a hairstyle identical to the Queen's. We didn't meet 'Derek' but he must be ten years older than her. So we had the works, which was fun: the secret door, the lovely Chippendale furniture opened for us, shown the secret drawers and beautifully matched doors etc. After 250 years everything still fitted and stood sturdily on curved legs: the quality of craftsmanship is breathtaking. At one point Mum, a bit overwhelmed, nudged me and hissed, 'If she offers tea say yes!' – but she didn't, so back we went to the Rose Garden and a dish of ice cream.

Kenny, Deb's (female) cat is *so* cute: a real little madam but with a delightful personality, she gets jealous when I'm working and bats everything on to the floor, then sits plonkingly on my lap. When I'd like her on my lap, she dances away skittishly and won't settle. Good company – she missed her Mum (Deb) on Sunday and yesterday and ignored her food, but like all good cats she rapidly transferred her affections and has been back to normal today. *Sic transit mater.*

Robin Oakley, the BBC political correspondent, was talking on the television news about the Littleborough and Saddleworth by-election, caused by the death of Geoffrey Dickens. It's clear he can't make up his mind who's going to win, or maybe he's been warned to be ultra cautious. I was there today and it looked pretty clear to me as I trudged up and down hills in a broiling sun – *we're* going to lose. We have the most peculiar man as candidate – a perky little local councillor like a small grey mouse, pointed nose and all. He was Dickens's agent for five years and I bet even that was a bit beyond him. The candidate's so dim we stopped having daily press conferences. It was too obvious he didn't understand the questions, let alone know the answers. Energy he has in plenty – he never stopped talking right through lunch, mostly about himself and his exploits on the council. When he got on to Mystic Meg he lost me (this is a character in the lottery draw programme on Saturday nights), but he clearly thought the reference was the height of sophistication. Still, the seat disappears with boundary changes and so will he. More interesting is the battle between the Liberals (who would normally expect to win) and Labour under Peter Mandelson's[180] expert hands, who are chasing hard and with great professionalism – posters everywhere, huge and audacious, show his touch. I'd guess Labour will get it, or be close. I had to see 'waverers' and I doubt if it was a good use of my time: four-and-a-half hours for thirty-eight addresses, of whom two-thirds were definite 'no's. I was told how Nick Winterton whinged about being asked to do the same duty at the weekend and ended up on TV

---

180 One of Labour's chief strategists; MP for Hartlepool since 1992.

declaring we'd lose, so I kept smiling and walking. And as at previous by-elections, not a single local helper, not one.

Colleagues are beginning to jump ship as the new boundaries become effective. George Walden announced yesterday that he's leaving politics deeply disillusioned, fed up with lying to the electorate and treating them like children. His electors think the economy's in a mess, he declared, and they're right. In *Buckingham*? Made a loss on property speculation is what they did and they're still wallowing in negative equity, with a government which won't raise inflation to bail 'em out.

Here in Huddersfield I've been keeping myself busy, rather artificially, as there's no revision to do. Linden is still copy-editing a novel for Richard and won't be able to start on *A Woman's Place* till next week (groan) and then goes on hols on 6 August, if her old cat's well enough to go to the cattery (groan) and if her husband's hand is well enough to drive (groan) as she never learned because (groan, groan)… Bloody irritating, actually. So I asked if she can do a quick skim for me, and the fact is I'll probably have to manage without. Richard is supposed to be looking at it again this weekend but may need nagging, which I hate to do. He was in Holland last week to referee the World Fencing Championships but must have known before he left that Linden couldn't help me much, which is why he's not returning my calls! That's how I know I'm dealing with an unformed adolescent, really… Still, Sue is complimentary, though distant. I just wish somebody else would take the book as seriously as me and not be so *complacent*.

Huddersfield, Tuesday 1 August

It's been horribly hot today, around 90°, so I stayed in till 5 p.m. and cracked on with Sue's revision, which is now basically done.

And Richard is coming to France. I can't quite believe it! 'Twenty-four hours,' he says, by which he means two nights. He will bring half of *A Woman's Place* done and do the rest there, so we'll have to keep our heads down. He has so much to cope with at the moment. His next business plan is due (actually late, just like the last one), and he should be talking to 3i[181] about further equity finance. When

---

181 The venture capital company.

I see him on Monday he'll give me the complete list of fifty-one books accepted by RCB up to 1998, of which he's immensely proud. His first three books have made £30,000 between them and more to come, but it'll all be swallowed up by the loss on Patrice Chaplin's 'biography' of her mother-in-law. The payment was made for world rights on the assumption of USA sales, which never materialised. Richard didn't read it properly and left it to Linden to edit. And the contract was defective, which is unforgivable – the money was payable on *delivery* and there's no mention of *acceptance*, so he could not refuse the manuscript or send it back. He commented ruefully that he's 'too soft' with women.

Meanwhile colleagues are still jumping ship at a rate of knots. The latest is Dudley Fishburn,[182] who's only been an MP since 1988: he's a most able man, associated with *The Economist* and Harvard University, and it was a bit of a puzzle why he wanted to be a lowly MP in the first place. We have too many MPs, he said (from 615 after partition in 1922, soon to rise to 659), and they have too little to do. That's caused great guffaws around the nation, especially following on our apparent change to a three-day week. I loved William Rees-Mogg's comment in *The Times*, that really Fishburn was saying he was bored: 'a willingness to be bored, and sometimes even to be boring, is an asset to a politician'. An asset increasing in value, especially in the current Parliament. There'll be more – Ken Baker is leaving, probably for much the same reason – as the more able souls decide not to sit on the opposition benches next time. Predictably we lost Little and Sad[183] – heavily, but not quite as badly as Christchurch. The Liberals took it with 16,000 votes, an increase of 2 per cent in their share, but Labour were breathing down their necks with 14,000, up from virtually nothing. Our vote was down to 10,000.

Ominous noises from the Balkans as Croatia prepares to go to war over Krajina, a patch of land next to Bosnia occupied by ethnic Serbs, I think. It looks as if Serbs and Croats are about to fight

---

182 Conservative MP for Kensington.
183 The Littleborough and Saddleworth by-election. The Conservative candidate came third.

each other again, trampling over the bodies of Bosnian Muslims as they do so. The Senate voted by a hefty majority to lift the arms embargo and the House of Representatives is debating it today: a green light for open civil war, in my view, and the end to the UN as an effective force for good. I felt almost sorry for the UN negotiator, a Japanese: but what can you expect, since we turned the Japanese into chickens after the war?

Les Tuileries, Thursday 17 August, 2.30 p.m.

Under the partial shade of the hibiscus tree in Mouliherne. Large withered buds keep dropping in my lap – the lovely pink flowers only last a day – and my head is surrounded by lazily buzzing bees. I may go off for a swim later. I feel *very* lucky, and overall generally content.

The new book is a much better book than *A Parliamentary Affair* in many ways: crisper, shorter, tighter, more exciting, the characters disturbingly real. Deb phoned me on Monday evening – 'Mum! It's brilliant!' – full of excitement; she had spent all day reading it and said she could not put it down. Her judgement is much sounder than it used to be, so I *was* pleased. Then Clare wistfully reminded me that she had read Chapters 1–24 and was dying to know the ending…! As for sales – Deb thinks it'll do as well as *A Parliamentary Affair* and Richard thinks better. Hope so – for I've just had my second batch of royalties, £39,000! That could mean *A Woman's Place* keeping the cash flow healthy from spring '94 to '98. I may well need it all by then if I lose South Derbyshire, as I expect to.

I am, as will be apparent from the writing, very tired; two nights this week I've had little sleep, and though I can still function it's not with any grace or talent. Richard, on the other hand, is completely knocked out by sleep deprivation, so the poor thing is probably right now on a plane to Mauritius or Milan rather than to London, if his previous travelling experience is any guide. He was supposed to come Monday evening – had to fly and then missed the TGV. Not smart. He didn't spot there was another forty-five minutes later, and a third just after midnight, but instead took the *slow* train (11 p.m.), arrived in Le Mans at 1.30 a.m., phoned (was I glad to hear from him!) and had to take a taxi which eventually reached here at 3 a.m. at a cost of 800F (over £100). The intelligent thing to do would have been to stay at Montparnasse overnight, get a good night's sleep and pop down here first thing in the morning – but no, not him. If there's a hard way to do it, he will.

He'd *said* he'd arrive with half of the book done for final edit, but of course he didn't. So I put my foot down, knowing where the weaknesses were, and we've dealt with these, just about. I resisted the idea of his starting at page 1, we'd never have finished – and demanded he prioritise. Given the clash between two perfection-ist personalities which followed, it's amazing we ended up working together at all. I suppose I should be grateful!

I brought a new laptop computer to France with me and succeeded in converting from the old one, virtually by myself – a couple of phone calls to Clare sufficed, whereas I'd been expecting endless problems. Then to my delight I got Richard in front of the old one, and within ten minutes he was playing with it and mutter-ing 'amazing' under his breath. He has taken it with him! One of his hobbies now is writing children's stories about a sports-mad slug called 'Henri'. The next one will be written on the computer, all being well. Progress! I also taught him how to heat up his break-fast orange juice in the microwave... *and* ironed his shirt. Boy, is he *stubborn*: persuading him to try or permit something new and unfamiliar is like climbing Kilimanjaro by your fingernails...

He continues to have trouble in his office for similar reasons. He *needs* a good administrator/secretary, so he's freed to edit. He keeps taking on dotty young girls – not a harem, but a coterie of gigglers – and regales me proudly with tales about this one or that one who wants to come and work for him. Idiot, say I, you aren't ready to be a pupil-master just yet; none of your staff would last five minutes in *my* office.

Switzerland, Tuesday 29 August, 10 p.m.

The end of a very pleasant few days with Susie, and nearly the end of the summer. We've 'done' Geneva very thoroughly since I arrived Saturday lunchtime: lunch on a boat on Lac Léman, then stroll around town trying (fruitlessly, partly) to get tickets; on Saturday night we saw an American production of *Hair*, on Sunday we went to Genève Plage and sunbathed, then to the marvellous Circus Knie – and last night to a movie, *The Usual Suspects*, which was excellent; Monday a bus trip up to Les Diablerets, where (instead of glorious sun and a fabulous view of mountains and glacier) it snowed hard at a temperature of –5°C, and today (Tuesday) on a two-hour train snaking up more mountains to Gruyères: damp and cold, but pretty, and predictably we ate fondu and had enough cheese to keep us content for a month.

Tower House, Wednesday 6 September, 5.30 p.m.

I'm feeling tired. Mostly, I suspect, because of the tablets, or lack of them: when I'm off the noresthisterone like this week, I'm whacked by 4 p.m. Now I know what it's like to be a normal woman, and I don't like it! The oestrogen alone is not enough: I need both, lower doses. It would be nice if I could just take them each morning for the rest of my life and not have these uncomfortable breaks, when I feel so sleepy and headachy all the time.

Alan Amos,[184] who was cautioned after gambolling on Hampstead Heath in 1992 and didn't contest the election (the incident I used in *A Woman's Place*), has joined the Labour Party and wants to be a Labour MP. I heard his flat, deadpan voice on Radio 4 yesterday morning saying, 'If you go to a Conservative Party Conference the only way you can get applause from the moronic majority is by bashing foreigners or by attacking minorities. I find that distasteful.' Does he, now? I don't recall him speaking up for minorities such as gays in the last three years. He could easily have expressed support for the age of consent debate, even privately, as Harvey Proctor[185] did. Mr Amos reckons he was stabbed in the back at the time of his resignation. Michael Brown said that wasn't true; several key people including Portillo and Gummer tried to help him, and Gummer even employed him after the election, paid, to help him find his feet. So in my view he's an unpleasant little twerp who simply wants to be an MP for any party which will have him,

---

184 Conservative MP for Hexham, 1987–92.
185 Former Conservative MP for Billericay, 1983–7; MP for Basildon 1979–83; exposed in a scandal involving homosexual sado-masochistic practices.

and hang any sincerely held views. I hope they squash him and his ambitions firmly!

Meeting Michael Brown was interesting, in fact. I'd been chased since March by Tony Hutt, one of the Tory gay activists, to come to supper with him and his partner Kenny who is an airline steward (and the original of Kenny in Michael Dobbs' *To Play the King*). I thought it would be cosy and laid back – in fact the table creaked with crystal, porcelain and delicately arranged flowers, and ten of us sat down to a splendid dinner cooked by the fastidious Kenny: aubergine and peppers in olive oil with fresh (warm) walnut bread; *salade tiède* with chicken livers; poached salmon with very pretty vegetables including the latest delicacy, a seaweed which resembles green beans (not bad, but why bother?); lovely cheese and raspberry tart with sour cream (or was it quark?) custard; coffee; mints, port etc... Jolly nice – I did feel pampered. Michael's current boyfriend is twenty-one years old, extremely handsome – dark hair and eyes, very pretty. Not sure whether it's the same chap he was caught with at twenty last year when it was still technically illegal – 'when I had my trouble', as Michael put it. Gummer helped him too, and phoned Michael's mother and talked to her for twenty minutes about what a good guy he was. (Yet he couldn't bring himself to vote for 16: rum!) It was so curious: nobody asked about Ray, as if it was quite normal not to be partnered. Will I have to tell anyone? Will I have to explain? Not yet, anyway, though I had steeled myself to do so last night to Tony and Kenny, if necessary, and was amused and relieved when the question did not arise.

Goodness, the future seems so uncertain – yet I just feel faintly exasperated about that, rather than scared. To complicate matters Richard phoned on Sunday morning while I was at the gym and got only a very curt Ray; he'd said he was just starting out on a journey to the airport on the way to New York and would call again, but didn't. *Exasperating.*

Clapham, Monday 2 October, 3.45 p.m.

What I *should* be doing is proofreading *A Woman's Place*, which arrived from the printers last week. But if I do, I'll doze off. Foolishly I worked till 12.45 a.m. on a review of Betty Boothroyd's life by Paul Routledge for the *Sunday Times* (fascinating but elusive subject, slapdash biographer). And at 5.30 p.m. I'm being collected to go and have dinner and speak at the RAF Staff College in Berkshire. So doing my diary, which has been gathering dust for a month, is both just and a suitable penance.

Actually I've been waiting to figure out what's happening with Richard. I kept sending faxes with dates to meet and he appeared to ignore them. By last Monday (25th) I'd had enough. He'd cancelled the one evening I'd stayed in for him. We'd had one half-hour chat on the phone: and that was it. All good intentions but no action. So I turned up at his office on Monday morning with various papers he wanted: and he was all charm, leaping around full of smiles. He hadn't got any of my faxes, none of them, because the machine had been on the blink for weeks. Then the sweet boyish smile, asking to be forgiven. 'So fix it,' I said, brutally, 'it's your bloody fax. What am I supposed to do?' and I walked out. He phoned as I drove to Derby and I cut him off (all these weeks he could have dialled that number and hasn't). Eventually he persuaded me to see him – Thursday night at Clapham.

We talked about RCB – I think it will be badly affected by the collapse last week of the Net Book Agreement, as it's so seriously undercapitalised and he tends to overtrade in his enthusiasm. It makes RCB a far less likely candidate for the next EC book, even if all other things were equal, which they're not.

The Hodder promotion meeting came and went and a new person entered the frame – Karen Geary, who's their new Publicity Director: slim, clever, dark, business-like, she took me to lunch at L'Etoile. Very nice, but I prefer the authentic French versions *in France*. It's a showbiz place; as we left I was accosted by a small cigar-toting, grey-haired gent who grabbed me, kissed me on both cheeks, waved the cigar and said, 'Loved the performance! Congratulations!' God knows who he thought I was. I flatter myself. Jane Lapotaire? Felicity Kendal?

Susie's now off at Cambridge – Ray took her on Saturday and said she had a nice room and seemed to settle in quickly. I spent this weekend with Deb and managed to spend quite a lot of money.

I was anxious about the terrible tin cans she has been driving, courtesy of Norman, the boyfriend: so, we visited seven garages on Friday night and found a nice little Mazda which will keep her going for a couple of years, from a family garage which will look after her.

Liverpool, Saturday 14 October, 5.40 p.m.

I spent the Conference week at Parrox Hall in Poulton-le-Fylde, which is jammed with original carved English oak four-posters, chests, linen-fold panelling etc. The land has been in the same family since the Conquest and now belongs to Harold Elletson[186] – the neighbourhood's littered with roads and pubs with the family name. 'Never had enough money to ruin it, thank God,' was the comment of a guest at Monday night's opening party, a surprisingly decorous affair attended by lots of MPs and partners – in a few cases, I suspect, not the right ones. We thumped the piano and sang lustily, ate Harold's mother-in-law's goulash and damson fool (made from fruit from the garden), and eventually retired up creaking stairs to damp bedrooms smelling of must and the roses which dripped petals prettily on ancient glossy dressers. Lovely, indeed. A couple of nights as I returned about 1 a.m., I joined in drinking whisky and gossiping around the table, with Harold, Peter Ainsworth,[187] Seb Coe[188] (who is now responsible for youth in the Party, but whose flat personality fails to make anything of a marvellous opportunity) and Cheryl Gillan. Gillan is edgy, endlessly smoking, alternately insecure – 'don't photograph me with a cigarette' (why ever not, since she's always *seen* with them?) – and aggressive – 'I voted for 21. I don't believe anyone should have sex young.') 'Oh,' says I, getting a bit fed up with this – she wasn't joking, and we were all a bit tiddly – 'so how old were you, then, first time?' She giggled: 'Mind your own business, how do you know I wasn't a virgin when I married at thirty-three?' I smiled sweetly. 'Poor you,' I murmured to general chuckles. But Ainsworth, impressively, drew the right conclusion –

186 Conservative MP for Blackpool North since 1992.
187 Conservative MP for East Surrey since 1992.
188 Conservative MP for Falmouth and Camborne since 1992.

'It isn't anybody's business what age adults have sex, or who with, and it shouldn't involve the law.' He and Harold were calm, dignified and good humoured, and both should go far, provided they can hold their seats. They told the tale of a neighbouring MP, Nick Hawkins,[189] who now has the sixth most marginal seat; as he went to be interviewed for a much safer constituency, a local Labour supporter arrived dressed as a chicken and danced around, clucking. This is the 'chicken run', as Tory MPs convinced they'll lose next time in the scramble for safe roosts.

In fact we'll be lucky to see next year out, for the official majority is down to five. (Richard Body has not resumed the whip.) On Sunday last Alan Howarth announced his defection to Labour. What a prize for them – former minister, former Vice-Chairman of the Party and head of CRD, founder member of the 'No Turning Back' Group, with a majority of over 20,000. He doesn't like the 'politics of divisiveness', he said – Labour is now the one-nation party. I was commissioned to do an instant piece for the *Daily Mail*, which I regard as a bellwether paper, and was intrigued that they wanted a sympathetic tone. Alan's been rubbished in a vitriolic way, predictably, especially by Gillian Shephard ('lowered the tone,' Alan sniffed), but it's clear he's suffered a mid-life crisis of massive proportions, having left his wife earlier this year and being seen in restaurants with Labour peer Lady Hollis, whose husband is away in the USA. George Walden put his finger on it – Howarth hasn't joined the Labour Party which we all know and despise, he's joined Tony Blair. That *is* scary, for Howarth is exactly the sort of soft-hearted, middle-class Englishman Blair's keen to lay his hands on. One or two journalists wondered if I'd cross the floor too, but the answer's firmly 'no'. I know too much about Labour, I guess. Unlike Howarth I've seen them in the raw, from Liverpool through local government through mining – pro-CND and anti-European most of the time, whatever they may claim to be now.

---

189 Conservative MP for Blackpool South since 1992.

Clapham, Wednesday 18 October, 2 p.m.

I'm very cross with myself: had most of the day with nowt to do and I've got virtually nothing done.

Anyway, to last week's Party Conference. The most significant event, which has reverberated since, was Portillo's disgraceful speech on Tuesday afternoon. It was the crudest bit of 'Brussels-bashing' I've ever heard; it would have been ghastly from a pimply seventeen-year-old Young Conservative, but from a Secretary of State for Defence it was unbelievable. 'Let Brussels at the army and they'll metricate cap badges!' (The armed forces have been metric for decades.) 'They'll have everyone going home after a forty-hour week!' (They're exempt from employment laws.) 'British soldiers will never fight for Brussels!' (They did just that, fifty-one years ago.) 'But only for British interests!' (Since when? What are we doing in Bosnia?) 'British soldiers will never be commanded by foreigners!' (They are, in NATO, and were in 1944–5.) And so on. More, he seemed to abrogate the bravery of British soldiers and the SAS to himself (muttered fury from uniforms) and ended with 'Who Dares, Wins!' (To which the Redwoodites – and I – responded: 'Well you didn't, did you?') Even Rees-Mogg in *The Times* was disgusted: 'Rabble-rousing... very immature... aggressive rhetoric... make it more difficult for Britain to exercise influence on European policy... gratuitously offensive,' etc.

The pro-Europeans erupted with furious protests – me included. John Gummer, who'd spoken at our CGE lunchtime fringe just before Portillo spoke, was said to have marched up the stairs of the Imperial Hotel and harangued the PM on it: for Portillo's people make it quite clear that No. 10 had seen and cleared the speech, and the PM joined in the seven-minute ovation which followed. The FCO was bombarded with angry queries from the European embassies, and (so I was told by Lutz Hermann from the Foreign Press Association) had to apologise to the German Ambassador. Much spin-doctoring hastily followed – this was only for domestic consumption, the foreigners were told.

Of course there's another agenda at play here. Portillo is still the heir apparent, as he's a much more attractive figure than Redwood, but his decision to stay put in July betokens not his loyalty but calculation, which the faithful are ambivalent about. So it suits Redwood to make Portillo uncomfortable. The question is, who would oppose them from the centre, with a fair chance if both decide to stand – and I can't see either making way for the other? Gill Shephard is my bet: she's shaping up nicely, avoiding controversy in her enhanced department, leaking any Treasury documents which suggest her budget should be cut, and ensuring that teachers get their pay rise in full next spring. Since 'education' is at the top of everybody's agenda, Blair's and Ashdown's too (and the PM spent twenty minutes on it), Gill is set to benefit. Everyone likes her: she comes across as no-nonsense and tough, a more emollient version of Mrs T. The problem for me, however, is that she doesn't appear to have an original thought in her head, nor to have any drive or commitment. This is a languages graduate, a former HMI[190] in languages: where's the push for more and better languages in our schools, starting at seven or eight? There isn't one. Here's a married woman MP who didn't get to Westminster till she was forty-seven – and she's in charge of employment and equality legislation. Where's the drive to get more women into the House of Commons? More women candidates in the Party? More childcare? She doesn't have to make a big fuss publicly if she pushes behind the scenes, but there's not a scrap of evidence that she does: rather the opposite. No inspiration, no sweat, no passion.

Monday I had lunch with Lisa, who is anxious that I don't encourage RCB to think they'll get my book. I agree, I told her sadly. Hey presto, I get back to Clapham and find messages from Richard on the answerphone wanting my correct address. His latest appeal for money has brought in £40,000, 'but most haven't sent their cheques yet'. Wishful thinking, I feel certain; though I've put him in touch with 3i and (now) NatWest, I don't think he has the management skills to convince those johnnies. Lisa says he needs a proper manager at around £40,000+, so that he (Richard) can get on with what he does well, commissioning and editing books and looking after authors.

190 Schools inspector.

Clapham, Monday 30 October, 9.40 p.m.

Today I have a 21-year-old daughter... Doesn't seem like two minutes, really, but what a lot of water has flowed under bridges since. In a way things started to go wrong with Ray not long after, for he was so put off by Deb's birth that he flatly refused to attend Susie's and I had nobody to hold my hand. 'You looked like a road accident,' was all he could say, helplessly, in mitigation (he meant, loads of blood). So *he* was suffering, was he? It was *my* blood. I put the thought grimly away. With two small children I could not even think of an alternative scenario. Not, that is, until they'd grown up: and here we are.

Anyway, the birthday girl hasn't been in touch this weekend, though we spoke during the week. She has decided not to be a teacher, hooray, because several of the other girls on her course will do the PGCE, and 'if people like that are becoming teachers, it's not for me.' They're dim and dull, she means. I talked her through once more the difference between being 'ordinary' and 'special' – how disappointed I'd be if my children decided resolutely to be ordinary, when they are both so bright and talented. In my view that gives them obligations, to *use* their brains to the full, and not just to benefit themselves. Ray, on the other hand, would be perfectly content if they chose to be ordinary.

On Thursday evening I went to see John Osborne's *A Patriot for Me* at the National in the Barbican. Ray would have found its homosexual theme tedious, and in fact I thought that was heavily overdone. It is the story of Alfred Redl, an officer in the Austro-Hungarian army who is blackmailed into becoming a double agent by the Russians, and is finally unmasked and shoots himself: really about the deterioration of a personality – a bit like *The Portrait of Dorian Gray*, I thought. But Osborne was trying to shock both himself and his audience in a very contrived way: lot of scenes in bed with (mostly) men and a girl, all naked, all done in much the same way – watching Wilby[191] put on his trousers got boring the fifth or sixth time, even if he, and all the others, looked lovely without them.

---

191 The actor James Wilby played the leading role.

On 22 October I'd been to the Equality Show at the Albert Hall. I took Susie (looking very glam in a short black silky dress and black tights) and her friend Si (wide eyed in a white shirt, and the typical awful manners of that generation – it never occurred to him to offer his seat to anyone else, though the box was so crowded that some people had to stand). Actually it wasn't nearly as much fun as last year, possibly because it *wasn't* sponsored by Absolut Vodka this time, possibly because there wasn't the frisson of fear as in 1994, when so many people were 'out' for the first time. On this occasion the only fresh face was Michael Barrymore, who looked very nervous when he first came on stage till a wag yelled in a deep voice, 'You were a bit late, but you're very welcome, darling' – which brought the house down. But I realised why I didn't enjoy it all as much – the lesbians have muscled in, and a more tedious bunch than short-haired dykes like Sandi Toksvig in dungarees I can't imagine. Even Lily Savage, who is usually gorgeous in sequins, did a skit from her 'Prisoner Cell Block H', in prison blue dungarees. What makes me catch my breath in admiration, I guess, is men in drag – *how* do they do it, is one question; but also they go much further than any woman would, really go to town, and it's wonderful. Since (again) there was no spouse on my arm, I got the occasional odd look, as if they expected *me* to come out: but, as my curious examination of all that splendid Austro-Hungarian equipment reminded me, I'm only one way inclined; and if I have a wistful expression it's merely because I'm not getting any!

I spent much of today taping the audio book of *A Woman's Place* with Mike Carrington-Wood, who's a most engaging and professional character, married (for twenty-nine years) to one of Jeffrey Archer's old girlfriends. As preparation I've been listening to audio tapes all summer and have just finished Philip Madoc's unabridged reading of *Dr Zhivago* – a magnificent experience: on Friday evening, as I drove to speak in Swindon, I nearly came off the road when Zhivago and Lara listened to the wolves and then she left with Komarovsky – brilliant, tragic, heart-wrenchingly moving. Then Saturday night (while Ray was at Nottingham dogs with his mates) I watched the video of the David Lean film, and awfully good that was too. So I've gorged on Pasternak and feel full of him – I hope it's had a beneficial effect on my rendition of the highly truncated version (18,000 words) of *A Woman's Place*!

Lane End, Nr Wycombe, Thursday 9 November, 7 p.m.

I'm sitting in Otto in a car park, waiting to speak to the Lane End and Piddington branch of Wycombe Conservatives in the village hall. I'm an hour early, but I didn't have anything much to do in London. The things we do for the cause...

In fact I've spent all day on the cause, attending my first NUEC meeting. The attendance was impressive – easily the best-supported Tory meeting I've been at in ages. Less marvellous was the chairing, with Basil Feldman[192] doing his Dalek act. That man has dull black pebbles for eyes, and behaves as if his job is to bat us all away like irritating midges. Much was plain depressing. When I asked what we were planning to do to bring young people in, since the Party's average age of sixty-three is getting to be a teensy bit worrying, he blinked and said he was open to ideas. Crumbs. Mawhinney spoke and was very smooth, to my surprise, smiling a lot and referring graciously to named members of the audience: at Westminster we see only his hard-man side.

Meanwhile what we didn't discuss at CCO, but which coloured every answer given, were the accounts now sent to me as a member of NUEC. What would you do with a political party that has reserves of only £1 million just before an election, and which paid out nearly £900,000 in interest on average borrowings of £13.5 million? These are coming down, they claim, by about £2 million (the surplus) a year, and now (31.3.95) stand at below £12 million. So 'don't expect any early PPBs,' warned Mawhinney, 'and if you want lots of poster sites during the election campaign, I have to have some money.' The Party still owes Saatchi (Cordant) £1.5 million. And they claim financial and economic competence sufficient to run the country?

On Tuesday the Select Committee on Defence reported on Gulf War Syndrome and gave the MoD a real rocket! A string of condemnations – appalled, unacceptable etc. – littered the report, especially over the delays in dealing with the complaints. Michael

---

192 Vice-President of the National Union of the Conservative Party.

Colvin[193] (the Chairman) told me later that Nick Soames (the minister) had spoken to him very arrogantly the night before and said the complainants were only after money, which isn't true: most of them would rather have their health and a decent job. They do not regard having Gulf War Syndrome as akin to winning the lottery.

Eurostar, Sunday 12 November, 11.10 a.m.

On Eurostar, travelling at 300km/h (187mph), on a splendid sunny morning. The train is full of Americans, thrilled at travelling under the Channel, and I must confess I am too. It's superb.

This is just a short break: back Wednesday morning (15th), partly to see the repairs being done at Les Tuileries, partly because I still need to *get away* and to be reminded in France, in that gorgeous house, of all I can achieve when I'm not even really trying. It's a good feeling – relief at not having to be a public person any more (I'm in jeans and no make-up) and pleasure in my own company, in being able to decide for myself exactly what I want to do. For a brief time it's a delicious pleasure, though I'm too gregarious to want it forever. Yet I've been isolated for such a long time without realising it. Talking to Deb by phone Thursday I was telling her about *The Master Builder* with Alan Bates, and how I'd started going to the theatre alone. 'Don't you miss the company? I'd need somebody to talk to about it,' she said. Well yes, a bit, I answered. But in practice I do find people to talk to, in the bar at the interval – and I make a point too of telling the next friend I meet, and of putting some thoughts in my diary. But for years, I now see, I went to the theatre and movies with Ray, and we *never* talked about them – and I never felt confident enough to discuss my reactions with anybody else. In fact I hardly had any conversations other than at work. I certainly don't *feel* half so lonely, or so frustrated, now. Rather content, in fact, though it would be lovely if some nice bloke were sitting opposite sharing my enjoyment.

I've been listening to Branagh reading Pepys's diary. Poor Pepys, so worried about going blind, and driven frantic both by his

---

193 Conservative MP for Romsey and Waterside since 1983; MP for Bristol North West, 1979–83.

Launch of the new Chairman and Vice-Chairman, European Movement, 1995.
L to r: Ming Campbell MP, EC, Professor Alan Watson, Giles Radice MP (chair),
Peter Mandelson MP, Emma Nicholson MP.

With Teresa Gorman MP, Glenda Jackson MP, Liz Lynne MP and Jean Corsten MP,
June 1993.

ABOVE Meeting of Conservative MPs with Prime Minister Rabin of Israel, Jerusalem, July 1993. L to r: Raymond Robertson, Liam Fox, EC, Yitzhak Rabin, David Evennett, Spencer Batiste, Bernard Jenkin, Charles Goodson-Wickes, John Sykes, Nigel Evans.

LEFT With daughter Debbie and Tony Banks MP in Trafalgar Square for the Gay Age of Consent rally, January 1994.

ABOVE House in France, Les Tuileries, in the Loire Valley.

LEFT The Tower House, EC constituency home 1984–97, Findern, Derbyshire.

HARDBACKS

THIS WEEK	General	LAST WEEK	WEEKS ON LIST
1	My Secrets / Joan Collins (Boxtree £14.99) Star's mental and physical plan for happiness and success	2	3
2	Bravo Two-Zero / Andy McNab (Bantam Press £14.99) Story of an SAS patrol behind Gulf war lines in Iraq	1	15
3	Great Railway Journeys / Clive Anderson et al (BBC £16.99) Celebrities take to the iron road — as seen on television	3	4
4	Life In The Freezer / Alastair Fothergill (BBC £18.99) Natural history of Antarctica, accompanied the television series	4	9
5	The Tiny Book Of Hugs / Kathleen Keating (Fontana £2.99) Hugs and cuddles for all occasions	—	8
6	Some Other Rainbow / J McCarthy & J Morrell (Bantam Press £14.99) Kidnapped TV journalist and campaigning lover recount the hostage years	5	42
7	Investment Made Easy / Jim Slater (Orion £24.99) Companion volume to financier's bestselling The Zulu Principle	—	1
8	A Brief History Of Time / Stephen Hawking (Bantam Press £14.99) Life, the universe and everything — still selling steadily	8	234
9	Mind Over Matter / Ranulph Fiennes (Sinclair-Stevenson £16.99) Story of the first unsupported trans-Antarctic walk	6	16
10	Diaries / Alan Clark (Weidenfeld £20) Impolitic life and loves of a lively politician	—	22

THIS WEEK	Fiction	LAST WEEK	WEEKS ON LIST
1	A Parliamentary Affair / Edwina Currie (Hodder £15.99) Ex-minister weaves a Westminster mystery	—	1
2	An Imaginative Experience / Mary Wesley (Bantam Press £14.99) Her first novel set in modern London explores personal tragedy	—	1
3	Disclosure / Michael Crichton (Century £14.99) Female sexual harassment — a male backlash novel	1	3
4	The Matisse Stories / A S Byatt (Chatto £9.99) Artistic vignettes from surprising places — such as a hair salon	3	5
5	The Touch Of Innocents / Michael Dobbs (HarperCollins £9.99) More high-level treachery involves Cabinet minister and television reporter	4	3
6	Paddy Clarke Ha Ha Ha / Roddy Doyle (Secker £12.99) Hilarious, poignant account of growing up in Dublin — the Booker winner	2	29
7	Pemberley / Emma Tennant (Hodder £9.99) A sequel to Jane Austen's Pride And Prejudice	—	8
8	The Power / Colin Forbes (Pan £14.99) A massacre in Cornwall and a bomb in London herald Tweed's greatest test	9	2
9	Mrs De Winter / Susan Hill (Sinclair-Stevenson £12.99) Manderley still haunts the characters of du Maurier's Rebecca	7	16
10	Copperhead / Bernard Cornwell (HarperCollins £9.99) Second in his new series about the American civil war	5	5

Sunday 13 February 1994, *A Parliamentary Affair* tops the *Sunday Times* bestseller list.

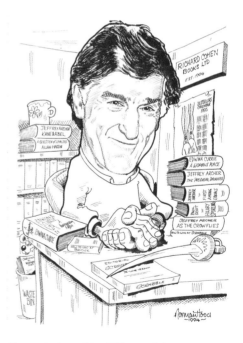

9.35 your time

You're not in, or have passed out drunk under the table. Either way, I can't tell you how good Ch. 23 now is.

R · X

Fax from Richard Cohen, 18 June 1994, the response all authors would like from their editors.

Commissioned by EC to celebrate the establishment of Richard Cohen Books Ltd.

Unbelievable: we have a No. 1! Celebrating the success of *A Parliamentary Affair.*

Promoting *A Parliamentary Affair* on London's red buses.

The 'launch' of *A Woman's Place*, 1996.

EC's 50th birthday party, St Ermin's Hotel, 13 October 1996, being upstaged by two daughters!

With mother in France, May 1992 (Villandry).

Daughters Debbie (left) and Susie
(right) 1994.

Debbie practising her microphone
technique with the TV remote
control, 1997.

The Mojams featuring Debbie Currie, as promoted by *The Cook Report*.

Noel's House Party, April 1997. 'What we do for votes...'

Driving a Warrior Armoured Vehicle in Bosnia, June 1996.

neurotic wife and his passion for Deb Willetts ('I would have her maidenhead...'). He's vain and silly, but his naïve enjoyment of his new coach ('mighty pretty') and his posh clothes is very endearing, and for me, from an equally modest background, entirely recognisable: that's exactly how I feel about Otto whenever I see him. Similarly his pride when he does something really well, such as his appearance before Parliament, and his delighted recording of *all* the nice things everyone says about him – bit like me keeping my press cuttings.

Brussels, Sunday 3 December, 5.30 p.m.

It's ages since I wrote anything and I'm ashamed of myself, but the weeks since the State Opening of Parliament have been 100 per cent busy. From Monday to Friday inclusive this week, for example, I worked seventy hours, including early mornings Monday, Wednesday, Friday and then Saturday to come here for the CGE Seminar. Leaves me tired – and fat, as I can't control myself so well when I'm whacked: a hot chocolate, or a muffin seems like such a good idea, so I'm up to 11 stone and heavier than I've ever been.

Both the Queen's Speech and the Budget were damp squibs, rather as I expected, but their limpness was all the more damaging as they'd been presold as the government's comeback. Instead, as NOP in the *Sunday Times* this morning showed, we've slipped back again 2 points to 25 per cent, Labour up 2 points to 57 per cent (i.e. 32 per cent ahead) with the Liberals on 15 per cent. Last week Peter Riddell in *The Times* pointed out that even if we recovered 20 points (and taking into account the anti-Tory bias in the polls, especially MORI and NOP), we could still lose as badly as in 1945, when Labour were only 6 per cent ahead. I sat next to Peter Kellner[194] at *The Spectator*/Highland Park lunch and asked him if he thought we could still win. Brow furrowed, he answered that he had honestly sought out that body of silent Tories whose votes would rescue us in '97, but hadn't found them – and was anxious to find them if possible, as commentators like him were so wrong last time.

---

194 A political analyst/psephologist, a regular contributor to the *New Statesman* and the *Evening Standard*.

Ken Clarke had little choice over the Budget. The PSBR this year will be £29 billion – still a staggering sum. As he said the figure a gasp went round the Commons, but Ken gave a little shrug, as if to say, 'What can I do? It's your choice to spend the money and not vote the taxes.' So we have 1p off income tax, down to 24p, and restored allowances and a few other tweaks, and that's it – except that it's paid for by the roads and hospital-building programmes being cut to ribbons, including the Derby Spur. So the 'feel bad' factor is likely to persist.

We're pretty certain to lose North West Leicestershire anyway,[195] especially if David Ashby stands. Friday was the eighth day of his preposterous libel action against the *Sunday Times* – win or lose, he's lost already. I should start by recalling that Ashby voted for 16 and has been very supportive of TORCHE (confirmed again by Tony Hutt when he and Kenny came for supper Thursday – my first dinner party, and successful). So David shouldn't regard being called a homosexual as an insult, even if he isn't one. The story in the *Sunday Times* about a holiday in Goa with a man friend is admitted as incorrect: it was given to the paper by David's sister and brother-in-law, in league with his ghastly Italian wife Silvana. Hence much of David's misplaced effort is revenge on his horrible family – but he seems to think remarks made in court about them, and about his constituency Chairman 'Big Val' in North West Leicestershire (who will be incandescent) support his case, whereas they just make him look nuts, and a hypocrite to boot, as he doesn't deny he shared a bed with other men – he just denies that makes him gay. I think he's very innocent about what constitutes sex. But the case will bankrupt him, and lose him (and us) the seat, for certain.

I went up to Leeds on 17/18 November and had a pretty grotty weekend, though comical in retrospect. The Coopers and Lybrand event was OK, then followed by Leeds West dinner (John Whelan's seat). Oh, they had worked so hard, but it was only a handful of around thirty people, several of whom were mad and most decrepit, in the 'ballroom' above a Conservative

---

195 Next door constituency to EC's South Derbyshire.

club, which was so poor it couldn't afford to turn on the heat. So we were freezing: the soup was stone cold before it touched our lips. To keep myself warm I bustled around, helping to serve slabs of overcooked rubbery beef and not quite defrosted Black Forest Gateau. Still, they made over £400 profit, so good for them. Next day, however, I'd agreed to go to a 'fashion house' in Leeds run by a Frenchwoman, and had rather assumed – since this *was* Leeds – that it was a factory outlet. To my horror it was just a shop and it was made very clear I was supposed to buy. But the stuff was horrendously expensive, outrageously so, a real rip-off. Clare was inveigled into trying on a green suit; as she began to pirouette, I reached in the pocket, found the price tag and told her grimly it was over £600. You can buy designer suits for much less in Selfridges. Deb was there, eyes boggling, as these awful shop assistants, pancake makeup and outlined lipstick and false cheeriness, followed us and the photographers round. One looked disapprovingly at my Mansfield suit (about £200, bought cheap at Gertrude's) and remarked, 'She is *ordinary*, isn't she?' When they realised Deb had heard, they said, 'Well, natural, rather...' As I left, the owner tried to press a sales leaflet on me and told me how Barbara Taylor Bradford had ended up buying all her outfits from them for a USA promotional tour. I nodded and smiled agreeably. Then *her* daughter, one of the sales managers, exploded: 'Someone'll get the sack – you've been here all this time and nobody's managed to sell you anything!' As neatly as I could, I extricated myself, left the leaflet on the counter, avoided shaking hands and walked out. *Yuk.*

Exeter, Saturday 16 December, 5.30 p.m.

I'm two hours into a five-hour train journey from Cornwall back to Paddington. Yesterday I went to Exeter for a sixth form conference for the local branch of the European Movement; and this morning came on a hot, packed little train down to Cornwall, through some of the loveliest country I've ever seen and over Brunel's magnificent 1859 Royal Albert Bridge to Saltash. Pity the weather was grey and bleak, but though arduous and tiring, it's been fun. Today's event was a lunch arranged by Judith Woodcock, a handsome, intelligent

55-year-old, for the Cornwall and West Plymouth Euro Council. I'm surprised to find it still exists. The seat was lost by Christopher Beazley, who (according to Judith) has been moping around miserable and virtually unemployed since. She doesn't think he'll try for the Euro Parliament again, at least not for the West Country, as his wife Christiane would not be keen. Shows how destructive this life is. I encouraged her to think of putting her name forward for South East Cornwall, where Robert Hicks[196] has just announced his retirement – the fifty-first Tory MP to do so. According to last weekend's *Sunday Times*, the Party is alarmed that so few women have been selected as candidates – Labour has thirty-nine women MPs and another thirty-nine selected so far, while we've only a handful. '150 low calibre men are to be culled from the list and replaced by women' ran the headline – an unconscious irony there! I attended (as a speaker) a class at CCO for women on the list chaired by Dame Joan Seccombe on Thursday, and it was dreadful – only eight women there and only one or two smart, intelligent and electable. Most needed basic training, e.g. in how to *smile*. Grim.

Grim prospects too in Staffordshire, where David Lightbown died last week. I will miss him – he was a gentle giant, a lovely man, and unusual in having been both a successful engineer and businessman and a thoroughly competent local government leader too. Not many like that on either side at Westminster: made the Alan Duncans and Graham Riddicks look even more puny and disreputable. His seat is highly vulnerable; like me he had succeeded in pushing up his personal vote since 1983, when he was first elected, but his majority had been eroded steadily over the years. He had no agent – in fact in the eleven Staffordshire seats we have but one, in Burton. Isn't that *awful?* David kept his people afloat with money from the office allowance, which of course adds to their weakness rather than reducing it. Tyrone will probably get pulled over to help in the by-election, which is not scheduled till April/May as there's so much to do. Could be local election day, then – get all the disasters out of the way in one hit.

---

196 Conservative MP for South East Cornwall since 1983; MP for Bodmin, 1970–83.

And yesterday was the Madrid EU summit, which (as far as I'm concerned) had a splendid outcome. 'It's going to be called the euro, and it's going to be the new Euro currency,' said Ken Clarke smugly to the British press, as if the matter had ever been in doubt. It has dawned on this morning's papers that the Europeans are *serious*: that it'll happen in 1999 or as soon after as is possible: that Britain will have to decide in mid-1998 whether we're in or not; and that, politely or otherwise, the rest will go ahead with us or without us. All that generates a distinct sense of shock, particularly the last bit. I spoke in a Commons debate on 7 December and had a similar letter in *The Times* yesterday, rehearsing the benefits of joining the single currency in due course, that the main restrictions would be on printing money (i.e. too high deficits) and fiddling with the exchange rate (i.e. devaluation), in both cases improving our economic management, stability and credibility no end. These are *positive* advantages a good Tory, a believer in sound money, can warm to, and have a more convincing ring than the tedious argument about not being left out, which in fact appeals to many Tory supporters as a distinct gain.

Had an entertaining lunch with Gwynneth Flower this week – I do enjoy her company; she is such a lively and interesting conversationalist, a woman who's lived a man's life. By contrast many women are so dull! Gwynneth looked lovely: tall, elegant, beautifully coiffed and manicured, in a dark blue suit with a pretty scarf, wedding ring (!), earrings, the lot – immaculate. Who else do I know with perfect red nail varnish? Or who starts a conversation by telling me her brain scan was great, it showed she really is a woman? Or who explains it's easy to pick up men, you just go walking in the park in a tracksuit and high heels with a borrowed King Charles spaniel? And full make-up, I'll bet – delicious – of course the hands are too large, and the ankle bones too; whatever the scan shows, a lot of male hormones were coursing through that body at key times in its development. But the gaze is blue eyed, direct and coquettish; I almost felt *I* was being flirted with. What a hoot! I do admire her sheer courage – and she gets on with her life too. She's almost as indignant as I am about prejudice against women; she told me that she was one of three women on the original list of twelve names headhunted for the Borrie (Nolan) job,[197] but Robin Butler allegedly had all the female names removed, as 'no woman would have the gravitas' (of course he may not know Gwynneth was a full colonel in the Army! Joke's on Robin…). She was told this by the lady head-hunter in charge, and I see no reason to doubt her. She also regaled me with another entirely plausible tale, of how she left a dinner in the House of Commons one evening recently, got a bit lost, and heard raised voices around a corner: a northern accent angrily saying, 'Well, you've never been a bloody socialist, have you?' At the sound of her approach they stopped; it was Blair and Prescott, who scuttled away.

Made me realise I miss Richard, for his conversation and the chance to talk both seriously and wittily. The reviews are coming through of some of his books; the £30 amalgam of Hilary Spurling's 'superlative' biographies of Ivy Compton-Burnett from 1974 and 1984 is clearly not edited at all, which really is a disgrace at that price. Penelope Mortimer, writing in the *Telegraph*, says that it 'makes for tedious reading… the result is a clumsy publication, unworthy of the skill and dedication with which both books were written.' Oh dear. I am beginning to realise that the only book Richard edited properly last year was mine, and that took a lot of hassle and bullying on my part. I hope he has a better year in '96, but it won't include any work of mine.

Tower House, Tuesday 26 December, 9.30 a.m.

I woke about 7.30 a.m. to find the sky yellow behind the power station and everything still: another hard frost. Now the sun is high and bright; I'd go for a walk if I hadn't done so the last two mornings, so today I'll write my diary, then swim, then do 'cold cuts' lunch. We have all four family here, plus Norman, Deb's current boyfriend. He's a tall, slim, black Yorkshireman with a kind of beauty, but no conversation whatsoever. Still, he is well behaved and helpful, which makes him an asset at Christmas time. As he polished off second helpings of everything at lunch yesterday I asked if it

197 Commissioner for Standards in Public Life, a post set up at the recommendation of the Nolan Committee.

met with his approval. 'Yes, it's gorgeous,' he responded wistfully in broad Yorkshire, thus telling a long tale of what he might have expected at home. I do wish, nevertheless, that Deb would take up with a bloke who was not only pretty, but bright and articulate. It'd make a change.

As far as I'm concerned the feast has been a success, though in one sense it only confirmed what I know already about this home and marriage. The worst moment was in the pub last night. It's a dismal little place – a small box that feels like a cage, with everyone crouching at small low tables or standing uncomfortably at the tiny bar wreathed in cigarette smoke. Quiz night: 'Do come, Mum,' so I did, and stayed all of ninety minutes. An old drunk at the next table was a pest, putting his arms around me and making me cringe; and I had no 'role', as I wasn't there as their MP but nor was I a normal person either, so everyone felt uncertain and embarrassed. After about seventy-five minutes, I began to feel I'd give an arm and a leg for a *conversation* – but the quiz is an elimination of chat except at the most trivial level. I'd be in the middle of an anecdote, only to be hushed for the next question. The rapt attention on Ray's face distressed me – he really did love it and was in his element, respected as the one who wins every week. I had two glasses of lager and a packet of crisps, fought off the drunk and shook his hand yet again, yawned ferociously a couple of times, and gave up. I walked back up the hill in the peaceful dark, the sky studded with stars, to catch the end of Osborne's *England My England* – about Purcell – on TV: pretentious and overblown, though Simon Callow and Bill Kenwright were fun and the music marvellous; then I sat till 1 a.m. drinking Drambuie and reading Peter Ackroyd's *Blake*.

David Ashby suffered a catastrophic defeat on Tuesday, when he lost his libel case against the *Sunday Times*. Hardly a surprising result: he sued on the grounds that their articles made him out to be a homosexual, a liar and a hypocrite. They countered that 'homosexual' was no longer a term of insult, which Ashby conceded; the issue was whether he was unfaithful to his wife at a time when he was extolling his adherence to family values in his election address. In the witness stand Ashby proved himself amply to be a fool and a pompous prat: that his wife went into the witness stand against him and he called his boyfriend on his own side proved everything else to the jury's satisfaction. David's objective, he told me, was to make £1 million out of the *Sunday Times*, but all such hopes must have been dashed in the last week of the hearing when Lord Mackay[198] set out new rules in damages cases, which will end the huge payouts gained by such as Archer and Gorman; nobody should get more for their reputation than a permanently disabled person gets for a damaged life. Now David is landed with costs estimated at £350,000–£500,000 – the case took *three weeks!* – though the *Sunday Times* hint they won't press for all theirs. He won't be bankrupt as he owns three properties, including a house in Putney, the marital home for twenty-five years, but he'll be cleaned out, and politically ruined.

On top of all this, the government was defeated the same night, Tuesday 19th, in a vote on fisheries. Fertile ground for the Eurosceptics: two (Cash and Carttiss) voted against the government and the rest abstained – Nick Budgen said cheekily that he had to attend Lightbown's funeral and couldn't return in time for the 7 p.m. vote. Sick men were brought in by both sides: Michael Colvin, who'd had a hip replacement five days before, strapped to a stretcher in an ambulance, John Fraser[199] with his head in a steel clamp after a car accident, and poor Roland Boyes[200] wandering the corridors, chattering amiably to everyone he encountered and telling them all about his Alzheimer's disease: I think he must have been on dope or something as he was irredeemably cheerful, but it was horribly sad. And Hugh Dykes decided to play silly buggers and voted with Labour 'out of despair at the government's drift over Europe'. Liam Fox, the whip, asked me to reason with Hugh; we all tried, but he was adamant. So the vote was 297–299 against the government.

I should add one more piece of miserable news: on the same front page as 'Ashby loses' was a piece about Lord Brocket, whose magnificent pile, Brocket Hall, I visited during campaigning for the Euro seat in spring 1993. Last year he was arrested on suspicion of

---

198 Lord Mackay of Clashfern, Lord Chancellor since 1987.
199 Labour MP for Norwood since 1966.
200 Labour MP for Houghton and Washington since 1983; he was only fifty-eight at the time.

an insurance scam, involving four disappeared classic cars worth £4.5 million. In court that day he pleaded guilty; he faces a longish jail sentence. I remember being hugely impressed with the house, with its fabulous hangings and wall coverings, all in pristine condition: i.e. brand new. But running the place as a conference centre would never raise enough to pay for the borrowing: the family just didn't have the money. In addition there was an unpleasant divorce after a twelve-year marriage – the settlement must have cost him a packet. How are the mighty fallen: a good-looking and personable guy of forty-three with everything going for him (so like a lot of my Tory MP colleagues), who blows it all by being *stupid*.

What is the Party coming to? Heather[201] asked me that, at 11 p.m. on Saturday night, but I was too tired to talk political and shooed her home, poor faithful Heather. She told me that the man who raped her daughter and was sentenced in 1988 was in court again in Derby for another series of rapes committed after his release: this time he got life, and sharp words from the judge about serving twenty years. The fact that this repeat could happen, after early release for a violent criminal, shows how this government has failed: it makes noisy speeches at Conference but eschews attention to detail or the hard work which ensures that a policy is carried out to the letter. So it isn't. God, I despair. As for the PM, he has become almost a non-person: watch him in the voting lobbies – nobody comes up to him to talk to him, only his invisible PPS John Ward[202] (who thinks very highly of him). Margaret used to be surrounded by a gaggle of hangers-on, supplicants and admirers, so thick she could hardly walk through the voting lobby; John is avoided, and eyes averted, as if he has a disease.

I should mention seeing Alan Ayckbourn's *Communicating Doors* by myself at a matinee (fun, beach farce, Adie Allen brilliant as Poupay), and *A Little Night Music* at the National, organised by Ray: tedious, I thought. First time I've been there, huge stage, everyone having to run to get into place; all ethereal, and at times quite beautiful, but none of the claustrophobic atmosphere the piece should

201 A South Derbyshire constituency worker.
202 Conservative MP for Poole since 1979.

have. I was grumpy much of the way through. I'd already decided I wouldn't go to Le Beaujolais with Ray after – that involved a trek across the river nearly to Tottenham Court Road and then back to Clapham, and I wasn't keen to spend hours artificially in Ray's company after weeks of successfully avoiding him. So I chickened out, and walked along a misty Embankment and across Westminster Bridge to retrieve my car: feeling a bit lonely, of course, but better than pretending.

1996

Les Tuileries, Monday 1 January, 9.15 a.m.

The Party continues to fall apart. Now Emma Nicholson has defected, this time to the Lib Dems. She won't stand for Westminster again, she says, but hopes to try for the European Parliament in 1999. As a Lib Dem? That seems barmy to me; Emma seems to have lost her marbles. The Party's drifted too far to the right, she says, and is too anti-Europe – much the same sentiments as Alan Howarth. Her radio interview included sententious references to 'the poor' – oh, Lady Caine,[203] if you knew what 'poor' was.

Radio 4 phoned me and we had a long chat, but it was clear they preferred the sharper comments of Hugh Dykes: five or six other disaffected people are also possible defectors, he said, and the government's got to shape up and stop kow-towing to the Eurosceptics. Who? Not Hugh, he declared soundly, not me; one possibility in my mind, Jim Lester, got his knighthood at last in the New Year's Honours List. David Knox,[204] maybe? Andrew Rowe? Tim Renton?[205] Patrick Cormack?[206] But though they qualify in terms of unhappiness with Party policy on a wide front, they all seem too sensible, or have strong incentives to stay put.

---

203 Emma Nicholson was married to the businessman Sir Michael Caine.
204 Conservative MP for Staffordshire Moorlands since 1983; MP for Leek, 1970–83.
205 Conservative MP for Mid Sussex since 1974.
206 Conservative MP for South Staffordshire since 1974; MP for Cannock, 1970–74.

Tower House, Sunday 14 January, 12.30 p.m.

In bed. Not feeling brilliant; horrible sore throat which I must look after, as we've twenty-three interviews (so far) arranged for the next two weeks. I'm blowing green gunk out of my nose in great globules and feeling a bit sorry for myself, especially as it's a lovely sunny day and would have been perfect for a long muddy tramp. Huh.

The promotion campaign is hotting up, and we will have more than enough coverage. The literary editors have been reading review copies over the holidays, then writing up *A Woman's Place* as a news story – couldn't be better – though they are prats, some of them. *The Observer* seems to think the novel's no more than a collection of political insults (so how come it'll sell well outside UK?); Max Davidson in the *Telegraph* writes it's 'more substantial' than that, but can't bring himself to say, as he did to my face, 'it's very good and I enjoyed it.' Patronising bugger! The *Express* wrote in effect a splendid review – 'sizzling page turner' etc., but chided me for forgetting Disraeli was a Jew: I must copy a page of a suitable history to show why he got baptised.

I dream about sex quite a lot: usually with whichever presentable man I've been chatting to during the day. And why not? If there is to be a lover, some day, he'll probably come from an unexpected source.

I was on *Question Time* on Thursday, with Peter Mandelson, Nick Harvey (Lib Dem MP for Newbury – looks and sounds like a small-town bank manager, prematurely tubby and bald, good humoured and not very bright), and Tina Knight, Chairman and MD of Nighthawk Electronics, who's now chairman of 'Women into Business'. She's a spunky lady, sharper and more aggressive than Teresa Gorman, pink hair, heavy jewellery, black suit and finger-nails, much bosom: she'll be shocked when she sees herself, as she really looked a witch. Can't say I like her, but she was entertaining, and scored points off Mandelson by demanding to know what the minimum wage will be. Peter has become a highly significant and rather sinister figure in the Labour Party. He's a bit of an android: expressionless face, taut body, disciplined, deliberately bland, watchful. I'm getting to know him quite well now through the European Movement. We had an excellent press conference on Monday – lots of good poll figures showing that the Europhiles in the UK still outnumber the Eurosceptics by 3:1. Peter must have a deep-seated commitment as he turns up faithfully despite a frantically busy diary, and he's reliable (and was pleasant to me on *Question Time*, so that's a bonus). But you can't get through to him at all.

Meanwhile our erstwhile Great Leader has been chucking the shit into the nearest fan. On Thursday night (while I was filming *Question Time*) she made her first big domestic speech in five years, the Keith Joseph Memorial Lecture. It had a curiously dated feel about it. While a much better, crisper speech than anything her successor could make, it had neither wisdom nor balance, nor any concern for its damaging consequences. She derided 'one nation' Tories and implied we're all federalists (Portillo recently said federalists had no place in the Conservative Party and should leave, the little squirt). She said the PM had let down the middle classes. Yes, she did have a go at Mr Blair; and yes, she did argue cogently for less state activity – though inconsistently she then demanded adherence to the 'rule of law', which implies a strong state and bureaucracy, not a weak one. Her supporters have claimed the reporting was biased, but that's disingenuous – it was easy as pie to dig out clippings of her ringing endorsements of 'one nation' Toryism in the 1970s when it suited her. But then in those days we were hungry for office, and we aren't now. One passage in particular about 'being prepared to state uncomfortable truths' and the necessity for debate within the Party is very revealing: she's referring to a time, '74–'79, when we were in opposition, which suggests such a period again would be a good thing.

It seemed to affect the PM quite badly. His tactics have shrunk to an appeal for unity. On a radio interview I offered the metaphor of the coachman who doesn't know where he's going: he thinks his sole job is to keep the horses, who are pulling in opposite directions, heading roughly the same way, and the carriage upright. What he doesn't realise is that he's the *lead horse*. If he stepped out smartly and boldly, with some sense of purpose, the other steeds would swing in behind him and trot along happily enough, only tugging at the reins occasionally. But on *Frost* last Sunday (an interview he must have requested) he merely bleated what sounded like a plea from the driver: 'Please, chaps, hold steady.' The 1922 Committee has refused to change the rules to prevent further leadership challenges before the election, which Fox had promised – that can't be doing John's morale much good, either, though (in fact) I doubt there'll really be a challenge so close to a general election. Who wants to be blamed for losing it, when a contest must occur immediately after anyway? The fact is, victory has been written off and everyone is busy making alternative plans.

Including me. I did quite well in France – got Chapter 1 of *LOL*[207] written, and now Chapter 2 is almost done. Once Chapter 3 is under my belt, I can send what I've done to Lisa. Deadline, end of this month.

On train from Derby to London, Monday 29 January, 3.50 p.m.

Did my first signing of *A Woman's Place* today at W. H. Smith in the Eagle Centre, Derby – not a brilliant success as nobody had advertised the event, and the hardback is very expensive at £16.99. No discounts either. Should do better on Saturday at Waterstone's in St Peter's Square – I gave them a plug on Radio Derby this afternoon.

Last Sunday I spent in London doing accounts. Boy, did the results give me pause for thought! My turnover in 1995/6 will top £150,000; I'll have to set aside a hefty chunk for tax. Now that means I'm running a serious business. This started as a bit of fun, a way of keeping myself busy. I feel very lucky, and quite scared.

I told Deb all this on the phone last night – we talked for ninety minutes, and it was *so* good. I wanted in part to convince her that, should she turn to writing at some future point, it could give her a damn good living. She said her boyfriend Norman is getting very serious; he has withdrawn all his cash from Junction 25, the car firm he works for, and is setting up on his own. He's written off too for courses he can study at home; he's become much more ambitious since knowing Deb. She protests (wisely) that she's only twenty-one, and isn't

---

207 *Leaving of Liverpool*, the provisional title of the book eventually published as *She's Leaving Home*.

ready for domesticity and babies yet! She came off the pill because it was making her edgy, which explains her rather moody behaviour over Xmas. For twenty minutes we compared our hormone intake. What a pair.

Meanwhile, Richard phoned late on 18 January (Thursday) and wanted to chat. I was dog tired and not very well, but obviously he needed to talk. It looks as if RCB is heading for disaster. At 31 December it had lost £¼ million (which means most of his share capital). Somebody has lent him £100,000 to bring the overdraft back down, but it's a highly perilous position. He's published sixteen books in six months, and not one has been a success. I think it's worse than that – most were late and not reviewed, and those that were reviewed were criticised as not very good, even from experienced writers like Sue Bradbury, whose novel was described as 'clichéd'. At once I suspected what was wrong. He edited only one book last year, and that was mine. To none other did he give half as much time, and to most none at all. The editing was done by the likes of Linden, who has neither the skill nor the authority to throw a book back at an author. It may even be that Richard's reputation as an editor meant some writers expected to leave a lot of the work to him; but as so many were late, there was no time for rewrites, though I think that in such cases he should have put his foot down and postponed the publication date until the work was good enough to bear the RCB imprint. He's been vanity publishing in a big way, and I fear the business is going to go bankrupt fairly soon.

Which gives me a (sort of) dilemma, as that would mean he'd be available to edit *LOL* if I wanted. He's excellent, no doubt of that. But taking him on means taking on all his hassle. I don't think I want to go down that route again.

The government had a splendid time last week, though when I congratulated the PM after Prime Minister's Questions on Tuesday he said warningly, 'We had a good wicket.' And so they did: Harriet Harman, not the most well-liked soul at Westminster, announced she'd decided to send her son to a grant-maintained grammar school in Orpington. Well! A selective school, no less, with some of the best exam results in the country. Harriet, the daughter of a surgeon and educated at St Paul's, is so middle class it hurts, but you'd think her husband Jack Dromey, head of a trade union, would have talked sense into her. Apparently she couldn't quite see what she'd done wrong, as at least she hadn't chosen a private school. Well – Bromley is a Tory borough which kept selection, Ms Harman, which your Party is pledged to abolish. That clear enough? Not only were we baying for her blood, but so were the PLP; at their weekly meeting she had to grovel and apologise, but she got Blair's full backing and did not have to resign from the front bench. (At the shadow Cabinet elections in November they'll have their revenge and vote her off like last time – and Blair will have to accept it.) It's really been a first-class row about hypocrisy, and about the modernisers vs. the old-timers in Labour; and perhaps too about education policy, given that neither Labour-run comprehensives nor Tory grammar schools are producing satisfactory results. This week the newly published test tables showed 50 per cent of eleven-year-olds weak in basic literacy and numeracy skills: very depressing.

I did envy her one thing, however: the staunch backing of her boss. If I'd had that in '88… who knows? And I'd done nothing wrong, nothing blatantly against Party policy: yet that support was not forthcoming. Ah well, I've made a success of my life since, which is more than can be said of Mrs T herself, or so many other people.

On the train from Derby, Monday 12 February, 9.45 a.m.

Otto's gone in for servicing after 34,000 wonderful miles – it feels like I've sent a friend in for a check-up. In my bag are the completed three chapters and synopsis of *LOL*, which I'll drop off with Lisa on the way to the House of Commons. She's coming in to dine tonight and we'll talk. So I feel I've done my duty, though I'm not exactly pleased with life.

This time in 1994 I had a No. 1 bestseller, *and* I'd been paid. In February '96 neither is true. *A Woman's Place* is at No. 15 in *Publishing News* and (I'm told) No. 11 in the *Sunday Times*, which means nowhere. By lunchtime today I'll have done eight signings and I can tell them why not: because at a penny under £17 it's too expensive.

The only signing which was a success was at Allders in Croydon (splendid people – proper meal after), where the price was £13.49.

That's more like it, and the book sold like hot cakes: twenty-four in an hour, plus fifteen paperbacks of *A Parliamentary Affair*, so that's one every seventy-five seconds, approximately. In Books Etc. in Victoria Street, by contrast (quick dry sandwich by the counter), we managed only eleven (plus paperbacks.) I reckoned Allders did over £300 of business and Books Etc. about £200. The No. 1 is Julian Barnes's *Cross Channel* at £13.99, discounted to £10 in Dillons. It doesn't help that we've hit W. H. Smith at a very bad time, when top management is changing, and all budgets are frozen. Their brains seem to have been frozen too: there we were in W. H. Smith Sloane Square with full-price books, staff with no name plates ('lost in the wash') and a cold, dead atmosphere. They'd put out no ads – if I'd been manager I'd have put the ad in the *Evening Standard* myself, sold the books and hassled to be reimbursed afterwards. After my arrival someone phoned HQ and got permission to discount; so I put the 'bargain price' labels on myself (to £10.99), but since nobody knew about it, they still didn't sell. Smith's are discounting throughout the country this week, but I've a horrible feeling we've missed the boat.

Greedy Hodder. I supported their efforts to break the NBA[208] because I do believe that cheaper prices sell more books. Mine was at the highest price in the *Publishing News* 20. Huh!

Tower House, Sunday 18 February, 10.38 p.m.

Wild, wet and windy out – it's been blowing a howling gale all weekend. At times it's felt as if this house were a rocket poised to take off from Cape Canaveral. Outside it's so loud, with the wind screaming in the poplars and around the roof, that you can't hear yourself think; instead there's a low moan round every corner, and sudden inexplicable draughts as if the place were haunted.[209]

A Woman's Place is in all the bestseller lists – No. 5 in the *Sunday Times*, No. 7 in *The Times*, No. 9 in *Publishing News*. Not good enough, but a bestseller at last. Lisa loved the new synopsis, and today I've tweaked it and the 23,000 words of Chapters 1–3 to suit her. I told her I hope we'll try simultaneously for the USA, for TV and

208 The Net Book Agreement, which regulated book prices.
209 Tower House was a windmill dating from 1716.

for a two-book agreement, hopefully with a new publisher as I'm worried Hodder's might want to jazz up *LOL* and spoil it. Onward, as Richard would say – though probably without him too.

Alas, no Valentines this year: not one, and I didn't send any. First year since God knows when. Left me feeling bereft and deeply unloved.

House of Commons, Monday 4 March, 9 p.m.

The PM has emerged unexpectedly in a cloud of credit. He met Bruton[210] on Wednesday after talking to him half the night on the phone, and it seems the two governments are *determined* to work together on achieving a settlement in Northern Ireland. Real progress – look how far we've come – instead of seeing the Irish government, and Clinton, and the EU and UN as interfering where they had no business, we welcome their help and effectively now share decision-making with Dublin; and instead of trying to reason with the gunmen, all preconditions about decommissioning arms have been dropped, and 'ceasefire restoration' is the sole require-ment. Instead of refusing to talk to Sinn Fein we do, all the time. Amazing. Andrew Hunter[211] and a few of the die-hard Tories are upset. Andrew said to me in the cloakroom, 'The government has taken another thousand-mile step towards the terrorists' – surpris-ingly eloquent for him, usually so dull.

And we've lost another MP: Thurnham has gone independent and voted the other way, joined by Quentin Davies. At the last minute Rupert Allason was persuaded to stay put, as was John Marshall.[212] But it confirms the appallingly weak position of the government, and given the Grim Reaper, nobody can now guaran-tee we'll get safely to May '97. I speculate about who'll pop off before then – Iain Mills[213] is drunk and swaying every night, so must be a candidate for a heart attack; Sir John Hunt,[214] lovely man, is look-ing distinctly rickety; Sir Dudley Smith looks florid and overweight;

---

210 John Bruton, leader of Fine Gael since 1990; Taoiseach since 1994.
211 Conservative MP for Basingstoke since 1983.
212 Conservative MP for Hendon South since 1987.
213 Conservative MP for Meriden since 1979.
214 Conservative MP for Ravensbourne since 1974; MP for Bromley, 1964–74.

and then there's our sick men, Jack Aspinwall and Julian Critchley. Lots of people waiting to leave, to get out… The whole thing is so shaky. In the tea room Elizabeth Peacock[215] (tiny majority) tells me she has no branch network left at all. So if we can't win the marginals, how do we hang on to power?

This lady could find herself out shortly. Ty came round to Tower House on Friday night with my constituency chairman, Michael Everington, and told more gloomy tales about plotting against me for 15 March (the AGM). I'm going to brief the Chief Whip about this, as I do take it seriously. There can be only one motion: that my name go forward, just mine. It'll be voted on. If 'yes', that's fine, I fight. If 'no' or equivocal, then presumably I stand down. I am certainly *not* taking part in any beauty contest. If thirteen years' hard work isn't enough for South Derbyshire Tories, then nothing else I can do or say is either, and they can find themselves another candidate.

I'm cross, though in two minds. What I want is to come out of this Parliament, but to do so graciously and with my reputation intact: fighting and *losing* would achieve both objectives nicely. Not fighting would be cowardly and looks disloyal. Not to be chosen to fight is a rejection.

Meanwhile the alternative career… W. H. Smith have sold only 1,000 out of 5,000 hardbacks: 'according to expectations', says Sue Fletcher, which I don't believe. We did exceptionally well in Belfast at lunchtime: seventy-seven hardback and fifty-five paperback sold, which took over an hour to sign. That's more like it!

Richard sent out his figures, which are as awful as he told me over the phone, except they're for end September, not 'year end', which I took to be Xmas. He's lost virtually all the independently subscribed capital and (as I suspected) has given a personal guarantee for a £100,000 loan, which also means he's run out of savings. Ghastly.

House of Commons, Monday 18 March, 11.05 p.m.
Waiting to vote at 11.30 p.m. Oh, weary, weary! But it's my own fault. Susie and I sat up late last night to watch *Citizen Kane* on video.

---

215 Conservative MP for Batley and Spen since 1983; her majority in 1992 was 1,408.

It was in many ways much better than I remembered – very atmospheric and clearly dramatically influential; but the ending seemed no longer a puzzle but trite. The 25-year-old Orson Welles came over as pure genius – quite amazing, a master. Pity he did so little of value after that (1941).

So: to business. The South Derbyshire Conservative Association AGM on Friday was quite an exciting affair. Stern-faced people queuing up to get in: everyone checked against the list of members paid up on 31.12.95. The place was stifling and the atmosphere electric. I spoke quite well, but was uneasy rather than confident – it was more like a selection committee, yet I didn't feel nervous; I suppose I know them too well. And in reality, if they didn't want me, part of me would give a small shrug. Yet I wanted that nomination. I was proposed, seconded, and then came the vote, done without fuss or preliminaries by secret ballot, and I trounced 'em: sixty-eight votes yes, thirteen no, a majority of 5:1. So that's it, for the moment. Except that I'm still quite sure we will lose in due course. In fact, barring accidents, I can't see how we can win. All the better, therefore, that Lisa's sent off my synopsis of *LOL* to Hodder: and now we'll see what they say.

Except that when Ray and I get home, he has a bombshell to drop. 'Can you spare a minute?' he asks, and as this is the first time he's suggested a talk in – goodness – years, I pour a couple of stiff drinks (I needed mine by then) and wait. He's lost his job.

It's come out of the blue: there's been some talk of restructuring, but the last thing that occurred to him is that the Arthur Andersen Training Department would be disbanded, with training done at local office level. I don't think it will be for long – I agree with him that there are huge benefits in doing it centrally, such as economies of scale and high standards. But from 30 June '96, a month short of twenty-nine years since he joined the firm, he will be redundant.

Is it just hindsight that makes me feel I saw it coming even if he didn't? He's been at the top of his scale for over a decade, which makes him expensive in a job a more junior person could do: the firm could commission its partners, to whom it pays outrageous sums, to give the big talks at no additional expense. I think he was lucky not to fall out during the recession, to be frank. It can't have helped that he tucked himself away in Westway: you have to be seen and touched, in the main HQ building, if you're to seem indispensable. And never being there from Thursday afternoon, not even being in London – that didn't help either.

Clapham, Saturday 23 March, 9.10 p.m.

I've just been to do *A Week in Politics*[216] and had three glasses of wine and a few crisps (all I'm allowed in the diet, which is working). The phone has started to ring, as I've an article in tomorrow's *Sunday Express* (ghosted by Simon Walters, recently transferred from *The Sun*) about BSE. Let me explain.

On Thursday a minister came clean at last. Stephen Dorrell took to Cabinet the terrifying advice he'd just received and forced them to accept that an immediate public statement was necessary. The ten cases of Creutzfeldt-Jakob disease (CJD), which had shown up in the UK in people under sixty-five, the first time ever, were a new strain, and the most likely source was contaminated meat from pre-1989. The beef had BSE – 'mad cow disease' – and that in turn was put into the food chain by feedstuffs containing ground-up sheep remains containing the 'scrapie' bug. The thing had crossed two species. Worse, it's not a standard bug but a 'prion', which survives to 130°C and thus isn't killed by normal sterilisation procedures. Oh God, I thought, here it comes.

I had the opportunity to meet my farmers quickly on Friday p.m. in the White Swan at Walton, but already the bottom had dropped out of the market. As I write, over twenty countries have banned UK beef imports, including Italy (the main destination for South Derbyshire beef), most of the EU with the backing of the Commission, and South Africa. An entire industry is about to be wiped out, just as the busiest time of the year is beginning. And it will get worse: gelatine, for example (according to the *Sunday Times*, who've just been on) is included in *most* products from yoghurt to pharmaceuticals, and it's made from – wait for it – boiled-up cattle backbone. Terrific... Education authorities have already banned

---

216 A television programme.

beef from schools, and the Co-op is talking about getting its beef from abroad for the first time in its 150-year history.

Ministers are telling everyone to wait till the scientists pronounce before deciding not to eat beef. But that's a totally unrealistic position, since three weeks ago ministers and scientists were saying there was no risk at all, and now they're declaring the opposite, nobody believes any reassurance whatever. As one of my farmers said to me, 'either the industry dies and we go bankrupt quickly, or something drastic is done. The public won't feel satisfied till they see dead cows burning on television.'

I felt *so* sad. Poor bloody farmers. One of my chaps said he'd been up calving at 3.30 a.m. – 'but what's the point? The animal's worthless. Nobody will buy him, not to eat, not to breed.' They pointed the fingers at MAFF, and so do I, especially at the obdurate Keith Meldrum, who was Chief Vet in 1988. (I think the *Mail on Sunday* is going to have a go at him. Hope so.) Somewhere around 1981 intensive farming became all the rage. Go for it, lads – more nitrate on the land for bigger yields, more feedstuffs bought in, and relax the controls to keep the cost down. By '85 the first cases of BSE showed up. By '87 we had serious (and new) infection in the fowl stock. By '88 I was up to my neck in food poisoning cases – and at the same time the first half-hearted attempts were being made on BSE, e.g. by banning the use of contaminated feedstuffs, though it was perfectly all right to use up existing stocks, chaps, and so they did. Just a precaution to satisfy a silly hysterical public, you understand. In '89 the entry of condemned animals into the food chain was banned, but only 50 per cent compensation was offered – it was another nine months before we got to that stage. At every point MAFF was grudgingly complacent and offhand in its reaction. So now we have young people dying slowly and horribly, and *at last* it's being taken seriously. Douglas Hogg,[217] the new Minister of Agriculture, said firmly on Friday morning radio, 'Public health is the top priority.' Music to my ears – and a contrast to John

217 Secretary of State for Agriculture since 1995; Conservative MP for Grantham since 1979.

Gummer, last but one, whose response was to stuff hamburgers down his unwilling daughter's throat.

As for me: I'm still eating beef, but only best quality – as far as I can ascertain. The damage was done, if it was, a long time ago. The whole business is really too horrible, too tragic to take in properly.

In all of this, the government's White Paper on Europe has been a complete damp squib – nobody can remember what the paper says, and it will be out of date once the first negotiation is out of the way. The debate on Thursday was, as I would have expected, an opportunity for our own Eurosceptic backbenchers to attack ministers. How naïve can you get? And there was Norman Lamont, like a pop-eyed frog, seriously advocating withdrawal. This country's stature shrinks daily, along with the value of its currency, while prats like Lamont and the upmarket version Redwood distract the Tory Party from its fight against socialism to a pointless, narrow, xenophobic tantrum against progress and the future.

The FET Conference at Lancaster House on Monday/Tuesday/Wednesday last week was *wonderful*. Oh, the speakers were run of the mill, mostly mediocre – but the delegates were wonderful – exactly right: over eighty people, all MPs, from a bizarre collection of thirty-four countries. I was worried by Bernard Jenkin, however. That man's a natural mischief maker and little else. He 'chaired' several discussions, including one on EMU which he dominated by paraphrasing the speakers, asking questions and challenging their replies – hardly any delegates who were pro-EMU got a word in edgeways. He plans to replace me as Joint Chairman when I lose my seat, I'm sure.

Deb and Susie are in Derbyshire tomorrow; Susie anyway as she has a party to attend, and Deb at my suggestion so her Dad can tell her his bad news. He and I went out to see *Sense and Sensibility* last night (quite brilliant – how astounding Emma Thompson is – she has really left Kenneth Branagh far behind in talent, courage and imagination), then to the Full Moon for a curry. 'Why did you arrange for Deb to come?' he asks. 'Because she has to know, and you have to tell her, and you made me promise I wouldn't tell, so I haven't,' I reply. 'I did not,' he says, and launches into a denunciation. But he did, and when I protested, accused me of playing word games... and suddenly the atmosphere turned very sour, and my heart sank. And I'd been daydreaming all week that maybe this was the moment when he might realise he had a friend, and might talk freely...

It's 10.30 p.m. and the flat is quiet, comfortable – and empty. There ought to be a lovely naked man in my bed and I ought to be playing with him and making him laugh, instead of talking to myself like this. If my status were clarified, I might get a chance!

On the train from Darlington to London, Sunday 31 March, 11.30 a.m.

What a trudge – up from London on Friday to York to speak in Northallerton to the local European Union of Women (excellent lamb lunch and sold fifty-five books), then to Harrogate for NUEC (Majestic Hotel grandiose and shabby, conference centre futuristic and stifling), then to Redcar to speak to local Conservatives, mostly bussed in from Whitby and Scarborough ('There's only really four of us in Redcar. Would you like to see Mo Mowlam's house?'). The Hotel Royal York at Redcar did its best, but what a horribly depressing environment, with ICI belching fumes on one side and the stalag of British Steel on the other. The whole area is dreadfully blighted – looks like eastern Europe, a British Bitterfeld. *Very* glad to leave it behind.

What a week! After the announcement Thursday (21st) that we'd managed to create a new disease, the nation held its breath and the markets collapsed. Abattoirs have shut, transport workers been laid off. All weekend a cull was discussed – Douglas Hogg said we'd do away with the whole 11 million herd if necessary. Come Monday morning (25th) most of Cabinet met, including Party Chairman Brian Mawhinney, Treasury, and Leader of the House Tony Newton. They decided to do – *nothing*. Statements thoroughly trailed by Dorrell and Hogg turned out damp squibs. The farmers went ballistic, and so did I. I went to see Tony after the 10 p.m. vote and rather laid into him. 'We've set up the scare, now we have to satisfy the customers and reassure them.' Actually I started the conversation with, 'Let's talk politics. Will today's announcements bring my voters flocking back?' Answer – no, of course not. It got worse, as the EU Commission backed a Europe-wide ban on British beef – then, as alarm mounted, and the French very publicly incinerated an affected herd in Brittany, put a worldwide ban on all UK beef exports. The idea is to protect the reputation of European meat exports, but the Eurosceptics seized on it, claimed huge cover-ups in France and Germany, and asserted that our beef was safer than theirs. The PM, silly fool, joined in, attempting to blame both 'Europe' and Tony Blair for the infection which *this* government had allowed both to enter and to persist in the human food chain.

By Thursday evening the rout was complete. British beef had been replaced in both McDonald's and Burger King, Birds Eye had withdrawn pies, sausages etc.; remaining prime cuts were on sale at £2 per lb in Tesco (and sold out, rather as I would expect). Most LEAs have banned all beef products from school dinners. Protests by ministers that they were only following scientific advice in *not* seeking a cull, and the meat was safe, were widely taken as abjuring responsibility – exactly the opposite of what was expected. In the tea room, MPs insisted to me that the whole scare was got up by a hostile press (the *Daily Telegraph?*). On the radio Dorrell quoted with ferocious exasperation *The Sun*'s headline, 'It's not the cows who are mad, it's the people' – including presumably those we want to vote for us. And another tea room pundit, a new MP (Spink,[218] I think) said gloomily to me, 'Whenever there's a row, it's always the government which has to carry the can.' Well, quite, I responded, that's what it's for. What do you think being a minister is all about – a life of glamour with red boxes, a chauffeur-driven Rover and immunity from criticism?

The Economist (30 March) did a superb three-page analysis of the causes of BSE. How did it happen? (1) We have scrapie and have had it centuries – few places have as much. (2) Nowhere else is 4–5 per cent of cattle rations made from meat and bone meal (banned – at last! – on Thursday. If that had been done ten years ago, I told the Redcar Tories, I'd have been... who knows... Foreign Secretary by now!) And (3) nowhere else allows rendering at below 100°C, at which temperature even humble bacteria can survive, let alone

---

218 Robert Spink, Conservative MP for Castle Point since 1992.

the prion, which can manage 130°C. As early as 1980 a committee of government experts warned that low temperatures could be
dangerous – but no action because cheaper. And other countries
react effectively at once – whenever a case pops up they destroy
the whole herd (Ireland, France). But we never bothered – in fact
that decision still hasn't been taken, and now probably won't be –
instead the cull is likely to be all animals aged over thirty months,
since not a single case has appeared in anything under thirty
months recently. Still taking a risk, aren't we, since maybe it just
doesn't show up? By contrast, the Dutch have this week ordered the
destruction of 65,000 British veal calves. They simply don't believe
in taking chances, and we do.

In Harrogate I ran into Val Pulford, 'Big Val' of the David Ashby
case. She'd been his Chairman in 1983 and had been unhappy at
his selection; she confirmed my suspicion that he was the best of
a rum bunch, and had the edge as 'Ashby for Ashby'.[219] I said she
should put in for the vacancy and she looked very wistful, but it's
too late – she and hubby have moved to Suffolk and are caring
for her three-year-old grandchild. And she's had health problems:
aged fifty-two, she's past it. Lucky stars, I thought, thank you for my
energy and health. I still have so much to do.

Meanwhile the alternative career moves on. Hodder have offered
£200,000 for the next two novels, which is clearly good news – I have
a sale, hooray – but Sue Fletcher's letter was a bit offhand, and as
I wrote to Lisa, sounds disappointed that I haven't offered another
dirty book. But I don't want to be Jilly Cooper – I couldn't maintain the parallel career of a politician if I did that, and being both
ambitious and conceited I do think I can do better. Sue talks about
'going back to the same £100,000 offer as for *A Parliamentary Affair*'
but, as Lisa spotted immediately, that's wrong. It was £102,000,
with audio on top (£4,000), and you could add 10 per cent inflation
since 1992, so the correct figure would be £116,000. So it looks like
an opening bid. We haven't resolved the issue of the editor yet, but
it almost certainly won't be Richard now, and my reaction is one

---

219 Ashby-de-la-Zouch was in David Ashby's North West Leicestershire
    constituency.

of relief. Lisa says it could be an interesting few weeks! Anyway it means I can buy Mum a flat, and I'm looking forward to that: it will feel like completing a circle.

I went to the South East Staffordshire by-election on Tuesday, with Toby Jessel,[220] Michael Fabricant, and a would-be agent called Dirk Russell, who drove. He told me he's met me before: he drove me to/from Telford Young Conservatives years ago and I ticked him off about smoking. So he stopped: 'Best thing I've ever done.' Fabricant and Jessel were both delightful travelling companions; Toby has a fund of anecdotes about long-dead politicians, none with the slightest hint of malice. Michael talked endlessly about sunbathing nude on beaches and how he wouldn't mind being displayed full frontal in a tabloid if a paparazzo caught him. He seems to have sex on the brain, but is so funny and engaging, like a naughty little six-year-old playing with his willy. I sat behind him in the car and in fascination examined the tufts of multi-coloured (orange and grey) hairs peeping from under this pink wig, and fought the impulse to raise this artificiality and check just how bald and shining the pate beneath. What an odd man!

Toronto, Thursday 11 April, 8.40 a.m. Canadian time

About to take off from Toronto for London. Boring airport! All I could get as souvenirs was smoked salmon and maple syrup. We moan about Heathrow, but the shops are sparkling. Now I'm in for a seven-hour flight which arrives in England at 9 p.m. tonight. Ghastly boring, even though the antics of Sir Jimmy Goldsmith in Ivan Fallon's 1991 biography *Billionaire* will keep me entertained.

The Canada trip was, I think, a great success. The tally was nine TV shows, four radio interviews, three print interviews (*Toronto Star*, *Ottawa Citizen* and *The Hill* – a dotty, snobby sheet read by the intelligentsia and political mafia in Ottawa). The best was Pamela Wakin's live CBC evening show: she's a cross between Gloria Hunniford and Barbara Walters, more cutting than the first and nicer than the second. We finished with the Press Club of Ottawa,

220 Conservative MP for Twickenham since 1970.

which was great fun – I did my usual speech and a short reading and answered questions.

And yet one wonders why publishers think such activity is worthwhile. Canada has 28 million people: half the UK. But only about 18 million are English speaking and they don't buy many books: 3,000 is a bestseller. Josephine Cox is being pushed up to 10,000 – and that's paperback. A Catherine Cookson is huge, at 30,000! Even in Ottawa the bookshops are small and old fashioned. I saw only one discounting (though books aren't expensive). There's only one proper chain, most are two- to three-shop independents. Nobody thought audio, and I suspect CD-ROMs are to be found elsewhere, certainly not in bookshops. (The newspapers are amazingly old fashioned – old fonts, no colour.) Makes you realise, as I saw in Washington, that Europe is in some ways well ahead. And the cost! Business-class flight £2,435, internal £220, hotel for three nights $922 = £460, meals, chauffeured cars for two days, etc. – well over £3,000, so they're going to have to shift all their books to make a profit. It's called 'building on an author', they told me, and they expect more in future from me. Oh well, not much to become famous in a country overnight, I suppose.

Last week Lisa and I had an hour's, not entirely satisfactory, meeting with Sue and Jamie Hodder-Williams at Hodder. Sue looked tired and I found myself paradoxically liking her for trying hard and being professional, even as her comments fell far short of what I wanted. Lisa said she's never seen Sue talk so much! Jamie was good – it looks as if he's decided the company is going places and he intends to rise with it. Good for him. They made a slightly comical pair, especially in their efforts to make *LOL* a more 'international' novel (if accusing worldwide Jewry of racialism and of losing their children through cruelty isn't a global topic, then I don't know what is). She said brightly, 'We'll fly you all over the world!' as if I'd find that attractive… and Jamie wants an Australian in it, or an Aussie setting. Why? 'Cause we're big in Australia,' he finished lamely. All of 10 million of them, and a twenty-one hour flight? No thanks. I told them rather bluntly that I'm not Thomas Keneally, but I suspect they'd rather I were Jilly Cooper. Anyway, Lisa will send the proposal off to six other publishers (*not*

HarperCollins, as they have both Archer and Dobbs), and we'll see what happens.

And Ray appears to have opted for an unrealistic view of the future, settled in the Tower House, hardly ever expecting to be in London. Doesn't want a secretary – will write his own letters – but will get a mobile phone. Will need a big computer (what for?) and is thinking of a second-hand one (dangerous: viruses). And doesn't want advice, thank you: 'I have run a business' (when?). Was surprised I do my own VAT returns. He thinks I'm earning a bit of pin money.

Tower House, Friday 19 April, 2.50 p.m.

Last Friday I went up to Liverpool, where Mum moaned at me about an article (written by a freelancer, Danny Danziger) in the *Daily Mail*, an interview done in February, in which he'd taken *only* the negative quotes about the city. Most were accurate, so hardly worth my complaining about, but the tone was rather nasty, and everything in the first person, as if I'd written it. Her 'friend' Bertha Crawford, the lady who runs the Sunday afternoon cultural club, didn't bother to ask for a response, but promptly wrote and cancelled my invitation for a Sunday in June. Oh, *good*.

Flat-hunting started with me very much on edge, therefore. In one (very nice) place Mum turned up her nose – she knew, she said, someone had died there (not true – the lady had gone into sheltered accommodation, a neighbour said). She would not have *this* one if I gave it to her free. 'I *am* giving it to you free!' I muttered between clenched teeth. As I put it to Deb over a Chinese dinner later – I couldn't face any more chicken – 'Does anybody realise just how hard I have to work to raise £60,000?' She does, of course, and told me later that Mum did make grateful noises, to her. But nobody in my family ever learned to say nice things to *each other*. No wonder we were dysfunctional!

We lost the South East Staffordshire by-election quite spectacularly – a 22 per cent swing to Labour, only the second largest in a by-election since the War. Our vote dropped by over half, whereas Labour's total increased from '92, despite only a 60 per cent turn-out. (Lib Dems lost deposit – tactical voting.) Don't tell me they're not winning votes from us; and don't tell me we'll get it back – I don't believe it.

Brian Mawhinney responded so angrily to a question about the PM's leadership on Radio 4's *Today* as to have heightened (instead of killing) speculation about the issue. Labour was on to it like a shot. At Prime Minister's Questions yesterday – one of the best I've seen for ages, with the PM in Prague – Prescott put it to Heseltine that he'd thought it was necessary to do away with MT – so did he think the same now about JM? Hezza bounced back with energy and wit; sadly it demonstrated how leaden is the boss, how self-righteous is Blair; their deputies are human beings and much more fun. But it's too late to sparkle now, Michael – the time was last July had you wanted the job, and then you didn't.

Forty thousand copies of *A Woman's Place* sold by 29 February '96, so Hodder tell me; I'm now getting on with *LOL*.

Clapham, Sunday 21 April, 9.40 p.m.

Whacked! Lovely sunny weekend, so I drove down to Heathrow yesterday to pick up Susie (now travelling light, thank heaven) and spent a splendid twenty-four hours in her company. She stayed overnight in Clapham and we went on to Cambridge at lunchtime, getting entangled with the dafter end of the London Marathon; the runners all looked totally exhausted in the heat. (Hottest event ever: would you credit it, yet last weekend we had frost in Derbyshire and the tips of my daffodils turned black.) But Susie was in good form, and last night I took her to see the stage version of Irvine Welsh's *Trainspotting*, brought down from the Edinburgh Fringe. The film is all the rage at present: the story of four heroin junkies in Edinburgh and the mess they make of their lives – the baby dies, someone gets killed, an innocent bloke gets addicted, and will catch AIDS or whatever. Powerful stuff, brilliantly done. The accepted wisdom is that it glorifies addiction by making it funny, but I thought it exposes the bleakness and dreariness of their lives – it would put loads of people off drugs. Certainly the play, which is very violent (though not a drop of gore on stage), made the audience squirm, and every few minutes someone who could take no more got up to leave. But I found it mesmerising, though the movie (lots of gore, real baby etc.)

would not be to my taste: I liked the theatricality and admired the enormous skill with which it was done. And by contrast, Cambridge in the sunshine looked fabulous.

Because I could not bring myself to write it at the time, I haven't mentioned the profoundly unsettling info my brother gave me on 25 January, actually at his birthday party in the River Café, the posh eatery in Fulham. It transpired that when I left home (to get engaged), my father held a funeral service for me. He actually sat 'shiva', as if I were dead. Even as I write this, I start to shudder. I did not know then, and nobody (through shame?) has ever told me in the twenty-four years since. But to do it at all required ten men: so I asked Henry if he was one, and the answer, with not a whisker of embarrassment, was, 'Oh yes; well, you know what Dad was like.' No, I didn't. Not the complete depth of the horror. I never thought he was capable of *that*. As for my brother, I asked him, 'You would have been – what? Twenty-three – a university graduate? Why didn't you just tell him he was crazy and you wouldn't dream of supporting him?' He shrugged and grinned, and my appetite vanished, and I changed the subject. For if he had said another word I swear I'd have poured the soup right over him and walked out. But what's the point?

Wicked man, wicked religion. It makes me burn to write that book – I just hope I can do it justice. Meanwhile the Israelis have been bombing the hell out of south Lebanon, in an effort (they say) to rid the neighbourhood of Hezbollah guerrillas who are bomb-ing northern Israel. They're killing and maiming civilians – terrible pictures of injured children. And Israeli citizens are demonstrating for more, not for peace. At times I *despair*.

House of Commons, Monday 29 April, 9.30 p.m.

A quick half-hour of quiet despair while waiting to vote. Last week we saw the Tory Party begin to break up. I am now completely certain that we will lose the next election by a landslide, and that Blair will be in office a long time, probably until his government is brought down in its turn by the weight of its own contradic-tions, just like this one. The Eurosceptics will hold their seats, while swathes of people like me will lose; then lots of the good guys will back out of politics.

What happened? I'm not sure exactly, but there's no doubt the tone changed. So many U-turns took place in the space of five days or so, that by the weekend the last vestiges of credibility had disappeared. We started the week with threats of retaliation against our Euro partners unless the beef ban was lifted. Now since the scare has spread rapidly through Europe, with markets collapsed in non-BSE countries like Belgium, everyone else recognises this as a European problem – except us. Nor would we strengthen our argument at the European Court of Justice that the ban is excessive and illegal if we were indulging in something similar. So on Tuesday the government backed down.

By Wednesday tempers were frayed as we had stayed up till 2 a.m. two nights running to debate the legislation for the Northern Irish Assembly elections. As long as Paisley's around you never can rest, but in the end there were no late votes either night. Wednesday was the day chosen for Lord Mackay's Family Law Bill (is it going to be called the Family Law Law after the Royal Assent, I wonder?) Over 200 MPs had buggered off by then, with barely 400 voting. Free votes were granted to everyone, including, fatally, Cabinet ministers. So four of them, including the Home Secretary, voted against their own Lord Chancellor – and flap around as he might, the PM could not undo the damage. There is now plentiful evidence that the right wing are well organised and large enough in number to defeat the government, who got the Bill through only with Labour support.

The same evidence turned up the day before, when sixty-six Tories voted for Iain Duncan Smith and John Redwood's ten-minute rule Bill to restrict the powers of the European Court of Justice. The fact that the Bill was defeated by eighty-three to seventy-seven didn't hit the public consciousness at all; but the presence of Portillo and Michael Forsyth from the Cabinet to give moral support was well reported. Bastards, the PM memorably called them. He failed to sack them on the LBJ principle, that it's better to have them on the inside pissing out, etc.; but when they're inside the tent, and pissing for all they're worth, those nearest get splashed most.

And Jimmy Goldsmith was holding court all week (from his suite in the Dorchester, which says it all), according to Frank Johnson in

The Spectator, an old pal. Goldsmith was invited to a hush-hush meeting with the PM, but refused: nothing silent for him. Mahomet came to the mountain, however, in the form of a slinky John Redwood. What a pair of wankers they looked on TV – swivelling eyes and slippery smiles everywhere. Goldsmith wants a full referendum on the European superstate, he says. By Wednesday night he was pushing his candidates forward, and I found myself live on *Newsnight* against no less than Sir Alan Walters, Margaret's old economic guru, who's temporarily abandoned Washington to stand for the Referendum Party. He really looked barmy, and I had a lot of fun with him: many complimentary remarks afterwards. That we should have to respond to such lunatics at all, instead of having a firm and loud blast of common sense from the government, is a measure of our disarray.

Elsewhere, successes and failures. I've now lost almost a stone, and feel and look much better, and can fit into loads of old clothes, including tight jeans which have been hanging forlornly in the cupboard for a couple of years. This is the longest I've ever dieted successfully and the most I've ever lost. I'll carry on for a few weeks more and get comfortably under 10 stone. Won't know myself. But I'm tired and need a holiday – I can't believe one-third of the year has gone already. I've booked ten days in France at Whitsun.

And I am still getting nasty letters about that *Daily Mail* Danny Danziger article, e.g. from someone called 'Joan Cohen' of whom I've never heard, who claims kinship through my eldest Uncle Morris's wife, Golda (not a recommendation – wealthy and snobbish people whom I hardly knew). Anyway, this lady knows me so well that she has to write to me c/o the South Derbyshire Conservative office. I got no further than the first couple of lines, registered that the rest was in the same self-righteous sneer, controlled my temper, wrote 'You shouldn't believe everything you read in the papers' across the top, and posted it back to her.

Iain Mills was found by the police face down at one o'clock on Friday morning, dead drunk. He must have tried to walk back to Dolphin Square and keeled over. At 6 p.m. this evening he was looking frightened and sober in the tea room, but by the 10 p.m. vote he was red faced and swaying again. What a tragedy: only fifty-six.

Clapham, Sunday 12 May, 11.06 p.m.

Ray's birthday yesterday, and the whole family made quite an effort. Both Deb and Susie came. I bought tickets to the RSC performance of *Twelfth Night* at Nottingham, a box, plus champagne and smoked salmon sandwiches in the interval: the play extraordinarily well done, all very funny, and Malvolio a figure of genuine pathos and dignity at the end. The Fool too big, strong and knowing and didn't sing well enough; Viola and Olivia both lovely, the Count a lovesick dolt, the trio (Belch, Aguecheek and Fool) a bit lightweight, though Aguecheek was very comical. A most successful and enjoyable evening, though the RSC road manager (who chose to come in as we drank our champagne) said occupancy had been only 55 per cent that week and even Saturday night wasn't full. At £17.50 top ticket maybe it was a bit dear for the provinces?

Cambridge 3–5 May with Susie was a dream – beautiful weather, fun being a tourist, Holiday Inn clean and smart and *good* food (smashing breakfast) and nice little pool – Susie being under nineteen stayed overnight, free – Fitzwilliam Museum a revelation, gorgeous stuff in there, Monet's poplar trees and orchard in spring, all light and air, breathtaking medieval stuff which formed the original collection, the William Blakes small, dark and disappointing – only three on show, rest *hidden* – how infuriating – everything visible bright and beautifully displayed, we felt drunk with it all. Sunday to Ely – my God, the cathedral is astonishing, tall and slender inside like a line of willow trees planted far into the distance – the Lady Chapel vast, its carving like fine lace.

Susie told me she passed her Maths exam (hooray), and got 64.7 per cent for her mock Part I, which is a whisker off a top 2:1. Next year she'll do a diploma in German and has been invited to Pakistan for holiday by a fellow student. Jammy beggar! She'll settle in year three to get her First – she's no taste for the infighting at the Union. Taken up ballroom dancing and can do the jive – she demonstrated as we crossed a golf course on our ramble this morning. Got some funny looks. Game kid!

How profound these thoughts are as I record them, and how evanescent only a month later. That's the value of writing them down I suppose, as well as getting them *out of my system*.

Business has got more complicated this week by Richard's re-emergence. On Monday evening he left a message on the answerphone, just 'hello', but by the time I picked it up on Tuesday I'd already written him a note to accompany a card for his birthday two days later. On Wednesday evening he phoned, late, and we talked for thirty minutes. He's keen to edit me again and doesn't want to lose touch with his 'protégée', so I suppose that means we'll meet, over lunch or whatever. This time, however, I have no illusions. The business is effectively in voluntary receivership: he invites all creditors to agree to accept 30p in the £ and carries on trading. Apparently everyone is being very friendly, though on top of that £¼ million he lost a further £70,000 in January and another £70,000 in February; then back came all the returns, which he had not budgeted for, and he and his accountant have parted, not friends. Nor has he yet got a non-executive Chairman. So being mixed up with him again is not a good idea.

Other business: the local elections were dire, and there's a distinct sense of time running out. In the country as a whole we got 27 per cent (2 per cent better than last time), with Labour on 43 per cent and the Liberals on 25 per cent. Tactical voting against us is occurring on a large scale. In Derby we held only three seats – two years ago we controlled the council. In the constituency as a whole excluding Mickelover: Conservatives 28 per cent, Labour 53.7 per cent, Lib Dems 15 per cent. Disaster is now taken for granted. It is only a matter of time.

I arrived home in the small hours of Saturday morning to find on the table an enormous folder from a constituent (who I wrongly assumed had come to the house with it), asking me to remove his four daughters from his alcoholic ex-wife. Except that the divorce court had believed *her*, not him, and I don't get involved in divorce cases – and what wise man would get an MP involved anyway? What is it with these people: do they think I have a magic wand – still? At the Advice Bureau next day (Saturday), case after case depressed me. Lunatics of the world unite. The middle-aged woman convinced that her senile 88-year-old mother is being mistreated in a nursing home: except that nobody else thinks so, including her own brothers and sisters who live nearer. Only she cares about Mother etc. – though it's another sister who's been entrusted with the cash. I didn't believe her at all. Nor did I find convincing the young heroin addict who says he now understands his problem and gave me *pages* of drivel he'd written about himself: I reckoned an inflated ego was at least part of it, but again I couldn't see what I could do, especially as he has several highly qualified people dancing attention on him and has had for years. Or the bunch of aggressive loud-mouthed people who came to complain about a loud-mouthed neighbour they want evicted – by the time they'd finished raising their voices to me too, it was my settled opinion that I wouldn't fancy any of them as neighbours or even within a mile of me.

The highlight of the week should have been lunch Wednesday 8th at No. 10, but a sticky camembert sauce which ruined the salad, followed by chicken (honestly), then more cheese and biscuits instead of pudding, depressed me no end. This time there were no flowers on the table of any kind. John's conversation was so *thin*, even though he was with friends – all Tory MPs – but he is always ten seconds behind and completely fails to spot nuances. For example he went on at length about how awful the press is, especially on sleaze. Sitting opposite were Tim Yeo, David Tredinnick[221] and Allan Stewart, who all squirmed. The PM was on his way to the Scottish Conference – I did him the courtesy of telling him his campaign to keep the UK united is honourable and brings him respect, but voters in South Derbyshire don't care a fig; it is a waste of time. He asked Allan why the Tories were so unpopular in Scotland (Conference was being held in Aberdeen where we did marginally better in '92, but because of fish that badly misfired.) You'd think a PM might have had the conversation before, but no. It is because we're seen as English, says Stewart, and our support used to depend on the old Protestant working class, which has in effect vanished. We turned 'em into middle class, I murmured, and now they vote Labour, or SNP, or Lib Dem. We could lose every seat up there.

On BSE and beef he told us nothing new. The first slaughter has only just started and everything is in disarray. But his approach was small-minded pragmatism at its very worst. We couldn't withhold our EC contributions, he explained, because (1) it's illegal, and

---

221 Conservative MP for Bosworth since 1987.

the Commission could get a court order 'within forty-eight hours'; (2) it'd need a vote in the House of Commons and he can't be sure of winning it (too bloody right); and (3) suppose they started to retaliate, e.g. scrapie?[222] God almighty, I muttered: never mind sheep, what about *cars*? And at what point, I wondered, did a PM utter a word of principle – like we don't even consider withholding contributions because it would be *wrong*, or adopt a truly practical approach like negotiating intelligently to convince customers, all of them? Amazing. Menzies Campbell[223] said recently that BSE now stands for 'Blame Someone Else'.

The PM did come to Toyota on Friday, when we did the turf-cutting ceremony for the next Toyota (Corolla) factory, which will push them up to 200,000 cars p.a. by 1998 and create 1,000 more jobs. I was relegated to table two and not actively involved, which was disappointing.

But the actual highlight of the week was the debate on gays in the military on Thursday evening, which turned into a real House of Commons event. After worrying about it, I used the Stonewall material and performed quite effectively; lots of those who attended out of politeness and had planned to slope off home stayed to listen, so we had a well-attended Chamber and lots of short excellent speeches. Labour had a free vote and all their Select Committee members voted against, with John Reid[224] barracked heavily by his own side. We had a 'relaxed three line' and eight of us supported the amendment, which to my surprise was only defeated by sixty-eight votes, 188 to 120. A very credible result, as I'd thought we'd be hammered and had only agreed to do it all out of a sense of *duty*. Stonewall had somehow acquired the legal advice given to Nick Soames which said he's likely to lose in the European Court of Human Rights in three to four years' time. I wonder if everyone realises how significant that will be. If people can't be dismissed from the Army on the grounds that they're gay, then that'd apply to all forms of employment –

222 I.e. by banning sheep products.
223 Liberal Democrat MP for Fife North East since 1987 and a prominent figure in the Party.
224 Dr John Reid, opposition spokesman on defence; Labour MP for Motherwell North since 1987.

and hey presto we have at a stroke an anti-discrimination ruling for all jobs, for all the 35+ signatories but most especially in the UK. Big stuff. Almost makes the job worthwhile – and certainly a lot more valuable than verbal abuse between neighbours. So I *shall* miss some of it, but not enough to fight to stay.

Tower House, Sunday 19 May, 10 a.m.

The new book is going well, but publishers don't seem so keen. No one else apart from Little, Brown has shown an interest – we see them tomorrow. One, Century, wrote back that I was heading into 'women's regional fiction, a crowded field'. What nonsense! They missed me last time too. Lisa sounds disappointed but cheery. The political novel field is pretty crowded, I'd say – Sarah Keays has one out in October, Steve Norris is putting pen to paper, Phillip Oppenheim has sent one (*On the Floor*) which sounds fun to A. P. Watt. The latter two are in a better position than I am to write about intrigue and shenanigans, and with far greater cynicism and nudge-nudge humour. That's not my objective at all. I'm trying to *expose* the unpleasantness, not connive in it.

And then there's Richard, who is being a pain. He's been badgering Lisa with an extraordinary proposition, that he as editor and Rosie Cheetham at Orion should jointly bid for *LOL*. Her question: should she start number-crunching the division of costs to give the idea serious consideration? Her view was that Orion was wrong for me. I agree, I said, this is a complication we don't need. It perpetuates the irritation of a separate editor, and it feels (I said to Clare but not to Lisa) like emotional blackmail – Richard is *saying* he doesn't want to lose touch with his protégée, but he's *hinting* that I can't do it without him. And I can; though I miss him it's better to leave him out of it, and seek a replacement.

And so to FET and Bosnia – I'm going on 31 May till 7 June, such excitement! The money came through from the Westminster Foundation on Wednesday, so it's off for my shots, warn my insurance company, sort out some robust hot weather clothes and off we go. I'm excited, and scared: such an honour to be asked, really, to represent all that's best about my country and to try to do some good in another country so ravaged by war, and now so reluctantly edging its way back to peace and normality. The Worcestershire Regiment will be there, with Derbyshire lads, so we'll be looked after very well. Susie is eating her heart out that she can't come, as her exams are that week: she has landed a summer job with the City Corporation at the Guildhall, where she'll be paid, and learn a lot.

On Friday I did a literary lunch at Windsor at Sir Christopher Wren's house, with Robert Goddard[225] and Carol Thatcher. Goddard was one of the dullest table companions I've ever come across – a clerk in the council office in Exeter who married his boss, he's now buried in Winchester and had nothing whatever of interest to impart. His books are complexly plotted thrillers which sell well in Germany and USA; he himself looks like a little hamster, with a tidy brown beard, bulging cheeks and bright little eyes. His talk was quiet to the point of inaudibility, but moderately intriguing. In front of us two customers fell deeply asleep and awoke only at the applause. Carol, aged forty-one, was splendid – goodness she is loud and vulgar, and cheerily attractive. Marvellous chunky jewellery, but too much of it. Smooth unlined face, very pretty, very little make-up, natural wispy haircut; big check jacket, black trousers, plump but sexy: I did warm to her. Her handwriting, on the cards from which she made her speech, is very like her mother's – large, flowing, aggressive. But Margaret was honed by science, and a natural caution which neither of her children have inherited. Carol was promoting *Below the Parapet*, her biography of Denis, her father, and did so very well – she made him sound wise and funny and clearly loves him very much, now if not earlier. As for mother – I asked as we settled to sign (she bought one of my books!) what her father thought of her book. Was he happy? 'Oh yes, very. He likes it – once he got used to the idea.' And mother? 'She hasn't read it. Haven't seen her for ages. You know she spends her time in America – swanning around with her Foundation...' Her face had a bitter look. You would have thought, that expression said, that Mum could have found time to come to the launch of her daughter's book about her husband – says much about Margaret's current regard for Denis, too, doesn't it?

225 A thriller writer.

Just taken a phone call from the *Daily Express* asking if, following all the stories a month ago about my being approached to defect, the PM, whips etc had been paying me undue attention. Now the original leak, or some aspects of it, came from the Eurosceptics, of that I'm sure. I suspect this suggestion has the same provenance. The answer's no, no special treatment – but lunch at No. 10 was long overdue, and the whips (especially Patrick McLoughlin) know more about what I'm up to than they do about most of their charges, since I do it in public.

But as for the Party and the leadership... oh, I despair. If I wasn't committed, I wouldn't fight the next election. And there are bad moments when I pray that Blair wins with a big majority to get this shower out, and that he governs with a radical agenda instead of pretending to be a Tory. The BSE crisis rumbles on: 4,000 cattle a day are now being slaughtered. So the dairy herds are costing a fortune in feedstuffs – it's been so dry recently that there's not much forage – and are producing milk over quota which will produce fines of 30p per litre (we buy it for less than that). Talk about turning a crisis into a shambles. Yet I listen to the NFU's complaints (e.g. yesterday) with a cynical air, for they'll be compensated. The abattoir workers, the packers, the transport companies won't – they'll go out of business, and nobody will notice or grieve. Meanwhile Hogg is forced to speed up the selective cull of younger animals as a bid to get a timetable for lifting the ban: which has come to mean declaring the meat safe. And 'Europe' is being blamed everywhere for being so rotten to our farmers and fishermen.

Llangoed Hall Hotel, mid Wales, Friday 24 May, 10.30 p.m.
I'm here for the Hay-on-Wye Literary Festival. I speak tomorrow (Monday is Bank Holiday), and then a dinner here for Brecon Conservatives, one of the seats we're likely to lose, despite the civilised, kindly Jonathan Evans QC as its MP. I walked down to the Wye this evening and sat in the late evening sun, watching its surging brown waters and feeling just as turbulent.

We still don't know who is going to publish *LOL*. On Monday we had a splendid presentation with Little, Brown. Alan Samson is small, trim, dark haired, quick, friendly and delicate of mannerism. He had a long list of *editorial* suggestions, most of which were perfect and the rest arguable. We talked for one-and-a-half hours. Even better, his wife is half-Jewish so we could get a lot of mileage out of that, and he's an expert on pop music – '1963 is too early for Sandie Shaw' – terrific! I liked him very much: he is exactly how Richard should be. Then we went in to see the 'Queen Bee' Philippa Harrison, who was called in to rescue the firm (which was Macdonald) after the Robert Maxwell demise, and has made a brilliant success of it. In '94 they won 'Publisher of the Year' at the book trade awards. Also present a Mike and a David from promotions and marketing, but neither said much. Lisa was wonderful: sharp and observant. Nobody outside Hodder, it turned out, knew that Richard had freelanced for me, or how we'd handled the promotion side with another freelance, Kerry Hood; Little, Brown were surprised and I suppose had assumed an in-house editor or Sue Fletcher. In truth Hodder published the book, but they didn't create it. PH and AS, however, shared my view that, well developed, *LOL* could be big and should go in the States. They were also surprised that the parliamentary novels hadn't been taken in the US. Lisa reported the agents' comments – 'Great stuff, but we must get an American woman Senator to write them.' The Little, Brown people grasped at once why a change of direction was also commercially desirable.

Afterwards, I felt exhilarated, and drained, like I'd been at a successful selection committee or the scholarship interview back in '64. I was incapable of stringing two words together, so I sat quiet and alone in a smoky pub for half an hour, reading *The Standard* and drinking a Beck's for which I'd paid an outrageous £2.50, until my brain came back.

Up till now I've been a politician who dabbled at writing, quite successfully. Monday at Little, Brown was so momentous, and their mood about *LOL* was so exactly mine, that suddenly I stopped feeling deep down that my writing was a bit silly – and began to feel passionate and serious about it – not as an adjunct to my life, but as its centrepiece. A bit *'époustouflant'*![226]

---

226 Mind-blowing.

Llangoed Hall, Saturday 25 May, 7.35 a.m.

Not my kind of hotel! Of course I can whinge. I have a 300-year-old house in Derbyshire and a 200-year-old one in France, the latter in particular with the cool air and clean lines I love. And most of the books fairly new, too.

I don't think I'm a literary festival person either, though I may pop in to hear Anthony Howard quiz Peter Mandelson at lunchtime, and Doris Lessing at 2 p.m. is a temptation. But I'll probably doze off, or want to ask questions and embarrass everyone; and my first reactions on reading the programme are (1) admiration at the effort required to get so many distinguished people together in one place, and at the imagination behind the clever matches made; and (2) embarrassment that while I've heard of some of them I haven't actually read their books or poetry. So I feel distinctly out of place.

On the boat back from France, Thursday 30 May, 4.15 p.m.

Just had a natter on deck with David Willetts[227] – oddly enough, he and his wife were on the boat out too, though I saw them only as we disembarked. He's spent the last few days writing and reading, and she painting. Good to get away from their children, he said, who are parked at grandparents'. Yet I loved having the kids with us. He's pleasant, and smart, and watchful; said Hezza (his boss at DTI) has been on duty all week. The old pro goes off on long official trips when the House is sitting – e.g. China most recently – and then volunteers to hold the fort while everyone, including the press, is away.

David invited me to agree that the government's new Eurosceptic viewpoint was in line with the views of most Tory supporters and Party members, and why was that? I answered bluntly, 'Because the Party's shrinking,' and he didn't argue. I meant that it's getting older, weaker and smaller, and relying too heavily on nostalgia; and from a woman's point of view it can all look very different.

---

227 Parliamentary Secretary in the Cabinet Office; Conservative MP for Havant since 1992; formerly Director of the Centre for Policy Studies; nicknamed 'Two-Brains'.

It's lovely outside in the Channel. My little cabin on 'B' deck is forward and overlooks the bow. The sea is navy blue and calm. On deck people are sunbathing – there's a lot of pink flesh on view, which will be very sore by the time we arrive.

The long-protracted negotiations were concluded late last night, and Little, Brown have got the next two books. Lisa reckons Alan Samson must have worked through the night, and came up with £350,000 for both books. Such a lot of money. Goodness, as Richard would say. Lisa says we'll earn out and not to worry. But the transition has happened, I can feel it: now writing takes precedence over anything else.

I managed to finish up to Chapter 7 this week, which involved a marathon nine-hour day on Tuesday. That brings me where I thought I'd be. I'll send it off to Alan if I'm not too late tonight, or when I get back next weekend. Then we need a real session. I like the writing process and there's no doubt that the characters keep putting on flesh before my eyes, especially the minor ones, just as in *A Parliamentary Affair*. This time it is more fun, and less mechanical than *A Woman's Place*. On the other hand I don't yet feel I'm in control. And pretty soon I'll have to start writing sex scenes – yet how will I do it, when inspiration has dried up?

Oh, I daydream of meeting somebody nice... for company, and for conversation, and for cuddles, and for bed. I suppose everyone assumes I'm happily wed, yet they never see me with this wonderful, supportive husband. He didn't even bother to phone me in France to satisfy any curiosity he might have felt about the negotiations – but then he never used to phone anyway. Is there anyone out there? Am I of any interest to anyone but me?

Hotel Bosnia, Sarajevo, Tuesday 4 June, 10.39 p.m.[228]

Outside a Bosnian band is playing a soulful tune complete with balalaika. It's a balmy warm night with occasional flashes of lightning which make the room lights flicker. Not that the electricity

---

228 The visit of several MPs was organised to help prepare Bosnia for free elections.

supply seems so secure here – much of the city is dark. Curfew at 11 p.m.

Opposite the hotel is a burned-out apartment building, gaunt and full of grief, yet people are living there: among the black holes, flower pots are neatly ranged on balconies, washing is strung to dry, and old gents take the air. Inside you can glimpse smashed chandeliers and neat tablecloths on ramshackle tables. The hotel itself has no roof, or top floor – it must have taken a direct hit. Only two hotels are functioning in the whole city, this one and the Holiday Inn, both full, so our drivers are being put up in private homes where there's no running water. We let them use our showers this afternoon or, nice boys that they are, they might have driven straight home to Zagreb. They did not know they were coming to Bosnia – the hire company assumed we would be trotting around Croatia for a week – so Sarajevo is not their idea of a picnic.

Where the rest of the crew are staying is far worse: a landscape of pure hell. Huge tower blocks stand gaunt and blackened. One is the Parliament building, or was. The Holiday Inn (built for the '84 Winter Olympics) is gloomy and filthy, with much of the exterior and ground floor badly damaged; one of its four wings has completely disappeared. In the bar I asked for a gin and tonic; the girl cheerfully poured a gin (one glass) and a mysterious cloudy liquid (second glass). 'It is tonic,' she assured us. It was bitter lemon. I asked for orange juice instead and got it; she poured the bitter lemon back into the bottle.

Spent much of today in the company of Bob Churcher, chief manager for Brown and Root, the main civilian contractors to the US Army. He was decorated for commanding our soldiers in Northern Ireland – was General Officer Commanding in Armagh for two-and-a-half years. B&R do all the housekeeping and construction: power, water, food, supplies etc. Bob is large, florid, unfailingly cheerful, committed and highly efficient. In a big white US Army Land Rover Discovery, which glided smoothly over potholes, we went to two camps, 'Guardian', the HQ of the Military Police, and 'Bedrock', one of the five main US Army bases in Bosnia, home to 1,200 troops. At the first the Commander invited me to address a gathering of around 300 military police from all over the country who'd come, coincidentally, for a briefing on the election rules. So there I was, thanking the US Army for its help, and explaining what we're up to here. What a thrill. The much bigger Camp Bedrock was impressive – enormous, well laid out, orderly: lorry loads of hardcore to combat the winter mud ('24 inches deep when we arrived') and raised boardwalks everywhere. Typical Americans, eating indoors in a sweltering tent whereas most Europeans would have rigged up a shelter and sat outdoors in the breeze. But the tables had chequered tablecloths and little pots of flowers (drooping roses with a heady perfume) brought in by the locals, while outside locals had planted trees, presumably in the hope that the Americans will stay. The unit is mainly engineering and a big field hospital complete with a mobile CAT scanner; its gleaming white side walls and roof fold down around it like a box for transportation, and the whole thing cost only $800,000. Amazing! (The orthopaedic surgeon is a tall thin blue-eyed man called Colonel Toon. 'Your ancestors came from South Derbyshire?' I asked. 'Yes, ma'am.' 'You're a Viking then.' 'Yes, *ma'am!*') The Chief Engineer explained why B&R mattered: 'While they're putting up huts and carting the garbage, my guys are clearing mines in the Hungarian sector, repairing bridges in the Turkish sector, carving out a road for UN humanitarian vehicles. We're doing our job, and they do theirs.'

The best bit of all was on Sunday, with the British army. I was flown out by 'copter from their base outside Banja Luka to the area (Previja) they patrolled south of Ključ. A briefing from the CO, Lt Col Patrick Mercer, and Major Fred Chedham, both *splendid*, tall, thin, rangy, handsome men, keen as mustard. They took me out in a Warrior armoured vehicle – just a quick dash down the road, you understand, with me in a headscarf, shades of Margaret Thatcher – and then up in the 'copter again further south, to the area called 'the Anvil'. We touched down in a tiny village (Ukov) which I suppose must have been Muslim, for we were made very welcome – one old lady gave me a hug and two kisses. The platoon had taken over a school as their barracks and the basic idea was to make it ready so that the children would have somewhere to go when they returned – we saw hardly any in the village, or young mothers, so I suppose they've been spirited away till it's safe to come back.

Then back in the 'copter to HQ and the General. 'Call me Mike!' he kept saying, and we kept teasing him by calling him 'General'. What a character. Major-General Mike Jackson MBE is close to fifty-five, a big, stooping, fast-moving paratrooper. Bit of a wise-cracking geezer but sharp as a needle, oh yes, and utterly engaging with it. It was clear all his men adored him. I'd love to serve under someone like that – plenty of action, no stupid risks, able people given their head, clean operations, tidied up afterwards, job well done. He met me briefly at HQ, looked me over, shook hands, and I suppose must have been satisfied; for he and his whole HQ top brass accepted the invite for our 7 p.m. reception, which really made it go with a swing, and took us back to HQ for supper. *Such* fun, oh rather! We polished off many bottles of Australian wine in a very jolly manner and I dutifully ate steak, only to be informed to general amusement that it was from Uruguay. But one does try.

7.30 a.m. Wednesday. Humid sunny morning.

The big news from home is that the ban on beef derivatives has been lifted, and that Rod Richards, Minister at the Welsh Office,[229] has resigned following revelations in Sunday's *News of the World* of an affair with a PR girl. Silly man. His place is taken by Jonathan Evans QC – so that's his third job in six months, and not a good move as he was doing well at the Lord Chancellor's Office; but then we're short of Welshmen. (I dreamed about Rod last night. He was shrinking. I had to get down under the table to talk to him.)

In the little park opposite Zagreb airport, Thursday 6 June, 12 noon

I was in the car yesterday for the journey from Tuzla (three hours) with Jonathan Steele, a senior *Guardian* journalist, and Malcolm Tyndall, Michael Portillo's agent. Jonathan is a tall, thin, spare man

---

229 Conservative MP for North West Clwyd since 1992, has been replaced as Minister in the Lord Chancellor's Office by Gary Streeter, Conservative MP for Plymouth Sutton since 1992.

with sharp eyes and a ready smile – he covered Russia in the 1980s so all this is familiar to him. Tyndall is a wiry Scot with a mouthful of sharp teeth, a broad accent, huge energy and a dominant personality. At home he's a special constable but he's more like a Brigadier or RSM: at meals it's always Tyndall who counts up, rather noisily, the orders for Cokes, beers, hotdogs etc. JS questioned us both about what would happen after an election. Would JM stay on? Not a chance, we both chorused, laughing. He might try – and if we win, he might reasonably wait till the November leadership contest. But, said I, were he to raise the possibility with two or three of his Cabinet colleagues they would tell him *they* wished to stand and if necessary would stand against him. Then if he persisted one would take one arm, a second the other, the third would open the window, and out he'd go. It's known as defenestration and was common during the Inquisition.

House of Commons, Monday 17 June, 8.45 p.m.

Waiting to vote on the Family Law Bill. I applaud James Mackay's efforts to take fault out of divorce; he's had a miserable time with the moral right-wingers. The sight of John Patten's face, with its collapsed jowls and puffy eyes, as he tells the rest of us how to behave is laughable rather than sinister, but I dislike this evidence of an organised agenda on the part of a number of colleagues. They can do a lot of damage, not least to the Tory Party. Gary Streeter, the new minister (following Rod Richards's demise), made a good job of defending the Bill and spoke well of his own marriage vows – he managed to sound sincere, a rare thing these days from the Dispatch Box.

The meeting of EU foreign ministers broke up today, with no agreement on the lifting of the beef ban. It won't happen the way the PM wants. Next weekend is the summit at Florence and he's hoping he'll get a framework, which will set out an agreed timetable – 'You do this, and we'll do that.' Tragedy struck with the revelation that back in 1988 when we banned (not very effectively) the use of contaminated offal in animal feed, we went on exporting the same junk, mainly to France – and indeed increased our exports there several times over. 'Well, it wasn't illegal,' one MAFF official said

lamely. The French press are apoplectic, so Chirac and his government have joined the opposition. *Quel scandale.* Serve us right.

The non-co-operation strategy is a disaster – *another* disaster, on
top of the avoidable mess of BSE. It's certain to do serious and
permanent damage to our standing abroad. 'What an example to
set to the new countries who want to join,' grumbled the Danish
Foreign Minister. 'They'll get the idea that this is a legitimate tactic.'
And I can't for the life of me see how vetoing the establishment
of Europol or the directive on fraud is going to help us present
scientific evidence over beef. Over fifty items have been vetoed –
that in itself is an eye opener. We're well and truly embroiled in
Europe, to a much greater extent than the public recognises or
ministers admit.

But the Tory Party is now well on the way to breaking up. The
row reached new heights last week. On Tuesday Bill Cash put
forward another ten-minute rule Bill, this time for a referendum
along the lines set out by Goldsmith – i.e. on whether we want
a federal Europe or not, real cloud cuckoo land stuff. Goldsmith
took out impressive full-page ads in the press to urge support for
this Bill. He also made it clear that any MP not voting for it would
face a Referendum Party candidate in the general election, though
he wouldn't guarantee that those who did would be safe. Mischief
maker.

But then arose the issue of Cash's cash. The *Newsnight* reporter
on Monday night inquired whether it was true that Cash's
European Foundation, of which he is chairman, receives money
from Goldsmith. Of course, was the answer. It has hardly been
a secret. But here he was, proposing a Bill to do exactly what the
government has turned down flat, and challenging the front bench
as blatantly as it was possible to do. With funding from the leader
of a rival party? At Prime Minister's Questions the PM was invited
by Blair to denounce such practice and totally failed to do so – in
fact John was dire. Blair put it so well – if he keeps running, they'll
keep chasing. By Wednesday morning the lolly had been repudi-
ated (though not returned). In steps Lady Thatcher and replaces
the donation with substantial dosh of her own. Then up pops John
Major, indignant and petulant: if she has money to spare it ought

to come to the Tory Party. Amazing! And he has the nerve to go to the Welsh Conference and say he's had a bellyful of the wrangling. So have we. Leadership, John, that's what it requires – and sadly you've managed to do and say exactly the wrong things, attack the wrong targets: Thatcher instead of Goldsmith, donations instead of policies, the EU instead of food infection. You must be the worst Prime Minister in a very long time.

I prepared for some of this by having the CGE officers in for supper, and getting them all fired up before the meeting with Rifkind[230] – not that it took much pushing. I need to make sure that when I stick my neck out, I'm not entirely alone. The negative 'heads down, chaps' approach of Whitney and the PEG people[231] won't do. So Rifkind got a roasting from a room packed with members from all over the country, and looked a little shaken. At that stage (Wednesday 12th evening) he was still talking up his chances of an agreement today. When we protested about the non-co-operation policy, he asked smoothly, 'But do you think we'd have got progress without it?' 'You haven't got it yet,' I replied grimly from the chair. 'What else might we have done?' he riposted, the smooth lawyer to his fingertips. 'Try convincing argument,' I said, and pointed at the next hostile questioner. I was so bloody angry!

Mum has agreed to let me buy the flat she wants, though the valuation has come in at £47,500 instead of the asking price of £51,000 and it needs everything doing to it. Apparently the owner won't negotiate. I feel I'm being conned, slightly. Thank goodness I can afford it. Debbie went to see it last weekend, and is full of good ideas for how it can be improved. I'll go there on 30 June and sign a cheque. Then we can get on with the rewiring, new windows, alarm system, new kitchen, bathroom, curtains, carpets. Oh well. What am I earning it for, if not to spend it on something worthwhile?

Richard came round to the flat on Sunday night (9th), and the papers for the company voluntary agreement followed a few days

---

230 Malcolm Rifkind was then Foreign Secretary.
231 Ray Whitney had been PEG Chairman since 1993.

later. He looked tired and scruffy – had been playing with his children, had taken Toby to see the Cézanne exhibition, so some part
of him is still functioning normally. Richard himself was a bit vague
about the figures, and I was appalled when I read them. The firm
lost £250,000 in the trading period up to the end of September,
as I already knew. But then it lost *another* £250,000 in the following
seven months to end April. It's clear that the investors have lost
their money. What made me particularly annoyed was that he owes
£140,000 to his suppliers – printers, delivery and the like, including
an unforgivable £1,088 to Linden Stafford, who can't afford to lose
it. The proposal is that creditors be paid 25 per cent and write off
the rest. Last time we talked he had fifty-one books; according to the
accounts, drawn up by insolvency practitioners, he has sixty. So he's
been buying more books, and paying the writers, while failing to
pay even the most basic bills. I call that a disgrace. He fell out with
his accountant in April and is now the sole director. In fact the
bank is running the show, so for the first time ever he is obliged to
watch the bills month by month, and managed to break even in
May. That, dear Richard, is how to do it.

Richard tried the charm, but I don't think we trust each other
like before – he doesn't trust me not to tell him constantly what
to do, and I don't trust him not to fantasise. His fantasy world is
so attractive, and dangerous, because unsettling. On the whole I
prefer equanimity.

Clapham, Wednesday 19 June, 10.50 p.m.
Just come back from a supper with the 'Blue Whips',[232] which
disturbed me very much. Judith Mayhew took the chair – she is
impressive, leader-elect of the City of London Corporation and
will be its first ever woman leader. No other woman Tory MP or
baroness bothered to come, though I think a lot were asked.

It was so depressing. Every woman there would make a first-class
MP, and not one is in a safe seat (not even me). Margaret Daly
thinks she is, but I doubt it. Some, like Judith and Elizabeth St Clair-
Legge, are potential ministers and Cabinet ministers, but they can't

232 Conservative women on the candidate list.

even get selected. At Guildford the final shortlist was three women and one man – and the bloke got it. In most cases the girls don't get past the first round.

Central Office is, in part, to blame. The list of attributes to look for now includes questions on 'family responsibilities', which any court would rule as highly discriminatory. The image of the ideal candidate as a 'Margaret Thatcher' has faded, to be replaced by identikit young men, a pattern adopted with alacrity by selection committees, most of whose members haven't experienced working women – at least not in peacetime. The executive (where safe seats make the final selection) is 200 or more old biddies – the '£5 a year members', one girl called them – who do little but turn up for the annual ladies' lunch and wouldn't know a voter if they fell over one. So much for all the PM's fine speeches: load of crap.

Some horror tales were told. One girl was pressurised into giving up office as constituency Treasurer when she got married. Her husband was Chairman, and the other officers objected that if they sat together on a selection committee they wouldn't be independent. Worse was the appalling story told by Geeta Sidhu, a wealthy and beautiful Indian, recently selected for Blackburn. No problem there about a woman candidate (it was Barbara Castle's seat), or her race. But when CCO heard she was pregnant, officials spent over four hours with her, she said, trying to persuade her to have an abortion. The way she told it was entirely credible, though if it had been me they'd have had barely four minutes.

What was creepy, however, was the accumulating evidence of some kind of conspiracy. Several present talked about the 'gay boys' who are winning seats, who all seem to know each other, who have friends in Central Office, who become special advisers and slide into other key posts. They've been targeting likely seats for years. They then hold key positions such as branch chairmen, and recruit like-minded people as members, so that the final selection stage may have 400 members attending, over half of whom are 'new'. It was only mentioned once that their views are very right wing and quite nasty, though my anxieties are raised as much by the fact that they are not open gays but have young women on their arms: they are cheats, liars and hypocrites. I hope to heaven they're not using

TORCHE (which has 400 members) as a front; I imagine leading lights such as Paul Barnes and Tony Hutt would be apoplectic at the thought of closet gays propounding right-wing moralistic views in order to get elected.

It sounds preposterous when I write it all down, but these women are not stupid, and all seemed to know to whom they are referring.

But if it's true – and if they come in to the next Parliament in fair numbers (how many are there? A dozen? Twenty? Who knows?) – then they really could destroy the Party. For once the scandal breaks, the press would be on to them like a shot. Just as this Parliament has been painted as crammed with adulterers when it isn't, it'd be relatively easy to paint the Tories in the next Parliament as a bunch of lying wankers. 'Could be very embarrassing!' as one of the girls put it. Some understatement.

Suddenly I'm really scared. If we get hammered and have, say, 200 MPs after the election; if the Party goes nastily right wing, so we lose the middle ground; if this 'infiltration' (a word used repeatedly) is a fact, then the Conservative Party could fall apart.

So I harangued the ladies, somewhat. It's our Party; we mustn't let this gang take over. And if they do… someday, sooner or later, a bunch of sensible Tories will meet and seize the Party back, restore it to its rightful electoral position (i.e. electable) and enable it to choose candidates of a more suitable tendency. In particular, more women like you! If you care about the Party, if you care about your country, you have to be ready. But I fear it could take a long, long time.

Tower House, Sunday 30 June, 10.30 p.m.
Richard is slowly climbing out of the mire. The creditors' meeting was on Thursday morning. He phoned the day before and found me struggling with Chapter 8 on a humid, sticky day, furious at being distracted by so many trivial phone calls. (As if I cared whether George Gardiner[233] was deselected or not – he wasn't. And French TV wanting an interview on what England

---

233 Sir George Gardiner, Conservative MP for Reigate since 1974; a prominent Eurosceptic and critic of John Major's government.

would be like with Tony Blair as PM – I ask you.) Anyway, to Richard – he told me he'd made a profit of £16,000 in May, despite £13,000 returns – most of his money comes from selling rights, not from selling books. Of course it helps that he can't contract any more books for ages, so he has to concentrate on adding value to what he's got. He has a mysterious new £50,000 backer and more to come – in Richard's eyes the promise of fresh cash had already grown to £150,000. Walter Mitty's not in it.

Tower House, Friday 12 July, 11.29 p.m.
Best news of the week was Deb's 2:1 from Huddersfield, which had her ecstatic on Monday afternoon. I was tickled that she'd run all the way back from the university to phone me – 'Mum! Guess what!' It's a good result, but I'm not surprised. In the last eighteen months or so she'd turned in a steady stream of A and B+ work. She plans to work for the next few weeks in the dispatch department of a factory earning about £160 p.w., so her finances will improve. She's such a sensible person these days, which makes me feel very confident about her future, and immensely grateful. It might all have turned out so differently: when you look at other people's horrible children – inarticulate, sullen and aggressive, or nasty little upstarts. It's fantastic to feel I've got one off my hands; it will be nice to get to 1998 or '99, when Susie starts earning money too!

Second bit of good news is that our parliamentary salaries are going up to £43,000 (from £34,000) from 1 July, so that means a hike in my redundancy money to nearly £24,000 – I can manage a year on that – and pension to (I think) about £11,000 a year. The vote was on Wednesday night, and without intending to I got heavily embroiled in the arguments, with appearances on *Frost* Sunday morning, the *Jimmy Young Programme* (Radio 2) Monday and a whole hour's Radio 4 phone-in, *Call Peter Snow*, which went very well but left me a bit limp and exhausted. Most critics think MPs aren't worth anything and several dottily suggested we should work for nowt. One guy wanted fewer MPs (agree) and that we should work 9–5 (impossible – and contradictory). Conflicting views came as to whether we *should* work outside – the Thatcher line: she famously declared in 1983, last time we had a Pay Review Body, that we should get a part-time salary for a part-time job, so we all dutifully voted for the pay to go from £11,000 (awful, even then), not to £19,000 as recommended but to £15,000, and have been regretting it ever since. In the last thirty years (last time we gave ourselves a serious hike was *1963*), MPs' pay has risen only by inflation and ministers' has halved, while average earnings are up 80 per cent in real terms. What stuck in our craw were two things: (1) the government had appointed the Pay Review Body in February '96, knowing perfectly well it would come up with big increases – had demanded a report and recommendations in record time – and then tried to ignore it entirely. Then (2) when it came to their own ministerial salaries, which will get a much bigger increase – so a PUS will get £66,000, a Cabinet minister over £100,000 and the PM £143,000 – the buggers sat on their hands and abstained, all of them. So they'd marshalled the payroll against our £43,000, then sat looking smug as we ensured their dosh. Angry? I could spit. When the result (253:49) was announced, there were furious shouts of 'Where's the payroll?' and one or two had the conscience to blush.

Tower House, Saturday 13 July, 11.05 p.m.
Lisa is getting married to her Andy, who's a hunk, and an author, but mostly in financial services in the City. I'm so pleased for her, and madly jealous! She's certainly been looking happier since he came along this spring. And she's setting up her own agency from 1 August, and I'll go with her; A. P. Watt will pay her a fee for administering all my contracts with them, including the new one, which I hope we will sign at last on 28 July. If it doesn't work out, I can always go back to A. P. Watt, or ask Alan who he thinks is the best: that's not likely to happen before '98/'99, by when she'll either have made a success of it or slid downhill. She's been superb with me.

Liverpool, Thursday 25 July, 10.20 p.m.
Humid night – surprising for Liverpool where it's usually fresh. Bad thunderstorms in London on Tuesday and Wednesday, with several women struck by lightning at a Buckingham Palace garden party.

I'm here to progress Mum's flat: the kitchen/bathroom people are getting on quite well though running up little extras, like a new radiator, the moment they see me coming. I'd mind less if they treated the flat with care, but there's junk all over the furniture and plaster ground into the carpet – not a cover anywhere, real cowboy stuff. Mum was sold a pup in the flat itself, which needed a lot of work – we'll be lucky to get away with only £16,000 worth; and allowed herself to buy all the beds there, a grim mistake as two of the mattresses turned out quite disgusting when lifted (which, since she thinks all Jewish people are totally honest, she didn't think to do first). We sorted out electrics today (new fuse box and plugs needed), plus windows (£2,800), curtains (£1,000) and carpets (£1,270). That leaves decorating, which Mum can look after herself. The carpet hunt angered me, and reminded me once more why coming to Liverpool is like arriving in a different country – a bit like Bulgaria, I imagine, though I've never been there – in which nothing is ever easy, straightforward, sophisticated or courteous. Minor examples at the theatre tonight included 'We don't have lemon and the ice is over there,' as I bought a G&T, and 'Crisps? No, we don't sell crisps,' as if that was a daft thing to request at a bar. If *only* somebody, in that accent so thick you can scrape off the wall, would say, 'Of course: let me get it for you,' or 'I must apologise...' We went to Carpet World and Allied Carpets at the retail park in Speke mainly to get 0 per cent credit, as my available capital has shrunk to zilch: cash flow problems for the first time in ages! In the former is a loudmouth salesman, who cackled at the idea of free fitting; said firmly the cheapest underlay was £3.49 (it wasn't), did all his sums terrifyingly in his head and wise-cracked his way round the shop. You won't get cheaper elsewhere, was his parting shot; ah, but I might get *politer*, was my muttered response, and I might be sure both Mum and I can trust both what's being said to us, and the after-sales service, among other things. We fared better with a patient young man at Allied Carpets – but oh! how I loathe all those Scousers that want to be Freddie Starr, and spend more time trying to guess (loudly) who I am than showing me their wares.

Took Mum to *Evita* tonight at the Empire. There was an odd moment when I thought of old love, and I suddenly felt very sad. I miss him so – it was *so* precious, while it lasted – and whenever I see actors embrace, mouth to mouth, it turns me over, for it's so long since anyone kissed me with passion and longing. Maybe there'll never be another occasion. Oh, misery.

Given half a chance (i.e. excuse) I won't stand for South Derbyshire again: I enjoy so much the three hours writing I can cram in to the morning, and so loathe wasting hours dining with constituents like last Friday night (how *can* people be so uninteresting – their hols in hotels in Cyprus… agh); or even, these days, the three hours at Advice Bureau, when I come to the conclusion that half the world's either mad or stupid.

Went to drinks with Tony Newton on Tuesday evening. Jacques Arnold[234] moaned about the bias of the Speaker (she's not biased, she's just useless). Rupert Allason blamed the press for everything, till I tartly asked what he'd do about the press and pointed out that effective gagging would never get through Parliament (and would be ruled out by courts, I'm sure). No more Parliamentary reforms are planned – a pity, since in fact Tony sees himself as a crusading, reforming Leader of the House. At a recent drinks session with William Waldegrave, No. 2 at the Treasury (Chief Secretary), canvassing ideas for the Budget, David Evennett[235] suggested a 5 per cent cut across the board of all public spending – as if we haven't been in power seventeen years and know it can't be done that way; Richard Alexander[236] wanted to *cut* tobacco taxes till I told him tartly (God, I get fed up with myself too) that he'd never get *that* through the House, as *I'd* vote against it, and so would several others. Sir John Hunt wants a tax on utilities and (I think) on 'fat cat' salaries paid to their chairmen – it'd be popular, he thought. Real *Daily Mail* area. The fact that we privatised 'em, and that as Tories we shouldn't join in the attack on *anybody's* salary, let alone in such a way as to suggest we have (or ought to have) a private sector pay policy, seems to have passed him by. So we have government

---

234 Conservative MP for Gravesham since 1987.
235 Conservative MP for Erith and Crayford since 1983.
236 Conservative MP for Newark since 1979.

by fools (5 per cent), pressure groups (tobacco) and populist rags (fat cats). Heaven help us.

Les Tuileries, Thursday 1 August, 3.45 p.m.

Under the hibiscus tree at Les Tuileries. Sunny but not too hot, faint breeze stirring the leaves, butterflies everywhere, honey bees above my head, and nothing more alarming than the faint 'plop' as a faded blossom, twisted into a crumple of purple crepe, falls to the gravel. Bliss.

Pity there's no one here to share it – but I always think that. Ray should be – doing what? When we came home from his niece's wedding in Northumberland, he just sat watching TV – the Tour de France, and the sailing at the Olympics. I joined him for a bit, but it was like watching paint dry. How *can* an intelligent man do that, for hours and hours? At least he now has a client, good news in which I rejoice without rancour. I'm glad I was wrong, and I hope he keeps it up. He certainly seems perkier.

The contract for *LOL* is signed, with a glass of champagne which promptly made me woozy and chatter on. Alan was happy with the chapters so far, particularly the flashback chapters which he feels work well, and made only superficial comments (e.g. about the chapter titles). Lisa and Alan were very hopeful that I'll meet useful people in New York – Time-Warner's editor, and Lisa's agent in the USA. Both should have seen the 78,000 words and synopsis, so we might conceivably be in business. For novel two, Alan seems interested in a 1970s sequel to *LOL*. Why not?

On the 'Pride of Portsmouth' in the Channel, Friday 23 August, 5.30 p.m.

Just eaten a rather disgusting plate of steak and chips – the latter thin, white, pallid, like strips of uncooked skin. I don't know why I do it: I wasn't hungry. In the three weeks in France I put on a couple of pounds, but not because I was eating badly – most of the time it was chicken, fish, salad (masses of it) and plums from our own tree, stewed in the microwave – delicious and good for me. Then I'd eat most of a packet of crunchy oat cereal (434 cals per 100g – and I could eat 400g at a sitting, i.e. most of a fresh 500g bag). Did that *twice*. Found some peanuts left over from New Year's Eve and did same with them. So it took a lot of hard work to put this weight on! And the daft thing is, I did my exercises faithfully every morning for twenty minutes, so it's all reasonably trim. Something very contradictory in there. Maybe I don't think I'm worthy of love or admiration, so I strive to be a slob. When I was a child my Mum was forever saying, 'Have *one*, Edwina,' and hoarding the rest (especially biscuits and sweet things – presumably because sugar was rationed?), and I get such a thrill of defiance when I go on eating and don't stop. Stupid!

It's the first time I've had the house entirely to myself all summer and *written* steadily – really got on with it, with few interruptions, and no frustrations. Not editing as in '93 and '95, and no emotional messes really.

In a list of working peers this week were included the names of Maurice Saatchi and Peter Gummer,[237] brother of John and the 'government's PR adviser'. Now that seems rum. I've no objections to their peerages – a lot of snobbery was flying around about PR people not being suitable. But it's odd to make the awards now, before the election which they are masterminding is won. Makes one wonder if it's part of a deal, and that they insisted on payment in advance knowing that afterwards (1) it could take years for CCO to cough up the cash, like last time, and (2) there'd be no guarantee of the honours, especially if JM moved on. Can't force him then! John Taylor, the loser at Cheltenham, is in too, so 'Marcus Carey'[238] is now a peer. Lord Taylor of – where? Solihull,[239] probably. I hope he loves every single minute!

Tower House, Saturday 7 September, 11.22 p.m.

Just been to my first South Derbyshire engagement since the hols, a 'meet your MP' event in Shelton Lock. Actually I'd met nearly all of them before; but these were among the 180 people who responded to our direct mail shot and survey in July asking if they wanted to join

---

237 As Lord Chadlington.
238 A character in *A Parliamentary Affair*.
239 In fact he took the title Lord Taylor of Warwick.

the Party. In all some twenty or so people attended, but that included more than half a dozen of our activists. So numbers are not exactly swelling in the area. The survey has been a success, however, with just under 5,000 returned, about 30 per cent; in Derby North and Erewash fewer than 3,000 have come in, though the mailing was roughly the same size. So they do take their politics seriously here.

And law and order remains the dominant issue (49 per cent), with NHS (21 per cent) and education (10 per cent). Nice to have a constituency which continues bang on the national averages! Twenty-nine per cent want a compulsory ID card – we discussed it tonight and the general view was that those who are against it (or don't want one) have a problem they wish to hide. None cared about the Eurosceptic argument, and none liked the government's muddled approach. Ty is convinced an election will be called for 7 November – Central Office is stepping up activity and gets frenetic at the least improvement in the polls – but it's the PM's decision and he is congenitally against speed. So I still think we'll see it out till the bitter end, and hope Labour continues to fray at the edges.

A good summer, in all. Aren't I lucky to have Les Tuileries and all the freedom it confers. I polished off my accounts during the Bank Holiday weekend in London, and then we had a most enjoyable time on *QE2*. *Far* better than two years ago: (1) a more agreeable companion in Susie – what a nice kid she is, so full of enthusiasms and excess, but so smart and intelligent; (2) the ship's been done up and looked splendid, and staff were much happier too; and (3) I didn't fight it, but let myself be lulled into relaxation and enjoyment. The motion of the ship is itself soporific, I decided: the whole place is enervating. But unless you fight it the effect is really rather nice, and you're too sleepy to get bored. I did manage twelve hours' writing in four days, but it was a supreme effort, and the results poor. And the two talks I gave went very well indeed, so I hope I get asked again. Next time it's Deb's turn, Susie and I decided, and I shall ask for the Caribbean cruise.

On board were Sir Ludovic Kennedy, looking decrepit, and his wife Moira Shearer, looking radiant and decades younger than her age – she must be seventy. Still red haired and very pretty. She told me she stopped exercising the moment she gave up ballet and has never done a scrap since, but she was upright and trim and elegant. Maybe good bones help, or a lifelong addiction to cigarettes – she has a deep husky voice, like sandpaper rasping on wood. Ludo had been invited to the States for the launch of an HBO film of his book on the Lindbergh baby case, so he rang the Cruise Director and offered to show it and talk about it, while Moira would introduce *The Red Shoes*,[240] in return for the passage; they leapt at it, as Ludo used to be a regular. Gary Rhodes, the punk TV cook, was on board talking too, and Jilly Goolden (wine expert and broadcaster), who, it turns out, is married to the DoH official on the cardiac desk (boyish, black curly hair, ready smile)... Paul something?[241]

So to New York, and that was far better than expected, cleaner, more fun. I told Susie my tablets make me more equable, which caused her to choke a bit, but in fact New York is *much* improved too. We stayed in the Paramount Hotel off Times Square, an old (?1930s) building recently done up by Philippe Starck in ultra-modern style. It took some getting used to – very weird furniture, strange mirrors, Yves Tanguy/Daliesque curves, dark everywhere, but with unexpectedly humorous touches – each lift illuminated in a different colour – blue, orange, green, red. I thought it was dotty till I saw its sister hotel, the Royalton, where the ideas were more boldly (and expensively) worked out. Bit like a half-finished railway station, I reckoned. I did get fed up with the air conditioning, which was so cold, but at least our bedroom was old fashioned enough to have its own controls. Someday someone will invent a quiet, dust-free air conditioner for small rooms, but it ain't happened yet. Perhaps fortunately the bedroom was a den of gloom, and much too dark to work in.

I did manage to get a meeting with Kathy Anderson of Lisa's agency, Scovil Chichak Galen. In some ways I wasn't very impressed – she was quite young and a bit scruffy, or at least dull – not a scrap of New York chic; and the office was (from what I could see) just a couple of small rooms in a nondescript office block on Park Avenue

---

240 The 1948 Powell and Pressburger film in which Moira Shearer starred.
241 Paul Marshall.

South, lined with books I didn't recognise at all, except Ackroyd. And I recall Ellen Levine took me to lunch, whereas this girl didn't even offer a glass of water on a boiling hot day – nor coffee, nor tea – nothing. It was also frustrating that she'd had the material and only just read it – she had only to Chapter 10, of course – but the Executive Vice-President of Little, Brown New York, Fredrica Friedman, had not, and 'thought it would be a discourtesy' to see me. Huh! Oddly enough, I didn't much mind – once I had one meeting, I could justify the $1,000 bill at the Paramount, and it was a bit too hot and stuffy to go trudging around. But the stuff's been in Lisa's hands since the end of July, so I did feel we could have done better. (Kathy said Fredrica and I would 'love each other'. Pity we didn't get a chance to find out.)

I was reminded of the rewards of my other life on returning home. The British Legion have put both mine and Alf Morris's[242] name forward for an award for our Gulf War Syndrome work – if agreed, I go to St James's Palace for a royal investiture. Now that would be nice. One always says one does this work for its own sake, but what delight if somebody says 'Thanks' in public.

Europejski Hotel, Warsaw, Saturday 21 September, 5.20 p.m.
I'm here in Poland for the latest conference of the FET, of which I'm now Joint Chairman. Terrific polyglot atmosphere. What fun this is, and how worthwhile! I'll skip the Berlin workshop in January '97, but hope to get to Estonia end February '97; whether I'll be allowed to go to the Georgia one in July I don't know, but after that I think I'll leave it to others. I don't fly too well – my right ear only 'popped' this afternoon, yet I flew out on Tuesday, and I suffered a bit at the start of the week as I stayed in a freezing cold house. I had to buy a coat or I'd have got pneumonia. It didn't help that the duvet, pillows etc. were all old feathers, so by yesterday morning my sinuses were blocked and I was feeling quite groggy and puffed up. Getting older, and at times like that I certainly feel it and long for a (slightly) quieter life.

---

242 Former Minister for the Disabled and opposition spokesman on the disabled; Labour MP for Manchester Wythenshawe since 1964.

I saw Alan two weeks ago as planned. He had detailed suggestions on Chapters 11–15, none of which sounded impossible. We lunched at Orso's,[243] and stayed till 3.40 p.m. talking over a pot of Earl Grey tea. One question I wanted him to mull over was what the next book should be, for if it is to be a sequel or use any of the *LOL* characters, we have to arrange that in final chapters. Afterwards talked to Lisa, who's quite optimistic about a US sale; the contract would probably stipulate that the second book must have USA setting, but after such an enjoyable time in New York City I can live with that. She'll press on. So: very hard work over Xmas hols to incorporate all Alan's points. But I am writing better and crisper – my only enemy is *time*.

Then I wasted some of that same evening with Richard. My own fault entirely, but it was a weird and distinctly unpleasant experience. Peter Ackroyd did a presentation at the National Theatre; I thought it'd be fun to see how someone else did it, and get him to sign my copies of his books after: it turned out I had four! – and now I have five, as I bought *Milton in America*, though it's had distinctly mixed reviews. I sent Richard a fax inviting him to join me, and he accepted with alacrity. We had a glass of wine, then went to eat. Why did I do it? Curiosity; I wanted to hear how he was getting on, and to tell him about my progress. So: RCB is still in trouble, as part of the rescue plan (to raise money through remainders) isn't working. I wasn't clear why, I must say. Well-reviewed books like the David Lean biography didn't sell – I guess because you need a marketing strategy, a retrospective of films or whatever, which Richard didn't have. The firm is thus still losing money. He said he has promises of £100,000 if only he raises another £50,000 etc., but really he's missed the boat with serious investment, e.g. from 3i. I should say the firm will fold after Xmas, and I got the distinct impression that he has rather lost interest. Lisa reckons he seeks easy happiness when times are tough. Whereas under pressure, people like her and me clear the table and get on with it. That's why we have achievements to our names, not debts written off.

243 A restaurant in Covent Garden.

Susie phoned: 'Hi, I'm in Moab. That's in Utah.' Having a smashing time and not run out of money yet. And Deb phoned in a tizz and then came to Derby for the Sunday (8th). Having a mid-life crisis, she said. Has decided Yorkshire is really too boring and undemanding – 'It's too easy to be best there' – and wants to move back down south, i.e. London, to look for a job in children's TV. Wow! I pointed out that she would have to cope with two things she's resisted so far – she'll have to exploit the fact that she's my daughter, and she'll become famous. She'd clearly thought about both: 'They'll go looking for skeletons in my closet, won't they?' she said cheerfully. 'Have you any?' I asked. 'Oh yes,' she responded cheerfully, 'dozens. Lost count. But if any old boyfriend went to the papers, I'd just say I couldn't remember him.'

Clapham, Sunday 6 October, 8.25 p.m.

The voters are still solidly with Labour. NOP in the *Sunday Times* makes gloomy reading: 52 per cent Labour, 29 per cent Tories (down 2 points), 13 per cent Lib Dems (whose Conference was very boring), and 5 per cent others. Labour's 23 per cent lead is back where it was in May. So much for our 'recovery'. What's more telling is that 53 per cent said simply 'it's time for a change' as the strongest reason to vote Labour – compared with only 14 per cent choosing their policies.

Neil Hamilton[244] and Ian Greer[245] abandoned their libel case against *The Guardian* on the grounds they couldn't afford it, they said: but in fact the previous week the defence had disclosed their case, as is now usual. That included numerous witnesses who had seen Hamilton accepting envelopes stuffed with £50 notes (£2,000 a time) from Mohammed Al Fayed: the bugger had even phoned and demanded to know if his envelope was ready. Over several years, as we all knew. Papers had been obtained on subpoena from No. 10, CCO and all over the place, so *The Guardian* has been having a field day publishing as much as it can. So much stuff has come out that

---

244 PUS, DTI, 1992–4; Conservative MP for Tatton since 1983.
245 Parliamentary lobbyist.

it's overflowed to other papers – e.g. a memo from David Willetts as a whip on how to nobble Sir Geoffrey Johnson-Smith's Privileges Committee, making 'good use of its Tory majority'. John Major was thumping the table on *Frost* this morning, saying 'I want to know the truth' and has promised all papers to Sir Gordon Downie, the Registrar (there are more?).

I went to Dublin Friday/Saturday to promote books, and had a truly marvellous time. The city looked splendid: very busy and smart, crammed with attractive young people who all dressed very Continental, slim and elegant. And Deb came too, to see around the RTE studios for *The Late Late Show*. It went well – I was on for nearly two hours. Goodness, isn't Gay Byrne a consummate professional: he won't use an earpiece or autocue, but concentrates, consults a few notes, and speaks direct to camera. The effect is relaxed and intelligent – a discussion on farm subsidies was lively to say the least, but got close to accepting that change is coming. Afterwards, as we drank red wine in the hospitality room, I asked Deb whether she liked the atmosphere: 'Oh *yes*,' was the answer. So next morning I took her shopping, replaced the tatty leggings with black leather trousers (not quite tight enough) and bought her an elegant grey suit with a tight little mini. Hardly expensive at £85, but she looked terrific. She has lost some weight and is now a size ten – the boobs no longer banging around and the thighs long and curvy. The Hodder lady took one look later and said, 'Does your daughter realise she's drop-dead gorgeous?' 'No,' says I, and I think that's true. Deb understands she's good-looking and sexy – I tried to explain to her about beauty, how the French understand it depends on line, and angle, and fluidity of movement: that a woman can be beautiful to them if she knows her body, has her hair cut perfectly, and moves with simple elegance. My daughter was *very* attentive, though she still twitches about her ears, which nobody but she will notice.

We discussed the possibility of her working in Irish TV. She made pals with Byrne's daughter Crona, and swapped addresses; they're in with the Riverdance crowd and will make contact when she comes to England to see the show. Deb will come with me to the *Frost* programme soon, and to Pebble Mill for *Call My Bluff* – that'll give her some idea of both London and provincial studios. But she'd need to learn her craft before making progress in London, and Ireland would be perfect, especially as a new TV channel is opening up there next year.

Les Tuileries, Sunday 20 October, 2 p.m.

I'm sitting in the garden in the sun: bliss! It was cold and misty when the boat docked at 6 a.m. – and pitch dark – but I got here by 10.15, opened the shutters, made the bed and headed into the village for the 'Foire des Pommes', the first time I've seen it.

Bit of a contrast to the slick operation of the Party Conference in Bournemouth this year. I was very apprehensive beforehand, but in fact it went well. All ministers, including the PM on Wednesday morning, made it clear that they won't be pushed into refusing the single currency now; our options stay open. It's the first time they've stated the same policy for two months in a row, in itself remarkable. The PM's session was a question-and-answer wheeze, but very well done. He clearly enjoyed the informality and gave much punchier and clearer responses to questions than his usual mealy-mouthed attempts to please. So the anti-Europeans went into retreat, or at least into abeyance; a truce has been declared till after the election.

At least, within the Conservative Party. Yesterday saw the Conference of the Referendum Party in Brighton, on which Sir James Goldsmith had reputedly lavished £¾ million, and a very lavish affair it was too, with free food and drink for the journalists and for many of the 4,500 delegates. Mostly Tories, it turned out: the type who thinks David Evans[246] is too lower class to be a Tory MP. According to *The Economist*, polls now suggest Goldsmith is getting 71 per cent of his support from ex-Tories – that's the appeal of money and charisma, both seen as missing from the modern Conservative Party. If he gets the 3.7 per cent gained by UK Independence Party (grossed up) in the election, then he could wreck as many as twenty seats for the Tories (i.e. cause them to be lost, mostly to Labour). And that'd scupper the election. I don't see it that way, frankly; if we lose in South Derbyshire (and we will), it

246 Conservative MP for Welwyn Hatfield since 1987.

won't be because of Goldsmith *et al*, but because my constituents decided to vote Labour some time ago.

So it was frustrating to hear Mawhinney talk as if it's possible to be in the Referendum Party and Conservative Party at the same time. Heseltine did lay into Jimmy from the platform, deriding his homes in Mexico and France and Venice, though the latter is Lord McAlpine's in fact (as Hezza must have known, because he went there after his heart attack). But the PM refuses to take the threat seriously, or to respond in an effective and direct fashion. There is no Party line, in fact; the loyal members don't know what to think.

Highlights from Conference: Ken Clarke at our CGE reception (a glittering affair!) bouncing around and announcing that we pro-Europeans have won. He did so well next day on the podium that he got a seven-minute ovation, in contrast to Portillo, whose earlier performance was wooden and sullen and whose dull speech read as if large chunks had been blue-pencilled out at the last minute, too late to rewrite. I do hope so. Redwood skulked sinisterly at the fringe, but was curiously ineffective. Tebbit snapped at Leon Brittan, but Quentin Davies emerged a star at the European Movement debate against Teddy Taylor. It felt good. And Ted Heath is in full swing, with a crisp well-thought-out attack on Thursday lunchtime against those who say they were deceived about the political aspects of European union. He was such a dull speaker when he was PM – pedantic and arrogant – but now is sharp, puckish and to the point. He got a standing ovation from the hall, which touched him and us: tears in eyes.

Of course the Conference won't make a scrap of difference. The Eurosceptics have their plans laid for *after* the election, not before. The voters are simply waiting, grim and cross. We came back to find Peter Thurnham (who gave up the whip in February) had joined the Lib Dems, which leaves them with the largest number of MPs since the 1950s.

And then there was my fiftieth birthday party on Sunday. I'm so glad we did it at St Ermin's:[247] no shopping, no hiring of staff, no

---

247 St Ermin's Hotel, off Victoria Street, near the Curries' flat in Carlisle
    Place and the Houses of Parliament.

mess, no crush, and no washing up afterwards. Lots of old friends I haven't seen for ten years or more. I brought down the Gresley Male Voice Choir as my main South Derbyshire representatives. They sang like angels and everyone loved them. Pink champagne and lots of good food, balloons and loads of flowers, my Mum sitting regally in an alcove as people came to chat, a table creaking under the weight of presents, which took two days to open: such treasures, such memories. The family gave me two days at a health farm (hoots of laughter from assembled pals), but Deb is keen to come too and try the massages etc. after hearing about the *QE2* from Susie. Gwynneth Flower made eyes at the elderly male choristers and they went home happy; I hadn't the heart to tell them…

I'm so glad I had the party. It made the transition into the second half of my life easy and fun, and I felt surrounded by love and affection, most of it of my own making. Strictly speaking it's the 'next third', when I think about it. The *first* third was 'childhood', up to the age of twenty, when I was forming. The *second* was 'the ambitious years' – ambitious in having kids, which I've realised is the most exposed and courageous thing anyone can do; and ambitious in terms of career. That lasted for me till quite recently, but the ambitions of my early twenties are satisfied. I certainly don't want to go back and repeat any of them, though what persists is those personality traits which were there in the first place: inquisitiveness, a low boredom threshold, a huge capacity for work, a delight in achievement, a masochistic pleasure in a fresh challenge. The desire to serve and be useful has waned somewhat, and been replaced more by a need to realise my own worth: but that's partly because time-wise the two are in conflict. I can *either* be a successful MP (or MEP), campaigning on behalf of constituents in particular or at large, or I can make the enormous effort to write decent books and make a lot of money. But I can't do both: there are neither the hours in the week nor the brain cells in my head. For the *third* 'third' of my life is the next twenty years when, if all goes well, I can build up some solid financial reserves: then the *fourth* 'third', which nobody ever plans for, will be seventy-plus, when I'll need every penny if I'm to have a comfortable old age. For me the ultimate luxury would be a companion (paid, if necessary) who'd have some of my tastes, and look after me, and not mind my imperiousness or bouts of misery, and share my joy in life, which mostly at the moment goes unshared.

Alan is very pleased with the new chapters. We discussed changing the title to make it less parochial: 'Taking Leave' sounds like Kingsley Amis, he said, but maybe 'Keeping Faith' would do. It's important to settle this, as it'd need to be explained in the last chapter. Up to 140,000 words now, so we're in the home straight, and I'll finish mid-January if no mishap. Then I'll fight the election, and lose; then recuperate, appear at Hay-on-Wye with the Little, Brown people; then do pre-production work, and plan next novel; then September, whoosh, next launch. I like Alan: he's cool, and bright, less reserved than at first, boyish and articulate but full of sharp observations. We talk about the characters as if they're real, which he seems to think needs an apology on his part: to me, that's the greatest compliment he can pay.

Back at the Commons the main row is about sleaze again. Honestly, John Major needs shooting. He should have sacked Neil Hamilton or better still, never have put him into government with his dodgy reputation in the first place. (Instead he should have insisted that I went back. Insisted, and found a way to persuade me, and a job I'd like. He's an idiot.) What John did, however, was set up an inquiry which (1) spun the thing out – Hamilton resigned all of two years ago – and (2) churned up the earth and found lots of other bones sticking out. Hamilton himself should have been warned off suing and the whips should have made it clear he was on his own. At Conference Mawhinney was busy *defending* Hamilton. In the back of my mind is fury and bitterness that they go to such lengths to defend an amoral shifty slob like Hamilton, and did nothing to help me; and I'd done nothing wrong, nothing whatever. His constituency are backing him too. Hope he loses, but he won't, and it'll take ages before the corrupt taint is washed away.

I'm beginning to feel more 'politician-y' as the election approaches: can't help it, I suppose.

London, Wednesday 6 November, 9.10 a.m.
Bill Clinton got re-elected last night, relatively easily, the first

Democrat since Roosevelt to be elected for a second term (but then Kennedy was killed). He took 50 per cent of the vote, up 7 per cent from '92, to Dole's 42 per cent (up 4 per cent) – the votes coming from Ross Perot (8 per cent). And while male voters split for Dole, women went heavily for Clinton – older ones worried about pensions and healthcare programmes, the younger ones fearful of being carers or needing them in future. Ah, these men; they discount women voters but we count, we count!

An odd experience therefore to be voting in the House last night, trudging through the lobbies, and surrounded by men in suits. My nose is at the level of their shoulder blades. I see their dandruff and their sagging chins. I'm more aware than they are of bulging bellies and shirts escaping from trousers and buttons missed. I can't see their shoes, but neither can they and many haven't been able to see them for years! Not an impressive lot. Politics attracts some rather mediocre people who would not be successful elsewhere: yet because you don't need capital or an education to keep going – indeed the main requirements are a ready tongue, stamina and determination – progress is possible for many real nonentities. That doesn't matter as long as meritocracy rules and the leadership is immensely clear headed, but neither is true in this administration.

Supper in the Members' Dining Room with Ann Widdecombe and Janet Fookes. Excruciatingly boring, though the food was lovely. Apart from boundary changes, what have we got to talk about? Janet and I had been in the gym earlier. Ann said we were mad. Yet she was the only one with nail varnish: and like us, she dyes her hair, though badly. God, what an aggressive personality – and awful to look at!

Clapham, Monday 25 November, 11.30 p.m.

Deb has been trotting round doing TV with me, and it has been fun, if hard work. Yesterday, for example, I accepted Sky TV at 10 a.m.; then (their) cab to Harvey Nichols, then tube to Selfridges, then late lunch – an expensive Angus Steak House meal – then *Art* at Wyndham's Theatre where I fell asleep, not surprisingly: it's a good play, but would be perfect on TV, not stage. All livened by a big butterfly in the middle of one tear-jerking scene, which put the audience into fits of guilty giggles. Then (their) cab to LWT for *An Evening with Bruce Forsyth*; he's getting old (sixty-eight) and his jokes all fell flat, but he sings and dances with conviction and skill, and can still turn a sketch like a trooper. Fun for Deb to see a huge light entertainment studio, and to meet the stars afterwards. She made eyes at footballer John Fashanu (who was extremely nice, it has to be said), and was offered a job by Dai Llewellyn! And she has her first paid appearance coming up next Monday, on *The Time, The Place*, on what it's like to be a famous person's child: £150 fee, which she's very tickled about. I've warned her not to try to live on bits: she needs training, and won't get it easily. She went home this afternoon full of plans to sell her house, move her cats and grow her hair. Let's hope the punk with tattoos has been left behind for good.

I ran into Virginia Bottomley on a train this week. She insisted on sitting at my table 'for a gossip', but instead told me all her plans and ideas etc. at National Heritage[248] – not one of which sounded interesting or worthwhile to me. And she wanted my opinion about the Millennium and how to get a Christian element into it. I was frankly puzzled, and told her that the churches would do that and governments shouldn't interfere. She'd called in the Chief Rabbi, who said he wasn't bothered by the Christian implications, but I reckon she had a nerve even asking him that.

Tower House, Saturday 7 December, 4.40 p.m.
An amazingly grotty week. I'd say it was the point at which the Tory Party fell apart, if I hadn't said so several times before. I'm so weary of it all.

Officially we've lost our majority. Sir John Gorst[249] has withdrawn his support (not left the Party, since he couldn't stand next time) because pledges of a 24-hour accident and emergency service at his local hospital have been abandoned. Hugh Dykes is equally

248 She had been Secretary of State for National Heritage since 1995; her responsibilities included plans for celebrating the forthcoming Millennium.
249 Conservative MP for Hendon North since 1970.

cross about it. The same evening Eurosceptics like Edward Leigh[250] ('Tory ex-minister calls for...') and Tony Marlow were demanding the resignation of Ken Clarke. The Chancellor, it appears, is the main reason why the PM is sticking to 'wait and see' or 'all options open' on the single currency. But in last Monday's *Telegraph* the PM let it be known that he wants to change the policy (which was agreed only last April). He'd like to rule out joining the euro now: not because it's right and proper – or good for the country – but to avoid further splits in the Party. Do that and we go, warns Clarke. Go, howl the sceptics. All the cartoons show a crumpling Major. And this lady is utterly disgusted.

No wonder the polls are getting worse, not better. According to Gallup in the *Telegraph* yesterday (6 December) the gap's widened to 37 per cent! We've slipped back to 22 per cent, Labour's up to 59 per cent. At the same point before the last election we were no longer level pegging but slightly ahead.

Oh, to hell with politics. Most other things are going OK. A photoshoot for *The Sun* on Monday should put Deb (and me) in the limelight – I hope it'll help her. Dinner at St James's Palace for the Royal British Legion with Susie and Prince Michael of Kent was a rather dull affair, except they have the best waitresses in the business – cool, efficient and quiet. Lots of bad art, ill lit, on display on scarlet flock walls. Yuk. Alf Morris and I had to dash back to vote on the Budget: majority = 5. Editorial with Alan on Thursday fine – we're within 10,000 words of 'The End', and he says it should be a huge commercial success. He's also keen for me to meet Fredrica from Little, Brown USA. His version: 'Little, Brown is rather a WASP company in the USA, but all its big hits are via Freddie, who's New York Jewish in a big way.' I offered to take the lady to the House of Commons and his eyes lit up! That might work.

Susie's in Pakistan by now – she tried on the *shalwar kameez* in the flat last night and looked rather splendid. Deb is trying to sell her house and finds she'll have to take a loss: well, she bought a private house and is selling a property in multi-occupation. She

---

250 Conservative MP for Gainsborough and Horncastle since 1983; PUS, DTI, 1990–93.

was so sweet about it – the main loser of course is me, to whom she owes £5,000: 'I'll pay it back with interest some day when I'm rich and famous.' Of course she will. In fact I'll lend her another £5,000 to make up the gap, so she can survive on work experience. She's written off to Dai Llewellyn, and has no end of offers of work experience whenever she likes.

Clapham, Sunday 15 December, 11.19 p.m.

Tired, so I won't write long. The drive up and down to Derby is proving problematic – once again this evening I started to doze off and had to stop at a service station and curl up for a snooze. The rest of the trip was done on chocolate again, which makes me feel sick, though wide awake. The alternative is to drink Coca-Cola and then I have to keep stopping for the loo. It's been a busy weekend, with a party at Tower House last night for the constituency workers. I'm ashamed that I couldn't put a name to quite a few, and we (both Ty and I) forgot to invite Jane. Still the food was great, and Ray busied himself magnificently with the booze and bar, hoovered, shifted furniture, removed doors, put up decorations etc.

The workers were in surprisingly good humour and chattered away nineteen to the dozen. Bit of a contrast to the polls, which continue terrible, both MORI and Gallup. The Barnsley by-election went to Labour as expected, with a 33 per cent turnout; we were in third place to Lib Dems, but at least we beat Scargill's lot,[251] who barely showed. So that's the end of him – barely a footnote in a by-election. But by Wednesday skies had darkened again when the Standards and Privileges Committee published their unanimous report castigating David Willetts, not so much for attempting to interfere with their predecessor in his first week as whip over the Neil Hamilton affair, but for lying to the Committee quite blatantly. He'd have done better to admit it, plead incompetence, or temporary insanity, and apologise profusely. His punishment is to be forever associated with the euphemism 'dissembling'; as his integrity was firmly impugned he resigned at once, looking hurt and bewildered.

---

251 The Socialist Labour Party, founded by the miners' leader Arthur Scargill.

Meanwhile we have our two-day Euro debate and the Dublin summit. To my surprise I was called early in the first day's debate, and said (as I've said before) that if the PM budges any further in the direction of the Eurosceptics, and in particular if he declares against our joining the single currency, then he can fight South Derbyshire without me. For in a constituency which has done so well out of Europe, I can't stand up with any conscience (or credibility) and explain why the Tories, the party of business, have suddenly turned their backs on their main customers. The declaration caused quite a stir, as I hoped it would, though the *Daily Telegraph* promptly got it wrong and said I'd threatened to resign and call a by-election. No point in doing that so close to a general election, not that I'd do such a thing, so it wasn't very bright of their reporter. Today's *Sunday Telegraph* says ten Tories are talking to the Lib Dems and quotes encouraging noises from Archy Kirkwood:[252] well, he would, but I don't believe the story. So many times at Double Eight we've determined to stay put; and the one or two who have talked wildly about forming a new party (e.g. John Stevens MEP) have quickly been reminded that all that's out there is the wilderness. Do a Gaitskell[253] and stay and fight, that's the best approach and the one most likely to succeed in the long term.

I worked out that it could be a *very* long term. If Blair wins comfortably this time, he could pick the date of the election after that – say 2001, four years on: and again in 2005. On recent form that third election will still be on the current boundaries. It won't be till after that, perhaps 2009 and 2010, that fresh boundaries might be helpful to us, especially if a large-scale reform had taken place (smaller Parliament, fewer seats for Scotland and Wales etc. You never know). Could be 'thirteen wasted years' all over again. Teresa Gorman will be eighty before we return to power, or nearly. I wonder what age she will be claiming then?![254] Writing books instead seems

---

252 Liberal Democrat MP for Roxburgh and Berwickshire since 1983.
253 Hugh Gaitskell, leader of the Labour Party, 1955–63, resolved to 'fight and fight and fight again to save the Party we love' when defeated at the 1960 Party Conference over unilateral nuclear disarmament.
254 Teresa Gorman announced in 1988 that she had knocked ten years off her age in order to gain selection as Conservative candidate for Billericay.

like a *very* good idea. Maybe something on 'The Strange Death of Tory England'? That's from a Robert Harris *Sunday Times* article on my wall. He's so sharp; today he pointed out that we are returning to the eighteenth-century pattern of politics which predated social-ism and capitalism, namely the Whigs and the Tories. The latter were traditionalist, conservative, imperialistic, Anglo-Catholic and distrustful of foreigners. The former were liberal minded, anti-Establishment, reformist and too ready to accept foreign influ-ence and criticism. They were also (as Harris didn't point out) the academics who wrote their view of history – the chattering classes of their day. Meanwhile mass suffrage created an electorate sympa-thetic to the other side – hence the dominance of the Conservative Party in British politics since. Until now?

The Summit went very smoothly, despite the inevitable 'Major stands alone' headlines. On the contrary, he capitulated gracefully – well, he does give in so quickly these days. His face, as they say, bears the imprint of whoever sat on it last. Unveiled in Dublin were the new euro banknotes, lurid in colour but bland in design in order to offend nobody. The bridges, arches and monuments are all vaguely familiar and completely fictitious. That's a shame, considering what magnifi-cence we have in reality – it's as if Beethoven's 9th had been rejected in favour of Little Miss Muffet because Ludwig was a German. Oh, be brave, and have the courage of your convictions; and show a little *taste*.

Clapham, Monday 16 December, 11.49 p.m.
On Tuesday Nick Soames announced that the government had in effect changed sides on Gulf War Syndrome: he admitted open involvement of pesticides (organophosphorus compounds), declassi-fied the medical records, allocated £1.5 million to a full-scale Medical Research Council effort, increased co-operation with the Americans, and apologised profusely and repeatedly. Mrs Adams, who raised the issue originally, sent me a lovely Xmas card, in which she says her son is much better now, and is continuing his career in the Army.

Meanwhile the government had a comfortable eleven majority tonight on fisheries, with most of the rebels toeing the line. It'll be like that till the end of February, I guess. Then the whole thing will finish with a whimper.

Les Tuileries, Friday 27 December, 7.10 p.m.

Golly, it's nice here. Fire in the hearth – dry wood lit up easily, unlike the damp chunks of poplar on offer in Derby. I filled the house with plants bought in Alençon – hyacinths and daffodil bulbs, anemones – and in a day or two the smell with be lovely. The furniture is cold to the touch, like this table, but the house was warm, with all the radiators blazing away. Outside the sky's like black velvet studded with diamonds, but it's cold enough to freeze your eyeballs; inside the only sounds are the steady roar and crackle of the fire, the squeak of the clock on the oven, and the flap of the piece of paper on the noticeboard above the radiator. Utter peace, and relative comfort.

John Major ended the year in style, winning the Radio 4 'Personality of the Year' poll. He got less than a quarter of the nearly 140,000 votes cast: about 4,000 of his were disqualified through multiple voting. But if we can buy telephone canvassing we can organise (modest) phone-ins, and he didn't have much opposition because Blair was disqualified when his own people were caught doing just that!

Another minister is leaving Parliament – Tony Nelson, Minister of State at DTI, who is a strong pro-European, a thoroughly nice guy and a big loss to the pro-European wing. Yet one can see why. Tony came into Parliament aged twenty-six, and is now forty-eight. He languished on the back benches for a long while and got a reputation as a playboy – one girlfriend was the gorgeous actress Fiona Fullerton. Margaret ignored him. Only in 1992 was he brought into government as Economic Secretary to the Treasury and has done very well since. But where would he be going? Into opposition for ten years, when he could be earning very good money in the City and having a much easier life? It's hard to blame him. But that kind of attrition leaves the parliamentary Party wide open for take-over after the election.

Two strange incidents before we broke up for the hols. One concerned John Hume,[255] the SDLP MP who has run a one-man crusade for peace in Northern Ireland. He looks like an ill-kempt

---

255 Leader of the Social Democratic and Labour Party since 1979; MP for Foyle since 1983.

walrus, and blinks earnestly at you behind his specs, but there's not a shred of doubt he means well, though JM's view is that he gets in the way. In the Library he reminded me of a previous conversation I'd forgotten, about his dialogues with the IRA, and asked if I'd passed the info on to anybody, e.g. Andrew Hunter, Chairman of the backbench Northern Ireland Committee. Now Andrew is well meaning but dim, and I'd not dream of sharing a confidence with him or anybody else, and I said so. Apparently shortly after Hume told me, Hunter started asking questions of the PM and the initiative was scuppered. But Hume is not a discreet man – and if he told me, he told lots of people; after all, he wanted to be a conduit for the IRA so it wouldn't have made sense to keep quiet. Then Hume told me another indiscretion: that Hunter approached him and asked if it would be possible to meet Gerry Adams. Hume didn't say whether the meeting took place, but I got the impression that it didn't because Adams wasn't keen. Organ grinders and monkeys: Adams wanted to sit at the table with the PM, and nobody else. The ceasefire is over, no doubt about that. Another bomb in Docklands, though it wasn't mentioned on the Radio 4 news this morning so couldn't have done much damage. I think a faction of the IRA started placing bombs independently last summer, and Adams decided to accept responsibility, partly to stop the movement splitting and to keep an eye on the wild men. But 'intelligence' has led to lots of discoveries of arms caches, especially in England. The loyalists are itching to start shooting Catholics again. Mr Hunter is paddling in very deep and murky water.

The other 'incident' involved Andrew Robathan[256] and ended up in the *Sunday Express*. Last week in the tea room I was munching a bun and trying to read Mayhew's[257] statement on public interest immunity. Jopling[258] and Bowen Wells[259] were at the same table. I

---

256 Conservative MP for Blaby since 1992.

257 Sir Patrick Mayhew, Secretary of State for Northern Ireland since 1992; Conservative MP for Tunbridge Wells since 1974.

258 Michael Jopling, Conservative MP for Westmoreland and Lonsdale since 1983; MP for Westmoreland, 1964–83.

259 Conservative MP for Hertford and Stortford since 1983; MP for Hertford and Stevenage, 1979–83.

was grumbling that the gym was being renovated and I couldn't get to it: Jopling's jowls wobbled and he quoted Oscar Wilde: 'Whenever I get the urge for exercise I go and lie down.' Yes, I said sourly, but Oscar would have done better if he'd lain down by himself. Guffaws all round, they like smutty jokes in the tea room. Over comes Andrew Robathan. 'Ah! I hear you're standing down,' he says to me. 'No, provided the government doesn't change its policy any more,' I replied, smiling sweetly. 'But you are standing down! You are leaving us! Aren't you going to Europe?' (Giggles from table behind.) He bends his face towards mine. By this time Wells and Jopling have slipped out, and I'm alone with this creature hovering at my shoulder. 'We should be sorry to lose you. You're a very pretty woman.' Currie gazes at him in disgusted disbelief. 'Fuck off,' I told him. And he did. Time was when Tory MPs didn't behave like that even to the opposition, let alone to each other.

1997

Les Tuileries, Wednesday 1 January, 9.00 a.m.

I cannot get this house warm: the cavernous rooms suck up the meagre heat from the convectors and leave everything chilly to the touch, while the tendency to overload and cut out, e.g. when the fridge switches itself on, is not conducive to calm thought! I've four layers on indoors, and two duvets on the bed, and I keep working with a hot water bottle tucked under my sweater. If it wasn't worse at home I'd have gone back, but England has blizzards and roads closed, so an early return would be an even worse idea. Here at least it's bright and sunny all day. I went for a walk this morning and met dozens of birds: robins, blackbirds, finches etc. – great fun. Tomorrow lunchtime, if I've earned it by several hours' work, I'll *walk* into Mouliherne and have a hot lunch at the Cheval Blanc. I've had a grotty cold a week now, but it is passing and my body's craving exercise, so we'll try it.

Just read Michael Dobbs's new novel *Goodfellowe MP* for a review for the *Daily Mail* (sent out by courier and arrived in Mouliherne within twenty-four hours – very impressive). It took me four hours to read the lot, so hardly demanding and a bit boring. Basic plot of a bumbling worthy MP and a rapacious corrupting newspaper tycoon very predictable but worked out quite well – the sub-plots much more interesting, i.e. difficult teenage daughter, Jewish secretary, Chinatown locations. Loose ends everywhere: HarperCollins are not looking after him editor-wise. I'm sure *LOL* is much better – indeed, in a different class. Worked hard on it Saturday/Sunday/Monday/Tuesday, taken a break today and then start again tomorrow and work through until Saturday. Hope that'll suffice at this stage. I'm keen to hand it in next week before I go to Berlin, and then we can start the next stage of revision and the real struggle after that.

Clapham, Monday 20 January, 11.30 p.m.

I gave up on France and came home on the 3rd. The weather reports threatened heavy snow, which the Loire had avoided till then. So dismal did it sound that I phoned P&O and got the next boat back. By then the external water supply had dried up – the washing machine went round but no water – and I was spending more time filling hot water bottles (*bouillottes*) and fetching logs than writing. In Clapham I settled in for a marathon session, then took the word processor to Berlin, and got the great work finished and delivered last Monday.

It's 192,000 words, which I do regard as too long. A bit repetitive in places, too. And this was going to be a shorter work! Detailed line editing is required; I hope Alan has time to do it thoroughly. We have a full planning meeting Thursday (23rd) and Lisa is coming to supper at the House tomorrow (21st). That will be a busy day, as I plan to spend the afternoon sorting out the transfer of the Victoria flat to Susie.

Best other news is that Deb has a job. We went to two TV progs in one week, on 7/1 *The Time, The Place* live, and on 9/1 *Esther* recorded – not shown yet. Both on being famous. At the latter we were early and Deb vanished. She had a cold and had been feeling grotty, but wasn't in the dressing room. Half an hour later she reappeared, looking very pleased with herself, and announced that the producer, Maggie Elliott, had offered her a work experience placement. Today I took her and Esther Rantzen to lunch at the Savoy, partly to thank Esther and to pick her brains, and partly to ensure she remembers Deb on set. Kate Patten, Chris's daughter, is a production secretary there, so a paid follow-on is a possibility. It's up to Deb, really. I wish she would be more cheerful: her tension and the cold feed on each other. To cheer her up I took her to Birmingham for a day's shopping on Saturday: five hours later and £400 lighter she was still as miserable as sin. Says she's bored, then stays in bed till 1.30 p.m. Huh!

Meanwhile, back at the ranch... nothing's changed: a Tory

MP is embroiled in a scandal, with Max Clifford playing the self-righteous card; another couple of MPs die in their fifties; Gordon Brown promises not to increase income tax rates; Stephen Dorrell wants to privatise local authority social services; Richard Branson attempts the round-the-world balloon record and comes down next day; and the government is still 20 points behind in the polls. What's new? It's just a matter of waiting at the death-bed till Father Time gives the recumbent body the old heave-ho. Could be any time after the new registers come in (16 February), I reckon. The government's virtually given up on many of its Bills.

The MP with his knickers in a twist is Jerry Hayes,[260] whose many visits to the Commons gym are now explained. From 1990 he had a dishy young gay researcher, quite pretty enough to turn any head; only he was a boy, and strictly speaking under age, and a little prat into the bargain. Jerry swears the relationship was not physical, but he wrote some soppy love letters which the boy took (via Max Clifford and £75,000) to the *News of the World*. Clifford swears that Jerry's a liar and a hypocrite, as he had unprotected sex while involved in AIDS campaigning; but the charge won't stick as Jerry is too nice and too transparently straightforward. He did the right thing and flew abroad immediately, so has largely been left alone. Today's *Daily Mail* had a go instead at Angela Knight:[261] her ex-husband says he was angered by her criticisms of House of Commons hours as inimical to family life. 'She never saw the kids,' he growled, 'she doesn't now.' To her credit, Angela reacted promptly and effectively: she slapped an injunction on him, restraining him from talking about their sons. Clifford was involved in this lot too. Makes you wonder how they know where to contact him. I bet he goes on fishing expeditions of ex-spouses, ex-researchers etc., with a filing system a mile high.

---

260 Conservative MP for Harlow since 1983.
261 Conservative MP for Erewash 1992–7; Economic Secretary to the Treasury 1995–7. Chief Executive of the British Bankers' Association 2007–12. EC's neighbour in Derbyshire.

Tower House, Friday 24 January, 8.25 a.m.

Upstairs Deb has been singing *Evita* loudly, but is now on her way to work. On Tuesday she had a message to ring Doug Carnegie at *Central Weekend*, and within the hour was in the Nottingham studios, working on this week's programme as a researcher (unpaid). She told him she really loved its buzz – at home people would stand up and scream at the TV – and she was in. She'll do ten days, then to BBC TV for the *Esther* programme, then…? Only two weeks left at Central before the Easter break, but she's determined that by then somebody will be paying her.

The government's announced that the single currency's not going to happen. Not on 1.1.99 anyway. Can't be done. Not just for us, but the whole of Europe. This smacks of Margaret's belief that the reunification of Germany couldn't be done overnight and they should wait five years, or (on a different scale) Tim Eggar's[262] assertion that there was no way Toyota could get the factory finished in time, i.e. by December '92. Both were wrong. Just because *we* find things difficult doesn't mean others do too – and I suspect the Cabinet half assumes that the whole thing comes into operation on 1.1.99, whereas that's only the start of a three-year process. We won't see notes and coins until two-and-a-half years into it, and retailing has all that time to switch. So I see no reason why it won't proceed on time. Meanwhile British business will be lulled into not making preparations, so that 'it won't happen' will become a self-fulfilling prophecy, at least for the UK. That's if anybody believes anything the PM says, which I doubt.

The PM himself doesn't give the impression of success. Two incidents: on Tuesday night, as our majority of seven was announced, there were calls of 'Ten more years!', as in 1989. I saw him on the second vote in the lobby and repeated it. He sagged as if demoralised and exhausted. 'You're supposed to look keen, John,' I chided. 'Let's try that again. Ten more years!' – and he straightened and grimaced a lopsided grin. Then on Wednesday at 6.15 p.m. he came into the tea room, alone: no acolytes. Got himself a meal (pork

---

262 Minister of State, DTI, since 1992; Conservative MP for Enfield North since 1979.

pie and beetroot: ugh). Sat down and started reading the *Evening Standard*. Whinged about an article by Roy Jenkins in a peevish voice. Astonished his companions (EC, Jim Lester, Tim Smith and a few others) by his petulance and aggression. Didn't chat (in which case why not send out for a tray?), didn't flatter, didn't converse. A little man in a big body. The quicker he's out, the better.

Much talk about successors. I think we can rule out Rifkind and Lang,[263] who both have only tiny majorities and are likely to lose their seats. Portillo and Redwood are each determined to try and may test their weight against the other, but that depends on persuading other right-wingers not to contest – and Howard wants to. Dorrell is also after the right-wing vote, so there could be a surfeit of such candidates. On the left, Clarke will stand and Heseltine will make way for him. Gill Shephard will aim to be the compromise candidate, and Hague[264] will ensure he's mentioned. Not that it'll make any difference, if Blair shows astuteness in government. It's the leader after next who'll have the best chance of office, and I'd bet that'll be Hague.

Talk in today's press about forty Europhile Tories breaking away to form their own party. I don't honestly know who that means, though I may have a better idea after a lunch with Peter Temple-Morris[265] and friends this week. But I've repeatedly warned of the dangers of the wilderness and the obligation to stay put: Gaitskell and Hattersley rather than Shirley Williams and David Owen. I won't leave, that's for sure, though I may drift away from politics for a while. At a drinks party the other night (Tesco introducing their new South African range, most of which I did not care for), Michael Brown tried to cheer me up by saying my personal vote should see me through; that's what happened last time, I thought,

263 Ian Lang, President of the Board of Trade and Secretary of State for Trade and Industry; Conservative MP for Galloway and Upper Nithsdale since 1983; MP for Galloway, 1979–83.
264 Conservative MP for Richmond (Yorkshire) since 1989.
265 Conservative MP for Leominster since 1974. In 1997 he won the seat as a Tory, then left the Party and took no whip before in 1998 joining the Labour Party. Several other Europhile Tory MEPs broke away at the time of the 1999 European elections.

and reflected how little work has been done to shore up Tory support in South Derbyshire. It's almost as if there isn't an election here: no canvassing, nothing. Fortunately the Labour Party are equally low key – I don't think Mark Todd's[266] given up his day job yet. Anyway I'm so *bored* at Westminster that it can't end soon enough; I try to focus on what I'd lose, including £1,000 a week plus staff and a parking place, and grit my teeth and carry on.

Tuesday 28 January
Scene: House of Commons car park. A small car with a prominent sticker: 'British Beef is Best.' The sticker is illustrated with Limousin and Charolais cattle. The car's a Peugeot.

Tower House, Wednesday 29 January
Back in December, following a routine inquiry, I had an interesting letter from Toyota at Burnaston, which included the remark 'Toyota strongly believes that it is essential for the UK to remain as an integral part of the European Union.' That was a surprisingly blunt comment for the usually circumspect Japanese. Today Hiroshi Okuda, President of Toyota, was much blunter and indicated that future investments would be on the Continent if we weren't part of EMU. It sounds as if that's the trend of their thinking anyway – 'further investment in the UK would be excessive'. But very much to be taken seriously, and I've been on TV and radio solidly since 4 p.m. to say so. The PM's approach was to dismiss this, and to say that it wasn't to be taken seriously. During a vote at 6.15 p.m. I tackled him. 'It wasn't anybody important, only the President of Toyota,' he replied, and my mouth dropped open. 'Anyway, the Japanese can't tell the difference between the single market and the single currency.' 'Say that again…' I gasped, and he did: 'The Japanese can't tell the difference between the single market and the single currency.' (Authoritatively) 'The Americans are the same. They don't understand the single currency at all.' I laid into him, telling him not even to think such things, and not to be rude about the Japanese; they mean it, and the PM's dismissive approach would

---

266 EC's Labour opponent in South Derbyshire.

accentuate their anxiety. Our conversation was cut short by the end of the vote, but it must have been pretty obvious that I was furious. Forty-five minutes later there's another vote; Michael Heseltine takes me to one side and asks me not to speak to the press: 'It would only incite the Eurosceptics to say their piece.' I must have looked at him as if he was daft, but at least to him I was civil. 'You're a couple of hours too late,' I pointed out. 'Anyway, the first person on to the media was Teddy Taylor.' Michael was puzzled. 'Too late? Have you been on?' So I told him about the real world, of top news programmes at 5 p.m., 5.40 p.m., 6 p.m. and Channel 4 at 7 p.m., all live and in the can. He appeared bemused. The naïveté of such a big cat, once a star performer, is just breathtaking – and infinitely depressing to boot. So tomorrow I'll be busy from 7 a.m. till 10.30 a.m., begging all concerned to see sense.

I *despair*. The quicker this government is defeated, the better. The PM is more stupid and ignorant than ever I realised – he's just *dim*, period. It's a disgrace, and a tragedy, for what we set out to achieve (a stronger economy) has certainly occurred, mainly due to foreign managers and money, a free market, taxes lower than they should be given the budget deficit, and a first-class Chancellor. But it'd be a kindness to all and sundry to shoot John Major: he's acting more and more like his dim brother, though it grieves me to say so.

A supper yesterday was almost as frustrating, and eventually I walked out. National Power, who own Willington power station, had invited a bunch of not very important Tory MPs, some from 'mining' constituencies: Richard Alexander, Michael Clarke, John Whittingdale,[267] Quentin Davies (late as usual) and a couple of others who said nowt and failed to impress their names on me! Our hosts were Chief Executive Keith Harvey, their 'corporate communications' man, and the Company Secretary, a steely-eyed lawyer called Andrew Swanson, to whom I slowly took a deep dislike. After a while I worked out that they think the best tactic is to keep their heads down over Labour's plans for a windfall tax on privatised utilities; more important is screwing some money out of the Labour government for clean coal technology in return for more

267 Conservative MP for Colchester South and Malden since 1992.

coal contracts. Blackmail, in other words – with the assumption that the windfall tax (which may be spread over several years) will be a one-off. Since Labour is bound to win, and has been pledged to do this for two years, there's no point in fighting it. At this point I suggested they'd invited the wrong people to dinner and went off to find something better to do…

Tower House, Saturday 8 February, 8.07 p.m.

Spent the afternoon canvassing in Repton, then some telephone canvassing. More frustration! Only one person to help. I could hardly whinge as my husband wasn't by my side, was he? Then the responses niggled me. So many of them were anti-Europe, when we, the Tories, used to be unquestionably the pro-European party. Such damage has been done by JM's weakness, it makes me feel quite ill. It's the most important issue for most of our Tory voters – and most disagree not only with me, but with the government too, so it's become paradoxically a way of pushing supporters away. Not to Labour – but if they don't vote for us it doesn't matter where they go. After another three-hour Advice Bureau full of lunatics for whom I had precious little sympathy, a succession of little Englanders was almost too much. Then one chap stopped me; he had been active in 'South East Derbyshire', he said, so it must have been at least twenty years ago. I knew his face, but not his name. Strongly anti-Europe, he said, all his life. Didn't agree with my views. And he rabbits on, 'My father always said you weren't to be trusted, being half-Jewish and half-Irish…' – to my face! 'Well,' I said, 'your father was wrong on both counts. And if those are your views I'd rather you didn't vote for me.' I left him standing, still mouthing '…seeing as you come from Liverpool.'

Otherwise an interesting week, and mostly productive. The final revise/line editing started and under Alan's guidance proved fruitful and fun, and *very* interesting. He's much better than Richard; when we did *A Parliamentary Affair* I wasn't very good, and with *A Woman's Place* he wasn't. But this time both author and editor are concentrating hard, and there's a real buzz. I am beginning to feel quite excited about the new book, though we still haven't settled the title – Liz Thomson of *Publishing News* suggested 'Close Your Eyes and I'll Kiss You', which I like very much.

Had a long whinge to Alan this week over lunch. Changes may be in the offing. I've had no money since mid-December and the account's slid from +£7,000 to -£4,000. When I saw this I sent faxes and phone calls flying off everywhere, and now have cheques for over £5,000 in my handbag. Takes hours to sort out! As important as these administrative niggles is the question of what we produce on 18 September. If we're not careful it'll be just a book – a bestseller maybe, but it could be much more. Where are the film and TV contracts? We failed to get them with *A Parliamentary Affair.* And what about foreign rights? *A Woman's Place* wasn't offered for foreign rights at all, which was very disappointing. Serialisation? Audio tape? Can a one-woman agency handle all these? I'm beginning to wonder. So it wasn't entirely accidental that I found myself chatting to Jonathan Lloyd of Curtis Brown (correction: MD of Curtis Brown). We met at the Nibbies[268] at the Hilton – Lisa wasn't there and should have been. Lloyd is a drop-dead gorgeous, film-star type, who in fact came over to my table to speak to me again later. Alan says he's not a nurturer of future great writers, but an excellent packager of big events – Curtis Brown is very strong in media, whereas I get the feeling A. P. Watt leaves it to luck a bit. A shift poses big problems nevertheless. And I'd feel horribly mean to Lisa; but I must have the level of service, and I'm desperately, fanatically keen to see the new novel a big success and not just in the bookshops. Later Alan told me that Channel 4 had been contacted – they have £150 million for films and are looking for British material. I think *LOL* (or whatever it'll be called) will be too big budget for TV alone, but film in all those locations would be perfect. Terry, the marketing man, says there's no such thing as 'synergy' in the business, but I don't see why we can't hint at the Warner connection to make Channel 4 nibble. *Exciting* stuff – and now I feel sure that *LOL* will bear the weight. I'm enjoying every word of it – it's coming out like *Behind the Scenes at the Museum* (by Kate Atkinson, 'Author of the Year') crossed with *Diary of Anne Frank*, with touches of *Captain Corelli's Mandolin.*

Fay Weldon came in for tea Wednesday. She's odd – sharp, bright,

---

268 The annual book trade awards, sponsored by *Publishing News.*

very pretty face, little dumpy figure in black. Doesn't look sixty-five – more like forty-five. The purpose was to ask about her facelift, which was highlighted in the press ('Facelift saved my marriage') soon after her novel *Affliction* came out. But I clearly hadn't done my homework properly – her surgery was eight years ago, and in Hollywood. 'So much better, and you can sue,' she trilled. Not me, I can't, Fay. I don't have that kind of money. Nor do I think it's necessary to go that far, though the results were obviously highly satisfactory. It was fun talking to her though: she writes all her novels and screenplays in shorthand and has a secretary to type everything out, then edits. But as far as the face is concerned it's back to the drawing board.

Deb's life took a fresh turn. *Esther* turned out to be horribly boring, and 'class ridden' (Hampstead!); the most demanding thing any of the work experience girls had to do on Monday was go down four floors to fetch Esther a bar of chocolate. Nobody was very friendly. So on Tuesday she phoned *Central Weekend* and asked if she could return; Doug Carnegie told her to 'get your ass up here!' And she starts there again on Tuesday, at £75 per week 'expenses'. Wednesday and Thursday our photo spread was in *The Sun*; and Wednesday was the day millions of extra copies were printed and handed out free as promotion for the midweek Lottery. Oh, wow! And the pics were lovely. Monday next is the *Esther* programme we were in; last Saturday was the Forsyth programme. So we've been 'in' quite a lot. She's talking about *TFI Friday* with Chris Evans for the summer and right now she's on a date with Adrian, one of the *Central Weekend* presenters, and having a wonderful time!

House of Commons, Wednesday 19 February, 5.21 p.m.

Money has dominated my thinking for the last fortnight. It turned out that I wasn't entitled to an additional £13,000 – though this was 'credited to my account', it referred to my royalty account, not my bank account. Lisa had blithely wittered on about 'royalties' when she meant 'royalty statements', she says: I had totally misunderstood. Caradoc at A. P. Watt, who is actually responsible for the *A Parliamentary Affair/A Woman's Place* contracts, wrote more than once as if the £13,000 was to be paid to me. In essence I hadn't understood that an account can slip in and out of the black. I'd assumed that, once a payment in excess of the advance had been paid, that meant the account was firmly in the black.

Oh, well. I'm calmer about it now, but was furious with all and sundry last Monday when it became apparent. And the following day I invited Jonathan Lloyd of Curtis Brown for a drink. I hope something comes of it, for two reasons: (1) I currently have two agents, and that's barmy. Lisa asks me to send her copies of correspondence, so I'm turning into a photocopying machine, and that won't do. The liaison between them generally is poor; (2) I'm more ambitious now – and A. P. Watt never managed to do more than just get the books published (and in the case of *A Woman's Place*, in English only). Meanwhile Lisa's answerphone is on. She tells me how she spends all day Saturday doing her filing, yet she couldn't find the correspondence from Caradoc. I'd be more impressed if she'd spent the day interviewing an assistant. What I need from an agent isn't a guided tour to setting up *her* business, but how she's going to help me pursue mine: and in so doing, earn her commission.

I'm happy with my publishers: they're all keen to sell more books. But perhaps I'm wrong to see an agent more like a manager – or perhaps I'm right. We shall see...

Clapham, Sunday 2 March, 4.15 p.m.

Beautiful sunny afternoon. Deb has gone to meet new boyfriend, Adrian Mills the *Central Weekend* TV presenter; he comes across a bit colourless, which is presumably why at the age of forty he's hardly a top star. Still, she thinks he's gorgeous, and he's certainly a step up from Croydon cameramen and Yorkshire car mechanics. She is burning the midnight oil somewhat; last night, after seeing *Highland Fling* at The Place in Kings Cross (what a dump – but the ballet, a precursor of *La Sylphide*, was very interesting and well done, and we got to meet Matthew Bourne at the party afterwards), we came back here by 10.45 p.m., both went to bed, and surfaced at 12 noon! And I'm still tired. I've had a persistent cold and bad chest for a fortnight now and am thoroughly fed up. One reason why I'm like this is the misery of waiting for an election which, when it comes, will be a huge disaster. Like waiting to die: lined up in the trenches, hearing the rumble of big guns not far away, and knowing our orders are to march straight towards them. Well, I will be walking *slowly*. Ty gave me my election address Friday and it does look good: bold, handsome and positive in tone, with photos of me at the University of Derby, in a hard hat at Toyota, and with those splendid Worcestershire and Sherwood Foresters soldiers at Banja Luka.

Susie wrote to *The Economist* for a summer job and was told she was too late – but two prize internships were available via a competition, for which she had to produce an 800-word piece in *The Economist*'s style on a subject of her choice. So she did 'The Baltics feel the chill',[269] and read it to me over the phone yesterday. I thought it was *splendid* – very well written, lucid, thoughtful and accurate. They'd be mad not to give her a job. Judith Mayhew has said she's welcome back at the City Corporation, while the *Independent on Sunday* has also made her an offer. So we'll have her here all summer, and starting to earn some money.

She may be able to use Carlisle Place, though I'd rather have her company here. It turns out that the damp patch in the bathroom – about which we had done nothing – was caused by a hole in the guttering, established as soon as somebody climbed out there to look. So that'll be fixed; the mortgage is applied for. Elsewhere Deb's house turned out to have rising damp in the cellar, but she'll knock the price down a bit. She's not bothered, as so many exciting things are happening to her elsewhere, with potentially lucrative outcomes. And Mum is close to completion of the sale of her house too. A one-family housing boom all by ourselves! Next campaign the sale of Tower House. Ray would have ample remaining from the sale to buy a comfortable house, and I'd have some capital for the first time in my life. I might settle some on the kids if it could be done tax efficiently, especially if they supported my efforts to get the much-loved old white elephant sold.

Deb phoned in great excitement on Tuesday night. She's been approached by the *Cook Report* to help with a splendid exposé – one which if it takes off could be hugely successful. The pop music world is full of fiddles, as one might expect. The *Cook Report* want to

269 EC had recently taken Susie on a working visit to Estonia.

expose these, by getting a record to No. 1 using all the fiddles. Deb is to make the record and star in the video. Did I think this was a good idea? Oh, definitely – after all, she *would* be No. 1 and famous, and if the contracts were written right she could be rich too. I've sent her to talk to Curtis Brown: on the phone Jonathan Lloyd said, 'But they'd say she was only No. 1 because of the scam – that she couldn't really sing.' My response was: (1) she can sing – and dance, and she looks gorgeous; (2) she doesn't care anyway, as she wants to be a presenter. 'Oh, we represent them too,' he murmured, and mentioned Barry Norman and Sue Cook (Adrian also said they're a good agency). I reckon Deb makes the Spice Girls look like a bunch of potatoes and I shall go on saying so. What fun, if it comes off!

Jonathan Lloyd entered my life properly on Monday night when he came in for a drink in the House of Commons. He seemed oddly diffident, and I got the impression he thought I was looking at several agencies. I explained all the hassles over having two agents – which he said shouldn't happen; my anxiety that we mustn't fail with this book; my feeling that it needed a broadly based effort which Lisa couldn't provide. It suggests my judgement was right – A. P. Watt is not the big agency for me, and Curtis Brown is. Now ensue some Byzantine negotiations, in which Curtis Brown takes over all collections and pays the royalties (possibly as much as 100 per cent) to A. P. Watt; they will make their money on new contracts, and if successful we should be able to double the value of the book contract for *She's Leaving Home*[270] and Book 2.

Editing is still going well, though the pre-Estonian session (20 February) was hilarious. We had seven chapters to do and managed only five by 1 p.m.; so we went off to Rules, 'Dickens's favourite restaurant,' said Alan, which was packed with men tucking into roast beef. The testosterone was tangible. We were stuck on a tiny table with mustard on the manuscript till the waiters (British – hooray!) took pity on us and moved us to a bigger one elsewhere. It was all done by 3 p.m. – no time for coffee – dash back to LB's office to collect rest of manuscript – car's at the House – leave there 3.30 p.m. and head to Heathrow – mad dash across Helsinki airport in

---

270 The eventual title of *Leaving of Liverpool*.

the snow – arrive Tallinn 12.40 a.m. 'Not many authors would edit on their way to Estonia,' said Alan. Not many have to, I muttered in return, high as a kite on antibiotics.

All this fits beautifully with the parliamentary timetable, as after the Wirral by-election last Thursday (27th) an early call seems most unlikely. God, we lost it badly – an 8,000 Tory majority became a 7,800 Labour majority, on a turnout of over 70 per cent. Our Tory voters turned out all right, but they voted for Blair, who took more than half the votes cast. We could have a similar result nationally: at present Blair leads 15–19 per cent, depending which poll you look at. He needs 7 per cent or so to form an administration with a comfortable majority. I think he'll have about 10 per cent, so his majority (depending what happens in Liberal-held seats in the south-west) will be 60–80. When I told Deb that she inquired whether she could place a bet on it!

I went with a group led by Peter Temple-Morris to have a drink with Ken Clarke on Wednesday night. Andrew Rowe, Tim Rathbone,[271] David Knox (who is retiring), Quentin Davies, Justin Powell-Tuck from the Tory Reform Group, Jim Lester and a couple of others. Not a powerful bunch – and Ray Whitney was not among them, I suspect because he was not invited. Ken was in cheery mood. He is getting fatter, and his eyes bulge out, as does his belly. Gillian[272] looks even worse – she brought in the wine, and when I asked for orange juice she rolled her eyes and said she thought she might have some upstairs. Ken was expansive – last week he had quite a spat with Rifkind about the single currency. In fact the 1.1.99 starting date is starting to look dodgy because of the poor economic figures in Germany and doubts about whether Kohl (who's sixty-six) will stand in October '98. Ken said he wished he'd never given in on the referendum issue, but it couldn't be helped, and he persisted in saying at every opportunity that he could see advantages in joining the euro, if it is well set up and run. Options open therefore, though his is a forlorn voice. He said Michael Heseltine is very good when he sticks his head over the parapet, but

271 Conservative MP for Lewes since 1974.
272 Kenneth Clarke's wife.

he doesn't do that much these days. John Gummer came to speak to a CGE meeting on Thursday, and demonstrated why he doesn't have the high profile he wants: asked to speak for 10–15 minutes, he went on, very entertainingly, for forty minutes, by which stage most of his audience had headed for the last train home. And he did it all without a note, so no press release was possible. Still a teenage debater, I'm afraid, though his heart is in the right place. Ken said there are 5–6 Eurosceptics in Cabinet, 5–6 pro-Europeans, and the rest are opportunists who will say whatever seems most popular at the time. No wonder the electors loathe us.

Peter T-M circulated the rules on Party leadership contests. It appears that JM *could* stay till the autumn if he wanted, God help us. But that would give Blair six months to make hay with a new Budget, Queen's Speech etc. Has John thought of the damage that could cause the Party? No, probably not. He probably believes staying put would be best for stability and unity. No political nose whatever, that man. How glad I am that I'll be out of it; but looking at the chaps drinking Ken's wine on Wednesday, I doubt whether they're going to put up much fight for the soul of the party.

Clapham, Thursday 13 March, 10.08 p.m.

An amazing week for us as a family. Susie got elected as Treasurer of the Cambridge Union, though only after a nail-biting election. Her slate actually lost, but her opponent was caught having done some (strictly forbidden) written canvassing. He was disqualified; had seventy-two hours in which to appeal; that was on Monday, and this evening her election was confirmed. Wonderful! This is for Michaelmas term. Only problems are: (1) she's left it too late to try for the presidency; history repeats itself,[273] though I wasted a great deal more time dithering and resisting the obvious than she did; and (2) she's already behind in her work. Would I accept her getting a 2:2 this year, she asked? No, I would not! Anyway, she now has that important extra line on her CV.

And Deb is set to be a pop star. On Monday afternoon we were

---

273 EC was elected Treasurer of the Oxford Union in 1968; afterwards she stood for President but was defeated, and did not have time to try again.

bombarded by calls from Carlton trying to locate her (she was out shopping in Derby). They had decided to go ahead if she looked the part – she walked in, sassy and terrific as usual, and it was all sewn up in another hour. Both she and her 'manager' Barry Tomes are to be under contract to the *Cook Report* – Deb will be on a presenter's scale of £400–£500 p.w. for three months, which she thinks is fabulous (it isn't). The record comes out on 12 May. Some 50,000 CDs will be pressed, at a cost of £40,000, all to be borne by the TV company, which will recoup all turnover. At least that's the idea at present; but Barry, who has represented over a hundred singers, including Lulu for seven years, says that's not good enough. *Cook* think they're making a TV programme (to be shown mid-June) about the manipulation of the charts; Barry knows they're making a star, and he wants it much clearer. After X sales, is there a percentage? For her, for him? He's doing it out of conviction: 'We want our charts back. Independently run. At the moment they're owned by the big companies.' Deb will describe it all in her own book, *You Can Make Magic* (the name of the song). I took a wonderful photo of her practising with the nail varnish remover bottle as microphone – how many millions of kids have done that?

The polls are now going backwards, with Gallup in the *Daily Telegraph* last Friday showing a 26 per cent gap. We all expect a landslide now – and possibly a high turnout. George Gardiner defected to the Referendum Party after his deselection; photos last weekend showed him looking lugubrious as ever with Mr Toad in green tweeds, aka Alistair McAlpine,[274] and Badger with rolling eyes, Sir James Goldsmith. Why does he always look as if he has forgotten his wig? That makes Gardiner Ratty, I suppose, but he's not nearly as nice as the character, though he has 'ratted'. Ugh! McAlpine's just published his memoirs, *Once a Jolly Bagman*, full of love for Margaret and disdain for those he sees as his enemies – in a memorable phrase, John Major 'used to hang round Chequers pretending to be curtains'. Oh, yes, got him exactly.

But then JM is so peculiar. He acts like he's not in government – so if things aren't right it isn't *his* responsibility. And since nobody

---

274 Lord McAlpine, former Treasurer of the Conservative Party.

else is in government, it follows that it's nobody's responsibility, so nothing is done. He joined us in the tea room on Tuesday. The table (Jacques Arnold, James Arbuthnot,[275] Jacqui Lait[276] and others) had just been talking about Conservative clubs. Somebody said the place he could be sure *not* to meet any Conservatives was in his Conservative club. James said his were Tories but wouldn't admit blacks. 'Or women?' I queried. 'Yes, they'll take women. But not black women,' James responded dryly. Jacqui pitched in with a reminder that even the Carlton won't have women as full members. 'I think that sort of attitude is terrible,' said the PM between mouthfuls of buttered teacake. We all blinked at him, then I said testily, 'Well, we could have done something about it. Removed the clubs' rights to ignore the law on discrimination. You'd have got it through the House with a big majority.' Someone else chipped in, 'There wouldn't have been a vote at all – who would have defended such discrimination?' The PM looked *so* surprised. It was clear the idea had never occurred to him. I was so disgusted I rose to leave, in case I said something very sharp to him.

As for the possible facelift: I'll talk more about Dr C when the time comes. I'd hoped Deb would help me in the forty-eight hours after surgery when I have to have cold compresses on my eyes, but this may not be possible now, and Susie is much too squeamish. C was small, bird-like, white coated; crooked teeth and rapid speech, but friendly and quick. He has a house next to Harrods with polished oak floors and a grand piano in the waiting room, which had a rapid succession of anxious blonde Sloanes, mainly in their thirties. Breast implants, at a guess. They were all too willowy to need liposuction – nowt to suck! It did occur to me that I'm accumulating plenty of useful background about coming to terms with fifty.

Clapham, Sunday 16 March, 10.45 p.m.
On Thursday I did a longish interview for John Pienaar of BBC Radio: he came to the flat. We talked about the next few months; I said how much I deplore the leadership contest which has been

---

275 Conservative MP for Wanstead and Woodford since 1983.
276 Conservative MP for Hastings and Rye since 1992.

under way for months now, and which has intensified recently, with Stephen Dorrell changing tack on Europe and popping up with a new announcement every five minutes, along with Gill Shephard, who has 'told friends' that she is interested, etc. JM has often said publicly that he wants a life outside politics, by which we all assume that he'll pack his bags after the general election (though if we win he might want to stay on. Not clear what for). So I thought nothing of talking of the necessity for him not to hang on, but to get the contest out of the way quickly, for the sake of the Party. If he decides to stay till October it could be a disaster, just like the long-running Maastricht Bill debate. However, my piece was spliced with interviews with John Biffen and Lord Blake,[277] both of whom implied or (in Blake's case) said we would lose, so the impression was created that I did too. The broadcast went out at lunchtime on Friday, just as the Central Council was arriving in Bath, then all hell broke loose. At 2.35 p.m. I get a call in my car from my whip, Matthew Carrington.[278] My whip? This is nothing to do with Parliament, remember. Charles Levington at CCO had phoned the Deputy Chief Whip; he phoned my whip; my whip phoned me. No doubt the calls were then reversed. Why, I puzzled, didn't Levington phone me at once, and then help put out a correction? It'd have killed the story stone dead. But no, so it ran on in the press all weekend. I refused to comment further, partly because that's the quickest way to kill it, and partly because I didn't want to answer any direct questions about our prospects.

Part of me feels deflated, but another part is indifferent. It's much too late now to worry about the election. The gap in all the polls is so wide, and widening, that it's best to look beyond; so my energies have been devoted to book-making, which will be my meal ticket in future.

I did some sums in the House of Commons Library. Even if I poll 5 per cent above the national average for the Party in South Derbyshire, I'm still going to lose by 6,000 or so votes. So I booked the ferry for a few days in France over Easter. Six weeks' campaigning? No, I don't think so.

---

277 Robert Blake, historian of the Conservative Party.
278 Conservative MP for Fulham since 1987.

House of Commons Library, Wednesday 26 March, 5.15 p.m.
Might be the last time I get to sit here, the best part of the whole
Palace of Westminster (except the car park, of course). I'm in Room
A, the first off to the left; lined with legal books, Scots law, Queen's
Bench records bound in maroon leather, statutes in force in smart
brown folders, health service and medical law in blue. Quiet, except
for the hum of a computer behind me on the International Desk.
I'm the only MP around.

As expected, the election for 1 May was announced last Monday
(17th) by the PM outside Downing Street, but the arrangements
were odd, to say the least: the campaign to start at once, Parliament
prorogued four days later on the Friday (21st), but dissolution not
till 8 April. The latter date is mainly determined by pension rules,
which give better results if the '97/'98 tax year is reached. But on the
Monday evening the government was embroiled in frantic negotiations over no fewer than twenty-five Bills, including flagship crime
and education Bills. Since they could have easily gone on till 3 or
4 April, i.e. another fortnight, and since it soon became clear they
were prepared to accept emasculation of both – what was going on?

Then it became apparent why the government wanted this
Parliament to end six weeks before the election (the last time
anything like this happened was in 1945). On Monday this week
Sir Gordon Downey was due to publish his report into 'cash for
questions'. The PM had promised it 'well before the election'. Now
his action has ensured that it cannot come out until afterwards.
And that in turn ensured that the guilty parties had their names
splashed all over the papers, so that the issue of the first week's
campaigning was 'sleaze'. *The Guardian* seemed to have access to
the MPs' evidence to Downey, in which they and Greer admitted
they'd lied before – to the 1990 Select Committee, to the whips, and
pretty obviously to the Inland Revenue. Now it comes out, and it's
all sickening; in particular, Tim Smith (who admits to accepting
twice as much as he originally said) and Sir Michael Grylls[279] (who
is standing down, but who got very big sums from Greer) have been

---

279 Conservative MP for North West Surrey since 1974; MP for Chertsey,
    1970–74.

pilloried. As for Hamilton, what was known about him has already been published: the man who emptied the mini bar at the Paris Ritz could not be shown to be more greedy or foolish than he's already been painted.

God knows what it'll do to the polls. I know what it does to me, and it leaves a very nasty taste in the mouth. Smith has the third safest Tory seat in Britain, but as Greer put it, he was a man on a low income, and thus willing to consider propositions. The PM came out of it very badly, I thought; Smith said he told all this to the Chief Whip in 1990, but he was still considered suitable to be appointed as a minister in April '92. 'Trivial,' bleated JM, 'I didn't know – I wasn't told.' Now that compounds the offence. For JM was a whip, and would have automatically known: and if not, should have asked. But since the links between Hamilton, Smith, Grylls *et al* and Ian Greer were common knowledge – plus the fact that neither Hamilton or Smith were wealthy men – Smith in particular should have been ruled out of office. Heavens, he was a Northern Ireland minister and subjected to positive vetting. There's no way the PM couldn't know.

This 'I didn't know – they didn't tell me' defence wears very thin after a while. If you didn't know, you should have done; you failed to create an atmosphere in which ministers took responsibility and action. Instead you fostered a cover-up mentality, where defensiveness protected your flank, and attacking critics was your only strategy. But if you *did* know, and didn't act? That suggests you didn't care. With few moral scruples, you thought it didn't matter. On both counts, therefore, I find you guilty: of incompetence, of shallowness, of evasion. Yuk.

Perhaps it's a good thing I'm a Conservative candidate in this election. At least that guarantees I'll vote. I'm so disgusted with this government, that I doubt I'd bother otherwise.

Lamont was in Le Caprice at lunchtime today – rather obviously the guest of Jeffrey Archer, who of course failed to acknowledge me at the next table! Lamont looks fat and puffy, and one wondered mildly why he wasn't campaigning in his Harrogate constituency (I know, I know – I was in South Derbyshire *yesterday*, and am on camera to prove it). In the far corner was the Princess of Wales, in a very nice grey suit – she sat in the corner facing everybody, and was determined to be seen; I found her antics most amusing. She was with an older woman and a man. You'd think she'd find somewhere more private. Personally I'd like better service. We didn't get our main course till 2.40 p.m., and even then had to nag for it. The food's no better than plenty of other places.

I was with Jonathan Lloyd, Curtis Brown Chairman Paul Scherer (is *he* a sweetie!) and Diana McKay, their Foreign Rights Director. First time into their office at 12 noon, a few photos (taken by me), and House of Commons humbugs presented. Jonathan seems a bit nervous. I found out that he was born in December '46, which did surprise me as he looks much younger. Mostly we gossiped and talked politics – I don't feel too ready to discuss my career with quite so many people, new faces all at once. Jonathan thinks I should do TV and journalism as a feature writer and I do too, though I'm not keen to make a living getting up at 3 a.m. for the *Big Breakfast*, especially if nobody is watching. And if I am dashing about to the States, South Africa etc. selling books, then it may be difficult to sustain a journalism contract. Anyway the book got finished at 2 a.m. last night. Tomorrow I hand over to Alan and we'll have lunch.

Deb meanwhile is still ON for the *Cook Report*. They thought that the story was blown and pulled the plug, though by then she had given interviews and got publicity which has gathered pace since – the photos are terrific, and she's talked willingly about sex, school, singing etc. The tabloids love that. Then it dawned on Carlton that they hadn't had a single phone call about it, so maybe it hadn't been blown after all. They decided to wait till last Sunday: loads of coverage, most of it snide ('Who does this girl think she is? You have to be able to sing first'), which had Deb and me in stitches. Last Friday she and I met Michael Morley (regional director of Carlton) and Peter Mannion (*Cook Report* producer) in the Donington Thistle Hotel, suitably obscure at East Midlands Airport. I nagged about a contract, and that seems to have done the trick, as Deb was *very* perky with a brown envelope containing £800 (= two weeks' wages) burning a hole in her pocket this morning. The advantages for her are: (1) she'll be paid; (2) there's no financial risk, as Carlton's putting up all the dosh; (3) everyone wants her to be No. 1. The joke is that in order to prove the charts are rigged against the independents she'll have to enter the charts lower down; but in a way they've picked the wrong girl as she could be a big hit anyway. If she's No. 1, that rather disproves their case, see? We should care! If she's No. 1, it'll be wonderful. She will get a royalty: 2 per cent, which works out at a few pence on a typical £4 CD. If she sells 100,000 copies she'll make £8,000. She can make more money with a book, and I'm sure she knows that. Jonathan wants to sell it now, and will do it on the basis that it's just about being a pop star. I said he needs to talk to Deb, as soon as there's a lull between making the record and video and her going out on the promotion tour.

Tower House, Saturday 5 April, 11.20 p.m.

The adoption meeting on Friday evening went off OK. I was nervous, but it was hardly packed out; apart from our council candidates and top table, there were only twenty-five people there. Plus Susie, who turned up in a great flurry, having said she wasn't coming because she'd promised her friend Ellen to be in Chesterfield for a dinner party at 7 p.m.; fine, I said to her on the phone, bear in mind that this may be the last time. Next time you get a phone bill you can get Ellen to pay it for you too. And put the phone down on her. So she came, and I was delighted she did. Deb didn't, but I wasn't surprised as on the phone (she's crashed out at Clapham) she sounded totally bushed.

Today was damp, cold and blustery. Ty wanted me to parade down Swad High Street, but that would have been an unmitigated disaster: it'd have invited Richard North[280] to tail us, and with only two women Party workers with me, it would have been ludicrous. So I said, I'll do that when he has ten people to go with me, of whom five are men. It's not danger, but appearances that I'm worried about. Anyway I got my way, and our doughty band of three went off canvassing in a new estate in Swad. Not bad: 30–40 per cent Tory, with less than that declaring themselves as Labour, and lots (about ⅓) saying they weren't sure. So that confirms the polls are right, if a few days out of date: nationally we're around 32–35 per

---

280 Candidate for the Referendum Party in South Derbyshire.

cent. But we are still going to get hammered. In the afternoon one of the women went home and was replaced by a man who'd never canvassed before. Three supporters all day, one of whom came from another planet. And when it's all over, I'll be accused of not having worked hard enough, and I'll bite my tongue to stop myself asking my accusers where they were on a cold, wet Saturday afternoon.

The room is full of the heady smell of hyacinths, blue and white: the pink ones appear to have vanished from the garden. Plus wallflowers, probably seeded naturally. And a bit of pussy willow, and a red tulip for colour. The garden, most of it, is rather splendid at the moment: I even found the urge surfacing yesterday, in good weather, to pull on gloves and spend an hour or two weeding. Alan Peat's[281] planted trees closer to the house, flowering fruiters like those we have in France, a legacy to leave behind for the next owners, whoever they may be.

Four weeks from now I'll be packing a bag to go to the clinic. It looks like I'll spend my first couple of days home alone, so I'll have to live on chocolate milk. I'll manage. I have to. Bit like fighting the election, I suppose. One foot in front of another, and you just keep going...

Tower House, Saturday 12 April, 7.18 a.m.

A fine pearly grey light outside, and dogs walking gingerly on hard ground frost. The land is white, ethereal. It's going to be a beautiful day. I'll spend the morning in Mickleover shopping centre with Javed Arain, our candidate for Derby South. He's a small, dapper, earnest young man whom I've never yet seen smile. Was I as committed, as devoted when I first started? Yet I had never fought a losing seat, so my enthusiasm and optimism were well founded. I went to his AGM at La Gondola on Thursday night: twenty people there. We want the Derby South people to come and help in South Derbyshire, but looking about it was clear that he'd be lucky to get his leaflets delivered, let alone have anyone spare.

I don't, in fact, think our useless campaign will make much difference to the voters, though it's wearing and frustrating. Thank

281 The gardener at the Tower House.

goodness for my hormone tablets – without their calming effect I'd be screaming at everyone. Not that there are more than a handful of people, mainly old ladies, to scream at! But the electorate have made up their mind, from what I can see. In Etwall yesterday, on my canvass, we could be sure of only just under 50 per cent, whereas in a Tory ward it ought to be 70–80 per cent. That confirms the polls, which continue to show we're on 30–33 per cent. I think that a large part of the Tory vote has collapsed; so many people hesitate when I ask, and drop their eyes. When I put it to them that they voted Tory last time they agree readily, but say this time they haven't made up their minds, or are thinking about it, or are 'not happy'. I stand on posh doorsteps, talking to well-heeled people with freshly decorated halls and immaculate gardens and door bells that work and two P-reg cars in the drive and a caravan bought with their TESSA tax-free bonus, and they tell me they're 'not happy'! And what, I inquire, could I do for them in addition to everything they've got, to make them happy?

Neil Hamilton got himself readopted on Tuesday night, though it's clear his association is split down the middle. So TV reporter Martin Bell ('the man in the white suit' in Bosnia) has come forward as an anti-sleaze candidate, to be endorsed by both Lib Dems and Labour. He could get elected, too; his daughter says he'd make a good MP, though I think he would hate every minute. Oddly enough, Bell looks wooden and confused on TV, Hamilton smooth and assured. But it's the effect on the rest of us, the other candidates, which is devastating, as we are all tarred with the same brush… It does not help that the PM, after some vacillation, decided to back Hamilton to the hilt, with much talk of 'innocent till proven guilty'; but there's a difference between a crime and dishonour, as the public (if not the PM) can well perceive, so this endorsement comes across as weakness or blindness, and a fuzzy attitude to the moral principles so loudly trumpeted at Party Conferences. Meanwhile a reputed 200 Tory candidates have accepted a businessman's contributions (Paul Sykes – about £2,000 each) for saying that they refuse to accept a single currency in their manifestos.

I should mention our rally with the PM at JCB in Rocester on

Thursday night – a miniature version of the end of Conference event, which I haven't stayed for in years. Yet this wasn't a mini speech: droned on for forty-five minutes, and frankly, despite a couple of good jokes and the entertainment of a couple of his usual mixed metaphors ('black hole/pull together/climb the mountain'), it was dire. A regurgitation of similar campaign speeches, nothing fresh. So his words don't get much press coverage. The audience was supposed to be enthusiasts, but *all* those near me had wangled tickets for a peep-show: they weren't even Party members, and were watching other people's enthusiasm with unfeigned curiosity. The only wild clapping from some sections of the audience came at the anti-Brussels table-thumping bit, at which point I remarked *sotto voce* to a neighbour that I'd heard that all before over BSE and other issues, and it didn't make a scrap of difference in Brussels itself. It was notable that many people fled for the exit the moment the PM and Norma (fetching in pink but looking very strained) had passed by. Depressing...

However! I went to London on Monday night and we had our planning meeting at Little, Brown with Jonathan present. He said afterwards to David Young[282] that he was 'underwhelmed', and that was true – it was poorly chaired, very laid back, with no sense of priority; until the cover and the proofs are ready we are stuck in many ways, yet the cover could have been available before Easter. The Lichfield photo shoot is a week on Monday, 21 April, so my 'old' face will adorn my books for several years to come: pity! A lot of the suggestions I've made, such as presentations to the trade, have been taken up, so I took an active part in the discussion – I wish I could have chaired it myself. Actually I'm not too worried, as I know this is a *good* book which everyone will enjoy. Jonathan called on Sunday to say it was 'much better than he'd expected', and does not read like a long book: praise indeed, if double edged, and I have teased him about it ever since. He took me on even though he thought I couldn't write... ho, ho.

I should see Deb's video soon. Apparently it's so sexy that they will have to recut it for children's TV. Heavens above! At the Savoy

---

282 Managing Director of Little, Brown.

she was showing Polaroids of the CD cover and some publicity stuff – taken naked except for her boots, and quite stunning: Jonathan blinked and grinned at me, but said nothing. Deb just shrugs: 'They're only pubes,' she said carelessly.

In bed at the Tower House, Sunday 20 April, 9.26 a.m.

The campaign is awful. Ghastly beyond words. It doesn't help that I've developed arthritis in my left foot, so that walking is really painful: I do it splay footed like a duck, and that gives me backache. However the street pounding is having only one result, which is to convince me that Labour will win.

My canvass returns are particularly disturbing, for they suggest that Blair's impact is strongest in well-off areas, so he could make serious inroads in the Home Counties. They recognise a man like themselves. They despise the ignorance, xenophobia and toe-curling nastiness of the Tory campaign, and are appalled at its organisational shambles. He could do very well in our 'heartlands', where his credibility is highest and ours lowest.

Deb put it rather well on the phone. Since she's on the register in Huddersfield with no postal vote, she's pretty certain not to vote anyway. But: 'I can't vote Labour, as I don't want to be paying 98 per cent tax when I'm rich and famous. And the Lib Dems – neither here nor there. But Mum, the Tories! At the moment I couldn't bring myself to vote for such a shower!' I agree whole-heartedly.

On the way to Nottingham to record a piece for ITN, through came a call from Michael Heseltine. 'Don't,' he said, 'Party unity and all that.' I nearly exploded. He's got a nerve, I thought, and quoted the PM at him: 'Backbenchers are entitled to express their opinions.' I also told him that he was too late, that I'd already done the *Today* programme. But then Michael never was one for assiduous attention to detail. And, says I, 'I'm a *supporter* of government policy. I'm the kind of backbencher you should be encouraging. Or is it only the Eurosceptics who are off the leash?' Next day it got worse. At the morning press conference the PM offered a free vote on the single currency. Not a bad idea, and one suggested last year by Hugh Dykes. Ted Heath gave a free vote in '71 on the principle of joining, but then put a three-line whip on the legislation itself, so he had a much bigger majority for the former (more than 100) than the latter (only eight on second reading). By midday he'd elaborated: if the voters were to get a free vote, i.e. a referendum, so should Parliament. Ken Clarke, asked if he'd been consulted, admitted not, but like me was content with the free vote. I was on standby for the five o'clock *PM* programme (actually, sitting in a lay-by on the A38 with the phone in my hand) in case Michael Heseltine didn't turn up. But he did, armed with a transcript of the press conference and nothing else. It was clear he had not been briefed on developments during the day, and when told what the PM had said at lunchtime accused the interviewer of wickedly distorting the PM's words. What a *shambles*. As for Ken Clarke – when challenged as to why he hadn't consulted our leading Europhile, the PM petulantly said, 'I was asked a question. I can't go round asking Ken Clarke, or – or Joe Bloggs how I should answer every question.' Crumbs. To equate KC with Joe Bloggs is a bit ripe: even you can see that, John, surely?

That evening the PM scrapped the planned PPB and instead spoke in impassioned tones on the need to keep our options open in Europe. He was in effect appealing to his Party's own candidates. Good, thought I, then there are at least two people in the Conservative Party sticking to the official line on Europe – him and me. Next morning it blew apart again, with a newspaper advertisement showing Blair as a glove puppet sitting on Chancellor Kohl's knee. 'Don't send a boy in to do a man's job,' ran the headline – i.e. send JM to the Amsterdam summit in June, not the inexperienced Blair. But the tone and picture were disgusting – anti-German, anti-Kohl: even KC burst out that Kohl's been a good friend to this country. I said that if we needed friends in Amsterdam, this wasn't the way to go about it; various German politicians interviewed on British TV (not the CDU or Kohl – very tight lipped about it) deplored this 'unintelligent' approach. Spot on. Had we shown Blair as a puppet of the unions, that might have hit home with wavering voters – the Essex firemen are out on strike right now. Intelligent, moderate Tory voters don't like such crude images, which serve only to confirm the nastier prejudices of our hard core, and to consolidate the remainder's appreciation of Blair's eloquent, elegant, articulate professionalism.

The Curries have been in the news a lot this week. A very nice full-page spread on Deb in the *Daily Telegraph*; me in *The European*, the *Sunday Times* and on TV and radio; and Ray interviewed in the *Daily Mail* – his answers, snappy as usual, are interpreted as a very private man protecting his privacy, which is about right. But it made me blink in places, as if I was seeing Ray's image of himself, which is rather different from mine. He says he 'loves' canvassing, yet in real life has to be persuaded to come out. Similarly, 'mad about sport' – but only on the box.

Tower House, Friday 25 April, 5.50 p.m.
A horrible wet day, but really we need the rain – everything's been so dry and dusty, more like August than April, and cold too. Not the easiest weather for elections.

The polls don't budge – only that rogue ICM poll last week which suggested the lead was down to 5 per cent. The only slight shift appears to be Lab to Lib Dem, possibly among schoolteachers and other public sector employees who like Ashdown's promise to tax more and put it in their pockets. The five main polls are so consistent – yesterday they showed our share as 31, 30, 32, 30, 29 per cent. South Derbyshire polling doesn't contradict any of this. So what's going on? Some's complacency. The polls were wrong last time, so they must be wrong this time. Some's indifference. For the truth is, the bulk of the electorate is not all that frightened of a Labour government under Tony Blair. We may profess to be, but it's not so. Instead, the deeper polling suggests the voters are far more alarmed at the prospect of a fifth Tory term. Gallup in yesterday's *Daily Telegraph* produced a list of fears if Labour wins: e.g. inflation (69 per cent fear), Social Chapter costing jobs (63 per cent fear), strikes (54 per cent), increased taxes (64 per cent). Then the fears if we win: and wham! Up the figures go – old people won't be looked after (87 per cent), pay more for health and pensions (86 per cent), NHS not good/not free (85 per cent), and so on; of the twelve fears, ten on the Tory list scored over 70 per cent and thus above any of the Labour fears. Tax increases under the Tories are feared by 78 per cent, compared to 64 per cent under a Labour government. So all our efforts to pin tax increases on Blair appear to be counter-productive... Blair has pitched his tent in the middle ground. He's made them frightened of *us*.

And, to continue the truthful theme, many of my voters like what they see in Blair. A middle-class public schoolboy who might have been a Tory: if he can vote Labour, so can they. He's one of them – and John Major, with his strangulated vowels, his plaintiveness and his inability to make himself effective, isn't. It occurred to me on some very posh Repton doorsteps that I was talking to middle (and upper) management types. They admire good management and deplore incompetence – and they know both when they see them. As one lady said, 'I was appalled at the handling of the BSE crisis. Yes, I know your views and I admire them. But I cannot vote for this government.'

So it's only a matter of days now, thank heavens. The book cover has come and is fine (though I still think the painting is muddled and dull). The Lichfield session was brilliant – Alan says they're sure to use him again, despite the expense. Patrick was hilarious, more like a dinner party host than a photographer. Rather like Snowdon, he established what kind of people we were, then told wonderful stories about Princess Margaret (his cousin) and other notables. My favourite was the tale of how he tried to buy a piece of land on Mustique adjacent to hers. The negotiations were long and ultimately unsuccessful. Following the last two-hour session with solicitors, Patrick gave up; as he left, he heard her say to Sir Michael Farrar, her solicitor, 'You see, Sir Michael, Patrick comes from the side of the family without the Jewish blood.' He showed us one of his books, a lovely collection of portraits; the frontispiece was Harold Macmillan at ninety in his Russian hat, overcoat and Guards tie. When Patrick was signing at Harrods he by chance wore the same tie. One American lady customer examined the book, then smiled sweetly. 'I must tell you, Lord Lichfield, that you look much better without the moustache.'

Afterwards I met Steve Kyte of Radio 5 Live. Roger Mosey of Radio 4's *Today* programme has taken over there; he and Steve were thinking about new presenters – Diana Madill is leaving, for example – when Steve suggested me. Now that would be fun, but I don't want to get too tied down with a daily programme, which would prevent me from promoting books. I've suggested I could do mornings June/July, then a weekend magazine programme from October onwards. I told him how much I earn from my books, and he didn't blink. I'd *love* to work for them: it'd be a lot of fun and not too arduous. But TV'd pay a lot better, I think. Anyway, hopeful stuff.

Deb is off up north at the moment – when we spoke on the phone this morning she'd just done Radio Cleveland. Tuesday's effort turns out to be Belfast not Dublin, so I am going too. Not much point in flogging a dead horse here, especially if not a single constituency worker can be bothered to come too. She has had some problems with the two girl singers, who are not keen to go slogging round the country to do the clubs. They haven't twigged that this is about to be a big hit, and they could be rich and famous, which is presumably what they'd like – so they're being difficult, and she may have to do it all alone. Of course she'd be OK, and they never did expect to take the whole band. But it emphasises once more the differences between those who'll put in the effort, who can see beyond the horizon and who will make it – like Deb – and those who won't or can't. Even if the latter make good money and have two mobile phones each! Of course neither band nor backing group knows anything about Carlton, though I doubt if they would see that in quite the positive light we would.

Tower House, Wednesday 30 April eve of poll, 2.44 a.m.

I didn't think the campaign could get worse, but it has. A month ago it was like swimming through mud: dark, sticky, with a sinking feeling. Then it became more like molasses: dark, sticky and with a bitter aftertaste. Now it's like a bath of hot shit: smelly, overpowering and contaminating. Come out of this in one piece with any friends left and I'll be doing well.

The fun side first, though. Yesterday I spent in Belfast with Ulster TV, recording their Friday night *Kelly* programme with Deb. That had its surreal side, as we had to do two different intros – one as if we'd won the election, and then, after a couple of questions, back out and start again as if we'd lost. Talk about virtual reality. Deb had to perform – first time on TV – and did it really well: she looked lovely, and everyone was singing along with her by the time she'd finished. The little green halter-neck dress didn't leave much to the imagination as she gyrated about, nor much room for the microphone box taped to her waist, but I was thrilled for her. Also got a copy of the CD, plus the postcard they're using for promotion. And what a mad world – the posters are about to go up; the budget's £3,000 to print, plus £1 for each one fly-posted throughout the country, another £5,000. Barry's also put out a story that the CD covers were too raunchy and had to be withdrawn. Sexy image? Don't ask.

Deb was tired and fractious after a late-night gig in Birmingham (we stayed over in the Metropole at the NEC), then an early morning call to catch a 7 a.m. flight to Belfast. She'll get even more tired when she's out promoting the disc for real. It makes relations strained between her and Barry, as she hasn't learned to pace herself or get up cheerful, ready for action after a catnap. She was snappy with everyone, which is not good. Yet the strain is having one (to me) beneficial effect – she doesn't think she wants to be a pop star, and is far more interested in a career as a TV presenter when all of this is over. 'I'll see what offers come in,' she said. 'I don't think I make a very good pop star, to be honest.' Not sure I agree, but she doesn't have the background of years in clubs learning her 'art', nor does she have a burning desire to be recognised for the quality of her singing voice. So I'm relieved in a way, as I'd much rather she be celebrated for other talents. Yet I hope what she's done will be recognised – that she's not only an undercover journalist, but in order to do this successfully has had to work her ass off to be a real pop star too. That takes class.

I'm almost looking forward to being cut about on Saturday morning and blind as a bat for five days as preferable to the torture that's going on at present. For some reason I can't fathom I'm being dropped in that hot smelly bath and held under; I'm really not that important as a minor backbencher (and soon to be ex-), unless it's that I've been the sole Tory voice, along with Ken Clarke, to speak up for Europe and what used to be Tory ideals. Last Saturday morning (before I wrote the last diary piece) I talked for a while on the phone to Simon Walters, formerly of *The Sun* and now political editor of the *Sunday Express*. On late night TV news that evening I hear that comments are being made about an article I've written for the *Sunday Express*. We don't get it (terrible rag), and I knew I hadn't written an article for anybody. It was nearly noon before I managed to get hold of a copy. Simon had really done the dirty, and written up my comments as to *why* we were going to lose, and thus why the campaign was so ineffective, as 'an exclusive article by Edwina Currie'. That broke the confidence, bad enough, but to put my by-line on it made me hopping mad. I promptly sent off an invoice – if anyone uses my name they should pay for it! – so in Tuesday's *Express* they printed that too. Deep shit, I tell you. But why bother? I'm really not that important, am I? They don't know what I've kept to myself. 'Landslide territory' (my description) is hardly big news when the polls still show us 15–20 points behind; and I'm hardly the first, nor will I be the last, to suggest we lost this election through ineptitude and poor leadership a long time ago. I don't get it, but maybe some day I'll hear the full story. Simon has never betrayed a confidence before, though he sails close to the wind; nearly everything he's written about me over the years has been friendly. By this morning it was his editor who was making the comments, so perhaps he was pressurised or leaned on. I hope so – I'd rather think well of someone I'd thought was a pal (even if naïvely) than add him to my collection of prize shits with no integrity at all.

Predictably the reaction here was cataclysmic. The press camped out on the lawn till I called the police (Ray didn't want to – 'I'll go out and tell them to go away,' he announced magisterially). The South Derbyshire Conservative Association officers called a meeting Sunday night – none of them, or Tyrone, had done me the courtesy of phoning to ask what was going on, and none has since. My fault, I suppose – I never built up any sort of relationship with them, and find my chairman sometimes hard to take for her sanctimony. But no benefit of the doubt existed, then or since, which is profoundly depressing. In effect, 'no action' was the course of the day; the eve of poll meeting for Tuesday was cancelled, not least because Tyrone hadn't put any notices out about it (should have been done ten days ago), so nobody knew it was happening. I suspect the recriminations will be just as bitter and personal all over the country, if more private.

Clapham, Wednesday 7 May, 6.10 p.m.

We got smashed. *Armageddon*. The *Sunday Times* poll had predicted that Labour would get 422 seats, us 165; in the event they were only two out – Labour got 419, while the Lib Dems snuck forty-six and act like they won, pompous gits. The share was Labour 44 per cent, us 31.4 per cent, Lib Dems 17.2 per cent.[283] Here in South Derbyshire the Referendum Party polled just over 4 per cent. It was a doubly historic event: the biggest Labour landslide ever, bigger even than 1945, with so many MPs they couldn't find a committee room in the Commons big enough for today's PLP gathering and had to go to Church House instead; and the biggest general election defeat for the Tories since the origins of modern democracy in 1832. Curiously enough, it all had an element of *déjà vu* for me, for the last national poll I fought was 1994, the Euros, at which we polled 28 per cent (i.e. even less). It felt exactly the same – the same grim expressions on the Party workers' faces, the same melting away of helpers till the office was virtually empty, the same lonely agent and the still-clacking fax machine churning out irrelevant rubbish from Central Office, the pitying looks on doorsteps as if a hideously injured beggar was standing there, instead of the smartly dressed middle-aged lady they normally see on the telly.

The count in South Derbyshire was almost a relief. I knew I was going to lose, and in the end was grateful I knew, for the certain knowledge of a landslide acted like a protective garment. It was as if I'd taken shelter, while others were swept away, psychologically as well as politically.

So many losers. The whole of Scotland – Rifkind, Lang, Forsyth (who will leave politics). Tony Newton at Braintree. The whole of Wales. More than forty seats lost in the Midlands – only Norman Fowler left in Sutton Coldfield, and Taylor[284] in Solihull, both a

---

283 In South Derbyshire the share was as follows: Labour 54.5 per cent, Conservative 31.3 per cent, Lib Dems 9.0 per cent, Referendum Party 4.2 per cent, UKIP 1.0 per cent.

284 John Taylor, Conservative MP for Solihull since 1983.

waste of breath these days. Most of London gone – only eleven seats, compared with forty-one before; Hugh Dykes out in Harrow, Olga Maitland[285] too, even Wimbledon lost, and two of the three Croydon seats; the Lib Dems took the five seats around Richmond. Some quiet cheers from me – Bell won in Tatton (11,000 majority), Lamont lost in Harrogate (6,000) and so did Marcus Fox in Shipley, who'd made some spiteful little remarks about me; serve him right. Ian Taylor hung on in Esher, Ted Heath in Old Bexley, Bob Walter got in for North Dorset and Damien Green in Ashford, Anne McIntosh in the Vale of York. But Tredinnick won in Bosworth – doesn't it make you sick? Most of the 'Nolan' MPs lost, including Aitken, Michael Brown, and David Mellor, so it's possible the Downey Report will be shelved now. Anyway, sleaze is no longer an issue: it sank us, and has now vanished like dew on a summer morning. The smell is sweet.

The voters were very clever. Having endured years of being talked about like dull children, they rose up and operated like a bunch of consultant surgeons: tactical voting to an astonishing degree. And where it wasn't necessary, such as here in South Derbyshire, they didn't bother – the Lib Dem vote at 9 per cent was exactly the same as in 1992. Deliberate abstention in fact counted for more here; the turnout at 75 per cent was a full 10 per cent down, probably all ours. Yet I'm not tempted to say 'serve 'em right' again. Many of them, like me, were attracted to Blair and New Labour, and deeply repelled by the nasty small-mindedness that had become the modern Tory Party. I suspect a fair number of the abstainers were pleased at the result. Somewhere deep down, I was thrilled to bits. For Blair played a blinder, right from the moment he won Brown's backing in the leadership contest: he has been a consummate performer, and now has the majority to do whatever he wants. I find him admirable, and from what little I know of him (like the age of consent debate) I think he's genuine, dogged and sophisticated, all qualities which could serve the country well in the next ten years or so, if his stamina and luck hold out.

285 Lady Olga Maitland, Conservative MP for Sutton and Cheam since 1992.

I'll do a note for Robin Hodgson,[286] setting out some 'must dos' if the Conservative Party is ever to be electable again. In the next five years it'll be mainly machinery – for if you think about it, to spend £10 million on these offensive, useless ads and then have fewer paid agents than in 1992 was *mad*. And the quality of the agents! This one a crook, that one a drunk, nobody in NW Leics or Derby South, and Tyrone only capable of doing one thing at a time (not that it mattered in Enfield, where Portillo had an enviably excellent agent in Malcolm Tyndall). We need seriously to address young voters, with a team of (say) twenty paid organisers going out to the universities and colleges. We need to gear up for local elections, for the new London authority, for elected mayors. We need to think about Party fund-raising, and our *lack* of dependence on local branch efforts. We need some democracy in the Party, and fast, so members will have a role instead of acquiescence – then maybe they'll talk sense and counterbalance Central Office, which was truly hopeless this time. And we need to start nurturing candidates for the future and seeing it as a long-term job.

But in the election of 2006 – the last one before boundary changes – we'll need a whole batch of new policies. Everything we fought in this election will be redundant:

- there'll have been a Scottish Parliament for nearly ten years
- we'll have been in the euro for some time, successfully if late
- the fastest growing economy in Europe will be Poland
- our troops will be serving in the Euroforce
- we may have given up on our nuclear deterrent, or pooled it through NATO
- our Security Council place will be held in rotation by the Presidency of the EU, or by the Germans.

And so on. So heaven knows what our policies will have to be then. But I'm quite sure Margaret Thatcher thought ten years ahead, and we'll have to do the same – if we are capable of it.

Brown too played a blinder on virtually his first day in office as

286 Chairman of the National Union of Conservative Associations.

Chancellor. He raised interest rates 0.25 per cent, which caused hardly a stir – the Stock Exchange rose – then announced that he was handing over responsibility for interest rates to the Bank of England. Just like that! An independent central bank! Eddie George looked pleased as Punch. It'll function much like the Bundesbank – the government will set the inflation targets and the Bank will do the rest. So, at a stroke, all the objections to the single currency are swept away. No more Norman Lamonts screwing up the economy and singing in the bath as they do so – just faceless bankers appointed in perpetuity and (hopefully) taking the firm line necessary with our inflationary tendencies. And the Chancellor can shrug and blame someone else when times get hard – though I have a suspicion they won't, not now, even though a tax hike is confidently expected in a summer Budget. I am *delighted* at the news and I hope he carries on in the same way.

One other element gave me great pleasure. Over 120 women have been elected this time (of whom eleven are Tories – a slight *increase* in the percentage on our benches, would you believe. Huh.) They look terrific – not only the young ones, but the middle-aged too: some Barbara Follett clones, but some cooler, smarter, more soignée altogether. Ruth Kelly[287] is eight months pregnant and stood up well in a breakfast TV interview this morning against Ann Widdecombe, who looked hideous and sounded harsh and aggressive: the milk of human kindness never flowed in those vast breasts. They're all pledged to social hours and a crèche (Ms Kelly will need it), and I envy them – the place is being sorted out just as I leave. But no, sisters, you're not the pioneers. Others were, years ago, including me; and your arrival should have taken place in such numbers ten years ago, and would have done, had Margaret cared enough. But she didn't, she preferred men. *Not* a sister.

And so to the Tory leadership contest. Ugh. Hezza is ruled out by an angina attack the day after the election: hospital and oblivion for him. Ken Clarke declares right away, and the Tory Reform Group will organise to back him – Clare will be at the heart of that. He will have about one-third of the votes of the parliamentary Party, but he'll be just as cheerful if he loses – you never feel he

287 The newly elected Labour MP for Bolton West.

cares quite enough, that he wants it enough. Redwood, slimy toad, declared quickly. I noticed he was careful to have dull nonentities about him this time – Marion Roe, looking like a forgotten doll in a toy cupboard, and Andrew Hunter: no sign of Marlow (who lost), or Budgen[288] (ditto), and no doubt Teresa was bound and gagged under the table.

In piled Howard, but not without some high farce. On Monday night he had Hague in for dinner, the last night in his official Home Office residence. Over champers they agreed a dream ticket – Howard as leader, Hague as deputy. Next morning, however, Hague said no, he'd prefer to stand himself. His press conference this morning at the Atrium was superb – polished and stylish and expensively mounted, backdrop and all, and applause from acolytes as he entered – so he'd been stringing Howard along all the time. Hague's against the single currency in principle, heaven help us, but he's for a 'Fresh Start' – i.e. thorough rethinking. If he carries on like that, he'll win it.

Peter Lilley declared himself, virtually unnoticed, with Gill Shephard in support. Oh, and Stephen Dorrell at his worst declared this morning on TV. He looked ghastly – exhausted, bags under eyes, still hoarse, shiny nose and in need of a haircut. The contrast with the smooth Hague a couple of hours before couldn't have been greater. All that uncut hair blowing around in the breeze (do it indoors! Comb your hair! Smile!) about a scowling, glowering face. Yet Dorrell was saying much the same as Hague: 'It is not the voters who were wrong last week, it was us: we have to listen to them.'

I don't fancy any of them much – that's why I invented a Roger Dickson in the novels. Ken is the most appealing to the electorate at large; he is clear, cool and straight, and pro-European. For all those reasons our MPs will prefer somebody else. Hague, I think, who is placing himself squarely against Blair, and (as he said) is a northerner, a comprehensive schoolboy who knows Wales, and therefore can credibly try to reform the Party. Dorrell is hopeless – no campaign, no constituency. Ditto poor Lilley, who looks lost

---

288 Conservative MP for Wolverhampton South West 1974–97; a prominent Eurosceptic.

without Portillo[289] (how odd that JM was proved right – 'Michael Portillo will never be Prime Minister' – but not like this). Redwood is organised, but he'll find his support is slippery – if they think Hague'll get it, they'll slide away to him, whatever they've promised and however much money went into his election coffers. Redwood will learn the hard way that a man who can't show loyalty – indeed whose disloyalty is his only trump card – can't expect it in return. And Howard – I hope! – will be a respectable also-ran. God, if the Party choose him, it'll be in the wilderness for ever.

Elsewhere – got my face chopped about on Saturday morning – five hours on the operating table and £7,700 lighter – and several pounds in weight, too, as my system goes into shock! I have these skinny legs and bony knees now, but my chin's tight (hooray) and the eyes are surrounded by yellow not black (my lower neck's gone a pale purple – apparently it's all the gunk sinking slowly back down). Stitches everywhere especially around my ears: I look like somebody tore them off in a fight. No pain, though my eyes are a bit pricky. Forehead (lasered) is horrible – shan't have that done again. When the dressing comes off and it's washed it stings to screaming point, then weeps for hours. Main stitches out on Friday, last ones Monday, then I'm nearly done. All rather exciting, though tiring. I think I'm going to like this result too.

Within weeks EC was working for BBC Radio Five Live, eventually presenting her own weekend programme, Late Night Currie. *The novel* She's Leaving Home *was published in September 1997. Debbie's record entered the hit parade and was then taken off the market by Carlton, who broadcast two programmes featuring her. Susie gained a 2:1 at Cambridge and went on to Stanford University, California.*

William Hague won the Tory leadership contest; he led the Party to a second landslide defeat in 2001, when Tony Blair was again returned to office.

The Curries were divorced in April 2001. A few weeks later EC married John Jones, a former senior detective in the Metropolitan Police, whom she met when he was a guest on her programme.

---

289 Michael Portillo had lost his seat in the general election and was therefore ineligible to stand.

Index